Advanced Python Development

Using Powerful Language Features in Real-World Applications

Matthew Wilkes

Apress®

Advanced Python Development: Using Powerful Language Features in Real-World Applications

Matthew Wilkes
Leeds, West Yorkshire, UK

ISBN-13 (pbk): 978-1-4842-5792-0
https://doi.org/10.1007/978-1-4842-5793-7

ISBN-13 (electronic): 978-1-4842-5793-7

Managing Director, Apress Media LLC: Welmoed Spahr
Acquisitions Editor: Celestin Suresh John
Development Editor: James Markham
Coordinating Editor: Aditee Mirashi

Cover designed by eStudioCalamar

Cover image designed by Freepik (www.freepik.com)

Photographs by Mark Wheelwright (Matthew), Stephanie Shadbolt (Jesse) and Niteo GmbH (Nejc)

Distributed to the book trade worldwide by Springer Science+Business Media New York, 233 Spring Street, 6th Floor, New York, NY 10013. Phone 1-800-SPRINGER, fax (201) 348-4505, e-mail orders-ny@springer-sbm.com, or visit www.springeronline.com. Apress Media, LLC is a California LLC and the sole member (owner) is Springer Science + Business Media Finance Inc (SSBM Finance Inc). SSBM Finance Inc is a **Delaware** corporation.

For information on translations, please e-mail rights@apress.com, or visit http://www.apress.com/rights-permissions.

Apress titles may be purchased in bulk for academic, corporate, or promotional use. eBook versions and licenses are also available for most titles. For more information, reference our Print and eBook Bulk Sales web page at http://www.apress.com/bulk-sales.

Any source code or other supplementary material referenced by the author in this book is available to readers on GitHub via the book's product page, located at www.apress.com/978-1-4842-5792-0. For more detailed information, please visit http://www.apress.com/source-code.

Printed on acid-free paper

Table of Contents

About the Author

Matthew Wilkes is a European software developer who has worked with Python on web projects for the last 15 years. As well as developing software, he has a long experience in mentoring Python developers in a commercial setting.

He is also very involved in open source software, with commits to many popular frameworks. His contributions in that space are focused on the details of database and security interactions of web frameworks.

About the Technical Reviewers

Coen de Groot is a freelance Python developer and trainer. He has been passionate about computers and programming since the late 1970s when he built his first "computer."

After nearly finishing his computer science degree at Leiden University, Coen has worked for a large oil company, small startups, software agencies, and others. He has written a lot of software in many different programming languages. And he has worked in software support, delivered training, led teams, and managed technical projects.

After about 20 years in IT, Coen tried something different, trained as a business coach, hosted a large community of coaches, and organized five conferences. But he quickly got pulled back into building websites and other IT services for coaches and others.

For the last 10 years, Coen has mostly been programming in Python, with hints of SQL, JavaScript, and others. And he still enjoys learning more Python and passing on that knowledge face to face, in writing or on video.

Geek since he was able to walk, **Nejc Zupan** developed his first computer game in primary school, won the national robotics championship in high school, and cofounded niteo.co while still in college. He has spoken at conferences in five continents, mostly relating to the Web, Python, and productivity. Whenever he is not coding, he is chasing big waves around the world.

Jesse Snyder began programming after many years of deferring graduate studies in ethnomusicology and was pleasantly surprised by how completely engrossing he found the challenges and rewards of software design. After several years in the Pacific Northwest nonprofit technology scene, he now works as an independent consultant. When not at work or playing Javanese gamelan music, he is likely out for a long run through the beautiful parks and neighborhoods around his home in Seattle, Washington.

Acknowledgments

Many people helped with this book in various ways. The thousands of contributors to Python's open source ecosystem must come first; without them there would be no book to write. Thank you to Joanna for encouraging me, despite the difficulty and long hours. Thanks also to the rest of my family for their unfailing support over the years.

For this book specifically, I'd like to thank Nejc Zupan, Jesse Snyder, Tom Blockley, Alan Hoey, and Cris Ewing, all of whom gave valuable comments on the plan and implementation. Thank you also to Mark Wheelwright of ISO Photography for his excellent work in getting a good photograph of me and to the team at Apress for their hardwork.

Finally, thank you to the people who continue to make the Web as weird and wonderful a thing as it was when I was first drawn into working with the Internet. Thomas Heasman-Hunt, Julia Evans, Ian Fieggen, Foone Turing, and countless more – I doubt industrial software would have captured so much of my attention without people like you.

Introduction

Python is a very successful programming language. In the three decades that it has existed, it has become very widely used. It ships by default with major operating systems; some of the largest websites in the world use Python for their back ends, and scientists are using Python every day to advance our collective knowledge. As so many people are working on and with Python daily, improvements come thick and fast. Not all Python developers have the chance to attend conferences, or the time to follow the work done by different parts of the community, so it's inevitable that some features of the language and ecosystem are not as well known as they deserve to be.

The objective of this book is to examine parts of the language and Python tooling that may not be known to everyone. If you're an experienced Python developer, you may well know many of these tools, but a good many more may be on your to-do list of things to try when you have time. This is especially true if you're working on established systems, where rearchitecting a component to take advantage of new language features isn't something that can be done frequently.

If you've been using Python for a shorter period, you may be more familiar with recent additions to the language but less aware of some of the libraries available in the wider ecosystem. A large part of the benefit of attending events like Python conferences is the chance to notice minor quality-of-life improvements fellow programmers have made and integrate them into your workflow.

This is not a reference book with stand-alone sections covering different features of Python: the flow from chapter to chapter is dictated by how we would build a real piece of software.

With many pieces of technical documentation, there is a tendency to provide simple examples. Simple examples are great for explaining how something works, but not so useful for understanding when to use it. They can also be tricky to build on, as complex code is often architected quite differently to simple code.

By following this one example, we are able to consider technology choices in context. You will learn what considerations to bear in mind when choosing if a particular approach is suitable. Topics that are related by how they're used will be covered together, rather than topics that are related by how they work.

This book

My objective in writing this book is to share knowledge from different parts of the community and lessons learned over 15 years of writing Python code for a living. It will help you to be productive, both with the core language and add-on libraries. You will learn how to effectively use features of the language that are not strictly essential to be a productive programmer, such as asynchronous programming, packaging, and testing.

However, this book is aimed at people who want to write code, not people who are looking to understand deep magics. I will not delve too far into subjects that involve implementation details of Python. You will not be expected to grok[1] Python C extensions, metaclasses, or algorithms to benefit from this book.

Substantive code samples are shown as numbered listings, and the accompanying code for this book includes electronic versions of these listings. Some of these listings also have output shown directly beneath, rather than separately as a numbered figure.

The accompanying code for this book is also where you'll find copies of the full codebase for the example on a chapter-by-chapter basis, as well as helper code for the exercises. In general, I would recommend that you follow along with the code by checking out the Git repository from the book's website or the code distribution and changing to the relevant branch for the chapter you're reading.

As well as listings, I show some console sessions. When lines which are formatted like code begin with >, that indicates that a shell session is being shown. These sections cover commands to be run from your operating system's terminal. Any that involve >>> are demonstrating a Python console session and should be run from within a Python interpreter.

The example

This book's example is that of a general-purpose data aggregator. If you work in DevOps, then it is very likely you use a program of this sort to track the resource utilization of servers. Alternatively, as a web developer, you may use something like this for statistics aggregation from different deployments of the same system. Some scientists use similar methods, for example, for aggregating the findings of air-quality sensors distributed

---

[1] A jargon word that became popular during the 1960s, when computing was a much smaller field. To grok something is to understand it on a very deep and intuitive level. It is derived from Robert Heinlein's novel *Stranger in a Strange Land.*

across a city. It isn't something that every developer will need to build, but it is a problem space that is familiar to many developers.

It has been picked not just because it's a common task, but because it allows us to explore many of the subjects we want to cover in a natural, unified way. You will be able to follow the complete example perfectly well using any modern computer running any modern operating system,[2] without purchasing any additional hardware. You may find you get more out of some of the examples if you have additional computers to act as remote data sources.

I will be using a Raspberry Pi Zero equipped with some aftermarket sensors for my examples. This platform is widely available for approximately 5 US dollars and provides lots of interesting data. There are commercial sensor add-ons available from many Raspberry Pi stockists.

Although I'll be recommending things specific to the Raspberry Pi to make following the examples easier, this book is not about the Internet of Things or the Raspberry Pi itself. It's a means to an end; you should feel comfortable to adapt the examples to fit tasks that are more relevant to your interests if you like. Any of the similar problems mentioned earlier would follow the same design process.

Choice of topics

The topics covered by this book have been chosen to shine a light on a variety of different aspects of Python programming. All are underused or under-understood by the Python community as a whole, and none are things likely to be taught as a matter of course to beginners. That's not to say that they are necessarily complex or hard to understand (although some certainly are), but they are techniques that I believe all Python programmers should be familiar with, even if they choose not to use them.

Chapter 1 will introduce you to different ways of approaching the writing of very simple programs in Python and, in particular, will cover Jupyter notebooks and an introduction to the use of the Python debugger. Although both are relatively well-known tools, many people are proficient in the use of one but not both. It will also cover ways

---

[2]However, if using Windows, I'd suggest you consider something like the Windows Subsystem for Linux, as most add-ons are written with Linux or macOS systems in mind and so may perform better under WSL.

of approaching the writing of command-line interfaces and some useful third-party libraries to support succinct command-line tool development.

Chapter 2 will cover tools that help you identify mistakes in your code, such as automated testing and linting tools. These tools all make it easier to write code that you can be confident in, whether it's a large codebase, one that you rarely need to edit, or one that will garner contributions from third parties. The tools covered here are all ones I would recommend; however, the focus will be on understanding their advantages and disadvantages. You may have used one or more of these tools, and you may have opinions on whether some of them are appropriate to use. This chapter will help you understand the trade-offs to help you make informed decisions.

Chapter 3 covers code packaging and dependency distribution in Python. These are key features for writing applications that can be distributed to others and for designing deployment systems that work reliably. We will use this to convert our stand-alone script into an installable application.

Chapter 4 introduces plugin architectures. This is a powerful feature; it's not uncommon for people who learn them to try and apply them everywhere, which means people can be wary of teaching them. For our example, a plugin architecture is a natural fit. It also covers some advanced techniques for command-line tools that can make debugging plugin-based systems easier.

Chapter 5 covers web interfaces and techniques such as decorators and closures to write complex functions. These techniques are idiomatic in Python but hard to express in many other programming languages. It also covers the appropriate use of abstract base classes. It's common for people to advise against using ABCs because of the tendency of people who learn them to want to use them everywhere. There are definite advantages to a restrained use of ABCs in particular circumstances, especially when combined with some of the tools from Chapter 2.

Chapter 6 expands our example with another major component, the aggregation server that collects the data. This chapter also demonstrates some of the most useful third-party libraries you will use as a Python programmer, such as "requests."

Chapter 7 covers threading and asynchronous programming in Python. Threading is often the source of subtle bugs. Asynchronous code can be used for similar tasks, but it is an idiom that many Python programmers haven't used because the program behaves quite differently to synchronous programming. This chapter focuses on the real-world use of concurrency to achieve a result, rather than demonstrations of a simple example or the limits of what asynchronous programming can do. The objective is working code that is usable in the real world and a thorough understanding of the trade-offs, not a stand-alone technology demonstration.

Chapter 8 goes further with asynchronous programming, adding in the testing of asynchronous code and the various libraries that exist to write code that deals with external tools (such as databases) in an async context. We will also look briefly at some advanced techniques for writing good APIs that are helpful for asynchronous programming, like context managers and context variables.

Chapter 9 sees us return to Jupyter to use its features for data visualization and easy user interaction. We will look at how to use our asynchronous functions with widgets in Jupyter notebooks as well as advanced use of iterators and ways of implementing complex data types.

Chapter 10 details how to make Python code faster, using different types of caching and for which situations they are an appropriate choice. It covers benchmarking individual Python functions in your applications and how to interpret the results to find the reasons for slowdown.

Chapter 11 extends some of the concepts we've visited earlier in the book to handle faults more gracefully. We'll look at ways that our plugin architecture can be modified to allow for handling errors seamlessly while retaining full backward compatibility, and we'll take a closer look at designing processes that handle errors that they encounter.

In **Chapter 12**, the final chapter, we use Python's iterator and coroutine features to enhance the dashboards we've developed with features that aren't passive data gatherers but actively introspect the data we've gathered, allowing us to build multistep analysis flows.

Python version

At the time of writing, the current release of Python is 3.8, and as such the examples in this book are being tested against 3.8 and first development versions of Python 3.9. I do not recommend using older versions. Very few code samples in this book do not work on Python 3.7 or Python 3.6.

You will need Python pip installed to follow along with this book. It should already be installed on your system if you have Python installed. Some operating systems intentionally remove pip from their default installations of Python, in which case you'll need to install it using the operating system's package manager explicitly. This is common on Debian-based systems, where it can be installed with `sudo apt install` python3-pip. On other operating systems, use `python -m ensurepip --upgrade` to have Python find the latest version of pip itself or find instructions specific to your operating system.

Electronic versions of code samples and errata are available from the publisher and the book's website at `https://advancedpython.dev`. This should be your first port of call if you encounter any problems working through this book.

CHAPTER 1

Prototyping and environments

In this chapter, we will explore the different ways that you can experiment with what different Python functions do and when is an appropriate time to use those different options. Using one of those methods, we will build some simple functions to extract the first pieces of data that we will be aggregating and see how to build those into a simple command-line tool.

Prototyping in Python

During any Python project, from something that you'll spend a few hours developing to projects that run for years, you'll need to prototype functions. It may be the first thing you do, or it may sneak up on you mid-project, but sooner or later, you'll find yourself in the Python shell trying code out.

There are two broad approaches for how to approach prototyping: either running a piece of code and seeing what the results are or executing statements one at a time and looking at the intermediate results. Generally speaking, executing statements one by one is more productive, but at times it can seem easier to revert to running a block of code if there are chunks you're already confident in.

The Python shell (also called the REPL for **R**ead, **E**val, **P**rint, **L**oop) is most people's first introduction to using Python. Being able to launch an interpreter and type commands live is a powerful way of jumping right into coding. It allows you to run commands and immediately see what their result is, then adjust your input without erasing the value of any variables. Compare that to a compiled language, where the development flow is structured around compiling a file and then running the executable. There is a significantly shorter latency for simple programs in interpreted languages like Python.

1

© Matthew Wilkes 2020
M. Wilkes, *Advanced Python Development*, https://doi.org/10.1007/978-1-4842-5793-7_1

Prototyping with the REPL

The strength of the REPL is very much in trying out simple code and getting an intuitive understanding of how functions work. It is less suited for cases where there is lots of flow control, as it isn't very forgiving of errors. If you make an error when typing part of a loop body, you'll have to start again, rather than just editing the incorrect line. Modifying a variable with a single line of Python code and seeing the output is a close fit to an optimal use of the REPL for prototyping.

For example, I often find it hard to remember how the built-in function `filter(...)` works. There are a few ways of reminding myself: I could look at the documentation for this function on the Python website or using my code editor/IDE. Alternatively, I could try using it in my code and then check that the values I got out are what I expect, or I could use the REPL to either find a reference to the documentation or just try the function out.

In practice, I generally find myself trying things out. A typical example looks like the following one, where my first attempt has the arguments inverted, the second reminds me that filter returns a custom object rather than a tuple or a list, and the third reminds me that filter includes only elements that match the condition, rather than excluding ones that match the condition.

```
>>> filter(range(10), lambda x: x == 5)
Traceback (most recent call last):
  File "<stdin>", line 1, in <module>
TypeError: 'function' object is not iterable
>>> filter(lambda x: x == 5, range(10))
<filter object at 0x033854F0>
>>> tuple(filter(lambda x: x == 5, range(10)))
(5,)
```

Note   The built-in function help(...) is invaluable when trying to understand how functions work. As filter has a clear docstring, it may have been even more straightforward to call `help(filter)` and read the information. However, when chaining multiple function calls together, especially when trying to understand existing code, being able to experiment with sample data and see how the interactions play out is very helpful.

If we do try to use the REPL for a task involving more flow control, such as the famous interview coding test question FizzBuzz (Listing 1-1), we can see its unforgiving nature.

Listing 1-1. fizzbuzz.py – a typical implementation

```
for num in range(1, 101):
    val = ''
    if num % 3 == 0:
        val += 'Fizz'
    if num % 5 == 0:
        val += 'Buzz'
    if not val:
        val = str(num)
    print(val)
```

If we were to build this up step by step, we might start by creating a loop that outputs the numbers unchanged:

```
>>> for num in range(1, 101):
...     print(num)
...
1
.
.
.
98
99
100
```

At this point, we will see the numbers 1 to 100 on new lines, so we would start adding logic:

```
>>> for num in range(1, 101):
...     if num % 3 == 0:
...         print('Fizz')
...     else:
...         print(num)
```

```
...
1
.

.

.
98
Fizz
100
```

Every time we do this, we are having to reenter code that we entered before, sometimes with small changes, sometimes verbatim. These lines are not editable once they've been entered, so any typos mean that the whole loop needs to be retyped.

You may decide to prototype the body of the loop rather than the whole loop, to make it easier to follow the action of the conditions. In this example, the values of n from 1 to 14 are correctly generated with a three-way if statement, with n=15 being the first to be incorrectly rendered. While this is in the middle of a loop body, it is difficult to examine the way the conditions interact.

This is where you'll find the first of the differences between the REPL and a script's interpretation of indenting. The Python interpreter has a stricter interpretation of how indenting should work when in REPL mode than when executing a script, *requiring* you to have a blank line after any unindent that returns you to an indent level of 0.

```
>>> num = 15
>>> if num % 3 == 0:
...     print('Fizz')
... if num % 5 == 0:
  File "<stdin>", line 3
    if num % 5 == 0:
     ^
SyntaxError: invalid syntax
```

In addition, the REPL only allows a blank line when returning to an indent level of 0, whereas in a Python file it is treated as an implicit continuation of the last indent level. Listing 1-2 (which differs from Listing 1-1 only in the addition of blank lines) works when invoked as python fizzbuzz_blank_lines.py.

Listing 1-2. fizzbuzz_blank_lines.py

```python
for num in range(1, 101):
    val = ''
    if num % 3 == 0:
        val += 'Fizz'
    if num % 5 == 0:
        val += 'Buzz'

    if not val:
        val = str(num)

    print(val)
```

However, typing the contents of Listing 1-2 into a Python interpreter results in the following errors, due to the differences in indent parsing rules:

```
>>> for num in range(1, 101):
...     val = ''
...     if num % 3 == 0:
...         val += 'Fizz'
...     if num % 5 == 0:
...         val += 'Buzz'
...
>>>     if not val:
  File "<stdin>", line 1
    if not val:
    ^
IndentationError: unexpected indent
>>>         val = str(num)
  File "<stdin>", line 1
    val = str(num)
    ^
```

```
IndentationError: unexpected indent
>>>
>>>     print(val)
  File "<stdin>", line 1
    print(val)
    ^

IndentationError: unexpected indent
```

It's easy to make a mistake when using the REPL to prototype a loop or condition when you're used to writing Python in files. The frustration of making a mistake and having to reenter the code is enough to undo the time savings of using this method over a simple script. While it is possible to scroll back to previous lines you entered using the arrow keys, multiline constructs such as loops are not grouped together, making it very difficult to re-run a loop body. The use of the >>> and ... prompts throughout the session also makes it difficult to copy and paste previous lines, either to re-run them or to integrate them into a file.

Prototyping with a Python script

It is very much possible to prototype code by writing a simple Python script and running it until it returns the correct result. Unlike using the REPL, this ensures that it is easy to re-run code if you make a mistake, and code is stored in a file rather than in your terminal's scrollback buffer.[1] Unfortunately, it does mean that it is not possible to interact with the code while it's running, leading to this being nicknamed "printf debugging," after C's function to print a variable.

As the nickname implies, the only practical way to get information from the execution of the script is to use the print(...) function to log data to the console window. In our example, it would be common to add a print to the loop body to see what is happening for each iteration:

Tip   f-strings are useful for printf debugging, as they let you interpolate variables into a string without additional string formatting operations.

---

[1]You'll be glad of this the first time you accidentally close the window and lose the code you're working on.

```
for num in range(1,101):
    print(f"n: {num} n%3: {num%3} n%5: {num%5}")
```

The following is the result:

```
n: 1 n%3: 1 n%5: 1
.

.

.
n: 98 n%3: 2 n%5: 3
n: 99 n%3: 0 n%5: 4
n: 100 n%3: 1 n%5: 0
```

This provides an easily understood view at what the script is doing, but it does require some repetition of logic. This repetition makes it easier for errors to be missed, which can cause significant losses of time. The fact that the code is stored permanently is the biggest advantage this has over the REPL, but it provides a poorer user experience for the programmer. Typos and simple errors can become frustrating as there is a necessary context switch from editing the file to running it in the terminal.[2] It can also be more difficult to see the information you need at a glance, depending on how you structure your print statements. Despite these flaws, its simplicity makes it very easy to add debugging statements to an existing system, so this is one of the most commonly used approaches to debugging, especially when trying to get a broad understanding of a problem.

Prototyping with scripts and pdb

pdb, the built-in Python debugger, is the single most useful tool in any Python developer's arsenal. It is the most effective way to debug complex pieces of code and is practically the only way of examining what a Python script is doing inside multistage expressions like list comprehensions.[3]

---

[2]Some text editors integrate a terminal precisely to cut down on this kind of context switching.
[3]Pdb allows you to step through each iteration of a list comprehension, as you would do with a loop. This is useful when you have existing code that you are trying to diagnose a problem with, but frustrating when the list comprehension is incidental to your debugging.

In many ways, prototyping code is a specialized form of debugging. We know that the code we've written is incomplete and contains errors, but rather than trying to find a single flaw, we're trying to build up complexity in stages. Many of pdb's features to assist in debugging make this easier.

When you start a pdb session, you see a (Pdb) prompt that allows you to control the debugger. The most important commands, in my view, are **step**, **next**, **break**, **continue**, **prettyprint**, and **debug**.[4]

Both step and next execute the current statement and move to the next one. They differ in what they consider the "next" statement to be. Step moves to the next statement regardless of where it is, so if the current line contains a function call, the next line is the first line of that function. Next does not move execution into that function; it considers the next statement to be the following statement in the current function. If you want to examine what a function call is doing, then step into it. If you trust that the function is doing the right thing, use next to gloss over its implementation and get the result.

break and continue allow for longer portions of the code to run without direct examination. break is used to specify a line number where you want to be returned to the pdb prompt, with an optional condition that is evaluated in that scope, for example, break 20 x==1. The continue command returns to the normal flow of execution; you won't be returned to a pdb prompt unless you hit another breakpoint.

Tip   If you find visual status displays more natural, you may find it hard to keep track of where you are in a debugging session. I would recommend you install the pdb++ debugger which shows a code listing with the current line highlighted. IDEs, such as PyCharm, go one step further by allowing you to set breakpoints in a running program and control stepping directly from your editor window.

Finally, debug allows you to specify any arbitrary python expression to step into. This lets you call any function with any data from within a pdb prompt, which can be very useful if you've already used next or continue to pass a point before you realize that's where the error was. It is invoked as debug somefunction() and modifies the (Pdb)

---

[4]These can all be abbreviated, as shown in bold. step becomes s, prettyprint becomes pp, etc.

prompt to let you know that you're in a nested pdb session by adding an extra pair of parentheses, making the prompt ((Pdb)).[5]

Post-mortem debugging

There are two common ways of invoking pdb, either explicitly in the code or directly for so-called "post-mortem debugging." Post-mortem debugging starts a script in pdb and will trigger pdb if an exception is raised. It is run through the use of python -m pdb yourscript.py rather than python yourscript.py. The script will not start automatically; you'll be shown a pdb prompt to allow you to set breakpoints. To begin execution of the script, you should use the continue command. You will be returned to the pdb prompt either when a breakpoint that you set is triggered or when the program terminates. If the program terminates because of an error, it allows you to view the variables that were set at the time the error occurred.

Alternatively, you can use step commands to run the statements in the file one by one; however, for all but the simplest of scripts, it is better to set a breakpoint at the point you want to start debugging and step from there.

The following is the result of running Listing 1-1 in pdb and setting a conditional breakpoint (output abbreviated):

```
> python -m pdb fizzbuzz.py
> c:\fizzbuzz_pdb.py(1)<module>()
-> def fizzbuzz(num):
(Pdb) break 2, num==15
Breakpoint 1 at c:\fizzbuzz.py:2
(Pdb) continue
1
.
.
.
13
14
```

---

[5]I once so badly misunderstood a bug that I overused debug until the pdb prompt looked like ((((((Pdb)))))). This is an antipattern as it's very easy to accidentally lose your place; try and use conditional breakpoints if you find yourself in a similar situation.

```
> c:\fizzbuzz.py(2)fizzbuzz()
-> val = ''
(Pdb) p num
15
```

This style works well when combined with the previous script-based approach. It allows you to set arbitrary breakpoints at stages of the code's execution and automatically provides a pdb prompt if your code triggers an exception without you needing to know in advance what errors occur and where.

The breakpoint function

The breakpoint() built-in[6] allows you to specify exactly where in a program pdb takes control. When this function is called, execution immediately stops, and a pdb prompt is shown. It behaves as if a pdb breakpoint had previously been set at the current location. It's common to use breakpoint() inside an if statement or in an exception handler, to mimic the conditional breakpoint and post-mortem debugging styles of invoking pdb prompts. Although it does mean changing the source code (and therefore is not suitable for debugging production-only issues), it removes the need to set up your breakpoints every time you run the program.

Debugging the fizzbuzz script at the point of calculating the value of 15 would be done by adding a new condition to look for num == 15 and putting breakpoint() in the body, as shown in Listing 1-3.

Listing 1-3. fizzbuzz_with_breakpoint.py

```
for num in range(1, 101):
    val = ''
    if num == 15:
        breakpoint()
    if num % 3 == 0:
        val += 'Fizz'
```

---

[6]You may find documentation recommending import pdb; pdb.set_trace(). This is an older style that is still quite common, but does the same thing albeit without some of the configurability and less readable.

```
if num % 5 == 0:
    val += 'Buzz'
if not val:
    val = str(num)
print(val)
```

To use this style when prototyping, create a simple Python file that contains imports you think you might need and any test data you know you have. Then, add a breakpoint() call at the bottom of the file. Whenever you execute that file, you'll find yourself in an interactive environment with all the functions and data you need available.

Tip   I strongly recommend the library remote-pdb for debugging complex multithreaded applications. To use this, install the remote-pdb package and start your application with the environment variable PYTHONBREAKPOINT=remote_pdb.set_trace python yourscript.py. When you call breakpoint() in your code, the connection information is logged to the console. See the remote-pdb documentation for more options.

Prototyping with Jupyter

Jupyter is a suite of tools for interacting with languages that support a REPL in a more user-friendly way. It has extensive support for making it easier to interact with the code, such as displaying widgets that are bound to the input or output of functions, which makes it much easier for nontechnical people to interact with complex functions. The functionality that's useful to us at this stage is the fact that it allows breaking code into logical blocks and running them independently as well as being able to save those blocks and return to them later.

Jupyter is written in Python but as a common front end for the Julia, Python, and R programming languages. It is intended as a vehicle for sharing self-contained programs that offer simple user interfaces, for example, for data analysis. Many Python programmers create Jupyter notebooks rather than console scripts, especially those who work in the sciences. We're not using Jupyter in that way for *this* chapter; we're using it because its features happen to align well with prototyping tasks.

The design goal of supporting multiple languages means it also supports Haskell, Lua, Perl, PHP, Rust, Node.js, as well as many others. Each of these languages has IDEs, REPLs, documentation websites, and so on. One of the most significant advantages of using Jupyter for this type of prototyping is that it allows you to develop a workflow that also works with unfamiliar environments and languages. For example, full-stack web programmers often have to work on both Python and JavaScript code. In contrast, scientists may need easy access to both Python and R. Having a single interface means that some of the differences between languages are smoothed over.

As Jupyter is not Python-specific and has built-in support for selecting what back end to use to run the current code, I recommend installing it in such a way that it's conveniently available across your whole system. If you generally install Python utilities into a virtual environment, that's fine.[7] However, I have installed Jupyter into my user environment:

```
> python -m pip install --user jupyter
```

Note   As Jupyter has been installed in user mode, you need to ensure that the binaries directory is included in your system path. Installing into the global python environment or through your package manager is an acceptable alternative; it's more important to be consistent with how your tools are installed than to use a variety of methods.

When prototyping with Jupyter, you can separate our code into logical blocks that you can run either individually or sequentially. The blocks are editable and persistent, as if we were using a script, but we can control which blocks run and write new code without discarding the contents of variables. In that way, it is similar to using the REPL, as we can try things out without any interruption from the coding flow to run a script.

There are two main ways of accessing the Jupyter tools, either through the Web using Jupyter's notebook server or as a replacement for the standard Python REPL. Each works on the idea of cells, which are independent units of execution that can be re-run at any

---

[7]In fact, many people prefer to create a virtual environment just for Jupyter and add that to the system path, to avoid any risk of version conflicts in their global namespace.

time. Both the notebook and the REPL use the same underlying interface to Python, called IPython. IPython has none of the trouble understanding indenting that the standard REPL does and has support for easily re-running code from earlier in a session.

The notebook is more user-friendly than the shell but has the disadvantage of only being accessible through a web browser rather than your usual text editor or IDE.[8] I strongly recommend using the notebook interface as it provides a significant boost to your productivity through the more intuitive interface when it comes to being able to re-run cells and to edit multiline cells.

Notebooks

To begin prototyping, start the Jupyter notebook server and then create a new notebook using the web interface.

```
> jupyter notebook
```

Once the notebook has loaded, enter the code into the first cell, then click the run button. Many keyboard shortcuts that are common to code editors are present, along with automatic indenting when a new block is begun (Figure 1-1).

---

[8]Some editors, such as the professional version of PyCharm IDE and Microsoft's VSCode editor, have begun to offer a partial equivalent to the notebook interface from within the IDE. They don't have all the functionality available, but it's surprisingly good.

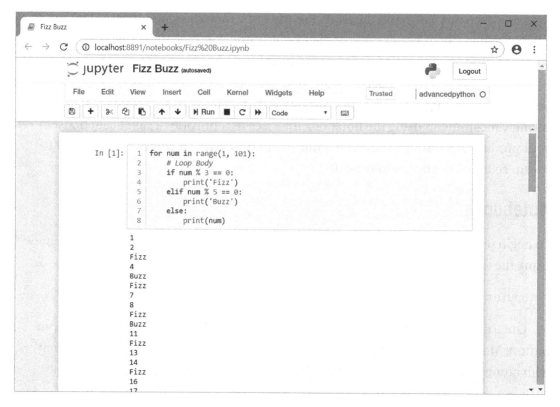

Figure 1-1. *fizzbuzz in a Jupyter notebook*

Pdb works with Jupyter notebooks through the web interface, interrupting execution and displaying a new input prompt (Figure 1-2), in the same way that it does in the command line. All the standard pdb functionality is exposed through this interface, so the tips from the pdb section of this chapter can also be used in a Jupyter environment.

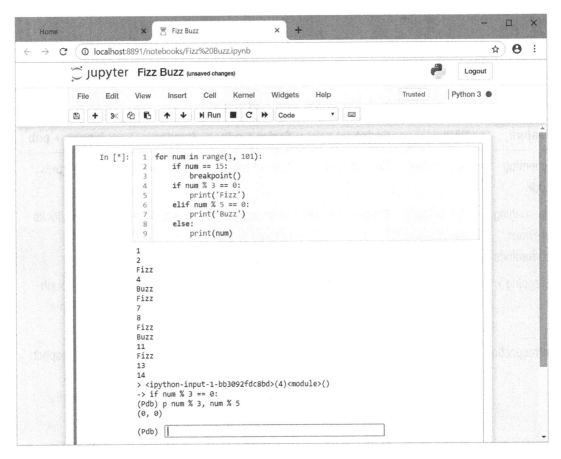

Figure 1-2. *pdb in a Jupyter notebook*

Prototyping in this chapter

There are advantages and disadvantages to all the methods we've explored, but each has its place. For very simple one-liners, such as list comprehensions, I often use the REPL, as it's the fastest to start up and has no complex control flow that would be hard to debug.

For more complex tasks, such as bringing functions from external libraries together and doing multiple things with them, a more featureful approach is usually more efficient. I encourage you to try different approaches when prototyping things to understand where the sweet spot is in terms of convenience and your personal preferences.

The various features of the different methods should go a long way to making it clear which one is best for your particular use case. As a general rule, I'd suggest using the leftmost entry in Table 1-1 that meets your requirements for the features you want

15

to have available. Using something further to the right may be less convenient; using something too far to the left may mean you get frustrated trying to perform tasks that are easier in other tools.

Table 1-1. *Comparison of prototyping environments*

Feature	REPL	Script	Script + pdb	Jupyter	Jupyter + pdb
Indenting code	Strict rules	Normal rules	Normal rules	Normal rules	Normal rules
Re-running previous commands	Single typed line	Entire script only	Entire script or jump to the previous line	Logical blocks	Logical blocks
Stepping	Indented blocks run as one	The entire script runs as one	Step through statements	Logical blocks run as one	Step through statements
Introspection	Can introspect between logical blocks	No introspection	Can introspect between statements	Can introspect between logical blocks	Can introspect between statements
Persistence	Nothing is saved	Commands are saved	Commands are saved, interactions at the pdb prompt are not	Commands and output are saved	Commands and output are saved
Editing	Commands must be reentered	Any command can be edited, but the whole script must be re-run	Any command can be edited, but the whole script must be re-run	Any command can be edited, but the logical block must be re-run	Any command can be edited, but the logical block must be re-run

In this chapter, we will be prototyping a few different functions that return data about the system they're running on. They will depend on some external libraries, and we may need to use some simple loops, but not extensively.

As we're unlikely to have complex control structures, the indenting code feature isn't a concern. Re-running previous commands will be useful as we're dealing with multiple different data sources. It's possible that some of these data sources will be slow, so we don't want to be forced to always re-run every data source command when working on one of them. That discounts the REPL and is a closer fit for Jupyter than the script-based processes.

We want to be able to introspect the results of each data source, but we are unlikely to need to introspect the internal variables of individual data sources, which suggests the pdb-based approaches are not necessary (and, if that changes, we can always add in a `breakpoint()` call). We will want to store the code we're writing, but that only discounts the REPL which has already been discounted. Finally, we want to be able to edit code and see the difference it makes.

If we compare these requirements to Table 1-1, we can create Table 1-2, which shows that the Jupyter approach covers all of the features we need well, whereas the script approach is good enough but not quite optimal in terms of ability to re-run previous commands.

For that reason, in this chapter we will be using a Jupyter notebook to do our prototyping. Throughout the rest of the chapter, we will cover some other advantages that Jupyter affords us, as well as some techniques for using it effectively as part of a Python development process, rather than to create stand-alone software distributed as a notebook.

Table 1-2. *Matrix of whether the features of the various approaches match our requirements*[9]

Feature	REPL	Script	Script + pdb	Jupyter	Jupyter + pdb
Indenting code	✔	✔	✔	✔	✔
Re-running previous commands	✘	⚠	⚠	✔	✔
Stepping	✘	✘	⚠	✔	⚠
Introspection	✔	✔	✔	✔	✔
Persistence	✘	✔	✔	✔	✔
Editing	✘	✔	✔	✔	✔

---

[9] ✔ indicates that our requirements are met, ✘ indicates that they are not, and ⚠ represents that our requirements are met, but with a poor user experience.

Environment setup

That said, we need to install libraries and manage dependencies for this project, which means that we need a virtual environment. We specify our dependencies using pipenv, a tool that handles both the creation of isolated virtual environments and excellent dependency management.

```
> python -m pip install --user pipenv
```

WHY PIPENV

There has been a long history of systems to create isolated environments in Python. The one you'll most likely have used before is called virtualenv. You may also have used venv, conda, buildout, virtualenvwrapper, or pyenv. You may even have created your own by manipulating `sys.path` or creating lnk files in Python's internal directories.

Each of these methods has positives and negatives (except for the manual method, for which I can think of only negatives), but pipenv has excellent support for managing direct dependencies while keeping track of a full set of dependency versions that are known to work correctly and ensuring that your environment is kept up to date. That makes it a good fit for modern pure Python projects. If you've got a workflow that involves building binaries or working with outdated packages, then sticking with the existing workflow may be a better fit for you than migrating it to pipenv. In particular, if you're using Anaconda because you do scientific computing, there's no need to switch to pipenv. If you wish, you can use `pipenv --site-packages` to make pipenv include the packages that are managed through conda as well as its own.

Pipenv's development cycle is rather long, as compared to other Python tools. It's not uncommon for it to go months or years without a release. In general, I've found pipenv to be stable and reliable, which is why I'm recommending it. Package managers that have more frequent releases sometimes outstay their welcome, forcing you to respond to breaking changes regularly.

For pipenv to work effectively, it does require that the maintainers of packages you're declaring a dependency on correctly declare their dependencies. Some packages do not do this well, for example, by specifying only a dependency package without any version restrictions when restrictions exist. This problem can happen, for example, because a new major release of a subdependency has recently been released. In these cases, you can add your own restrictions on what versions you'll accept (called a *version pin*).

If you find yourself in a situation where a package is missing a required version pin, please consider contacting the package maintainers to alert them. Open source maintainers are often very busy and may not yet have noticed the issue – don't assume that just because they're experienced that they don't need your help. Most Python packages have repositories on GitHub with an issue tracker. You see from the issue tracker if anyone else has reported the problem yet, and if not, it is an easy way to contribute to the packages that are easing your development tasks.

Setting up a new project

First, create a new directory for this project and change to it. We want to declare ipykernel as a development dependency. This package contains the code to manage an interface between Python and Jupyter, and we want to ensure that it and its library code is available within our new, isolated environment.

```
> mkdir advancedpython
> cd advancedpython
> pipenv install ipykernel --dev
> pipenv run ipython kernel install --user --name=advancedpython
```

The final line here instructs the copy of IPython within the isolated environment to install itself as an available kernel for the current user account, with the name advancedpython. This allows us to select the kernel without having to activate this isolated environment manually each time. Installed kernels can be listed with jupyter kernelspec list and removed with jupyter kernelspec remove.

Now we can start Jupyter and see options to run code against our system Python or our isolated environment. I recommend opening a new command window for this, as Jupyter runs in the foreground and we will need to use the command line again shortly. If you have a Jupyter server open from earlier in this chapter, I'd recommend stopping that one before opening the new one. We want to use the working directory we created previously, so change to that directory if the new window isn't already there.

```
> cd advancedpython
> jupyter notebook
```

A web browser automatically opens and displays the Jupyter interface with a directory listing of the directory we created. This will look like Figure 1-3. With the project set up, it's time to start prototyping. Choose "New" and then "advancedpython".

We now see the main editing interface for a notebook. We have one "cell" that contains nothing and has not been executed. Any code we type into the cell can be run by clicking the "Run" button just above. Jupyter displays the output of the cell underneath, as well as a new empty cell for further code. You should think of a cell as being approximately equal to a function body. They generally contain multiple related statements which you want to run as a logical group.

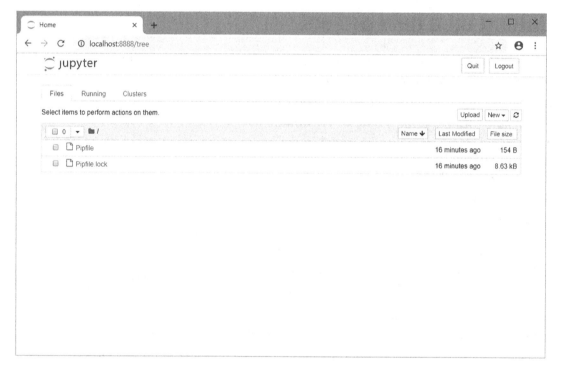

Figure 1-3. *The Jupyter home screen in a new pipenv directory*

Prototyping our scripts

A logical first step is to create a Python program that returns various information about the system it is running on. Later on, these pieces of information will be part of the data that's aggregated, but for now some simple data is an appropriate first objective.

In the spirit of starting small, we'll use the first cell for finding the version of Python we are running, shown in Figure 1-4. As this is exposed by the Python standard library and works on all platforms, it is a good placeholder for something more interesting.

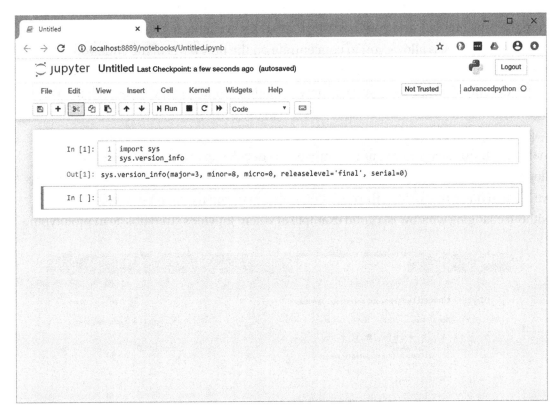

Figure 1-4. *A simple Jupyter notebook showing sys.version_info*

Jupyter shows the value of the last line of the cell, as well as anything explicitly printed. As the last line of our cell is `sys.version_info`, that is what is shown in the output.[10]

---

[10]This means that if your cell ends with an assignment, it won't show the value being assigned. This is because assignments in Python do not evaluate to a variable. It's common to explicitly show this with

```
version = sys.version_info
```

```
version
```

While you could also use Python 3.8's "walrus" operator, (`version := sys.version_info`), as that does evaluate to the value being assigned, it looks rather strange so I recommend against using it for a stand-alone assignment. This operator is best used in the condition of loops and if statements, where it looks a lot more natural as the parentheses are not required in such cases.

Another useful piece of information to aggregate is the current machine's IP address. This isn't exposed in a single variable; it's the result of a few API calls and processing of information. As this requires more than a simple import, it makes sense to build up the variables step by step in new cells. When doing so, you can see at a glance what you got from the previous call, and you have those variables available in the next cell. This step-by-step process allows you to concentrate on the new parts of the code you're writing, ignoring the parts you've completed.

By the end of this process, you will have something similar to the code in Figure 1-5, showing the various IP addresses associated with the current computer. At the second stage, it became apparent that there were both IPv4 and IPv6 addresses available. This makes the third stage slightly more complex, as I decided to extract the type of address along with the actual value. By performing these steps individually, we can adapt to things we learn in one when writing the next. Being able to re-run the loop body individually without changing window is a good example of where Jupyter's strengths lie in prototyping.

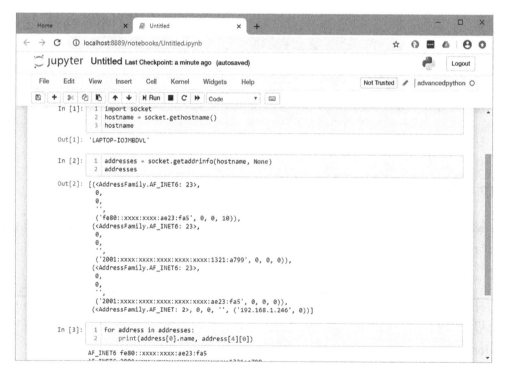

Figure 1-5. *Prototyping a complex function in multiple cells[11]*

---

[11]Part of the world-routable IPv6 address has been censored in these screenshots.

At this point, we have three cells to find the IP addresses, meaning there's no one-to-one mapping between cells and logical components. To tidy this up, select the top cell and select "Merge Cell Below" from the edit menu. Do this twice to merge both additional cells, and the full implementation is now stored as a single logical block (Figure 1-6). This operation can now be run as a whole, rather than all three cells needing to have been run to produce the output. It is a good idea to tidy the contents of this cell up, too: as we no longer want to print the intermediate values, we can remove the duplicate addresses line.

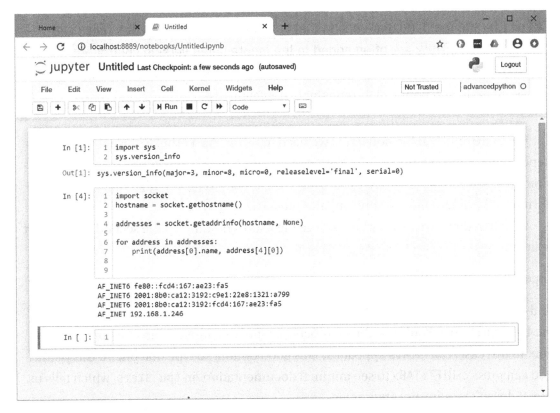

Figure 1-6. *The result of merging the cells from Figure 1-5*

Installing dependencies

A more useful thing to know would be how much load the system is experiencing. In Linux, this can be found by reading the values stored in /proc/loadavg. In macOS this is sysctl -n vm.loadavg. Both systems also include it in the output of other programs, such as uptime, but this is such a common task that there is undoubtedly a library that can help us. We don't want to add any complexity if we can avoid it.

We're going to install our first dependency, psutil. As this is an actual dependency of our code, not a development tool that we happen to want available, we should omit the --dev flag we used when installing dependencies earlier:

```
> pipenv install psutil
```

Note   We have no preferences about which version of psutil is needed, so we have not specified a version. The install command adds the dependency to Pipfile and the particular version that is picked to Pipfile.lock. Files with the extension .lock are often added to the ignore set in version control. You should make an exception for Pipfile.lock as it helps when reconstructing old environments and performing repeatable deployments.

When we return to the notebook, we need to restart the kernel to ensure the new dependency is available. Click the Kernel menu, then restart. If you prefer keyboard shortcuts, you can press <ESCAPE> to exit editing mode (the green highlight for your current cell will turn blue to confirm) and press 0 (zero) twice.

With that done, we can start to explore the psutils module. In the second cell, import psutil:

```
import psutil
```

and click Run (or, <SHIFT+ENTER> to run the cell from the keyboard). In a new cell, type psutil.cpu<TAB>.[12] You'll see the members of psutil that jupyter can autocomplete for you. In this case, cpu_stats appears to be a good option, so type that out. At this point, you can press <SHIFT+TAB> to see minimal documentation on cpu_stats, which tells us that it doesn't require any arguments.

Finish the line, so the cells now read:

```
import psutil

psutil.cpu_stats()
```

---

[12]This shortcut only works if the variable is available to the kernel, so you may find you have to run the cell that defines it before you can use the autocompletion. If you're overwriting the same variable name with different data, then you may see the wrong information, but I'd recommend against doing this where possible as it can be confusing.

When we run the second cell, we see that `cpu_stats` gives us rather opaque information on the operating system's internal use of the CPU. Let's try `cpu_percent` instead. Using `<SHIFT+TAB>` on this function, we see that it takes two optional parameters. The interval parameter determines how long the function takes before it returns and works best if it's nonzero. For that reason, we'll modify the code as follows and get a simple floating-point number between 0 and 100:

```
import psutil
psutil.cpu_percent(interval=0.1)
```

EXERCISE 1-1: EXPLORE THE LIBRARY

Numerous other functions in the psutil library make good sources of data, so let's create a cell for each function that looks interesting. There are different functions available on different operating systems, so be aware that if you're following this tutorial on Windows, you have a slightly more limited choice of functions.

Try the autocomplete and help functions of Jupyter to get a feel for what information you find useful and create at least one more cell that returns data.

Including `psutil`'s import in each cell would be repetitive and not good practice for a Python file, but we do want to make sure it's easy to run a single function in isolation. To solve this, we'll move the imports to a new top cell, which is the equivalent of the module scope in a standard Python file.

Once you've created additional cells for your data sources, your notebook will look something like Figure 1-7.

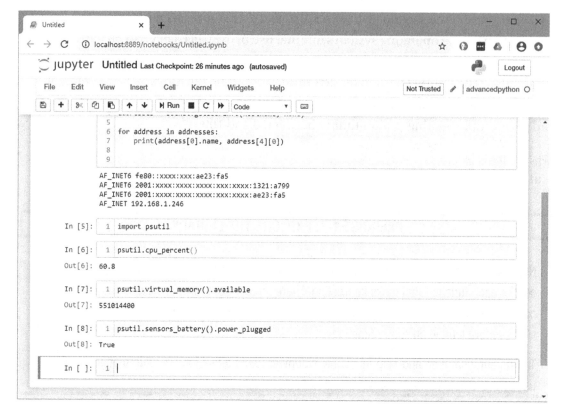

Figure 1-7. *An example of a complete notebook following the exercise*

While you've been doing this, the numbers in square brackets next to the cell have been increasing. This number is the sequence of operations that have been run. The number next to the first cell has stayed constant, meaning this cell hasn't been run while we've experimented with the lower one.

In the Cell menu, there is an option to Run All, which will run each cell in sequence like a standard Python file. While it's useful to be able to run all cells to test the entire notebook, being able to run each cell individually lets you split out complex and slow logic from what you're working on without having to re-run it each time.

To demonstrate how this could be useful, we'll modify our use of the `cpu_percent` function. We picked an interval of 0.1 as it's enough to get accurate data. A larger interval, while less realistic, helps us see how Jupyter allows us to write expensive setup code while still allowing us to re-run faster parts without waiting for the slow ones.

```
import psutil
psutil.cpu_percent(interval=5)
```

Exporting to a .py file

Although Jupyter has served us well as a prototyping tool, it's not a good match for the main body of our project. We want a traditional Python application, and the great presentation features of Jupyter aren't useful right now. Jupyter has built-in support for exporting notebooks in a variety of formats, from slideshows to HTML, but the one we're interested in is Python scripts.

The script to do the conversion is part of the Jupyter command, using the nbconvert (notebook convert) subcommand.[13]

```
> jupyter nbconvert --to script Untitled.ipynb
```

The untitled notebook we created is left unchanged, and a new Untitled.py file (Listing 1-4) is generated. If you renamed your notebook, then the names match the name you assigned. If you didn't, and want to rename it now as you hadn't noticed that it was just called Untitled.ipynb previously, click "Untitled" at the top of the notebook view and enter a new title.

Listing 1-4. Untitled.py, generated from the preceding notebook

```
#!/usr/bin/env python
# coding: utf-8

# In[1]:

import sys
sys.version_info

# In[4]:

import socket
hostname = socket.gethostname()

addresses = socket.getaddrinfo(hostname, None)

for address in addresses:
    print(address[0].name, address[4][0])
```

---

[13]IDEs and editors that offer notebook compatibility usually have a feature to do this from within the editor window, too.

```
# In[5]:

import psutil

# In[6]:

psutil.cpu_percent()

# In[7]:

psutil.virtual_memory().available

# In[8]:

psutil.sensors_battery().power_plugged

# In[ ]:
```

As you can see, each cell is separated from the others with comments, and the standard boilerplate around text encoding and shebang is present at the top of the file. Starting the prototyping in Jupyter rather than directly in a Python script or in the REPR hasn't cost us anything in terms of flexibility or time; rather it gave us more control over how we executed the individual blocks of code while we were exploring.

We can now tidy this up to be a utility script rather than bare statements by moving the imports to the top of the file and converting each cell into a named function. The # In comments that show where cells started are useful reminders as to where a function should start. We also have to convert the code to return the value, not just leave it at the end of the function (or print it, in the case of the IP addresses). The result is Listing 1-5.

Listing 1-5. serverstatus.py

```
# coding: utf-8
import sys
import socket

import psutil

def python_version():
    return sys.version_info
```

```python
def ip_addresses():
    hostname = socket.gethostname()

    addresses = socket.getaddrinfo(hostname, None)
    address_info = []
    for address in addresses:
        address_info.append(address[0].name, address[4][0])
    return address_info

def cpu_load():
    return psutil.cpu_percent()

def ram_available():
    return psutil.virtual_memory().available

def ac_connected():
    return psutil.sensors_battery().power_plugged
```

Building a command-line interface

These functions alone are not especially useful, most only each wrap an existing Python function. The obvious thing we want to do is to print their data, so you may wonder why we've gone to the trouble of creating single-line wrapper functions. This will be more obvious as we create more complex data sources and multiple ways of consuming them, as we will benefit from not having special-cased the simplest ones. For now, to make these useful, we can give users a simple command-line application that displays this data.

As we are working with a bare Python script rather than something installable, we use an idiom commonly called "ifmain". This is built into many coding text editors and IDEs as a snippet as it's hard to remember and very unintuitive. It looks like this:

```python
def do_something():
    print("Do something")

if __name__ == '__main__':
    do_something()
```

It really is quite horrid. The __name__ [14] variable is a reference to the fully qualified name of a module. If you import a module, the __name__ attribute will be the location from which it can be imported.

```
>>> from json import encoder
>>> type(encoder)
<class 'module'>
>>> encoder.__name__
'json.encoder'
```

However, if you load code through an interactive session or by providing a path to a script to run, then it can't necessarily be imported. Such modules, therefore, get the special name "__main__". The ifmain trick is used to detect if that is the case. That is, if the module has been specified on the command line as the file to run, then the contents of the block will execute. The code inside this block will *not* execute when the module is imported by other code because the __name__ variable would be set to the name of the module instead. Without this guard in place, the command-line handler would execute whenever this module is imported, making it take over any program that uses these utility functions.

Caution   As the contents of the ifmain block can only be run if the module is the entrypoint into the application, you should be careful to keep it as short as possible. Generally, it's a good idea to limit it to a single statement that calls a utility function. This allows that function call to be testable and is required for some of the techniques we will be looking at in the next chapter.

The sys module and argv

Most programming languages expose a variable named argv, which represents the name of the program and the arguments that the user passed on invocation. In Python, this is a list of strings where the first entry is the name of the Python script (but not the location of the Python interpreter) and any arguments listed after that.

---

[14]This is usually pronounced "dunder main" for "double underscore" as saying "underscore" four times adds 12 syllables and feels silly.

Without checking the argv variable, we can only produce very basic scripts. Users expect a command-line flag that provides help information about the tool. Also, all but the simplest of programs need to allow users to pass configuration variables in from the command line.

The simplest way of doing this is to check the values that are present in sys.argv and handle them in conditionals. Implementing a help flag might look like Listing 1-6.

Listing 1-6. sensors_argv.py – cli using manual checking of argv

```python
#!/usr/bin/env python
# coding: utf-8

import socket
import sys

import psutil

HELP_TEXT = """usage: python {program_name:s}

Displays the values of the sensors

Options and arguments:
--help:    Display this message"""

def python_version():
    return sys.version_info

def ip_addresses():
    hostname = socket.gethostname()
    addresses = socket.getaddrinfo(socket.gethostname(), None)

    address_info = []
    for address in addresses:
        address_info.append((address[0].name, address[4][0]))
    return address_info

def cpu_load():
    return psutil.cpu_percent(interval=0.1)

def ram_available():
    return psutil.virtual_memory().available
```

```python
def ac_connected():
    return psutil.sensors_battery().power_plugged

def show_sensors():
    print("Python version: {0.major}.{0.minor}".format(python_version()))
    for address in ip_addresses():
        print("IP addresses: {0[1]} ({0[0]})".format(address))
    print("CPU Load: {:.1f}".format(cpu_load()))
    print("RAM Available: {} MiB".format(ram_available() / 1024**2))
    print("AC Connected: {}".format(ac_connected()))

def command_line(argv):
    program_name, *arguments = argv
    if not arguments:
        show_sensors()
    elif arguments and arguments[0] == '--help':
        print(HELP_TEXT.format(program_name=program_name))
        return
    else:
        raise ValueError("Unknown arguments {}".format(arguments))

if __name__ == '__main__':
    command_line(sys.argv)
```

The command_line(...) function is not overly complicated, but this is a very simple program. You can easily imagine situations where there are multiple flags allowed in any order and configurable variables being significantly more complex. This is only practically possible because there is no ordering or parsing of values involved. Some helper functionality is available in the standard library to make it easier to create more involved command-line utilities.

argparse

The argparse module is the standard method for parsing command-line arguments without depending on external libraries. It makes handling the complex situations alluded to earlier significantly less complicated; however, as with many libraries that offer developers choices, its interface is rather difficult to remember. Unless you're writing command-line utilities regularly, it's likely to be something that you read the documentation of every time you need to use it.

The model that argparse follows is that the programmer creates an explicit parser by instantiating `argparse.ArgumentParser` with some basic information about the program, then calling functions on that parser to add new options. Those functions specify what the option is called, what the help text is, any default values, as well as how the parser should handle it. For example, some arguments are simple flags, like `--dry-run`; others are additive, like `-v`, `-vv`, and `-vvv`; and yet others take an explicit value, like `--config config.ini`.

We aren't using any parameters in our program just yet, so we skip over adding these options and have the parser parse the arguments from `sys.argv`. The result of that function call is the information it has gleaned from the user. Some basic handling is also done at this stage, such as handling `--help`, which displays an autogenerated help screen based on the options that were added.

Our command-line program looks like Listing 1-7, when written using argparse.

Listing 1-7. sensors_argparse.py – cli using the standard library module argparse

```python
#!/usr/bin/env python
# coding: utf-8

import argparse
import socket
import sys

import psutil

def python_version():
    return sys.version_info

def ip_addresses():
    hostname = socket.gethostname()
    addresses = socket.getaddrinfo(socket.gethostname(), None)

    address_info = []
    for address in addresses:
        address_info.append((address[0].name, address[4][0]))
    return address_info
```

```
def cpu_load():
    return psutil.cpu_percent(interval=0.1)

def ram_available():
    return psutil.virtual_memory().available

def ac_connected():
    return psutil.sensors_battery().power_plugged

def show_sensors():
    print("Python version: {0.major}.{0.minor}".format(python_version()))
    for address in ip_addresses():
        print("IP addresses: {0[1]} ({0[0]})".format(address))
    print("CPU Load: {:.1f}".format(cpu_load()))
    print("RAM Available: {} MiB".format(ram_available() / 1024**2))
    print("AC Connected: {}".format(ac_connected()))

def command_line(argv):
    parser = argparse.ArgumentParser(
        description='Displays the values of the sensors',
        add_help=True,
    )
    arguments = parser.parse_args()
    show_sensors()

if __name__ == '__main__':
    command_line(sys.argv)
```

click

Click is an add-on module that simplifies the process of creating command-line interfaces on the assumption that your interface is broadly similar to the standard that people expect. It makes for a significantly more natural flow when creating command-line interfaces and encourages you toward intuitive interfaces.

Whereas argparse requires the programmer to specify the options that are available when constructing a parser, click uses decorators on methods to infer what the parameters should be. This approach is a little less flexible, but easily handles 80% of typical use cases. If you're writing a command-line interface, you generally want to follow the lead of other tools, so it is intuitive for the end-user.

As click isn't in the standard library, we need to install it into our environment. Like psutil, click is a code dependency, not a development tool, so we install it as follows:

```
> pipenv install click
```

As we only have one primary command and no options, click only requires two lines of code to be added, an import and the `@click.command(...)` decorator. The `print(...)` calls should all be replaced with `click.echo(...)`, but this isn't strictly required. The result is shown as Listing 1-8. `click.echo` is a helper function that behaves like print, but also handles situations where there is a mismatch in character encodings, and intelligently strips or retains color and formatting markers depending on the capabilities of the terminal that called the program and whether the output is being piped elsewhere.

Listing 1-8. sensors_click.py – cli using the contributed library click

```python
#!/usr/bin/env python
# coding: utf-8
import socket
import sys

import click
import psutil

def python_version():
    return sys.version_info

def ip_addresses():
    hostname = socket.gethostname()
    addresses = socket.getaddrinfo(socket.gethostname(), None)

    address_info = []
    for address in addresses:
        address_info.append((address[0].name, address[4][0]))
    return address_info

def cpu_load():
    return psutil.cpu_percent(interval=0.1)
```

```python
def ram_available():
    return psutil.virtual_memory().available

def ac_connected():
    return psutil.sensors_battery().power_plugged

@click.command(help="Displays the values of the sensors")
def show_sensors():
    click.echo("Python version: {0.major}.{0.minor}".format(python_version()))
    for address in ip_addresses():
        click.echo("IP addresses: {0[1]} ({0[0]})".format(address))
    click.echo("CPU Load: {:.1f}".format(cpu_load()))
    click.echo("RAM Available: {} MiB".format(ram_available() / 1024**2))
    click.echo("AC Connected: {}".format(ac_connected()))

if __name__ == '__main__':
    show_sensors()
```

It also has many utility functions which make creating more complex interfaces easier and compensate for nonstandard terminal environment on end-user systems. For example, if we decided to make the headers bold in the show_sensors command, in click we can use the secho(...) command, for echoing to the terminal with styling information. A version that styles headings is shown as Listing 1-9.

Listing 1-9. Extract from sensors_click_bold.py

```python
@click.command(help="Displays the values of the sensors")
def show_sensors():
    click.secho("Python version: ", bold=True, nl=False)
    click.echo("{0.major}.{0.minor}".format(python_version()))
    for address in ip_addresses():
        click.secho("IP addresses: ", bold=True, nl=False)
        click.echo("{0[1]} ({0[0]})".format(address))
    click.secho("CPU Load: ", bold=True, nl=False)
    click.echo("{:.1f}".format(cpu_load()))
    click.secho("RAM Available: ", bold=True, nl=False)
    click.echo("{} MiB".format(ram_available() / 1024**2))
    click.secho("AC Connected: ", bold=True, nl=False)
    click.echo("{}".format(ac_connected()))
```

The *secho(. . .)* function *prints some information to the screen with the formatting specified.* The nl= *argument allows* us *to specify if a new line should be printed or not.* If you're not using click, the simplest method would be

```python
BOLD = '\033[1m'
END = '\033[0m'
def show_sensors():
    print(BOLD + "Python version:" + END + " ({0.major}.{0.minor})".
    format(python_version()))
    for address in ip_addresses():
        print(BOLD  + "IP addresses: " + END + "{0[1]} ({0[0]})".
        format(address))
    print(BOLD + "CPU Load:" + END + " {:.1f}".format(cpu_load()))
    print(BOLD + "RAM Available:" + END + "{} MiB".format(ram_available() /
    1024**2))
    print(BOLD + "AC Connected:" + END + " {}".format(ac_connected()))
```

Click also provides transparent support for autocomplete in terminals and a number of other useful functions. We will revisit these later in the book when we expand on this interface.

Pushing the boundaries

We've looked at using Jupyter and IPython for doing prototyping, but sometimes we need to run prototype code on a specific computer, rather than the one we're using for day-to-day development work. This could be because the computer has a peripheral or some software we need, for example.

This is mainly a matter of comfort; editing and running code on a remote machine can vary from slightly inconvenient to outright difficult, especially when there are differences in the operating system.

In the preceding examples, we've run all the code locally. However, we are planning to run the final code on a Raspberry Pi as that's where we attach our specialized sensors. As an embedded system, it has significant hardware differences, both in terms of performance and peripherals.

Remote kernels

Testing this code would require running a Jupyter environment on a Raspberry Pi and connecting to that over HTTP or else connecting over SSH and interacting with the Python interpreter manually. This is suboptimal, as it requires ensuring that the Raspberry Pi has open ports for Jupyter to bind to and requires manually synchronizing the contents of notebooks between the local and remote hosts using a tool like scp. This is even more of a problem with real-world examples. It's hard to imagine opening a port on a server and connecting to Jupyter there to test log analysis code.

Instead, it is possible to use the pluggable kernel infrastructure of Jupyter and IPython to connect a locally running Jupyter notebook to one of many remote computers. This allows testing of the same code transparently on multiple machines and with minimal manual work.

When Jupyter displays its list of potential execution targets, it is listing its list of known *kernel specifications*. When a kernel specification has been selected, an *instance* of that kernel is created and linked to the notebook. It is possible to connect to remote machines and manually start an individual kernel for your local Jupyter instance to connect to. However, this is rarely an effective use of time. When we ran `pipenv run ipython kernel install` at the start of this chapter, we were creating a new kernel specification for the current environment and installing that into the list of known kernel specifications.

To add kernel specifications that use remote hosts, we can use the helper utility `remote_ikernel`. We should install this to the same location as Jupyter, as it is a helper for Jupyter rather than a specific development tool for this environment.

```
> pip install --user remote_ikernel
```

We then need to set up the environment and kernel helper program on the remote host. Connect to the Raspberry Pi (or another machine that we want to send code to) and create a pipenv on that computer as we did earlier:

```
rpi> python -m pip install --user pipenv
rpi> mkdir development-testing
rpi> cd development-testing
rpi> pipenv install ipykernel
```

Tip   Some low-performance hosts, such as Raspberry Pis, may make installing ipython_kernel frustratingly slow. In this case, you may consider using the package manager's version of ipython_kernel instead. The ipython kernel does require many support libraries which may take some time to install on a low-powered computer. In that case, you could set up the environment as

```
rpi> sudo apt install python3-ipykernel
rpi> pipenv --three --site-packages
```

Alternatively, if yOou are using the Raspberry Pi, there is a repository of precompiled wheels at `https://www.piwheels.org` which can be enabled by adding the following new source to your Pipfile, in addition to the existing one:

```
[[source]]
url = "https://www.piwheels.org/simple"
name = "piwheels"
verify_ssl = true
```

You would then install the ipython_kernel package as normal using `pipenv install`. If you're using a Raspberry Pi running Raspbian, you should always add piwheels to your Pipfile, as Raspbian comes preconfigured to use PiWheels globally. Not listing it in your Pipfile can cause installations to fail.

This will install the IPython kernel program on the Raspberry Pi machine; however, we still need to install it on our host machine. To start with, we'll install a kernel pointing at the pipenv environment that we've created. After this, the Raspberry Pi will have two kernels available, one for the system Python install and one called development-testing for our environment. After installing the kernel, we can view the configuration file for the specification:

```
rpi> pipenv run ipython kernel install --user --name=development-testing
Installed kernelspec development-testing in /home/pi/.local/share/jupyter/
kernels/development-testing
> cat /home/pi/.local/share/jupyter/kernels/development-testing/kernel.json
{
"argv": [
```

```
"/home/pi/.local/share/virtualenvs/development-testing-nbi70cWI/bin/
python",
"-m",
"ipykernel_launcher",
"-f",
"{connection_file}"
],
"display_name": "development-testing",
"language": "python"
}
```

This output shows us how Jupyter would run the kernel if it were installed on that computer. We can use the information from this specification to create a new remote_ikernel specification on our development machine that points at the same environment as the development-testing kernel on the Raspberry Pi.

The preceding kernel specification lists how the kernel is started on the Raspberry Pi. We can verify this by testing the command over SSH to the Raspberry Pi, for example, by changing -f {connection_file} to --help to show the help text.

```
rpi> /home/pi/.local/share/virtualenvs/development-testing-nbi70cWI/bin/
python -m ipykernel –help
```

We can now return to our development computer and create the remote kernel specification, as follows:

```
> remote_ikernel manage --add --kernel_cmd="/home/pi/.local/share/
virtualenvs/development-testing-nbi70cWI/bin/python
-m ipykernel_launcher -f {connection_file}"
--name="development-testing" --interface=ssh --host=pi@raspberrypi
--workdir="/home/pi/developmenttesting" --language=python
```

It looks a bit intimidating, spanning five lines of text, but it can be broken up:

- The --kernel_cmd parameter is the contents of the argv section from the kernel spec file. Each line is space separated and without the individual quotation marks. This is the command that starts the kernel itself.

- The --name parameter is the equivalent of display_name from the original kernel spec. This is what will be shown in Jupyter when you select this kernel, alongside SSH information. It doesn't have to match the remote kernel's name that you've copied from, it's just for your reference.

- The --interface and --host parameters define how to connect to the remote machine. You should ensure that passwordless[15] SSH is possible to this machine so that Jupyter can set up connections.

- The --workdir parameter is the default working directory that the environment should use. I recommend setting this to be the directory that contains your remote Pipfile.

- The --language parameter is the value of the language value from the original kernel spec to differentiate different programming languages.

Tip   If you're having difficulty connecting to the remote kernel, you can try opening a shell using Jupyter on the command line. This often shows useful error messages. Find the name of the kernel using jupyter kernelspec list and then use that with jupyter console:

```
> jupyter kernelspec list
Available kernels:
  advancedpython
C:\Users\micro\AppData\Roaming\jupyter\kernels\advancedpython

  rik_ssh_pi_raspberrypi_developmenttesting
C:\Users\micro\AppData\Roaming\jupyter\kernels\
rik_ssh_pi_raspberrypi_developmenttesting

> jupyter console --kernel= rik_ssh_pi_raspberrypi_developmenttesting
In [1]:
```

---

[15]Use ssh-copy-id user@host to set this up automatically, rather than manually editing the authorized_hosts file.

At this point, when we reenter the Jupyter environment, we see a new kernel available that matches the connection information we supplied. We can then select that kernel and execute commands that require that environment,[16] with the Jupyter kernel system taking care of connecting to the Raspberry Pi and activating the environment in `~/development-testing`.

Developing code that cannot be run locally

There are some useful sensors available on the Raspberry Pi; these provide the actual data that we are interested in collecting. In other use cases, this might be information gathered by calling custom command-line utilities, introspecting a database, or making local API calls.

This isn't a book on how to make the most of the Raspberry Pi, so we will gloss over much of the detail of exactly how it does its work, but suffice it to say that there is a large amount of documentation and support for doing exciting things using Python. In this case, there is a library that we want to use that provides a function to retrieve both temperature and relative humidity from a sensor that can be added to the board. Like many other tasks, this is relatively slow (it can take a good portion of a second to measure) and requires a specific environment (an external sensor being installed) to execute. In that way, it is similar to monitoring active processes on a web server by communicating through their management ports.

To begin with, we add the Adafruit DHT[17] library to our environment. We have currently got copies of a pipfile both on the Raspberry Pi and locally. The remote copy only contains the dependency on ipykernel, which is already in the local copy, so it's safe to overwrite the remote file with the one we've created locally. As we know that the DHT library is only useful on Raspberry Pis, we can restrict it so that it only installed on Linux machines with ARM processors, using the conditional dependency syntax:[18]

```
> pipenv install "Adafruit-CircuitPython-DHT ; 'arm' in platform_machine"
```

---

[16]If you prefer a console environment to the web environment of the Jupyter notebook, you can see a list of available kernels using `jupyter kernelspec list` and open an IPython shell connected to the specification of your choice with `jupyter console --kernel kernelname`.

[17]This is part of Adafruit's excellent CircuitPython ecosystem. They have a lot more information on these sensors and how to use them in a variety of projects at `https://learn.adafruit.com/dht`

[18]This is defined by PEP508 at `www.python.org/dev/peps/pep-0508/`. There is a table on that page which lists the valid filters, although more may be added in future.

This results in the `Pipfile` and `Pipfile.lock` files being updated to include this dependency. We want to make use of these dependencies on the remote host, so we must copy these files across and install them using Pipenv. It would be possible to run this command in both environments, but that risks mistakes creeping in. Pipenv assumes that you use the same version of Python for both development and deployment, in keeping with its philosophy of avoiding problems during deployment. For that reason, if you're planning to deploy to a set version of Python, you should use that for development locally.

However, if you do not want to install unusual versions of Python in your local environment, or if you're targeting multiple different machines, it is possible to deactivate this check. To do so, remove the `python_version` line from the end of your Pipfile. This allows your environment to be deployed to any Python version. However, you should ensure that you're aware of what versions you need to support and test accordingly.

Copy both `Pipfile` and `Pipfile.lock` files to the remote host using `scp` (or your tool of choice), and then on the remote machine, run `pipenv install` with the `--deploy` flag. `--deploy` instructs pipenv only to proceed if the exact versions match, which is very useful for deploying a known-good environment from one machine to another.

```
rpi> cd /home/pi/development-testing
rpi> pipenv install --deploy
```

Be aware, however, that if you've created your `Pipfile` on a different operating system or a different CPU architecture (such as files created on a standard laptop and installed on a Raspberry Pi), it is possible that the pinned packages will not be suitable when deploying them on another machine. In this case, it is possible to relock the dependencies without triggering version upgrades by running `pipenv lock --keep-outdated`.

You now have the specified dependencies available in the remote environment. If you've relocked the files, you should transfer the changed lock file back and store it, so you can redeploy in future without having to regenerate this file. At this stage, you can connect to the remote server through your Jupyter client and begin prototyping. We're looking to add the humidity sensor, so we'll use the library we just added and can now receive a valid humidity percentage.

The Raspberry Pi that I copied these files to has a DHT22 sensor connected to pin D4, as demonstrated in Figure 1-8. This sensor is readily available from Raspberry Pi or general electronics suppliers. If you don't have one to hand, then try an alternative command that demonstrates that the code is running on the Pi, such as `platform.uname()`.

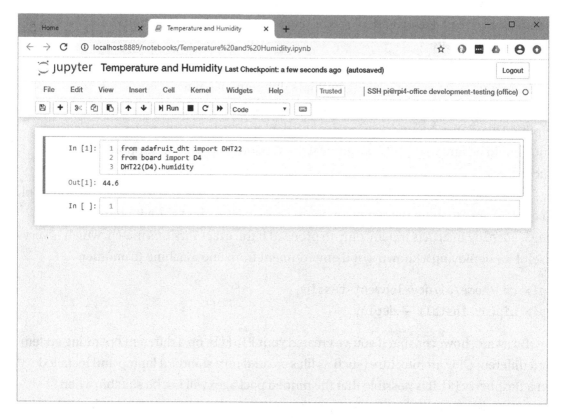

Figure 1-8. *Jupyter connected to a remote Raspberry Pi*

This notebook is stored locally on your development machine, not on the remote server. It can be migrated into being a Python script using `nbconvert`, in the same way as before. However, before we do that, we can also change the kernel back to our local instance to check that the code behaves correctly there. The objective is to create code that works on both environments, returning either the humidity or a placeholder value.

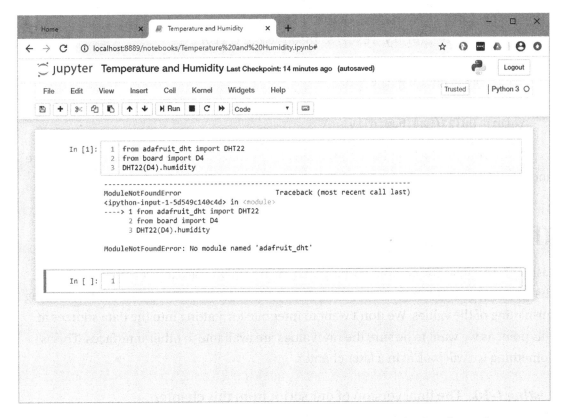

Figure 1-9. *Demonstration of the same code being run on the local machine*

Figure 1-9 demonstrates that the code is not suitable for all environments. We would very much like to be able to run at least some of the code locally, so we can adjust our code to take the limitations of other platforms into account. When this has been converted to the more general function form, it will look something like

```
def get_relative_humidity():
    try:
        # Connect to a DHT22 sensor on GPIO pin 4
        from adafruit_dht import DHT22
        from board import D4
```

```
    except (ImportError, NotImplementedError):
        # No DHT library results in an ImportError.
        # Running on an unknown platform results in a NotImplementedError
        # when getting the pin
        return None
    return DHT22(D4).humidity
```

This allows for the function to be called on any machine, unless it has a temperature and humidity sensor connected to pin D4 and to return a None anywhere else.

The completed script

Listing 1-10 shows the completed script. There are still hurdles to overcome to ensure that this is a useful library, most notably the fact that the show_sensors function is doing formatting of the values. We don't want to integrate formatting into the data sources at this point as we want to be sure the raw values are available to other interfaces. This is something we will look at in a later chapter.

Listing 1-10. The final version of our script from this chapter

```
#!/usr/bin/env python
# coding: utf-8
import socket
import sys

import click
import psutil

def python_version():
    return sys.version_info

def ip_addresses():
    hostname = socket.gethostname()
    addresses = socket.getaddrinfo(socket.gethostname(), None)
```

```python
        address_info = []
        for address in addresses:
            address_info.append((address[0].name, address[4][0]))
        return address_info

def cpu_load():
    return psutil.cpu_percent(interval=0.1) / 100.0

def ram_available():
    return psutil.virtual_memory().available

def ac_connected():
    return psutil.sensors_battery().power_plugged

def get_relative_humidity():
    try:
        # Connect to a DHT22 sensor on GPIO pin 4
        from adafruit_dht import DHT22
        from board import D4
    except (ImportError, NotImplementedError):
        # No DHT library results in an ImportError.
        # Running on an unknown platform results in a NotImplementedError
        # when getting the pin
        return None
    return DHT22(D4).humidity

@click.command(help="Displays the values of the sensors")
def show_sensors():
    click.echo("Python version: {0.major}.{0.minor}".format(python_version()))
    for address in ip_addresses():
        click.echo("IP addresses: {0[1]} ({0[0]})".format(address))
    click.echo("CPU Load: {:.1%}".format(cpu_load()))
    click.echo("RAM Available: {:.0f} MiB".format(ram_available() / 1024**2))
    click.echo("AC Connected: {!r}".format(ac_connected()))
    click.echo("Humidity: {!r}".format(get_relative_humidity()))

if __name__ == '__main__':
    show_sensors()
```

Summary

This concludes the chapter on prototyping; in the following chapters, we will build on the data extraction functions we've created here to create libraries and tools that follow Python best practice. We have followed the path from playing around with a library up to the point of having a working shell script that has genuine utility. As we continue, it will develop to better fit our end goal of distributed data aggregation.

The tips we've covered here can be useful at many points in the software development life cycle, but it's important not to be inflexible and only follow a process. While these methods are effective, sometimes opening the REPL or using pdb (or even plain `print(...)` calls) will be more straightforward than setting up a remote kernel. It is not possible to pick the best way of approaching a problem unless you're aware of the options.

To recap:

1. Jupyter is an excellent tool for exploring libraries and doing initial prototyping of their use.

2. There are special-purpose debuggers available for Python that can be integrated easily into your workflow using the `breakpoint()` function and environment variables.

3. Pipenv helps you to define version requirements that are kept up to date, involve minimal specification, and facilitate reproducible builds.

4. The library click allows for simple command-line interfaces in an idiomatic Python style.

5. Jupyter's kernel system allows for seamless integration of multiple programming languages running both locally and on other computers into a single development flow.

Additional resources

Each of the tools we've used in this chapter has a lot of depth to it, while we've only skimmed the surface to achieve our ends.

- The Pipenv documentation at `https://pipenv.pypa.io/en/latest/` has a lot of useful explanation on customizing pipenv to work as you want, specifically with regard to customizing virtual environment creation and integration into existing processes. If you're new to pipenv but have used virtual environments a lot, then this has good documentation to help you bridge the gap.

- If you're interested in prototyping other programming languages in Jupyter, I'd recommend you read through the Jupyter documentation at `https://jupyter.readthedocs.io/en/latest/` – especially the kernels section.

- For information on Raspberry Pis and compatible sensors, I recommend the CircuitPython project's documentation on the Raspberry Pi: `https://learn.adafruit.com/circuitpython-on-raspberrypi-linux`.

CHAPTER 2

Testing, checking, linting

Python is famously "duck" typed,[1] that is, you're expected to write code without explicit type checks. If you write a function that implements some algorithm on numeric types, it should work equally well when presented with `int`, `float`, `decimal.Decimal`, `fractions.Fraction`, or `numpy.uint64`. As long as the object provides the right functions and those functions have the correct meanings, they work correctly.

Python accomplishes this through the related features of *late binding* and *dynamic dispatch*. We will come back to this topic in more depth later, but suffice it to say dynamic dispatch is the difference between being able to run

```
some_int + other_int
some_float + other_float
```

and having to use[2]

```
int.__add__(some_int, other_int)
float.__add__(some_float, other_float)
```

That is, functions are resolved through an object to find the proper implementation for that type. Late binding means that this lookup happens when it's time to call that function, rather than when the program is being written. The combination of these two makes for what we call duck typing and allows for functions to be written that trust underlying object implementations without knowing what they are in advance.

---

[1] Derived from the phrase "If it walks like a duck and quacks like a duck, then it probably is a duck." In this context, it means that Python doesn't check that the type of a variable matches an existing declaration; rather it will accept any object in the place of any other so long as all the methods and attributes required to execute the code are present.

[2] Strictly speaking, it's the difference between `some_int.__add__(other_int)` and `int.__add__(some_int, other_int)`. Python will convert `x + y` to `x.__add__(y)` automatically, but I don't want to suggest that this is an appropriate way to add integers.

© Matthew Wilkes 2020
M. Wilkes, *Advanced Python Development*, https://doi.org/10.1007/978-1-4842-5793-7_2

However, this also means that Python programs don't benefit from the same level of automated checking that languages with *early binding*[3] offer.

Up until now, we've been writing simple functions that operate on Python's built-in data types, such as float. This works well for trivial functions, but as the program becomes more complex, it becomes harder and harder to write code that has no formal relationship to other parts of the code.

In the previous chapter, we added a humidity value to the data collection, but it's coming from a sensor that also collects the ambient temperature. The sensor returns this in degrees Celsius. We can add a matching temperature sensor, as demonstrated in Listing 2-1.

Listing 2-1. A simple temperature sensor function

```
def get_temperature():
    # Connect to a DHT22 sensor on GPIO pin 4
    try:
        from adafruit_dht import DHT22
        from board import D4
    except (ImportError, NotImplementedError):
        # No DHT library results in an ImportError.
        # Running on an unknown platform results in a NotImplementedError
        # when getting the pin
        return None
    return DHT22(D4).temperature
```

However, we might want to allow users to see this in different formats. When we write a conversion function, we know from our understanding of what the program does and the name that we give the function that it operates on numbers to convert from one temperature system to another, but that relationship is purely one of the developer's understanding, it isn't implied by any of the code. The code we'd write to do this is shown in Listing 2-2.

---

[3]Early binding is the requirement that the exact function that will be used is known when the program is being written.

Listing 2-2. Conversion functions for Celsius to Fahrenheit and Celsius to Kelvin

```
In [1]:  1  def celsius_to_fahrenheit(celsius):
         2      return celsius * 9 / 5 + 32
         3
         4  def celsius_to_kelvin(celsius):
         5      return 273.15 + celsius
```

```
In [2]:  1  celsius_to_fahrenheit(21)
Out[2]: 69.8
```

```
In [3]:  1  celsius_to_kelvin(21)
Out[3]: 294.15
```

As you can see from the screenshot, these work correctly for integer arguments. They also return the correct value if they are supplied with a Fraction,[4] Decimal, or float argument. Our functions will actually return values for any numeric type. Python's type system would throw TypeError if we were to call celsius_to_fahrenheit("21"), as the divide operation is not specified on strings, but our functions are only meaningful on real numbers, not just objects that implement a divide method. We haven't captured this requirement anywhere, so if someone were to pass some numeric values that we aren't expecting, these functions would still produce an output (Listing 2-3).

---

[4]The fractions.Fraction(...) class isn't used much, which is a real shame. It allows manipulating fractions without any loss of precision. The precision of floating-point numbers is enough for most calculations, but if your values represent meaningful fractions, then they can be useful. Imagine you've cut a cake into quarters, then you eat two thirds of a slice. Which of the following makes it clearer how much you've eaten?

```
>>> from fractions import Fraction
>>> 1/4 * 2/3
0.16666666666666666
>>> Fraction("1/4") * Fraction("2/3")
Fraction(1, 6)
```

Listing 2-3. The result of converting a complex number or a matrix from Celsius to Fahrenheit

```
In [3]:    1  celsius_to_fahrenheit(0.1 + 2j)
Out[3]: (32.18+3.6j)
```

```
In [3]:    1  import numpy
           2  celsius_to_fahrenheit(numpy.identity(3))
Out[3]: array([[33.8, 32. , 32. ],
               [32. , 33.8, 32. ],
               [32. , 32. , 33.8]])
```

The first two concepts this chapter covers are shown in these examples. Testing is the process of determining that a function works correctly. Checking, or rather static type checking, is the process of identifying the types that function operates on at the time that it is written rather than the time it's run. When writing a library, it is normal to write tests for the code. You may be the only person that ever runs these tests; they are to bolster your confidence in the code and aid in contributions.

On the other hand, any type checking you add is of direct benefit to anyone who uses your code as a source of library functions. You may derive less confidence in your code from these checks personally (although they certainly help you catch errors), but their real power is in making your code easier to use for people who are not as intimately familiar with it as their author. That's not to say that you will derive little benefit from type checking; the hints they provide are invaluable for making subtle misunderstandings clearer. Many IDEs even use the extra information they provide to offer a more user-friendly programming experience.

Testing

Untested code is broken code.

Python has built-in support for testing, in the form of the unittest module in the standard library. This offers a TestCase class which wraps individual tests with setup and teardown code, as well as offers helper functions for asserting relationships between values. While it's possible to write tests using this module alone, I strongly recommend using the add-on module pytest.

Pytest negates much of the need for boilerplate in setting up a test system. Compare the following tests written in unittest style (Listing 2-5) and pytest style (Listing 2-6). These are testing the temperature conversion function we prototyped earlier, shown as Listing 2-4.

Listing 2-4. temperature.py being tested

```
def celsius_to_fahrenheit(celsius):
    return celsius * 9 / 5 + 32

def celsius_to_kelvin(celsius):
    return 273.15 + celsius
```

Listing 2-5. Unittest style of testing the conversion function

```
import unittest
from temperature import celsius_to_fahrenheit

class TestTemperatureConversion(unittest.TestCase):

    def test_celsius_to_fahrenheit(self):
        self.assertEqual(celsius_to_fahrenheit(21), 69.8)

    def test_celsius_to_fahrenheit_equivlance_point(self):
        self.assertEqual(celsius_to_fahrenheit(-40), -40)

    def test_celsius_to_fahrenheit_float(self):
        self.assertEqual(celsius_to_fahrenheit(21.2), 70.16)

    def test_celsius_to_fahrenheit_string(self):
        with self.assertRaises(TypeError):
            f = celsius_to_fahrenheit("21")

if __name__ == '__main__':
    unittest.main()
```

Listing 2-6. Pytest style of testing the conversion function

```
import pytest
from temperature import celsius_to_fahrenheit

def test_celsius_to_fahrenheit():
    assert celsius_to_fahrenheit(21) == 69.8

def test_celsius_to_fahrenheit_equivlance_point():
    assert celsius_to_fahrenheit(-40) == -40

def test_celsius_to_fahrenheit_float():
    assert celsius_to_fahrenheit(21.2) == 70.16

def test_celsius_to_fahrenheit_string():
    with pytest.raises(TypeError):
        f = celsius_to_fahrenheit("21")
```

The clearest difference is that between `self.assertEqual(x, y)` and `assert x == y`. These both do the same thing, but the pytest style allows for significantly more natural code. The unittest style wraps most operations in helper functions, which both perform the comparison and generate an appropriate error message if the assertion fails. For example, if x and y are differing lists, `assertEqual` calls `assertListEqual` which compares the list and generates a diff of missing and additional elements and marks the current test as failed. Table 2-1 demonstrates the ways that pytest's assertion style is clearer than the unittest assertion style.

Table 2-1. *Some common assertion formats in unittest and pytest styles*

Comparison	Unittest	Pytest
Values are equal	`self.assertEqual(x, y)`	`assert x == y`
Values are unequal	`self.assertNotEqual(x, y)`	`assert x != y`
Value is None	`self.assertIsNone(x)`	`assert x is None`
List containment	`self.assertIn(x, y)`	`assert x in y`

(continued)

Table 2-1. (*continued*)

Comparison	Unittest	Pytest
Floating-point numbers differ by less than 0.000001	`self.assertAlmostEqual(x, y)`	`assert x == pytest.approx(y)`
Exception is raised	`with self.assertRaises(TypeError):` `    doSomething()`	`with pytest.raises(TypeError):` `    doSomething()`

In addition, unittest has a `TestCase` class which is used as the base class for all groups of tests. These test cases can have common setup and tear down functionality for ensuring that common variables and data are in place. The `unittest.main()` function called in the ifmain block is the entrypoint into the testing system. That function *collects* all test classes in the current module and executes them. For larger projects, there are usually multiple files containing tests which are *discovered* by the test loader and their contents collected and run.

Pytest behaves somewhat differently; running the executable begins test discovery, rather than relying on the Python source files to collate the tests. Once tests have been discovered, any filters passed as command-line arguments are applied, and the remaining tests are run.

The split between code defining the tests and a separate executable doing the setup and discovery allows for much more control over the Python environment where the tests are executed, for example, allowing for the use of bare `assert` statements rather than requiring wrapper functions for assertions.

When to write tests

There are a lot of strong opinions in software engineering about when is the appropriate time to write tests, should they be written before the code is written or after the code is written. Writing the tests first is often called test-driven development (TDD), and it has very vocal proponents. There's a good reason for this; it can be very satisfying to work in a test-driven environment, as it makes the triumphant feeling of getting a feature working the last part of developing a feature. If you plan to write the tests afterward, they can feel like an unnecessary chore.

In many situations in software engineering, there's a best choice for any given problem, but I believe that TDD vs. writing tests later is a more personal choice. I firmly believe that developers can be productive either way, but some people are naturally attracted to writing tests first, and others feel it makes for a slow start that they want to avoid. It's also very possible that which one you prefer depends on your mood or how familiar you are with the codebase on which you're working.

I generally prefer to write tests first, as I find it helps me think through the implications of the code before I get too deep into implementation details, but often I find myself wanting to get something working quickly and then polish it later. Both approaches are entirely valid; writing tests before you've written the code is no more correct or proper than writing them afterward. Try them both and see which feels more natural to you.

In some cases, you may even decide tests are not worth writing, or you may have a client or manager that pressures you not to write tests to save time. I'm not going to tell you that this is a good idea, but equally, there are times when it's a valid approach. If you're writing a program that will only ever be run once, or working with a complex existing codebase that is untested, the cost/benefit ratio of writing tests is skewed away from where it typically is. It's perfectly acceptable to decide in these situations that tests are not a priority for time investment. However, if this happens, you should remember that the decision is not irreversible. If you find yourself manually testing the same thing repeatedly and getting frustrated, that's generally a sign that you should have written tests. Don't let the sunk cost of the time you've spent manually testing dissuade you from spending some time adding tests if you think it'll save time.

EXERCISE 2-1: TRY TEST-DRIVEN DEVELOPMENT

In this chapter, we are writing the tests after we've written the code. There's no particular reason for this; the choice was made to make the flow of the chapter more natural. If you'd like to try writing tests first, this is a great opportunity. If you'd prefer to write tests after and follow the flow of the chapter, then feel free to skip this exercise.

Pick one of the sensors we looked at in the previous chapter and write some tests for it. You will find an environment that is set up with the code from the previous chapter in the support code for this chapter. It also contains documentation for how to run the tests.

If you do complete this exercise, be aware that the structure of the code you end up with may be quite different from what's suggested in this chapter. Remember that future chapters will build on this and you do not know all the requirements yet. There are many ways of approaching this problem; this exercise aims to help you get a feel for the kind of decision-making you need to do as part of test writing in a TDD process; there is no right answer here.

Creating formatting functions for improved testability

In the previous chapter, we created a simple script to print the values of individual sensors as a simple command-line script. This involved manually calling multiple functions from a prewritten `main()` function and handling their formatting independently. Although this served as a proof of concept, this isn't a sustainable way to build a large system. For each sensor value, we need a way to extract the raw value for quantitative analysis as well as a formatted value for display to end-users.

Another significant reason to do this split is to make sure that functions have a strict separation of concerns. We want to be able to test that the correct value is extracted and that values are formatted correctly without having to do them both at once. If we had a tightly coupled data extraction and formatting function, we wouldn't be able to check that a range of different values are formatted correctly. We would only be able to check the value of the machine currently running the tests, which may vary wildly from run to run.

To achieve this, we will expand the functions into a Python class that provides both the raw value retrieved by the sensor and a helper function for formatting it appropriately (Listing 2-7). This approach makes it easier to display the current value of the sensor in user-facing environments like the command-line script as there is no special casing of individual sensor values in the surrounding script.

For example, the sensor that determines how much RAM is available should display the number of bytes formatted into an appropriate unit. Previously we did this by assuming that the megabyte[5] was a suitable unit and statically scaling the number with `"{:.0f} MiB".format(ram_available() / 1024**2)`. This was both too complex to be appropriate for a one-liner and too simple to be generally useful.

---

[5]Technically, *mebibytes*: 1024 × 1024 bytes rather than 1000 × 1000 bytes. While the term megabyte (and the corresponding abbreviation MB) is frequently used with both definitions, the mebibyte (abbreviation MiB) refers exclusively to the larger, binary definition.

Listing 2-7. New temperature sensor implementation from sensors.py

```python
class Temperature(Sensor[Optional[float]]):
    title = "Ambient Temperature"

    def value(self) -> Optional[float]:
        try:
            # Connect to a DHT22 sensor on GPIO pin 4
            from adafruit_dht import DHT22
            from board import D4
        except (ImportError, NotImplementedError):
            # No DHT library results in an ImportError.
            # Running on an unknown platform results in a
            # NotImplementedError when getting the pin
            return None
        try:
            return DHT22(D4).temperature
        except RuntimeError:
            return None

    @staticmethod
    def celsius_to_fahrenheit(value: float) -> float:
        return value * 9 / 5 + 32

    @classmethod
    def format(cls, value: Optional[float]) -> str:
        if value is None:
            return "Unknown"
        else:
            return "{:.1f}C ({:.1f}F)".format(value,
                cls.celsius_to_fahrenheit(value))

    def __str__(self) -> str:
        return self.format(self.value())
```

The most significant difference between this and the original version is the switch from function to a class. This is a simple class that does not inherit from a base class, so there are no parentheses after the class name containing the bases. The most straightforward method,[6] value(), is the direct analogue of the original ram_available() function in that it extracts the data without any formatting.

The format(...) method is the equivalent of the formatting that was previously happening directly in the display logic for the command-line program. By making this a method on the sensor class, we implicitly associate the formatting functions with the data retrieval functions they work with. This makes it easier to understand what code is related and reduces the cognitive load in understanding the module as a whole, as compared to dozens of functions all at the global scope.

INSTANCE, CLASS, AND STATIC METHODS ON CLASSES

The celsius_to_fahrenheit(...) function has been defined as a staticmethod with a decorator just above, and the format(...) method has been defined as a classmethod, with first argument as cls rather than self.

These methods behave slightly differently to a standard instance method. When you define a function on a class, it takes self as a first parameter. This makes it an instance method; it can only be invoked on instances of the class and has access to attributes set on that instance as well as other methods. Temperature().value() will return a result, but Temperature.value() raises a TypeError.

In the typical case, when a function is defined on an object in Python, it has an argument of self in the first position. This is bound to an instance of the class, so each function can access the data stored in the class and can invoke functions that have the same access. When the class object is called with Temperature(), an instance of the class is returned, and when a method on that instance is called, it will automatically have the instance passed as the first argument. This means that Temperature().value() is all that is needed to retrieve the value. So long as you're calling a method by accessing it through an instance, you never need to explicitly pass the self argument.

---

[6]A function that's defined on an object rather than at the global scope is traditionally called a method.

A class method takes cls[7] as the first argument, which points to the class rather than an instance. The function can still access other functions on the class as well as any attributes stored on the class, but it cannot call instance methods as it doesn't have an instance of the class available. Class methods can be invoked on instances as normal or on the class directly. They're useful for writing custom constructors (such as `from_json(...)`) or for utility functions that use other functions or attributes of the class. A class method can be invoked on the class (`Temperature.format(21)`) or an instance (`Temperature().format(21)`); it will receive the class as the first argument in either case.

Finally, a static method is a method that has no implicit first argument. There are no significant advantages to a static method over a class method, but the absence of the implicit argument makes it clear to readers of the code that it's a completely stand-alone method that is only being grouped with the class for reasons of convenience. It can also be invoked on either the class or an instance, as `Temperature.celsius_to_fahrenheit(21)` or `Temperature().celsius_to_fahrenheit(21)`.

The preceding sensor code is intended to retrieve and format sensor data. It's possible that the `__init__()` method of some sensors may perform some expensive[8] setup that's required to make `value()` work. The reason we're marking the `format(...)` method as a class method is to ensure that we can still format the data without instantiating the class. This allows us to format data without having an instance of the relevant sensor, just its class.

The `__str__()` method is a Python internal convention; it determines how an object is converted into a string representation.[9] As this is only ever used on instances of the class, we can make this a shorthand way of saying "retrieve the current value and format it." As such, the code for displaying all sensor values is considerably shortened and easier to understand:

---

[7]Or klass. `class` is a reserved word so it can't be used for variable names. Both cls and self argument names are only conventions, but I strongly recommend you follow them.

[8]Expensive in terms of time or memory. Although some APIs can cause real money to be spent, I'd recommend against ever writing code where this happens implicitly just by instantiating a class.

[9] `__str__()` is used when an object is converted to a user-facing string. This happens when an object is printed or is used in string manipulation methods such as `"{}".format(obj)`.
`__repr__()` is used by Python internally for programmer-facing string representation, such as in tracebacks and typing its name into the REPL prompt. You can explicitly choose which you'd like to see by using the built-in `str(obj)` and `repr(obj)` functions.

```
@click.command(help="Displays the values of the sensors")
def show_sensors():
    for sensor in [PythonVersion(), IPAddresses(), CPULoad(), RAMAvailable(),
                   ACStatus(), RelativeHumidity()]:
        click.secho(sensor.title, bold=True)
        click.echo(sensor)
        click.echo("")
```

The work of displaying the sensor values has almost entirely been delegated to the sensor itself. All that is required is that the sensor has a __str__() method that returns a formatted version of its current value and that it has a title attribute that contains a header for the display.

Now that we've reorganized the code to have independent formatting and value extraction functions, we can write tests to ensure that values are formatted as we expect them to be. As always, you can find the reorganized code in the support files for this chapter, available on the book's website.

pytest

The first thing to do to be able to run our tests is that we need to install pytest itself. We consider this a development package, as it's not required for the system to be used, just to allow developers to be confident that it is behaving as intended.

```
pipenv install --dev pytest
```

This creates a new pytest script available in the environment for our project. At this point, we can run pipenv run pytest and see the results of our test run, which is that 0 tests ran. To test that we have a working environment, we can create a sample test. This is often done by code skeleton generators, where the test will be something like assert 1 == 1. We are going to assert that the file that contains our cli script has one of the sensors we expect to see.

To do this we create a new tests/ directory and add an empty __init__.py and a test_sensors.py as follows:

```
import sensors

def test_sensors():
    assert hasattr(sensors, 'PythonVersion')
```

Unit, integration, and functional testing

The hardest part of writing tests is knowing which tests to write. It can be tempting to write tests that run the entire application and check the output, effectively interacting with the code in the same way that an end-user would. This is known as **functional testing**. Functional testing is especially popular with web frameworks, where there may be many different layers of code interacting to provide services such as authentication, sessions, and template rendering. While this does effectively test that the correct output is generated, it can be difficult to write tests that go further than confirming the common case.

If we took this approach with our command-line script, we'd be looking to see that the script returns the values that we are expecting when it's run. The immediate problem that we'll come up against is that it's challenging to know what the correct values we're expecting are. The easiest of our sensors to predict is the Python version as there are only a handful of possible values, but even then it's not possible to know in advance which version of Python is being used.

For example, the following test uses the `CliRunner` helper tools from click to simulate running the command-line tool and capturing the output:

```python
def test_python_version_is_first_two_lines_of_cli_output ():
    runner = CliRunner()
    result = runner.invoke(sensors.show_sensors)
    assert ["Python Version", "3.8"] == result.stdout.split("\n")[:2]
```

This looks fine, until the first time someone runs it on Python 3.7 and sees the failure:

```
_____ test_python_version_is_first_two_lines_of_cli_output _____

    def test_python_version_is_first_two_lines_of_cli_output():
        runner = CliRunner()
        result = runner.invoke(sensors.show_sensors)
>       assert ["Python Version", "3.8"] == result.stdout.split("\n")[:2]
E       AssertionError: assert ['Python Version', '3.8'] == ['Python Version', '3.7']
E         At index 1 diff: '3.8' != '3.7'
E         Use -v to get the full diff

tests\test_sensors.py:11: AssertionError
```

For many people, the natural thing to do at this point is to change the test to detect the Python version that the system is running and use that to determine what to expect, something like

```
def test_python_version_is_first_two_lines_of_cli_output():
    runner = CliRunner()
    result = runner.invoke(sensors.show_sensors)
    python_version = "{}.{}".format(sys.version_info.major,
    sys.version_info.minor)
    assert ["Python Version", python_version] == (result.stdout.split("\n")[:2])
```

It will successfully run on any Python version. This is a perfectly reasonable change to make, but it's important to realize that you're no longer testing the same thing. Remember that the implementation of the PythonVersion sensor is

```
class PythonVersion:
    def value(self):
        return sys.version_info

    @classmethod
    def format(cls, value):
        return "{0.major}.{0.minor}".format(value)
```

So, if we strip away all the function call indirection involved in the sensor script, our test is effectively testing the following:

```
assert "{}.{}".format(sys.version_info.major, sys.version_info.minor) ==
"{0.major}.{0.minor}".format(sys.version_info)
```

Writing a test where the results of assertions are calculated rather than known in advance often results in a tautological test. It may not be this obvious, but in all cases it is suboptimal. It's not *wrong*, the test is still checking the header, the ordering of the sensors, and that the value displayed is based on sys.version_info, but it looks like it's testing the version detection and does not look like it's checking sensor order.

This test is now only testing that the Python version "sensor" comes first in the listing and that an appropriate header is shown. It is no longer testing any of the behavior of the Python version sensor.

To ensure that the sensor is behaving correctly, we break down the test into smaller units. The things we want to know about the PythonVersion sensor are

1. The sensor's value is equal to sys.version_info.

2. The sensor's formatter returns a version string like "3.8", that is, major.minor.

3. The sensor's string representation is the formatted version of the current value.

4. The CLI output contains the header "Python version" and then the result of formatting the value on the first two lines of the output. This is the test we started with.

These should all be independent tests, as they're all potential failure modes. If we only had the functional test that checked the output of the script and saw a failure, it would be impossible to know if the value, formatter, or script integration was incorrect without debugging the failing test and understanding the whole context of the tool.

For some of these tests, we can call functions in total isolation and look at their inputs and outputs. For example, the formatter takes an input and returns an output with no side effects.[10] This kind of tests is called **unit tests**, as we are testing a single logical *unit* of source code at one time.

Unit tests are the kind of tests that are hardest to write on complex code. If the structure of the code is not conducive to testing, it may be impossible to write useful unit tests. If we think back to the version of the script at the end of the previous chapter, the logical units are not as well defined as they are in the class-based implementation.

Each of the functions we've written involves calling some other functions to get their data, and the formatting logic is tightly bound up with the command-line processing logic. Unit tests are also some of the most useful types of tests to have because a failing unit test very accurately narrows down the broken code to a single location. Unit tests also generally execute very quickly and require minimal test setup, making for a more satisfying experience as a developer.

Other functions, such as the __str__() method, are more complex and call out to other functions to find their results. Finding the string value involves getting the value, which delegates to library methods, then formatting that value. This type of function

---

[10]This is called a "pure function": its output is determined only by its inputs. Functions that behave inconsistently, like random.random(), are not pure functions and are harder to test.

requires some setup to be tested effectively, as we need to write tests that override the behavior of the library functions the code is calling, so that they return known values. These types of test are best described as **integration tests**, but an exact meaning is difficult to define. An integration test generally tests a small number of related functions as one, but there is some flexibility in what different developers consider to be integration tests.

Integration tests are a happy medium between unit tests and functional tests. By writing tests that cover a group of related functions, they ensure that a logical component of the codebase is working correctly on given inputs and outputs. It's harder to really check edge cases with an integration test, but they're a great choice for tests that known-good or known-bad data is correctly processed.

The four planned test types mentioned earlier fall roughly into these three categories of test. The first of these tests that very simple functions behave correctly. For more complex sensors, it's possible that these would be more like integration tests, but the distinction is to help us reason about tests, it's not something that should concern us.

The third test is an example of an integration test. The string representation function calls the two functions tested in the previous step and ensures they work correctly together. These tests should complement each other; it's normal for an integration test to test multiple things in passing, some of which may overlap with the explicit unit tests that have been written.

Finally, we have a functional test to ensure that the sensor is being used in the output of the CLI program. Like the integration test, this inevitably tests things that are more appropriately tested elsewhere; you shouldn't concern yourself with trying to minimize this. What is important is that it's clear from the functional test's name and comments what it's intended to test. Often functional tests are deliberately wide ranging without explaining their logic, which is counterproductive when they fail due to a change later on. If it's not clear what a test is doing, then it won't be clear where a bug has been introduced when it starts to fail. Many different issues can cause failing functional tests, some of which may not appear to be related at first glance.

Tip   When an integration or a functional test fails due to a change to part of the codebase, it's a good idea to write a more specific test to cover this case. That is, if a functional test fails, try to add a unit or an integration test to isolate the issue. A test demonstrating a bug that was fixed is a much more useful artifact to have than an aging JIRA ticket, especially if that bug is ever reintroduced.

Pytest fixtures

For all but the most basic functions, it's likely that there will be a few different cases being tested, all of which should have their own test function. It's quite common that there will be setup code required, for example, instantiating classes if the function is a class member rather than an importable function. One way of doing this is to organize the tests into classes that contain both all related tests and setup code that is shared by all these tests.

All test frameworks have some method of providing common setup and teardown code to support tests. In pytest these are called "fixtures" and allow for a very flexible way of picking and choosing between different pieces of support code. Pytest fixtures are automatically invoked to match the arguments to the test function.

A good way of structuring tests is to define a class to contain related tests and any fixtures that are specific to these tests only and to keep more generally useful fixtures available for other tests to use as they like. This allows for using a style often referred to generically as "Subject Under Test" style, or SUT. The *subject* changes depending on the context. You may see FUT (Function Under Test), MUT (Method Under Test), OUT (Object Under Test), and so on.

In this layout of tests, each class has a fixture called something like MUT(), method(), or subject() which returns the function to be tested.[11] A fixture for a FUT might just import the function and return it, whereas a MUT, being a class method, likely involves creating an instance of a class and returning the specific method from that instance. This allows the individual functions to test a callable without having to worry about how that callable is obtained, which can be especially useful when testing methods of classes that take many arguments for their construction.

To begin with, we'll create a test class designed to test the Python version number sensor's formatter and give it a range of values to test. This consists of a test file (Listing 2-8) for the version sensor which provides a sensor fixture that represents the sensor being tested and a TestPythonVersionFormatter class that defines a MUT as the format method of that sensor, using the subject fixture.

---

[11]This is a matter of personal style. You might find it clearer to name the fixture something that makes it clear what the function is.

Listing 2-8. Initial version of test_pythonversion.py

```python
from collections import namedtuple

import pytest

from sensors import PythonVersion

@pytest.fixture
def version():
    return namedtuple(
        "sys_versioninfo", ("major", "minor", "micro", "releaselevel", "serial")
    )

@pytest.fixture
def sensor():
    return PythonVersion()

class TestPythonVersionFormatter:
    @pytest.fixture
    def subject(self, sensor):
        return sensor.format

    def test_format_py38(self, subject, version):
        py38 = version(3, 8, 0, "final", 0)
        assert subject(py38) == "3.8"

    def test_format_large_version(self, subject, version):
        large = version(255, 128, 0, "final", 0)
        assert subject(large) == "255.128"

    def test_alpha_of_minor_is_marked(self, subject, version):
        py39 = version(3, 9, 0, "alpha", 1)
        assert subject(py39) == "3.9.0a1"

    def test_alpha_of_micro_is_unmarked(self, subject, version):
        py39 = version(3, 9, 1, "alpha", 1)
        assert subject(py39) == "3.9"
```

The version fixture provides a structure that appears similar to the result of sys.version_info, as the particular object type that Python uses internally there cannot be instantiated with new values. This ensures that we can create values that behave the same way as sys.version_info but where we control their values.

These tests can be run with pipenv run pytest tests, and they pass, but any readers who have used other unit test frameworks may be concerned that we've moved too much into the fixtures and that it may be difficult to debug problems. Specifically, it's not clear at a glance of the code to what subject refers. To demonstrate that this is fine, we'll add a new failing test to cover a feature that we would like to add.

Our formatter here only shows the major and minor components of the release, on the assumption that the micro versions do not contain any changes significant enough to highlight. However, as I write this, there is a new Python version in the alpha stage, where the difference between alpha versions is significant in terms of new feature additions. To this end, it may be useful to special-case prerelease versions of the first micro release in a new minor line. I'll add a pair of new tests to demonstrate that we expect a different output for 3.9.0a1 (but to go back to the default for 3.9.1a1).

```
def test_prerelease_of_minor_is_marked(self, subject, version):
    py39 = version(3, 9, 0, "alpha", 1)
    assert subject(py39) == "3.9.0a1"

def test_prerelease_of_micro_is_unmarked(self, subject):
    py39 = (3, 9, 1, "alpha", 1)
    assert subject(py39) == "3.9"
```

One of these two tests fails, and the other passes. The reason for adding two tests here is to make it clear that the alpha tag only matters for cases where the micro version is 0. Without the second test, we'd have a passing test suite if all prerelease versions showed the full version string, which is not the feature we're looking for.

If we now re-run the tests, we'll see the failure of the test_prerelease_of_minor_is_marked test and the amount of contextual information that pytest automatically includes:

_____   TestPythonVersionFormatter.test_alpha_of_minor_is_marked _____

```
self = <tests.test_pythonversion.TestPythonVersionFormatter object at 0x03BA4670>
subject = <bound method PythonVersion.format of <class 'sensors.
PythonVersion'>>
version = <class 'tests.test_pythonversion.sys_versioninfo'>

    def test_alpha_of_minor_is_marked(self, subject, version):
        py39 = version(3, 9, 0, "alpha", 1)
>       assert subject(py39) == "3.9.0a1"
E       AssertionError: assert '3.9' == '3.9.0a1'
E          - 3.9
E          + 3.9.0a1

tests\test_pythonversion.py:28: AssertionError
=============== 1 failed, 3 passed in 0.11 seconds =========================
```

The first thing that is reported is the name of the test that's failed, followed by representations of the fixtures that are being used. These are displayed at the top of the failure information, so we can see at a glance that the subject fixture is the format method of an instance[12] of the PythonVersion class.

The next thing to be shown is the body of the test method up to the line that caused the error, followed by the formatted error. In this case, it's an assertion error as the assert line failed. We see the expanded version of the assertion, so we can see what subject(py39) evaluated to, then below we see a diff of the two strings. In this case, a diff is not especially useful, but with longer strings it is handy to get a line-by-line diff.

If we were to change the formatter method to be

```
@classmethod
def format(cls, value):
    if value.micro == 0 and value.releaselevel == "alpha":
        return "{0.major}.{0.minor}.{0.micro}a{0.serial}".format(value)
    return "{0.major}.{0.minor}".format(value)
```

and re-run the tests, we would instead see a confirmation that all the tests in test_pythonversion.py have passed.

---

[12]The representation of the method says "bound method," which means it's a method which is attached to an instance.

Categorizing test functions

We've decided to write multiple different types of tests for our code, covering everything from unit tests to full-stack functional tests. As functional tests are significantly slower than unit tests, we may want to exclude them from test runs from time to time, running only the fast subset of tests quickly. If we're expecting to see test failures, this can save a significant amount of time, so we can avoid running the longer verification tests until we know there are no failures in the fast, unit tests.

This can be done using the @pytest.mark decorator. We will use the "functional" marker to mark our test_python_version_is_first_two_lines_of_cli_output as being a functional test.

```
@pytest.mark.functional
def test_python_version_is_first_two_lines_of_cli_output():
    runner = CliRunner()
    result = runner.invoke(sensors.show_sensors)
    python_version = str(sensors.PythonVersion())
    assert ["Python Version", python_version] == result.stdout.split("\n")[:2]
```

This allows us to invoke tests with pytest -m functional to run only the functional tests

```
============ 1 passed, 5 deselected, 1 warnings in 3.17 seconds ============
```

or using pytest -m "not functional" to run all but the functional tests:

```
============ 5 passed, 1 deselected, 1 warnings in 0.11 seconds ============
```

The overhead for running the functional tests is huge, with running one functional test taking 30 times longer than running the five unit tests. A 3-second test run isn't so slow that it would discourage you from running tests, but we're just starting to write our test suite. When it's 10x larger, it will be the difference between 30 seconds of tests and 1 second. If your tests are too much hassle for you to want to run, then they will not be nearly as useful.

It's possible to create arbitrary markers just by using @pytest.mark.something as a decorator, but a warning is generated to advise you that it has not been explicitly declared. These warnings are useful for spotting typographical errors in your marker names, so we should create a pytest.ini file that declares that we use a functional marker.

```
[pytest]
markers = functional: these tests are significantly slower
```

Coverage

Code coverage is a metric for how extensive a test suite is. It represents the proportion of an application's codebase that is executed during the test run. Some people feel very strongly about a high level of test coverage being necessary, often going as far as saying that 100% coverage should be expected of all software.

I'd encourage you to take a more pragmatic view. The most important thing a test suite can do is to give you confidence that the software is behaving as expected. A high coverage percentage is usually correlated with confidence, and I'd encourage you to aim for a high level of coverage, but it shouldn't give you a false sense of security. In particular, as you approach 100% test coverage, it becomes harder and harder to ensure the last lines are covered, but the benefit remains constant. It's better to have a lower amount of coverage and an easily understood test suite than an overly complex one that hits 100%.

To enable code coverage, we need a pytest plugin to collect the data. The easiest way to approach this is to install the pytest-cov plugin, using `pipenv install --dev pytest-cov`. Once this is done, the `--cov` argument becomes available on the pytest executable. This argument takes a path to part of your codebase as an optional parameter. When this is provided, the coverage report only shows the coverage data for that subpath. To see the coverage of all the code, use just --cov, as follows:

```
> pipenv run pytest tests --cov
```

We should also create a `.coveragerc` file to configure the coverage report we'd like to see. The most important thing is to exclude the test directory, as the proportion of test files that were executed while running tests is not a useful metric and skews our average.

```
[run]
branch = True
omit = tests/*
```

We also add the branch configuration parameter, which changes the calculation of coverage to only consider an if statement to be covered if both the True and False conditions are encountered. If we run the tests with the --cov flag, we can see the coverage of our project to date:

```
----------- coverage: platform win32, python 3.8.0-alpha-1 -----------
Name            Stmts   Miss Branch BrPart  Cover
------------------------------------------------
sensors.py       121     17    22      7     83%

======================= 8 passed in 3.23 seconds =========================
```

This shows that our test run detected that 83% of the code has been covered by the test suite, which demonstrated exactly why we should be skeptical of coverage figures as a measure of test quality. Remember that we've only written tests for one of the seven sensors in our script, so the suggestion that 83% of our code is tested in any meaningful way is clearly wrong. This has been caused by the functional test that runs the script and looks at the output, as it causes all of the code to be executed. If we re-run the tests excluding the functional tests, we get

```
----------- coverage: platform win32, python 3.8.0-alpha-1 -----------
Name            Stmts   Miss Branch BrPart  Cover
-----------------------------------------------
sensors.py       121     62    22      1     43%

================= 7 passed, 1 deselected in 0.38 seconds =================
```

Forty-three percent still seems like an overestimate, given what we know about the number of tests we've written, but the coverage option lets us see which lines are covered and which are missed. There are a few different ways of displaying this, but they're all controlled by the --cov-report flag. A number of machine-readable formats are included, like an XML format, which is useful if you're using continuous integration, but for direct human consumption, the two most useful are --cov-report html and --cov-report annotate.

The HTML report format creates a directory called htmlcov which contains an index.html file that lists the overall coverage and the coverage of each file. By clicking the filename you're interested in, you see a listing of the file contents with lines color coded by their status in the coverage report, as shown in Figure 2-1.[13]

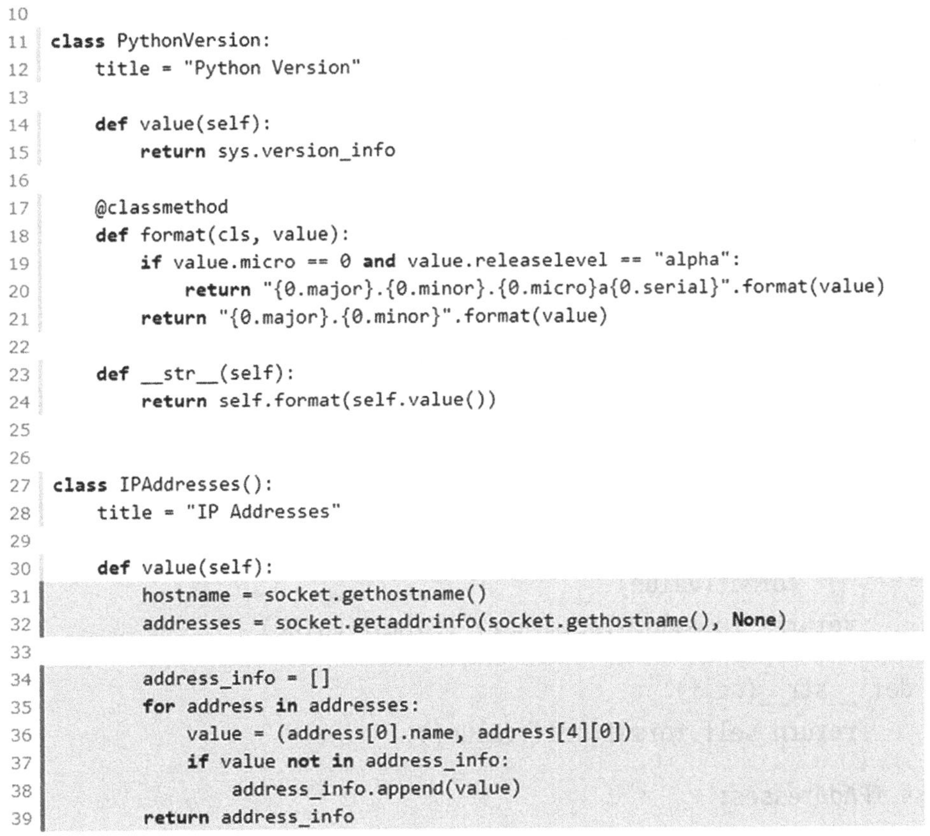

```
10
11  class PythonVersion:
12      title = "Python Version"
13
14      def value(self):
15          return sys.version_info
16
17      @classmethod
18      def format(cls, value):
19          if value.micro == 0 and value.releaselevel == "alpha":
20              return "{0.major}.{0.minor}.{0.micro}a{0.serial}".format(value)
21          return "{0.major}.{0.minor}".format(value)
22
23      def __str__(self):
24          return self.format(self.value())
25
26
27  class IPAddresses():
28      title = "IP Addresses"
29
30      def value(self):
31          hostname = socket.gethostname()
32          addresses = socket.getaddrinfo(socket.gethostname(), None)
33
34          address_info = []
35          for address in addresses:
36              value = (address[0].name, address[4][0])
37              if value not in address_info:
38                  address_info.append(value)
39          return address_info
```

Figure 2-1. *Visual representation of covered and uncovered lines when not running functional tests*

Lines with a green border and no shading are covered lines. The test suite has executed these lines. Lines with a red border and red shading are uncovered lines. These were not executed. Assuming that branch coverage is enabled, some lines may have a yellow border and be shaded yellow. These are lines that are partially covered, such as the if __name__ == "__main__" construction at the bottom of the file. As the body of that if statement is red, it's clear that the case where the condition evaluated to False was covered but the case where it evaluated to True was not.

---

[13]For those reading this in black and white, the red lines are below the green.

Alternatively, the `annotate` report type creates a `sensors.py,cover` file in the same directory as sensors.py. Lines prefixed with a > are covered or partially covered; lines prefixed with a ! are uncovered. The section of `sensors.py,cover` that matches the preceding HTML screenshot is shown as Listing 2-9.

Listing 2-9. sensors.py,cover representing coverage when not running functional tests

```
> class PythonVersion:
>     title = "Python Version"

>     def value(self):
>         return sys.version_info

>     @classmethod
>     def format(cls, value):
>         if value.micro == 0 and value.releaselevel == "alpha":
>             return "{0.major}.{0.minor}.{0.micro}a{0.serial}".
              format(value)
>         return "{0.major}.{0.minor}".format(value)

>     def __str__(self):
>         return self.format(self.value())

> class IPAddresses:
>     title = "IP Addresses"

>     def value(self):
!         hostname = socket.gethostname()
!         addresses = socket.getaddrinfo(socket.gethostname(), None)

!         address_info = []
!         for address in addresses:
!             value = (address[0].name, address[4][0])
!             if value not in address_info:
!                 address_info.append(value)
!         return address_info
```

I find the HTML report easier to work with, but your preferences may vary. Either way, we can see that the function bodies of the various sensors other than

PythonVersion are all uncovered, but the class and function definitions are all covered. This makes sense, as the Python interpreter has to execute the declaration lines to know what functions, classes, and class attributes are available. As our function bodies are relatively short, the tested function bodies plus the class and function declarations do make up almost half of the lines with statements on them.

EXERCISE 2-2: EXPANDING THE TEST SUITE

We've written the tests for one of the most straightforward sensors, but there are still several others that are untested. Practice writing some tests by adding tests to the other sensors.

Most of the sensors follow the same pattern, with the exception being the temperature and humidity sensors, which are somewhat harder to write tests for that cover the value method.

If you can write a test suite that covers 75% of sensors.py when running with -m "not functional", then you have a test suite that should give you great confidence in the program as a whole.

Type checking

The work we've done on a test suite gives us a lot of confidence that the code we've written behaves as we intend it to, but it doesn't help so much with confidence that we're using it correctly. We make heavy use of the psutil library in many of the sensors without writing any direct tests for this. Some programmers fall into the trap of writing tests that do more to test their dependency libraries than their own code.

If you feel yourself needing to write tests to cover the workings of the libraries that your code depends on, then you should step back and consider what the best course of action is. It's a lot easier to write tests for a library as part of its test suite, rather than in a consumer application's tests.

What people generally need when they use a third-party library is the confidence that they are using it correctly: passing arguments consistently, handling exceptions and unusual return values, and understanding what functions are intended to do. There's no automated way of checking our understanding, but type checking does allow us to check some of the other cases.

If you've used a programming language like Java, you'll be familiar with the impact a thorough type checker can have on code: it's not possible to overlook an exception or to call a function with an invalid value, but to other people it can feel quite restrictive.

Python has recently gained syntax to optionally annotate variables with types, to allow for type checking to be built on top of the base Python language. Python itself does not do any type checking for you, but the mypy project offers a program for running static type checks on your Python code.

Installing mypy

Mypy is distributed as a Python module, so it is installed in the same way as our other development dependencies, using

```
> pipenv install --dev mypy
```

This adds the mypy executable to our environment, as well as installs the mypy type-checking library and the typeshed collection of type definitions. The Python standard library does not include type-checking hints, and at the time of writing, most third-party libraries do not either. Type annotations were always intended to be an optional feature, so it shouldn't be surprising that many developers choose not to use them. Typeshed is a project of the Python Software Foundation that maintains a set of type declarations for the standard library and various commonly used third-party libraries.

That said, many libraries neither provide type annotations nor have entries in the typeshed, so when we run type checking on code that uses them, it generates typing warnings. If we invoke mypy on our code, we see such errors about psutil, as well as the optional dependencies adafruit_dht and board.

```
> pipenv run mypy sensors.py
sensors.py:9: error: No library stub file for module 'psutil'
sensors.py:9: note: (Stub files are from https://github.com/python/
typeshed)
sensors.py:116: error: Cannot find module named 'adafruit_dht'
sensors.py:116: note: See https://mypy.readthedocs.io/en/latest/
running_mypy.html#missing-imports
sensors.py:117: error: Cannot find module named 'board'
```

There are two approaches to this problem: ignoring it and fixing it. In almost all cases, it's a more effective use of time to configure mypy to ignore these problems, rather than to add type hints to all the dependencies your code uses. To do that, we need to add a mypy configuration file, either as mypy.ini or as part of a setup.cfg file, which can contain configuration for multiple different tools. Add the following as setup.cfg and re-run mypy to see it complete with no warnings:

```
[mypy]
ignore_missing_imports = True
```

Adding type hints

As our code is currently relatively simple, it's not difficult to go through the sensors and add type hints. The format Python uses is

```
def function_name(argument: type, other: type) -> type:
```

So, our CPULoad sensor would look like

```
class CPULoad:
    title = "CPU Usage"

    def value(self) -> float:
        return psutil.cpu_percent(interval=3) / 100.0

    @classmethod
    def format(cls, value: float) -> str:
        return "{:.1%}".format(value)

    def __str__(self) -> str:
        return self.format(self.value())
```

The return value of the value function is always the same as the value parameter of the format function. Once this has been added, we can experiment with mypy directly. For example, we could create a new file that misuses the sensor, shown in Listing 2-10.

Listing 2-10. incorrect.py

```
import sensors

sensor = sensors.CPULoad()
print("The CPU load is " + sensor.value())
```

Mypy can pick up this error by analyzing the file with the incorrect code and the sensors.py file, resulting in the following error:

```
> pipenv run mypy incorrect.py
incorrect.py:4: error: Unsupported operand types for + ("str" and "float")
```

However, some of the sensors are more complex. The ACStatus, Temperature, and RelativeHumidity sensors all have a value that can be None if for whatever reason the value cannot be determined. For these, we need to declare the return type differently. Python's typing allows for types to be wrapped into containers, in a similar way to generics in other languages. The typing.Union type defines a type that is one of a number of different options. In our case, ACStatus.value returns typing.Union[bool, None] and the temperature sensor returns typing.Union[float, None].

We can further simplify this by using the Optional type. Optional is a special case of Union, which takes one type argument and Unions it with None. It doesn't behave differently; it's just easier to read. Therefore, our ACStatus.value() function becomes

```
def value(self) -> typing.Optional[bool]:
    battery = psutil.sensors_battery()
    if battery is not None:
        return battery.power_plugged
    else:
        return None
```

Finally, the IPAddresses sensor's value is a more complex object. Each IP address is represented by a two-element tuple, containing a string representation of the address family and the address itself. The sensor returns a list of these 2-tuples. We could declare this as

```
def value(self) -> typing.List:
    ...
```

but if we did, a return value of [None, None, None] would be considered valid. We can declare some more of the internal structure of the list to ensure that mypy can be strict with its checks. The syntax for declaring the internals of List is the same as that of Union. For a list of (str, str) 2-tuples, we would use

```
def value(self) -> typing.List[typing.Tuple[str, str]]:
    ...
```

This does not prevent any mistakes where the data structure matches what's expected, as we still can't automatically check semantics, but it does prevent several classes of typographical errors and oversights. For example, we're not protected from mixing up the two values inside the tuple, but we are protected from assuming that a tuple is returned directly or that the return type is a list of strings containing IP addresses with no address family information.

For this sensor, we may wish to loosen the symmetry between the return type of value and the argument type in format. In all the other sensors, these have been exactly the same, as we only want to be able to format the data that we've received. In a few cases, it may be useful to be more flexible in the formatter. The type definition of the formatter should represent the data that may be formatted, not the data that we're expecting. We can format any iterable that contains an indexable sequence of at least two elements, both of which are strings. Our formatter code works if we pass in a tuple of lists just as well as it does when we pass in a list of tuples.

The following types would all be valid choices:

- List[Tuple[str, str]]
- List[Sequence[str]]
- Sequence[Tuple[str, str]]
- Sequence[Sequence[str]]
- Iterable[Tuple[str, str]]
- Iterable[Sequence[str]]

all with slightly different semantics. Using Sequence rather than List allows for the outer variable type to be a list or a tuple, and using Iterable as the outer type allows for it to be a list, a tuple, a set, or a generator. If we use Sequence[str] over Tuple[str, str] for the inner type, we gain the flexibility for the inner type to be a list, but we lose the assertion regarding the internal structure of that sequence. Of these, I believe the best choice is

```
def format(cls, value: Iterable[Tuple[str, str]]) -> str:
```

as it is the least restrictive type hint that does not allow invalid data.

Tip   Rather than importing all these marker types individually, you may wish to `import typing as t` and then use `t.Union[...]`, `t.Sequence[...]`, and so on. This makes the fact that these types are part of the typing hints clearer to casual readers of the source code and avoids having to manage imports when adding functions with a new type signature.

Subclasses and inheritance

Perhaps the most confusing thing for Python developers not used to using type hinting when writing code that is checked by mypy is that a much stricter view of type inheritance is used, as compared to what they are used to. In our sensor file so far, we have many classes that share the same __str__() method implementation. It is natural to want to move these to a superclass. You may naturally think that this would have great benefits for type hinting, as it would allow code to be written that explicitly operates on a subclass of Sensor.

The problem with doing this is that we do not have a common interface for Sensor. We have several subclasses that behave similarly, but they are not interchangeable. If you know that you have an instance of Sensor, then you know you have a value function, but you have no more concrete guarantees about what the output of that function is.

If we were to add a __str__() method to a superclass, then that method would need to be type-checked on the superclass itself. If either a value() or a format(...) method were missing, then type checks would fail, regardless of if those methods are implemented on subclasses. The type check must fail as the base class itself would not work in isolation. Equally, if we do define stub value() and format(...) methods on the superclass, then those definitions are used for determining if the __str__() method is correct, not the definitions on the individual subclasses.

This is the crux of the difference between static typing and dynamic typing. In a dynamically typed language, you can rely on things that *happen* to be true, whereas in a static typing environment, your assertions must *necessarily* be true.

Imagine the superclass that we would define here. The basic one we'd write untyped Python would be

```
class Sensor:
    def __str__(self):
        return self.format(self.value())
```

Writing this in a typed context, with __str__(self) -> str, would cause the function to be type-checked and therefore raise errors that "Sensor" has no attribute "format". So, we need to add placeholder format(...) and value() methods. The problem is, what type should the value method return? We have sensors that return float, Optional[bool], Optional[float], or List[Tuple[str, str]]. The stub methods can't use any one of these return types as they are incompatible with the other options. If we use the special typing.Any type, it effectively disables type checking for this method. If we use the extremely verbose Union[float, Optional[bool], Optional[float], List[Tuple[str, str]]] for the value() method, then we're saying that all of these types are equally valid as an output for any given sensor.

If we try to use that same Union as the argument type for the format(...) method, then we hit a more subtle error. All subclasses are bound by the type restrictions of their superclasses, but this manifests in different ways. When specifying the output of a function, the subclasses must return a value that is as specific or more specific than the definition of the superclass. So

```
class Sensor:
    ...
    def value(self) -> Union[float, Optional[bool], Optional[float],
    List[Tuple[str, str]]]:
        raise NotImplementedError

class ToySensor(Sensor):
    ...
    def value(self) -> Optional[bool]:
        return True
```

is completely valid as any consumer that expects a Sensor and is given a ToySensor will always find a value method that returns Optional[bool] when it's expecting one of several possible values, including Optional[bool].

This cuts the opposite way when working with function arguments. In the case of the format(...) function, the type definition of the superclass is guaranteeing to users of the class that *any* of the passed value types is acceptable; the subclass cannot restrict this as it means that the calling code would have to know specifically which sensor is being used. As such, the following code fails:

```
class Sensor:
    ...
    def format(self, value:Union[float, Optional[bool], Optional[float],
    List[Tuple[str, str]]]) -> str:
        raise NotImplementedError

class ToySensor(Sensor):
    ...
    def format(self, value: Optional[bool]) -> str:
        return "Yes"
```

with the error

```
Argument 1 of "format" incompatible with supertype "Sensor".
```

There are two approaches we can take here, and which you choose will very much depend on how much benefit you gain from type checking. The simplest is leaving some of the functions untyped, either implicitly or explicitly. Leaving this untyped would mean that we would not receive significant benefits of type checking when working with sensors in general, only when working with specific individual sensors. This may be sufficient for many applications and would certainly be simpler. To achieve this, we would create a Sensor superclass as follows:

```
class Sensor:

    def value(self) -> Any:
        raise NotImplementedError

    @classmethod
    def format(cls, value: Any) -> str:
        raise NotImplementedError
```

```
def __str__(self) -> str:
    return self.format(self.value())
```

and all of our code in future will restrict the type checking to the fact that the __str__()
and format(...) methods always return strings. No checking will be done on the value
type.

Generic types

The alternative is to go all in on the type checking. We've already seen that the
typing.List type can take arguments to specify what the contents of the list are.
In the same way, we can tell the typing system that the Sensor base class takes a single
type argument that represents the type this sensor operates on.

Adding the ability to specify contained types is called making the type *generic*. We
need to convert Sensor to be a generic type with a single type variable, which is used as
both the return type of the value function and the argument type of the superclass.

```
T_value = TypeVar("T_value")

class Sensor(Generic[T_value]):

    def value(self) -> T_value:
        raise NotImplementedError

    @classmethod
    def format(cls, value: T_value) -> str:
        raise NotImplementedError

    def __str__(self) -> str:
        return self.format(self.value())
```

Here, T_value isn't a type; it's a placeholder for a type of the value which is specified
using the square bracket syntax on Sensor. If there is a variable of type Sensor[str],
then mypy associates T_value for that variable with str, and therefore the value() and
format(...) methods are both associated with str. Importantly, the type associated
with T_value varies from sensor to sensor; it's not bound to a single type but rather is
dynamically associated with the subtype of Sensor that is declared by any particular
piece of code.

The sensors themselves use Sensor[type] as their base class, but still need to declare their own typing hints on functions. While the typing hints of the parent class are analyzed by mypy, it requires that any subclasses must still define type hints for them to participate in type checking. It may seem like a waste of time, but this makes it clear to anyone reading the code what the types required are without having to read the superclass. It also allows for checking both that the code is internally consistent within a subclass and that it is consistent with the assertions of the superclass. The result is that real sensor implementations look like Listing 2-11.

Listing 2-11. Typed version of sensors

```
class CPULoad(Sensor[float]):
    title = "CPU Usage"

    def value(self) -> float:
        return psutil.cpu_percent(interval=3) / 100.0

    @classmethod
    def format(cls, value: float) -> str:
        return "{:.1%}".format(value)
```

Caution   In the preceding CPULoad sensor example, we have value(self) -> float, but we can change this to value(self) -> int or even value(self) -> bool without seeing any error. This is an unfortunate design decision to support easier duck typing. The argument is that any function that accepts a float can accept an integer, which although not entirely true is close enough for most purposes. In addition, in Python bool is a subclass of int, so functions that accept floats can also accept bools without raising an error. Therefore, a function that is expected to return a float but returns a bool is seen as returning something that's compatible. I hope that this might generate warnings in future. For now, you should bear this limitation in mind.

A surprising consequence of the fact that T_value is bound to the specified subtype is the meaning of Sensor[Any]. This would appear to mean any valid Sensor, but in fact it means a Sensor that whose value is not type-checked. Using Sensor[Any] still has benefits over not using type checking at all. Although the type checker won't be able to check code that runs over a loop of `Iterable[Sensor[Any]]` for type safety in its handling of the value parameter, the assertions about the presence of a `title` attribute and the common `__str__()` method are common across all sensor types and so can still be checked.

Debugging and overuse of typing

When working with mypy, it can sometimes be useful to view debugging information. Mypy does not have an interactive debugger, so if we have problems with understanding why an error has occurred, we have to resort to printf style debugging, through the reveal_type function.

For example, let's create a test script that uses some of the code from sensors.py in an incorrect manner:

```
from sensors import CPULoad

sensor = CPULoad()
print(sensor.format("3.2"))
```

If we invoke pipenv run mypy broken.py, we will get the following expected error:

```
broken.py:4: error: Argument 1 to "format" of "CPULoad" has incompatible
type "str"; expected "float"
```

but if we update broken.py to be a little more complex

```
from sensors import CPULoad, ACStatus

two_sensors = [CPULoad(), ACStatus()]
print(two_sensors[0].format("3.2"))
```

then re-run mypy, the error we see is more basic:

```
broken.py:4: error: "object" has no attribute "format"
```

In this case, mypy appears to have inferred an incorrect type for the two_sensors list. We can add reveal_type(two_sensors) to the source file anywhere after it is defined to see what mypy discovered. Be aware, reveal_type isn't a real function. It doesn't require importing as it's a construction of the mypy parser, not Python code. If you leave it in your code, then it will cause errors when the code is run. Only add it as a temporary debugging aid when running mypy. When reveal_type(two_sensors) has been added, we see the following additional line in the mypy output:

```
broken.py:4: error: Revealed type is 'builtins.list[builtins.object*]'
```

showing that mypy has interpreted the variable as a list of objects, not a list of sensors. If we import the appropriate names from the typing module and add an explicit type to the two_sensors line, such as

```
two_sensors: List[Sensor[Any]] = [CPULoad(), ACStatus()]
```

then the output of mypy becomes

```
broken.py:6: error: Revealed type is 'builtins.list[sensors.Sensor[Any]]'
```

As mentioned earlier, the use of typing.Any is a mixed bag. This definition means that any sensor retrieved from this list is of type Sensor[Any], so two_sensors[0].format("3.2") would no longer be detected as an error by mypy.

In the current example, we have two sensors, one that returns a float and one that returns an Optional[bool], so we could declare the list as

```
two_sensors: List[Union[Sensor[float], Sensor[Optional[bool]]]] = [
CPULoad(), ACStatus()]
```

meaning that two_sensors will only ever contain those types of sensor, but this is still not especially helpful. We now get the pair of error lines:

```
broken.py:7: error: Argument 1 to "format" of "Sensor" has incompatible
type "str"; expected "float"
broken.py:7: error: Argument 1 to "format" of "Sensor" has incompatible
type "str"; expected "Optional[bool]"
```

showing that mypy has indeed determined that the call is incorrect, but based on the information, it cannot know if float or Optional[bool] is the correct choice. We can see more information about the format method it's complaining about with reveal_type(two_sensors[0].format), which returns

```
broken.py:6: error: Revealed type is 'Union[def (value: builtins.float*) ->
builtins.str, def (value: Union[builtins.bool, None]) -> builtins.str]'
```

That is, mypy knows that it's one of two function signatures, one that takes a float called value and one that takes a bool or a None called value, both returning str. Either one of these is equally valid according to the typing hints. We wouldn't be able to cause mypy to detect the one correct function unless we declared the type as

```
two_sensors: Tuple[Sensor[float], Sensor[Optional[bool]]] = (CPULoad(),
ACStatus())
```

These are absurd lengths to go to. This demonstrates how quickly your code can become unmaintainable if you approach typing too dogmatically. In such a situation, you have a choice, to accept a lower level of type checking or to completely rearchitect your program to allow for easier type checking by avoiding situations where you have mixed types together. Personally, I would pick opting for less checking.

When to use typing and when to avoid it

Type hinting, in general, is very much an optional feature in Python. Some people prefer the more rigorous style that static typing encourages, but if this style doesn't feel natural to you, then I wouldn't recommend making the switch just because it makes tooling easier.

Approach type checking as a way of helping yourself, not as a way of detecting all possible errors. You will have to make judgments in your coding about the benefits of individual bits of typing being correct, weighed against the disadvantages of increased code complexity. There is usually a clear middle ground, where any additional typing is much harder to represent correctly, and any less typing does not markedly simplify the code.

For example, much later in this project, we will want to chart the output of some of the sensors over time. The sensors that return float or int are easy to chart, as they're a quantitative value. Sensors that return a list of lists of strings or sys.version_info do not have a natural way of being translated into charts.

For these, we could imagine writing code that uses a sequence of sensors that all use numeric types (or optional numeric types) as their input. That would allow us to limit the expected types returned from the value function and ensure the rest of that function was type-safe without us having to ensure that the exact type of every sensor was maintained in all variables throughout the codebase.

More generally, not all projects benefit hugely from static typing. If a project has a relatively simple set of functions that return known types, it can be a real benefit. As soon as you start to require extensive use of Union or custom generic types, the argument in favor of typing becomes weaker.

The overriding consideration, in my view, is if the people developing the software want to use static typing. If you and your colleagues like the rigor that this way of working enforces, then it is likely to be a good idea to use static typing. If you spend lots of time and effort on code review and testing, then the benefits of adding testing may be significantly less.

If you're writing a library to be used by others, then it's nice to have at least the external interfaces type hinted, as it allows your users to use type hinting without marking your library as excluded from the type-checking process.

Throughout this book, we will include type hints for our code. As the code is being written by one person who does not object to type hinting, there is no particular reason to avoid it. The benefits are twofold. Firstly, books are hard to update if a small bug is found in a code example. Using type hinting makes it easier to get code right the first time. Secondly, it is much easier to have good intuitions on if this feature is going to be useful in your projects if you've used it before. As we build the example up through the chapters, you may find yourself disagreeing with the type hints I've picked. Don't dismiss these thoughts, knowing what feels natural to you is half the battle with designing test suites and static checkers.

Keeping type hints separate from code

An alternative to using type hints in your code is to define them alongside your code in a pyi file. These act like .h files, for those familiar with C programming. The structure of your code is maintained, but no implementations are present. This can be beneficial if the majority of developers working on a piece of software do not use the type hints (e.g., if they're intended for external consumers of the code) or if your type structure is so complex that it makes the code appear messy. A partial implementation of this would look like that shown in Listing 2-12.

Listing 2-12. Partial sensors.py file without inline type definitions

```
#!/usr/bin/env python
# coding: utf-8
import math
import socket
import sys

import click
import psutil
```

```python
class Sensor:

    def value(self):
        raise NotImplementedError

    @classmethod
    def format(cls, value):
        raise NotImplementedError

    def __str__(self):
        return self.format(self.value())

class PythonVersion(Sensor):
    title = "Python Version"

    def value(self):
        return sys.version_info

    @classmethod
    def format(cls, value):
        if value.micro == 0 and value.releaselevel == "alpha":
            return "{0.major}.{0.minor}.{0.micro}a{0.serial}".format(value)
        return "{0.major}.{0.minor}".format(value)
```

Matching sensors.pyi for the preceding partial file

```python
from typing import Any, Iterable, List, Optional, Tuple, TypeVar, Generic

T_value = TypeVar('T_value')

class Sensor(Generic[T_value]):
    title: str
    def value(self) -> T_value: ...
    @classmethod
    def format(cls: Any, value: T_value) -> str: ...

class PythonVersion(Sensor[Any]):
    title: str = ...
    def value(self) -> Any: ...
    @classmethod
    def format(cls: Any, value: Any) -> str: ...
```

These stub files can be generated by mypy from a standard Python file. These generated files must be edited before they can be used, as they will not contain any type declarations other than typing.Any. The files are generated with the stubgen tool, as follows:

```
> pipenv run stubgen sensors.py
> cp out/sensors.pyi ./sensors.pyi
```

In my opinion, this format should be avoided unless there are strong reasons for using it. It is harder to maintain, as new functions need to be added to the pyi file as well as the py file, and using the type annotations is slightly more difficult in some cases. For example, in the combined syntax, Sensor[float] is valid Python, but in this split form, the Sensor base class has no __getitem__ method inherited from Generic, so Sensor[float] is only valid in pyi files, not in py files. If we ever wanted to use Sensor[float] in a py file rather than just in a pyi file, we'd have to use the legacy comment syntax for defining the type:

```
sensor = [CPULoad(), ]  # type: List[Sensor[float]]
```

EXERCISE 2-3: EXPANDING THE TYPING COVERAGE

We've got a base class for the Sensors and have looked at how we apply that to one Sensor.

Go through the rest of the sensors in the sensors.py file and update them to use the Sensor base class with appropriate type hints.

You may want to try the --strict command-line flag to mypy to see additional warnings that aren't raised by default, for example, because we've ignored external modules.

There are a few choices you'll have to make, particularly regarding how to handle the untyped variables coming from psutil and one particular sensor that is difficult to type.

Linting

Linting is a general term for many different types of static analysis of code. In a way, the static analysis done by mypy in the previous section is a very technical, computer science–driven type of linting. The linting we're going to discuss in this section is a lot less involved and is much easier to introduce to existing projects than type checking is.

My linter of choice is flake8, a reference to the Python Enhancement Proposal (PEP8) that defines a style guide for Python code.[14] Flake8 and other linters go much further than this style guide to produce code that matches best practice and the opinions of some well-respected Python developers. You may find that a different linter integrates particularly well with your code editor of choice, in which case I'd recommend using that one.

You will inevitably find that some linters perform checks that you don't feel are important or may miss some checks that you think should be enforced on your code. For this reason, flake8 is very customizable, allowing the author of a piece of software to define how its code should be checked. As the author or maintainer of a piece of software, you are able to set these values how you like, so you get the most benefit from the linter. If you find yourself contributing to code maintained by someone else, then their choices for their flake8 configuration help you to know if you've written some code that they're likely to dislike the style of before you even submit your patches. It can be frustrating to have to adjust your code to pass an overly zealous linter, but it's less frustrating than having to go through comments one by one on a pull request as they're noticed by the maintainer.

As many of the complaints that linters have are based on formatting, there is a growing trend for the linter to fix the formatting to be consistent itself. The runaway leader in this field in the Python community is black.[15] Black automatically reformats your code in a consistent fashion. There are many advantages to using black over other linters. The main one is that it's emotionally a lot easier to accept having no control over the formatting of your code than it is to deal with a large number of seemingly insignificant changes being demanded. Not having to placate the linter on whitespace is a big advantage to using black.

Caution   If you're contributing to a codebase that does not use black, make sure you only contribute the changes you intend to. The git command `git add --patch` is an excellent tool for choosing exactly what changes are staged for commit. If you make a commit to a project that reformats code unrelated to your change, it is likely that the commit will be reverted and people will be upset.

---

[14]Technically, the name flake8 is actually based on the pyflakes and pep8 libraries, both of which are static analysis tools. The pep8 library is named after PEP8 as it attempts to check for PEP8 compliance.

[15]Black has very few configuration options; it does what it thinks is best. Its name is a reference to the Henry Ford quote: "Any customer can have a car painted any color that he wants so long as it is black."

Installing flake8 and black

We're going to install and set up both flake8 and black to run against our code. Both of these are development dependencies, not core dependencies, and so are installed with the --dev flag.[16]

```
> pipenv install --dev flake8 black
```

Fixing existing code

We can then run flake8 against our code (or our tests) with

```
> pipenv run flake8 sensors.py
> pipenv run flake8 tests
```

If you do run either of these, you'll see several required changes. Many of these are whitespace changes, but others are to do with code formatting. We don't want to make all these changes manually, so let's use black to reformat our code.[17]

```
> pipenv run black sensors.py tests
```

Now that these files have been reformatted, we'd expect flake8 only to report errors not resulting from formatting. However, there are a couple more things we need to do. Firstly, black's default line length is 88 characters, but flake8's is 80 characters. We need

---

[16]At the time of writing, the authors of black have been promising to imminently remove the prerelease flag from black for the last 18 months. If this still hasn't been done by the time you're reading this, you may need to add the --pre flag to pipenv to allow this to be installed. Despite it claiming to not be production ready, it's my opinion that it is.

[17]When converting a project to use black, you should add black to the environment in one git commit and make all the automated changes in a second commit. It's easier to drop the second commit and re-run black if merge conflicts occur later on. The commit that contains the reformatted code should be done as

```
git commit -m "Apply initial black formatting" --author="Black Formatter
<black@example.com>"
```

to ensure that the fact that this is an automatic reformatting is clear to developers in future. If you don't specify an author, then you will forever be assumed to have been the last person to touch various parts of the codebase.

to update the flake configuration to use the same value as black. This is done by adding a [flake8] section to setup.cfg, alongside the existing mypy configuration.

```
[mypy]
ignore_missing_imports = True

[flake8]
max-line-length = 88
```

When we run pipenv run flake8 sensors.py, we still see a couple of errors. These are because we have overly long comments, and as comments are intended for humans rather than the Python interpreter, black does not split them for us. The changes required to make sensors.py pass a flake8 test are minimal, but when we run against the tests, we see several real mistakes to fix.[18]

```
> pipenv run flake8 tests
tests\test_acstatus.py:2:1: F401 'socket' imported but unused
tests\test_acstatus.py:41:26: E712 comparison to True should be 'if cond is
True:' or 'if cond:'
tests\test_acstatus.py:46:26: E711 comparison to None should be 'if cond is
None:'
tests\test_acstatus.py:51:26: E711 comparison to None should be 'if cond is
None:'
tests\test_cpuusage.py:2:1: F401 'socket' imported but unused
tests\test_dht.py:2:1: F401 'socket' imported but unused
tests\test_dht.py:57:13: F841 local variable 'f' is assigned to but never
used
tests\test_ramusage.py:2:1: F401 'socket' imported but unused
tests\test_sensors.py:1:1: F401 'sys' imported but unused
```

In this output, we are given the filename, followed by the line number, followed by the column number within the line (or 1 if not applicable). Finally, we're given the flake8 code number for the style error and a human-readable explanation. The code number is what is used to exclude checks from being run, by adding them to an ignore= line in setup.cfg.

---

[18]Some of these I've been pretending not to notice so there would be things to find in this section, others I had not noticed. It's very easy to miss things when refactoring code, even when you're paying attention.

Each of these complaints is quite clear; it's a relatively mechanical task to go through line by line and make the changes suggested. I would recommend starting from the bottom of the list of errors and working upward. If you start at the top and work your way down, then the line numbers may not be correct due to removing unneeded import lines to fix F401 errors.

Running automatically

It's certainly possible to run linters by hand, but we've now got four different checks to remember to run to ensure that the code is acceptable. It's very easy to miss one of these and accidentally commit something that isn't up to standard. Once it's committed, making a fix is much more difficult; either the commit needs to be edited to include the fixes or a new commit containing only those fixes is needed. It's somewhat common to see commit messages like "PEP8", "Fixes", or "Flake8" in projects that use linters but do not use them consistently.

One of the main reasons to use a linter is to get things right the first time, so to get the most benefit, it should be run for every commit, not just every push or when the author feels like it. This is especially important if the codebase accepts external contributions or work from more than one developer as if some developers are not running the linter, then errors it picks up are not guaranteed to be related to the change you're working on.

For this reason, the last tool that I'll be recommending in this chapter is called pre-commit. This is a tool for managing the hooks that Git offers for determining if a commit should be allowed or not. It's written in Python and so can easily be installed in the same method as all our other development tools.

```
> pipenv install --dev pre-commit
```

We need to configure pre-commit to know about the three things we want to run by entering them into the .pre-commit-config.yaml configuration file. Pre-commit has extensive support for using community-written configuration through GitHub, which is the officially recommended way to configure hooks. However, I find that for many, it's faster to write a manual hook directly in the repository, as shown in Listing 2-13. There are many externally maintained hooks for you to choose from if you prefer, but this explicit approach is usually sufficient.

Listing 2-13. .pre-commit-config.yaml

```
repos:

- repo: local
  hooks:
  - id: black
    name: black
    entry: pipenv run black
    args: [--quiet]
    language: system
    types: [python]

  - id: mypy
    name: mypy
    entry: pipenv run mypy
    args: ["--follow-imports=skip"]
    language: system
    types: [python]

  - id: flake8
    name: flake8
    entry: pipenv run flake8
    language: system
    types: [python]
```

We are not automatically running pytest as part of this suite, as we expect pytest to become slower as the project progresses. The static analysis tools should never become much slower as the codebase grows, but tests may well do.

Once this file is in place, pre-commit is configured. Every user needs to enable pre-commit in their checkout, which is done with

```
> pipenv run pre-commit install
```

From this point on, all commits are guarded by these three checkers. It is possible to skip the checks (e.g., if making a quick work-in-progress commit that you intend to change later). Skipping the checks is done with the `--no-verify` parameter in your git commit call or by setting the `SKIP` environment variable to be the names of the checkers to skip.[19]

Tip   I often use `git add --patch` to interactively stage "hunks"[20] of my work rather than adding entire files at once. If you also work this way, you may be wary about linters and formatters as, when you're making a commit, there may already be code in place for the next commit you intend to make.

The pre-commit program handles this excellently. Any unstaged changes will be stashed in an independent store managed by pre-commit (it doesn't interfere with your existing stashes), so the validators and reformatters only work on the code you have staged. In my opinion, this is the "killer" feature of pre-commit.

Running on pull requests

Modern front ends to version control software like GitHub and GitLab support continuous integration hooks. These allow external services to run verification on your commits, branches, and pull requests and annotate them with the results in the user interface. Many different products offer this, all with different feature sets and pricing structures.

Github offers a simple docker-based CI runner, as well as many commercial offerings. The GitLab approach mirrors GitLab itself in that all are open source and available to be configured to your requirements. The number of different approaches here makes it impossible for me to give a single recommendation that would be useful to everyone, so this section only covers the general approach. Personally, I usually use Github's actions.

There are two intended users of the information provided by continuous integration software. The obvious one is the maintainer of the package. If you have some code that other people have access to, either open to public patches or just from your colleagues, you will want to know if a suggested patch has any obvious errors in it. It can be very hard

---

[19]For most shells other than Windows cmd.exe, this can be done as `SKIP="mypy" git commit`.

[20]I'm not sure why the authors of GNU diff chose to call a group of changed lines a hunk, but it has since become the standard term.

work maintaining a piece of software; if you have to check out a branch and build it on your local computer to find out that the submission has a typo that prevents it from working, then it gets even harder. Continuous integration reduces your workload by performing the common checks that you would always do and lets you concentrate on reviewing the code.

The less obvious user of the information is the author of the change. Whenever you're contributing to some software for the first time, it can be nerve-wracking making sure that you've not made a trivial mistake. Nobody likes to make mistakes, especially in public or in front of your peers. Continuous integration helps by warning you if something has gone wrong without any active interaction from other people. When you submit a pull request, you can watch the individual checks pass and be sure that your contribution isn't going to be seen as wasting someone's time because of a simple error.

This is especially useful for projects that have very slow test suites or test suites that rely on specific operating systems or dependency versions. It's possible to set up continuous integration to run your software on Linux, Windows, and macOS. The Django test suite runs against each of the supported database architectures, including nonfree databases like Oracle. It wouldn't be feasible to ask all people submitting a patch to run tests against all these different configurations, so the CI server handles it.

Summary

Throughout this chapter, we've extended our worked example from a handful of basic functions to classes that implement the functionality in a way that makes it easier to build upcoming features. We've implemented automated testing so we can be confident that the changes we're making are not breaking things along the way as well as type checking and linting to catch basic errors that creep in.

We've looked at three broad categories of software (testing, type checking, and linting) that help you as a software engineer to write code that you're confident in. You may often see people advocating for these three approaches and for specific philosophies that should be applied to their use, such as 100% test coverage. The value of these approaches is in the time it saves you and the people who contribute to your software, and that should be the standard by which you judge how you will use them.

In general, the approaches that involve the most effort have the most significant payoffs. As such, testing your code has the highest potential payoffs and is widely regarded to be a good idea. The relative advantages of test-driven development and writing tests after the main development, as well as of 100% test coverage, and the benefits of different types of tests are much less significant. For anything more involved than a toy project, I strongly recommend writing at least *some* tests. They don't have to be great tests, but some level of testing usually helps you over time.

Static type checking has significant benefits, especially when writing large, complex code. It also requires some decision-making regarding how to approach the process, and there is a significant learning curve. Developers who are not proficient with tests are not confronted with the details of the test suite at every turn; that's not the case with static typing. There is evidence of the typing work throughout the codebase, and writing a new function requires some thought about static typing. For this reason, I'd recommend only using static typing if you have a good reason to. The best reason, in my view, is that the development team believes it is helpful. Others such as an expectation of high code complexity or that future users may want to use type checks on their code are also quite convincing.

Finally, linting is very easy to implement, but the benefits are relatively minor. It will certainly save you some time (and perhaps some bikeshedding[21]), but it will only find relatively shallow bugs and stylistic improvements. It's worth doing, but it's not worth stressing over. I would strongly recommend all Python projects use some sort of linter, and I would encourage any projects where multiple people are going to be contributing to use a code formatter. That said, don't be afraid to disregard certain classes of warning if you don't find them helpful.

In the next chapter, we will package this software in an installable way and provide a way for additional sensors to be added to the available set through a plugin architecture.

Additional resources

The following resources provide additional information on the topics covered in this chapter:

- The typeshed library contains type hints for the standard library and many third-party libraries. It and its documentation are a great place to look for examples of complex typing done well. Its Git repository is available at `https://github.com/python/typeshed`.

---

[21]"Bikeshedding" is focusing on a trivial aspect of a design rather than the important parts. The name is a reference to the idea that when presented with detailed plans for a nuclear power plant, people are more likely to comment on something trivial but universal, such as the color of the bike shed, than something complex, such as the power plant design.

- The documentation for pre-commit has a lot of information on advanced features and prewritten hooks for various tools. See `https://pre-commit.com/` for more details.

- PEP561 defines how type hints can be distributed, especially as packages that just provide hints for existing packages. We'll be looking at packages in the next chapter, but `www.python.org/dev/peps/pep-0561/#stub-only-packages` provides information on this which may be useful for developers who are considering if adding stubs to an existing codebase is practical.

- A list of error codes used by flake8 is available at `https://flake8.pycqa.org/en/latest/user/error-codes.html`, which are used in addition to the pycodestyle list at `https://pycodestyle.readthedocs.io/en/latest/intro.html#error-codes`.

## CHAPTER 3

Packaging scripts

We want the Python code that we've developed so far to run on several different computers, but as it's currently stored as a directory of Python files, it's difficult to deploy updated versions and to ensure that all deployments are synchronized. We've already interacted with package management in Python throughout the last two chapters with our use of the pipenv script, but the next step is to use this system ourselves, rather than only depend on it.

The packaging process used in Python has been in flux for several years. The overall process has been improving steadily, and changes are still landing frequently. For many years, the setup process has been mediated through a file called `setup.py` which declares dependencies and metadata in a function call. That function is imported from one of several helper libraries (usually `setuptools`, but not always).

Perhaps the biggest problem with this approach is that some packages want to make use of dependency libraries to calculate the metadata in `setup.py` (e.g., for extracting version information from version control), but this dependency needs to be specified in `setup.py` itself. This leads to a chicken and egg situation, where it's not possible to determine the dependencies required to run the script that declares the dependencies.

This isn't a great situation to be in, but as most software doesn't make use of this feature, this has been somewhat of an academic problem. There has also been a profusion of distribution formats, the common ones were for many years `tar.gz` and `zip`, which are simple archives of the source code. They're the easiest to create but suffer from the circular dependency problem and require that code is executed to perform an installation. If installing into a system Python environment, this means running code downloaded from the Internet as root, which is enough to scare most information security teams.

For this reason, a standard zip-based format called *wheel* was developed in 2012. Wheel allows for installation of Python packages without executing any custom code. In fact, all that is required to install a Python wheel is to extract the contents into the

103

M. Wilkes, *Advanced Python Development*, https://doi.org/10.1007/978-1-4842-5793-7_3

correct directory.[1] Wheel is similar to an earlier distribution format called egg which also allowed for Python code to be installed without arbitrary code execution at install time, but made some different technical choices. You generally won't need to interact with egg files, but it's good to be aware of what they are in case you come across one.

There have been many changes in the way Python files are packaged over the years. Indeed one of the persistent criticisms leveled against Python over the years has been related to the packaging story. Almost every professional Python developer has experienced issues with packaging not working as intended. Still, in the last few years, the reliability of package installation seems to have improved. Most innovation now seems to be around better user experience for environment management, rather than fixing broken systems. There is still a way to go and a few different ways to approach the problem of packaging Python software, some of which may well overtake the methods this chapter recommends as the current best practice in the coming years. It's currently unclear which (if any) of these pieces of software will win the race.

Terminology

Some of the terms used in this chapter are sometimes misused in casual speech, more so than most programming terms. It's usually clear from the context what is meant, and the specific meaning of each term isn't something that developers need to concern themselves with on a day-to-day basis, but it is important to make sure the meaning used in documentation is clear.

File, *script*, and *module* are often used to mean the same thing when talking about Python code. A Python file is the foo.py file on the filesystem that contains the code. A script is a file that can be executed directly as a logical unit. A module is what you get when importing that code from a Python environment.

Similarly, *directory* (or *folder*) and *package* are conflated. The *directory* is the location on the filesystem where the *files* are stored; a *package* is an importable container for *modules*. If import foo.bar is valid, then foo must be a *package*, but bar could be either a *package* or a *module*. In this case, the code that does import foo binds foo to be the *module* backed by the file foo/__init__.py. If there's a need to differentiate packages from the packages that they contain, they are called *top-level packages* and *subpackages*.

---

[1]This is a slight simplification. For some packages, there is also parsing of various configuration files and copying of subtrees depending on their contents. The crucial factor is that no arbitrary code execution occurs.

The most confusion comes from the fact that the act of preparing a group of *files* and *folders* for distribution to users is called *packaging*. The result of this, a zip, a tar.gz, or a wheel file, is called a *distribution*. A *distribution* can contain multiple *top-level packages* (and their contained subpackages and modules) and/or *modules* directly.

In informal speech, it's common to refer to an independently distributed library or application as a package, using the top-level package as a placeholder for the distribution itself.

Directory structure

The first thing we should do to package up our code is to move it into a directory to house the related code. This isn't strictly required, and some packages like the Python 2/3 compatibility shim *six* are distributed as a single six.py file, rather than a six/ directory, but it is by far the most common approach. Most Python packages are installed in a flat namespace, where a directory contains Python files and subdirectories, and that directory is added to the import namespace. For example, django is packaged in a directory called django/, so it can be imported as import django. The result of importing django is a module object corresponding to django/__init__.py which is stored in the Python environment's internal site-packages/ directory. In general, this is the structure that you should adopt for your software.

An alternative is to use *namespace packages*. Namespace packages are directories in the module namespace that are guaranteed not to contain any code, only other packages. This allows developers to create multiple different distributions of code that install their software into a single location. This is usually overkill for simple programs, but very large applications may have multiple loosely coupled components for which this is a good fit. This multiple package approach can be an advantage and a disadvantage. It allows for different logical components of an application to be versioned and released independently, at the cost of adding substantial overhead to the release process if it's likely that all the components will be released together.

If it does make sense to release your code as multiple distributions, there are a few different ways to name them. Namespace packages themselves do not have many inherent advantages; there is very little practical difference between import apd_sensors and import apd.sensors; the namespace layout appears slightly cleaner, so I generally use it when working on code that is distributed as multiple packages.

Tip   As a rule of thumb, foo should be a namespace package if you anticipate creating foo.bar, foo.baz, and foo.xyzzy but never foo itself.

It makes sense for us to create an apd namespace for our examples. This allows our apd.sensors package to sit alongside the apd.collector package that we will create in a later chapter to collate and analyze the data we find.

We need to move our sensors.py into a new directory structure that matches the packages we want to offer, so it becomes apd/sensors/sensors.py. This apd/sensors directory needs an __init__.py to be a valid package, but we can leave that empty. It's required that namespace packages do not contain an __init__.py (as multiple pieces of code can be in the same namespace, there could otherwise be multiple __init__.pys that are equally valid).[2]

This directory layout is widespread in Python projects, but there is an alternative that I strongly recommend, often called "src layout". When using this layout, the apd/ directory is stored inside an src/ directory, so the sensors.py file is found at src/apd/sensors/sensors.py. The reason for this is that Python allows importing of code from the current working directory, so import apd.sensors automatically reads code from apd/sensors/__init__.py if available. The src/ structure ensures that this cannot happen, so the version imported is always the one installed in the environment.

Up to now, we've been relying on this trick to make our code importable. The sensors.py file is in the working directory, so the test code can import it. Being able to import code from the current working directory may, therefore, seem like a benefit. It means that the code you're working on is always available to Python, but it can make for confusing bugs in some situations.

Pipenv supports a flag -e which means "editable" which provides a structured way of achieving the same thing. When we install code into an environment, the relevant files are copied into the internal directories of that environment, so there is a consistent place for Python to find all the files. When something is installed with this flag, the code isn't squirrelled away inside the virtual environment. Instead, a link is set up between the internal directory of Python files and the files in your working directory (or checked

---

[2]This requirement wasn't always the case. You may come across some older packages that have __init__.py files in their namespace packages. These always include some special code to cause them to be disregarded and nothing else.

out from version control system, if a VCS URL is given rather than a filesystem path – see Table 3-1 for details of how this flag affects different installation types). This means that any changes made to those files are reflected immediately in the virtual environment.

Table 3-1. *Behavior of installing packages from different sources with and without the editable flag*

Installation source	With -e	Without -e
Filesystem path `./six`	Packages defined in setup scripts are installed in place as a reference.	Packages defined in setup scripts are copied to the virtual environment.
VCS path[3] `git+ssh://git@github.com/ benjaminp/six.git#egg=six`	Repository is checked out to `$(pipenv --venv)/src` and installed in place as a reference.	Repository is downloaded, then copied into virtual environment.
Distribution from PyPI `six`	Not supported. Packages are downloaded and installed as normal.	Packages are downloaded and installed as normal.

This approach allows us to ensure that the code we're editing is in use by the Python interpreter, but also gives us confidence in the packaging of the code by using the same dependency and environment management system that end-users will be using.

Given we have a way of ensuring that the local files are used in the environment, there is no reason to rely on the current working directory trick. Indeed, it can, on rare occasions, cause confusion. If there is a problem with the installation into the virtual environment, for example, due to an error in the metadata files for the code, it can result in an installation that partially works (rather than not working at all, as we'd expect). This behavior would often be inconsistent, behaving differently depending on which working directory commands are issued from.

---

[3]Note the use of #egg=six here. This is one of the few places you'll see the egg terminology in modern Python development. The reason this is here is to assist with dependency resolution when installing multiple packages at once.

Our rearrangement of the code gives us the following directory structure:

```
apd.sensors/
├── src/
│       └── apd/
│               └── sensors/
│                       ├── __init__.py
│                       └── sensors.py
├── tests/
│       ├── __init__.py
│       ├── test_acstatus.py
│       └── ...
├── .pre-commit-config.yaml
├── Pipfile
├── Pipfile.lock
├── pytest.ini
└── setup.cfg
```

Setup scripts and metadata

In the introduction to this chapter, we mentioned that the metadata for a Python package is traditionally stored in a setup.py file. This file contains a call to a special setup(...) function, with the various metadata about the package given as parameters. For our package the minimum we'd require the following setup.py:

```python
from distutils.core import setup

setup(
    name="apd.sensors",
    version="1.0",
    packages=["apd.sensors"],
    package_dir={"": "src"},
    license='MIT'
)
```

With this file in place, our packaging of the code is at a minimally functional stage. We can install the package in the current directory into our isolated environment and run the script that's defined in the sensors module of apd.sensors:

```
> pipenv install -e .
> pipenv run python -m apd.sensors.sensors
```

Dependencies

We now have an environment that includes all our dependent libraries and our code installed into the environment just like any package available on PyPI. However, the dependencies are still managed by Pipenv rather than being resolved through the apd.sensors package. We've only added a total of eight development dependencies to our environment, but their dependencies, both direct and indirect, have added 70 packages to our environment. We don't want our users to have to manually install the libraries that apd.sensors requires to work correctly; to achieve this we move the hard dependencies of the library to setup.py.

The contents of [packages] in Pipfile are our nondevelopment requirements, which looks like

```
[packages]
psutil = "*"
click = "*"
adafruit-circuitpython-dht = {markers = "'arm' in platform_machine",
version = "*"}
apd-sensors = {editable = true,path = "."}
```

We can see that there are three dependencies declared. Of these three, none have any version limits set, as shown by the fact that the version set is "*", but one has a platform marker. If we translate this to the format that setup.py expects, it becomes

```
from setuptools import setup

setup(
    name="apd.sensors",
    version="1.0",
    packages=["apd.sensors"],
```

```
    package_dir={"": "src"},
    install_requires=[
        "psutil",
        "click",
        "adafruit-circuitpython-dht ; 'arm' in platform_machine"
    ],
    license='MIT'
)
```

At this point, we can remove the extraneous lines from `Pipfile`, either manually or using `pipenv uninstall psutil` (and so on).

Caution   Conditional dependencies defined in `Pipfile` are always added to the `Pipfile.lock` file, regardless of whether they're required on the current platform. Conditional dependencies of the packages you install are only added if they are required for the current platform. For us, that means that we need to re-run `pipenv lock` on a Raspberry Pi to lock the ARM-specific dependencies. In general, a `Pipfile.lock` file creates reproducible builds on a given computer. It is not *guaranteed* to produce a reproducible build that works on a range of different Python versions, operating systems, or processor hardware (although it often does).

This is the minimal usable form of the `setup.py` file for generating distributions for use by other people. The command `pipenv run python setup.py sdist` generates a source distribution that can be shared with other people to allow for easy installation of the code. A source distribution is the most common format for Python software distribution. This file is stored in the `dist/` directory and can be shared online, in which case users can install it by URL.

Declarative configurations

So far, we've followed the `setup.py` approach that most Python packages use, but setuptools does allow for a more declarative configuration approach using `setup.cfg`. The approach is newer, and I prefer it, as it provides helper functionality for a variety of features that people commonly want for their metadata management.

The following section explains three common requirements for package metadata, all of which can cause problems when using the setup.py style. While some are possible to achieve with setup.py, all are trivial in the setup.cfg style detailed in the subsequent section.

Things to avoid in setup.py

It's best to avoid any logic in setup.py as environment management tools make several assumptions that expect setup.py to behave as though it calls setup(...) only. Any additional logic can cause these assumptions to be faulty.

Conditional dependencies

A common pattern in the past was to conditionally include dependencies based on detection of the state of the host machine. For example, we only need the temperature sensor code on the Raspberry Pi. We've achieved this using a dependency definition with a built-in condition. Consider the following (made-up) example showing a manual system for use of conditional dependencies:

```python
if sys.platform == "win32":
    dependencies = [
        "example-forwindows"
    ]
else:
    dependencies = [
        "example"
    ]
setup(
    ...
    install_requires=dependencies
)
```

This would broadly work as expected for most people. The preceding code listing represents using a fork of the example package that is distributed as example-forwindows when installing on a Windows computer. Although not very common, it's not unheard of for a package to be forked when users want to use it on a very different platform, but the maintainers don't want to maintain that compatibility.

The problem with this approach is that there is no *guarantee* that setup.py is executed on the installation target machine (or, indeed, that it isn't executed on other machines). If we were working with this code on both a Windows development environment and a Linux production environment, we would see the consequences of this. When the developer runs pipenv lock, then Pipenv executes the setup.py scripts of each dependency to find the full set of dependencies needed.[4] It would, therefore, determine that the package here depends on example-forwindows and would lock the latest version (including saving verification hashes of all installation files that are permissible) for example-forwindows without ever looking at example. This procedural declaration of conditional dependencies makes it possible for users to declare conditional dependencies in such a way that the setup(...) function (and therefore, the package manager) does not know they are conditional.

If this Pipfile.lock is then used to install the software on a production host, then it's the windows fork library that pipenv installs. At best, this won't work, but it could also create an inconsistent installation environment. If other packages depend on the example library using the proper conditional dependencies, then both distributions could be installed at once.

These forks often use the same name in the global package namespace, so code works seamlessly regardless of which version of example you're using. If both versions are installed at once, then one overwrites the files of the other.[5] Pipenv disables dependency resolution at install time, performing it only at the time the lock file is generated,[6] meaning that only packages mentioned in the lock file can be installed.

The correct way of representing this, as we've seen in earlier chapters, is by unconditionally declaring dependencies that are themselves conditional, such as

```
dependencies = [
    "example-forwindows ; sys_platform == 'win32' "
    "example ; sys_platform != 'win32' "
]
```

---

[4]It may use cached metadata instead of executing the scripts, if such files are available.

[5]It's actually worse than this. Any files present in only one of the two distributions will be present and can be imported from, so you wouldn't just have one version or the other, but a mixture of both.

[6]When using pipenv install example, the dependencies are resolved because example is added to the pipfile, which causes the lockfile to be seen as out of date.

```
setup(
    ...
    install_requires=dependencies
)
```

This causes Pipenv to investigate appropriate versions of both packages and their versions to be locked, with the appropriate metadata annotated to ensure that only the correct one is used at install time. You can see this already by looking at the Pipfile.lock of our running example, as one of the packages is only used when running on an ARM processor.

Readme in metadata

A more common reason to have code in setup.py other than the setup(...) call is to avoid duplication, especially in the long_description field. It is normal for this to be the contents of the README file, or a concatenation of the README and HISTORY files, or similar. Developers sometimes achieve this by reading those files in setup.py:

```
with open("README") as readme_file:
    readme_text = readme_file.read()
setup(
    ...
    long_description=readme_text
)
```

There are a couple of problems with this example. Firstly, open(...) has two optional parameters that should be specified. These are mode and encoding. As we haven't passed an explicit mode, we're effectively using mode rt, and therefore Python is handling the encoding and decoding of strings to bytes for us. As we haven't specified an encoding, this is dependent on settings of the computer we're using. The two default values of this function result in a situation where the behavior is not consistent across different computers. We have added an implicit assumption that this file will only ever be read on systems where the default encoding matches the encoding this file is saved as.

FILE MODES

By default, the mode in which files are opened is rt for read-only text. Instead of r it is possible to use the following:

> w (open a file in write-only mode and discard any contents, if present)

> x (open a file in write-only mode and raise an exception if it already exists)

> a (open a file in write-only mode and position the file pointer after the existing contents)

> r+ (open a file in both reading and write modes but position the file pointer at the start of the file)

> w+ (open a file in both reading and write modes and discard any contents if present)

The b modifier can be added to any of these access modes in place of t to indicate that the file is being opened in binary mode, meaning that read and write calls should use bytes rather than strings. It is common for t to be omitted, as it is the default, but I recommend keeping r for clarity despite it also being the default mode.

Encoding issues have become much more commonplace with the rise in popularity of emojis. Many people who speak European languages have been able to ignore encoding and have text handling seemingly work correctly. They're now experiencing bugs where emojis break applications, as these characters are not handled properly by their systems' default encoding.

The main reason for this is that the *Latin-1* encoding (and the very similar *Windows-1252*) and the UTF-8 encoding use the same bytes to represent most characters commonly used in European languages. Therefore, switching between these three encodings still produces the correct values for most characters used by European languages.

As the default encoding in Windows is Windows-1252 and the default encoding in Linux is UTF-8, any program that runs on both of these operating systems produces inconsistent output files unless an encoding is specified.

One character that differs in encoding between Windows-1252 and UTF-8 is £, the symbol for the British Pound. Table 3-2 shows the effect of failing to include an encoding in file operations that involve this symbol.

Table 3-2. *Implicit encoding problems across operating systems*

Result of writing "£100" to a file and reading back	Windows reading	Linux reading
Windows writing	"£100"	UnicodeDecodeError
Linux writing	"Â£100"	"£100"

When the same system is used to read and to write the file, there is no problem with this character.[7] When there is a mismatch, there's a chance of an error occurring. This could take the form of a garbled character being read (such as "Â£" rather than "£"), an exception being raised, or it could work as intended. The exact result depends on the combination of the two default encodings.

To go back to our long_description example earlier, if my README file included "Thanks to Company X for supporting the development of this package with a donation of £1000," I might experience this problem. If I wrote this on a Windows computer that saved the data in the default Windows encoding, then setup.py would not be executable on Linux hosts.

This would mean that the source distribution file we created for the package would not work for most users, and users who specified this package as a dependency would find that their invocations of pipenv install and pipenv lock would fail on Linux hosts.

It is possible to correct these shortcomings and have a reliable setup.py by correcting the use of the open call. The following is an improved example of loading README to long_description:

```
with open("README", "rt", encoding="utf-8") as readme_file:
    readme_text = readme_file.read()
setup(
    ...
    long_description=readme_text
)
```

---

[7]This isn't true for all cases, just the case for this example. Writing "😊" to a file on a Windows machine without specifying an encoding will result in UnicodeEncodeError being raised immediately.

115

It is still possible that open(...) could raise an exception, such as if the README file is missing. Still, any exceptions raised in this case would likely be transient or symptomatic of underlying issues that would cause the installation to fail regardless.

Some people do even more involved processing of the input files in setup.py, for example, converting between different markup languages, but this increases the likelihood of accidentally introducing buggy code that would cause exceptions to be raised when running on other hardware.

Version numbers

Finally, many packages include their version number in a way that is accessible to Python code. This is often stored as __version__ or VERSION in the highest level __init__.py in the package. We previously left apd/sensors/__init__.py empty; let's now add a version number:

```
VERSION = "1.0.0"
```

This version number can be imported as apd.sensors.VERSION. Making version numbers available in code is useful for users of our library. It means they can easily log what version of a library a piece of data was generated with or even view the value in an interactive session or in a debugger to confirm what version of a dependency is installed in a given environment.

Tip   If you want to include many other things in your __init__.py file, you may want to set the version in a version.py file instead. You can then import that value in __init__.py for convenience or access it from version.py to be sure there are no side effects from your other code in __init__.py.

The problem is adding this attribute means two places need to be updated every time a new version is released, both setup.py and src/apd/sensors/__init__.py. This can lead to mistakes, where one version is updated but not the other. If these two numbers are ever out of sync, it becomes useless to offer both as users cannot trust them. Therefore, they must be kept absolutely synchronized.

The attribute needs to be accessible from the `setup.py` script, but the `setup.py` script is executed before the code is installed (except when upgrading, in which case a previous version is available), so it cannot just `import apd.sensors`.

Although this is a very useful feature, there is no advisable way to achieve this when using `setup.py` style of metadata. There are a few methods that try to work around this problem, such as tools that synchronize the version number automatically.

Using setup.cfg

We can achieve the same results without writing any code in `setup.py` by declaring the information that would usually be passed as parameters to `setup.py` in the `setup.cfg` file.

Converting our existing `setup.py` to declarations in `setup.cfg` is quite straightforward. Rather than all the values being stored in the flat namespace of the arguments to the `setup(...)` function, they are stored within sections in the ini file. Two of the more complex patterns we saw earlier have been baked into the configuration language in Listing 3-1 (highlighted in bold).

Listing 3-1. setup.cfg

```
[mypy]
ignore_missing_imports = True

[flake8]
max-line-length = 88

[metadata]
name = apd.sensors
version = attr: apd.sensors.VERSION
description = APD Sensor package
long_description = file: README.md, CHANGES.md, LICENCE
keywords = iot
license = MIT
classifiers =
    Programming Language :: Python :: 3
    Programming Language :: Python :: 3.7

[options]
zip_safe = False
include_package_data = True
```

117

```
package-dir =
    =src
packages = find-namespace:
install_requires =
    psutil
    click
    adafruit-circuitpython-dht ; 'arm' in platform_machine

[options.packages.find]
where = src
```

setup.py

```
from setuptools import setup

setup()
```

PYPROJECT.TOML AND PEP517

This approach is specific to setuptools, the default and recommended build system for Python packaging, but this is one of the areas of the packaging process that is in flux. A pair of standards called PEP517 and PEP518 defined that `pyproject.toml` can be used to pick between many different packaging tools. This is an important step, as it clarifies some implicit understandings about how Python packages are built.

PEP517 has enabled some alternatives to setuptools already, such as *poetry* and *flit*. One or both of these tools may become the clear best practice in the future, but at the time of writing, they are promising minority approaches.

However, some important questions raised by PEP517 have not yet been resolved. The one that affects us is that we use `pipenv install -e .` to install our code as an editable dependency. This instructs the setuptools build system to create links to our code in our environment, so the code is loaded directly rather than needing to be copied.

This feature is specific to setuptools, and while other build tools offer equivalent features, they have not yet been standardized. Any codebase that contains a `pyproject.toml` file is considered to have opted in to only use the PEP517 build system, so there is no guarantee that `pipenv install -e .` will work as expected.

Some tools (like mypy) use `setup.cfg` as a place to store their configuration, but others (like black) store their configuration in `pyproject.toml`. As more and more tools start storing their configuration in this file, it'll be more likely that you'll need to create it and therefore opt in to PEP517.

For now, I must recommend that you avoid adding a `pyproject.toml` file to any codebase that uses setuptools. If, however, you experiment with other build systems (such as flit and poetry), these generate a `pyproject.toml` file which you must not remove, or else users will not be able to install your package. Hopefully, the problems with editable installations will be resolved soon, but in the meantime we'll take a brief look at the general structure of this new feature.

The `[build-system]` section of the file declares which tooling is responsible for building releases of this software and comprises a `requires` line and a `build-backend` line. The following is the `pyproject.toml` for using setuptools. It declares that building requires setuptools and wheel format support and uses the modern setuptools builder (as opposed to the legacy setuptools builder).

```
[build-system]
requires = [
    "setuptools >= 40.6.0",
    "wheel"
]
build-backend = "setuptools.build_meta"
```

With this in place, the `setup.py` file is completely optional, but editable installations are not guaranteed to be possible.

Custom index servers

It's a good idea to use an *index server* to allow people to download your code. The Python Software Foundation offers an index server called PyPI.[8] PyPI is managed by the Python Software Foundation for the benefit of all Python developers and is financed through

---

[8]This is often pronounced "pie pie," but to avoid ambiguity between PyPI and the Python implementation PyPy, a better way might be "pie pee eye."

donations, both cash and in-kind donations like web hosting from large technology companies. This is appropriate for open source libraries that anyone could depend on, but not for private projects. You shouldn't be afraid of publishing code on PyPI if you're happy for other people to use it.

There are a few open source projects which act as alternatives for PyPI that allow you to store your private packages, following the requirements documented in PEP503. The code that runs pypi.org is called Warehouse and is available as an open source project. This may seem like an attractive place to start, but it's likely that your requirements are nothing like the requirements of PyPI.

There is another open source implementation of the same interface that PyPI provides, imaginatively called pypiserver. To be clear, pypiserver is not used to host pypi.org; rather, it is a server that provides an alternative to pypi.org.

Both implementations provide for browsing of projects through the Web and downloading distributions by name. The version of the site that humans access (through https://pypi.org) is different from what is accessed by pip and setuptools when finding a package. The "simple" index is used by dependency management tools, which is also HTTP based but not intended to be used by humans. You can see it for yourself at https://pypi.org/simple/: it is an unstyled page consisting only of the names of the 200,000 or so packages available on PyPI. If you click one of these links, you'll see the filenames of each distribution that has been uploaded and a download link.

This simple listing is the minimum required for a repository of distributions. Warehouse and pypiserver also offer an upload API that is common to both systems. The API can be accessed using the tool twine, which uploads any distributions you give it to the index server of your choice.

When you upload a package using twine, you may need to provide credentials. Warehouse checks that you can authenticate yourself as a user who is authorized to upload new releases to the project in question. Only users who have been authorized by the initial uploader of a project (directly or by others that the original uploader delegated access control to) may upload new releases. This prevents malicious change being made by members of the public.

Per-package delegated permissions are excessive for a private index server used by only a few people who trust each other. Pypiserver protects actions in a flat hierarchy; if you're allowed to upload a distribution to an instance of pypiserver, you may upload **any** distribution without having to be explicitly authorized for each individual project.

This is a much better fit for commercial environments, as all developers (or, a subset who are responsible for handling releases) can add new distributions of any internal packages without worrying about coordinating access levels. If you and a group of colleagues are regularly creating new releases of packages you've written, then pypiserver is an excellent way of managing this.

There are alternatives which offer fewer features but are even easier to set up. As the index server only requires a listing of packages by name which each link to a listing of files, a web server that serves a directory of files and is configured to generate directory listings is enough. This can be done with Apache, Nginx, or even simply `python -m http.server` from the appropriate directory.

This cannot support direct uploads as there is no logic backing the server, but it does allow for hosting your dependencies on any standard web server at the cost of making the upload process more complicated. This approach does not provide the same metadata information that full index servers do, so tasks such as having Pipenv lock dependencies take much longer. I would, therefore, not recommend this approach.

Setting up pypiserver

We will create an index server the code we're developing, so we can publish it to a repository without having to clutter up PyPI with multiple versions of this tool. This index server should be set up in a new isolated environment; you should not install the index server as part of your development environment for `apd.sensors`.

I will be installing the index server on a Raspberry Pi 4B. To do so, I connect to the Raspberry Pi and create a new user account for the index server and follow the on-screen prompts. A different user account allows for better separation of concerns between the main user of the system and its role as the index server.

```
rpi> sudo adduser indexserver
```

We should also run `sudo apt install apache2-utils` to install the `htpassword` utility, as we will need that to configure authentication information in a moment.

Now, change user to the indexserver user, either with `sudo -iu indexserver` or reconnecting via SSH as indexserver. We can now install pipenv for this user, add it to the user's path, and set up our new environment.

```
rpi> sudo -iu indexserver
rpi> pip install --user pipenv
rpi> echo "export PATH=/home/indexserver/.local/bin:$PATH" >> ~/.bashrc
rpi> source ~/.bashrc
```

```
rpi> mkdir indexserver
rpi> mkdir packages
rpi> cd indexserver
rpi> pipenv install pypiserver passlib>=1.6
rpi> htpasswd -c htaccess your_desired_username
```

We then need to configure the Raspberry Pi to run this server automatically on startup, which we do with a *systemd* file.[9] This should be done as the default pi user, as it involves using sudo to edit system files. Create the file in Listing 3-2 to configure the system.

Listing 3-2. /lib/systemd/system/indexserver.service

```
[Unit]
Description=Custom Index Server for Python distributions
After=multi-user.target

[Service]
Type=idle
User=indexserver
WorkingDirectory=/home/indexserver/indexserver
ExecStart=/home/indexserver/.local/bin/pipenv run pypi-server -p 8080 -P
htaccess ../packages

[Install]
WantedBy=multi-user.target
```

We can then enable and start the service with

```
$ sudo systemctl enable indexserver
$ sudo service indexserver start
```

From this point on, the service will start up automatically when the machine is powered up and listen on http://rpi4:8080 or whatever hostname or IP address is associated with the Raspberry Pi on your network.

---

[9]This varies by operating system. These instructions are for the default Raspberry Pi operation system, Raspbian.

Durability

When running your own index server, it's important to consider what would happen if there were to be a catastrophic hardware failure on your infrastructure. Distributions themselves are not stored in version control, although the versions of the source code they're generated from should be tagged for easy access in future; regenerating the distributions from the same tag may result in files with different check hashes being generated. Ensuring the exact same files are always available is key to being able to rebuild older versions of the software.

Pipenv automatically records the hashes of all distributions that were available when it last locked, so as long as the same files are available in future, the same environment can be reconstructed.

Therefore, the distribution files being stored on your index server should be treated as being as important to keep backups of as your main source tree. As all dependencies are required to rebuild the environment exactly, many Python developers choose to also keep backups of all their dependency distributions on their private index server. This allows for builds of the application to happen without access to PyPI, such as on private networks or during planned maintenance windows.

There are many ways of doing this, such as specialized proxy servers that cache packages as they are downloaded. It's easy to overcomplicate this, however. I recommend using a tool like `wget` to create partial mirrors of pypi for the packages you depend on.

The full set of packages that are needed for a given environment can be extracted using `pipenv lock -r` and `pipenv lock -r --dev`. These will output a listing of the dependent packages as well as the version that was picked and any conditions that apply to that dependency. You can use these command outputs to create a list of required packages.

Alternatively, the open source project jq provides for an easy way to extract data from JSON files, like the `Pipenv.lock` file. The command `jq ".default + .develop | keys" Pipfile.lock` extracts the names of each package referenced in the main and development dependency lists and their dependencies.

Confidentiality

In a situation where you're running your own index server, you will almost certainly have packages that you do not wish to become publicly available. Generally, these are closed source packages developed on a commercial basis, where their release would be a problem for the relevant copyright owner. They could also be tools that are so specific that they won't be generally useful. They could even be open source packages that have been forked, so long as the relevant license terms are being upheld; even if you have a legal obligation to share the code with someone who requests it, there is no requirement to provide access to an index server for their use.

Confidentiality is the property of an index server that ensures that people who are not authorized cannot access the distributions that it stores. This usually also includes preventing people from accessing the names of packages it stores unless so authorized.

The best way of approaching this problem depends very much on your appetite for risk and your expectations for what kind of people may try to find your code. For most companies, there is a relatively low risk of direct, targeted attacks against infrastructure aimed at extracting source code. For these companies, it's probably acceptable to use the security features afforded by pypiserver or a web server like Apache or Nginx.

A slightly higher level of control can be achieved by using a private network, such as running the index server from within a physical office or in a cloud hosting provider's virtual network offerings, ensuring that only computers that are connected via a company-controlled network can access the index server. Network-based security would generally be combined with a more traditional authentication system, for additional protection.

It is important to remember that developers are not the only consumers of the index server; production deployments are generally granted access to the same index server to facilitate automatic downloading and installation of application code.

I find that confidentiality is often the least important of these three pillars, due to the lack of a convincing potential threat for most developers. You should certainly apply at least one level of protection to your index server, both to prevent spiders from indexing your code and to protect against casual snooping by people, but you should absolutely balance an assessment of the likelihood of someone trying to gain access (and the effects it would have on your business) with the amount of effort and hassle it would be to set up a more secure system.

Integrity

The final of the three pillars is integrity, that is, can you be sure that a distribution has not been changed by a malicious third party. This is generally accomplished by recording the list of cryptographic hashes that are available when a package is added to the dependency set or its version is updated. When installing the packages, the downloaded files are examined and their hashes are calculated. If the hash doesn't match the list of allowed hashes, then the file will be rejected as incorrect.

An important one is that we expect distributions to never change. If we are installing version 1.0.3 of a piece of software, then it should always have the same bugs as other copies of 1.0.3. Unfortunately, this is not always the case outside of PyPI. Some developers have been known to surreptitiously replace distributions that they have made public when noticing what they consider to be an embarrassingly simple error. These "brown bag" releases are quite dangerous, as it's not possible to know if you have the fixed or broken version other than through checking the hash of the distribution that you downloaded (or manually auditing the code).

There is another, less commonly used, aspect of integrity checking: distribution signing. The PyPI server supports uploading a cryptographic signature at the time a distribution is added. These signatures are available through the same interfaces as the distribution files themselves and can be used to check that the distribution was uploaded by a specific trusted party.

This makes sense only if the threat model you're using is that your index server cannot be trusted to only allow uploads by authorized people. A very few people may legitimately distrust public index servers like PyPI. However, it's unlikely that anyone with a risk appetite that does not include trusting PyPI is happy to trust individual contributors to PyPI. I do not use the signing feature.

Wheel formats and executing code on installation

As a general rule, you should not use `sudo pipenv` (or `sudo pip`, `sudo easy_install`, or `curl ... | sudo ...`) when installing anything, as this allows for the execution of unseen downloaded code as root. It would be best if all developers always audited third-party code before trusting it, but that is not practical for the vast majority of people. If you are lucky enough to work in an environment where this happens and is done efficiently, then running an index server is the perfect way to ensure that only code that has passed your organization's gate keepers is available for installation.

If you do audit third-party code before allowing its installation, or if your organization's security policies do not allow for the running of code during installation, you should make sure that all dependencies are available in the wheel format.[10] As mentioned in the introduction to this topic, the wheel format allows for the installation of Python packages in a purely mechanical fashion. Many software authors make a point of uploading wheel-formatted distributions to PyPI, as it's trivially easy for pure Python packages.

Warning   While creating wheel distributions is trivial for pure Python packages, if you are using code that involves a compilation of libraries in its installation process, then you should bear in mind that you will need to produce a wheel for every environment that you want to use the wheel in. Wheels are tagged with the environments they support, with the -manylinux tag being a popular one to indicate that it will work on most distributions of the GNU/Linux operating system.

If you are using such packages, you will need to generate the wheel on a system that closely matches the target it will be installed on. I would recommend you generate wheels for both the production environment and development environments, if they differ. A wheel is significantly faster to install than a distribution that involves compilation; your fellow developers will thank you.

Creating wheels from existing distributions

It is possible to convert an existing distribution to wheel format, even if it's a distribution of a package that you are not the maintainer of. This *could* be done by recreating the development environment of the package, but that is not always an easy task, so I would not recommend doing it. Instead, you can use the existing package installation infrastructure to build wheels. This uses the tool pip (which Pipenv is built around) to download and build the wheels.

Firstly, we should create a fresh Pipenv environment, as any packages that are being built into wheels may define build or setup requirements.

---

[10]Any package installed from a .tar.gz or a .zip file *may* execute arbitrary code during installation, no matter how it is installed. This is something that many infrastructure security teams are unaware of, thinking that only python setup.py install has the chance to run arbitrary code.

```
> cd ~
> mkdir wheelbuilding
> cd wheelbuilding
> pipenv install
```

Warning   Pipenv does not allow for nested environments. If you've created a Pipenv environment in your home directory, then you cannot have other environments in subdirectories. This shouldn't happen, as you'll want each environment to be self-contained rather than floating in your home directory, but if it does just run `pipenv --rm` from the home directory and move the `Pipfile` and `Pipfile.lock` files to a more appropriate location.

Using a fresh pipenv to run the tool will ensure that these build requirements do not pollute our other environments. The command to build a wheel of a given package is `pipenv run pip wheel packagename`.[11] You may also need to run `pipenv install wheel` first, depending on your Python version and installation method.

If we want to build wheels of all our dependencies, we can use a Pipfile.lock file from one of our other environments. Pip itself cannot read the `Pipfile.lock` file format, so we would need to extract the information. As we saw in the durability section, this can be done with `pipfile lock -r > ~/wheelbuilding/requirements.txt`.

EXERCISE 3-1: EXTRACT A BETTER REQUIREMENTS.TXT

The `Pipfile.lock` file has more information than is exported by `pipenv lock -r`, specifically the hashing information.

For example, I see

```
adafruit-pureio==0.2.3
```

---

[11]If you have already downloaded the file that you want to convert to a wheel, you can provide the path to the file instead of the name:

```
> pipenv run pip wheel ./packagename-1.0.0.tar.gz
```

rather than

```
adafruit-pureio==0.2.3 --hash=sha256:e65cd929f1d8e109513ed1e457c2742bf
4f15349c1a9b7f5b1e04191624d7488
```

so my generated requirements list does not have the hash checking enabled. Write a small Python script to extract this additional data and save it to a `requirements.txt` file. This is a good opportunity to practice prototyping and testing, as in previous chapters. There is a sample implementation in the code accompanying this chapter for you to check your work.

Once you have your requirements list file, you can pass it to the pip tool to generate wheels. This is done with

```
> cd ~/wheelbuilding
> pipenv run pip wheel -r requirements.txt -w wheels
```

The generated wheel files are then stored in the `wheels/` directory, ready to be uploaded to your custom index server.

In the first chapter of this book, we added the PiWheels server to our Pipfile. The process we've just completed is very similar to what PiWheels does. PiWheels automatically downloads every distribution available on PyPI and converts it to a wheel and makes it available on their alternative index server.

The PiWheels process is a little more complex, as they have a custom wheel build process to generate files that are likely to work on many different Raspberry Pi hosts with different software versions installed, but the idea is the same. Distributions that only use Python code are very easy to convert to wheel format, but it is possible to add compiled components that would then require appropriate libraries and tools to be installed.

The benefit we get from this is that packages such as `sysv_ipc` and `psutil` which would otherwise involve length build steps on every Raspberry Pi installation target are much faster to install. In general, if a package has a wheel available for the environment you're targeting, then you no longer need to install a compiler and build chain on production servers. Being able to do any compilation in advance on a nonproduction server is a very appealing benefit for many systems administrators.

Installing the console script using entrypoints

We're now able to build distributions that install cleanly on other users' environments without error, but our invocations of the command-line tool have changed again. Over time we've used `python sensors.py`, `python src/apd/sensors/sensors.py`, and `python -m apd.sensors.sensors` to invoke the script. None of these are acceptable solutions for users, and the change is a symptom of a lack of indirection in our setup.

We want users to be able to run the script as though it were any binary installed into their environment. Python provides for this using the console_scripts feature of packages. When a distribution is installed that has values in the console_scripts metadata field, these are created in the binaries directory of the install location as executables.

For example, in the first chapter, we installed pipenv into our global environment. This puts the Python code into `C:\Users\micro\AppData\Roaming\Python\Python38\site-packages\pipenv\__init__.py` on a typical Windows machine. When invoking pipenv on the command line, the file that's executed by the shell is `C:\Users\micro\AppData\Roaming\Python\Python38\Scripts\pipenv.exe`. This is a real executable file that runs natively, not a batch file. That said, it is not self-contained; this is just a wrapper that invokes Python with the appropriate options, the code itself isn't compiled into the executable. If we look at Pipenv's `setup.py`, we can see

```
entry_points={
    "console_scripts": [
        "pipenv=pipenv:cli",
        "pipenv-resolver=pipenv.resolver:main",
    ]
},
```

as part of the `setup(...)` call. This declares two python callables that should be wrapped up as executables that can be run directly. The format for these lines starts with the name that should be exposed as an executable. In the case of the first entry here, that's `pipenv`. Then an = separates the executable name from the reference to the callable that should be invoked. This is a dotted name to a module followed by a colon, then the name of the callable within that module. In this case, `cli` is available as `from pipenv import cli` from Python code.

We want to make the show_sensors callable in apd.sensors.sensors available as a command-line script, so we will add the following to our setup.cfg file, which is the equivalent of the dictionary of lists from the preceding setup.py example:

```
[options.entry_points]
console_scripts =
  sensors = apd.sensors.sensors:show_sensors
```

These executables are only created at install time, so we need to re-run the installation process so that this new script is processed. This hasn't been necessary for most changes as we've installed the directory in editable mode, meaning changes in Python code are picked up immediately. This is another advantage of the setup.cfg approach rather than setup.py, as it could be counterintuitive that changes to setup.py require a reinstallation as it is also a Python file. Putting the metadata in setup.cfg might make it easier to remember that this is installation metadata, not normal Python code.

To trigger this installation, we run pipenv install. At this point, the script is now runnable as pipenv run sensors. We're almost at the stage of having a complete first version of the software; all that's missing are the documentation files.

README, DEVELOP, and CHANGES

If your instinct toward writing these files is that they are less important than other parts of the packaging system, you've been very lucky in your time as a developer. When approaching a new project, having sufficient documentation to hand to get started is invaluable. Best practices change over time and knowledge of how to use tools that are no longer in common use fade. More than that, it's common to want other developers to get started working on a piece of software with a minimum of trouble.

Sometimes the most challenging part of getting started on a new project is understanding what patterns the developers have followed. Do you use pipenv to install the dependencies or an older system like virtualenv and pip? What command do you run to start the tests or to start the program? Do you need to configure API accesses or load sample data? All this information is strictly necessary to be able to work productively in a new environment.

We need to write up a README file for our apd.sensors package that explains what the package is, how to install it, and how to use it. This file will be the first thing that users see when they visit the GitHub[12] repository and the PyPI information page by virtue of it being used to form the `long_description`. Most users will never extract the archive to see the other files in the distribution. In fact, in some distribution formats, the README won't even be included. The contents may only exist as the metadata for the package.

PyPI supports README files in plain text, reStructuredText and Markdown formats. reStructured text is familiar to many as the format that is used by the popular Sphinx documentation, and Markdown is used by many sites, such as GitHub, Bitbucket, and Stack Exchange. As git hosting providers tend to use Markdown and Markdown is easier to read when viewed as plain text than reStructured text, I generally recommend picking Markdown as the format to use for README files.

The selection is declared by filling in the `long_description_content_type` parameter of the `setup.cfg` file to be `text/plain`, `text/x-rst`, or `text/markdown`.

Markdown format

Readme files in the Markdown format are stored with the .md extension, so we will create a `README.md` file in the root of the project directory to begin with. We can then start writing a simple description of the project under a heading. In Markdown, headers are represented by leading # symbols, so the minimal `README.md` would be

```
# Advanced Python Development Sensors

This is the data collection package that forms part of the running example
for the book Advanced Python Development.
```

Other aspects of the formatting are likely to be quite familiar to many readers, as they're now commonly used online. An extended example is shown as Listing 3-3.

Listing 3-3. cheatsheet.md

```
# Header 1
## Header 2
### Header 3
#### Header 4
```

---

[12]Other distributed version control hosting providers are available.

italic **bold** **_bold and italic_**

1. Numbered List
2. With more items
    1. Sublists are indented
    1. The numbers in any level of list need not be correct
3. It can be confusing if the numbers don't match the reader's expectation

* Unordered lists
* Use asterisks in the first position
    - Sublists are indented
    - Hyphens can be used to visually differentiate sublists
    + As with numbered lists, * - and + are interchangeable and do not need
    to be used consistently
* but it is best to use them consistently

When referring to things that should be rendered in a monospace font,
such as file names or the names of classes, these should be surrounded by
`backticks`.

Larger blocks of code should be surrounded with three backticks. They
can optionally have a language following the first three backticks, to
facilitate syntax highlighting
```python
def example():
    return True
```

> Quotations are declared with a leading right chevron
> and can cover multiple lines

Links and images are handled similarly to each other, as a pair of square
brackets that defines the text that should be shown followed by a pair of
parentheses that contain the target URL.

[Link to book's website](https://advancedpython.dev)

Images are differentiated by having a leading exclamation mark:

![Book's cover](https://advancedpython.dev/cover.png)

Finally, tables use pipes to delimit columns and new lines to delimit rows. Hyphens are used to split the header row from the body, resulting in a very readable ASCII art style table:

```
| Multiplications | One | Two |
| --------------- | --- | --- |
| One             |  1  |  2  |
| Two             |  2  |  4  |
```

However, the alignment is not important. The table will still render correctly even if the pipes are not aligned correctly. The row that contains the hyphens must include at least three hyphens per column, but otherwise, the format is relatively forgiving.

reStructured text format

Readme files in the reStructured text format are stored with the .rst extension, so if we were using this format, we would create a README.rst file. This may not be in the root directory, as rst formatted README files are often used to tie in with the use of the Sphinx documentation system. In this case, they're likely to be stored in a docs/ directory in the project. The equivalent file to the preceding markdown readme would be as shown in Listing 3-4.

Listing 3-4. cheatsheet.rst

```
Header 1
========

Header 2
--------

Header 3
++++++++

Header 4
********

*italic* **bold** Combining bold and italic is not possible.
```

1. Numbered List
2. With more items

   #. Sublists are indented with a blank line surrounding them
   #. The # symbol can be used in place of the number to auto-number the list

3. It can be confusing if the numbers don't match the reader's
   expectation

- Unordered lists
- Use asterisks in the first position

    - Sublists are indented with a blank line surrounding them
    - Hyphens can be used to visually differentiate sublists
    - As with numbered lists, * - and + are interchangeable but must be
      used consistently

- but it is best to use them consistently

When referring to things that should be rendered in a monospace font,
such as file names or the names of classes. These should be surrounded
by ``double backticks``.

Larger blocks of code are in a named block, starting with ``.. code ::``. They
can optionally have a language following the double colon, to
facilitate syntax highlighting

.. code:: python

   def example():
       return True

..

   Quotations are declared with an unnamed block, declared with ``..``
   and can cover multiple lines. They must be surrounded by blank lines.

Links have a confusing structure. The link definition is a pair of backticks with a trailing underscore. Inside the backticks are the link text followed by the target in angle brackets.

`Link to book's website <https://advancedpython.dev>`_

Images are handled similarly to code blocks, with a ``.. image::`` declaration followed by the URL of the image. They can have indented arguments, such as to define alt text.

```
.. image:: https://advancedpython.dev/cover.png
   :alt: Book's cover
```

Finally, tables use pipes to delimit columns and new lines to delimit rows. Equals signs are used to delimit the columns as well as the top and bottom of the table and the end of the header.

```
=============== === ===
Multiplications One Two
=============== === ===
One               1  2
Two               2  4
=============== === ===
```

The alignment here is essential. The table will not render unless the equals signs all match the extent of the column they define, with no discrepancy. Any text that extends wider will also cause rendering to fail.

README

We are not writing a large documentation piece, so Markdown is the most appropriate choice for the README. We should include a simple description of what the package does as well as any important information that prospective users should know (Listing 3-5).

Listing 3-5. README.md

```
# Advanced Python Development Sensors

This is the data collection package that forms part of the running example
for the book [Advanced Python Development](https://advancedpython.dev).

## Usage

This installs a console script called `sensors` that returns a report on
various aspects of the system. The available sensors are:

* Python version
* IP Addresses
* CPU Usage
* RAM Available
* Battery charging state
* Ambient Temperature
* Ambient Humidity

There are no command-line options, to view the report run `sensors` on the
command line.

## Caveats

The Ambient Temperature and Ambient Humidity sensors are only available on
Raspberry Pi hosts and assume that a DHT22 sensor is connected to pin `D4`.

If there is an entry in `/etc/hosts` for the current machine's hostname that
value will be the only result from the IP Addresses sensor.

## Installation

Install with `pip3 install apd.sensors` under Python 3.7 or higher
```

CHANGES.md and versioning

We should also create a CHANGES.md file that indicates what changes between versions in the apd.sensors package. This will let people understand when they need to upgrade the version to gain access to new features they want or bug fixes they need.

Our `setup.cfg` is configured to join the contents of the `README.md` and `CHANGES.md` files to form the `long_description` which will be shown on PyPI, so we need to match the format and make this a Markdown file too. We should also be aware of making sure that the heading levels are consistent.

CHANGES files have a very standard format; for each version there should be a header (of an appropriate level, 3 in our case) followed by the version number and the release date in parentheses. Then, there should be an unordered list of changes, optionally with the author of the change in parentheses, as shown here:

```
## Changes

### 1.0.0 (2019-06-20)

* Added initial sensors (Matthew Wilkes)
```

The version numbers themselves are not inherently meaningful; they do need to follow PEP440 which defines how Python code should parse version strings. Generally speaking, version numbers are series of integers separated by periods, such as `1.0.0` or `2019.06`. Some other additions to this are commonly used, such as `a1`, `b1`, or `rc1` suffixes, to identify a distribution as being a prerelease[13] of the otherwise specified version number.

Semantic versioning

A good rule of thumb is to follow the principles of semantic versioning (`https://semver.org/`). It is a versioning policy that is intended for libraries, but it is possible to use something broadly similar for application versioning. Semver assumes three position version numbers, with the positions being called the **major**, **minor,** and **patch** versions.

The major version number should be incremented whenever there is a backward incompatible change to the API, no matter how small. Examples of this include any new required arguments to functions, functions being renamed or moved to a different module, or a change in the intended return values or exception behavior of a function that makes up the public API. Making any of these changes to functions that aren't part of the public API does not require incrementing the major tag, so long as it's clear which functions make up the public API. It's also fine to change the behavior of functions to

---

[13]`a1` means the first alpha, `b1` the first beta, and `rc1` the first release candidate.

fix bugs, so long as it's not foreseeable that people will depend on the broken behavior. The intention is that a consumer can upgrade to any later version within a major version series and have a guarantee that the code will work.

The minor version number is incremented whenever there is a change in the public API that does not break backward compatibility. This includes new functions being added or new optional arguments to existing functions. This allows users to specify in a two-digit version number what the minimum version required that offers the required feature set is.

Finally, the patch version number is incremented if there are bug fixes in the software without adding any features to the public API. Patch releases are the smallest increment; they should be completely invisible to end users who are not triggering the error case.

Calendar versioning

Another popular scheme for version numbers is to use the date of the release as a version number. Calendar versioning (`https://calver.org/`) makes deciding on a version number much easier, as there is no need to consider the impact of changes on your users. The downside is that the version numbers are not a good predictor of the difference between two versions.

Calver is really useful for projects where releases are always a big adjustment or always very minor. If there is a mixture of big and small changes, then it's not a good choice. There are a few variations of how dates are formatted for calver version numbers, but they're usually quite recognizable as starting with a year rather than a major version number.

Upstream dependency version pins

Consumers of libraries will want to set a limit to the versions of the library that they are willing to accept, starting with the lowest version they require up to just before the next major version. To demonstrate this, we'll look at the direct dependencies we have in apd. sensors and determine what pin ranges would be appropriate.

It is very hard for end-users to override version numbers that have been set in the install_requires lines, so you should err on the side of loose version specifications. You should certainly exclude any version that you know will not work, but the end-users of your application will be pinning versions too. Some library developers go too far with pinning and will pin single versions that are known to work or a narrow range that they expect to work. This can cause more problems than not pinning versions at all.

To demonstrate this, imagine we pinned the psutil library to version `5.6.3`, the latest version at the time of writing. Then, sometime later, somebody wants to build an application that uses the sensor functions we've developed as well as those from some other library that itself depends on a later version of psutil. There would then be conflicting version requirement which the application developer would have to resolve manually, judging for themself which version of psutil is the correct one to use.

If we had used a less restrictive version specification than ==`5.6.3`, then the dependency resolution system may have been able to find a mutually agreeable version for the two libraries, without needing manual intervention from the downstream developer.

Loose pins

The loose version pinning strategy involves setting version pins only to exclude versions that you know don't work. This involves either searching for the particular versions or leaving a version unpinned. The latter is much more common than the former, because of the amount of work required.

One way of determining these pins would be to run `pipenv install psutil==4.0.0` and similar, making a note of which the earliest version is that passes the test suite. As the latest version of the software works, we cannot set an upper bound that we know is incompatible. On the machine I am currently using, `psutil==5.5.0` is the earliest that installs cleanly (although earlier versions may work on different systems, it provides precompiled wheels for Python 3.7 on MS Windows), `click==6.7` fails to complete the test suite, and `adafruit_circuitpython_dht` appears to work at any version. We have rather weak confidence that the version pins `psutil >= 5.5` and `click >= 7.0` would be appropriate.

Given we don't know of any versions that absolutely will not work, it may be more appropriate to list all of these dependencies as unpinned, until we become aware of real limitations. In this case, it is important to document a known good set of dependencies, such as having a `Pipfile.lock` committed. This will allow future users a starting point where they know versions that did work if they have to construct pins for a future, unmaintained version. The following is the recommended version pins in the loose scheme:

```
install_requires =
    psutil
    click
    adafruit-circuitpython-dht ; 'arm' in platform_machine
```

Strict pins

An alternative is to use knowledge of the versioning scheme in use (or, assumed to be in use) to set a relatively wide range of pins that should definitely work. This is one reason that semantic versioning is so useful; it allows developers to reason about what is a safe range to pin without having to examine the code or changelog to decode your intentions.

The `click` library does not use semver; however, from looking at the changelog, it appears that they use a major.minor version scheme that is relatively close in meaning to semver. Therefore, we'll assume that it is safe to update minor versions but not major versions. As we are currently using version 7.0, we will set a version pin that contains >=7.0. We also want to allow versions 7.1, 7.2, and so on but not 8.0. You may be tempted to specify <8.0, but 8.0a1 would be caught by this (as 8.0 is a later release than 8.0a1). Instead, we will want the version pin >=7.0,==7.*, meaning any 7.x version that is at least 7.0. This is such a common pattern that it has its own alias: ~=7.0.

`psutil` is similar; it also doesn't follow semver, but does not appear to introduce backward incompatible changes in minor versions. Again, this is a judgment call, but it feels likely that 5.x version later than the 5.6.0 would be safe to use, so we will use ~=5.6 as the version specifier.

Finally, our third dependency is `adafruit-circuitpython-dht`. This is the trickiest one, as it doesn't declare that it follows semver and it doesn't include a changelog. The earliest version to be released was 3.2.0 and the newest at the time of writing is 3.2.3, which makes reasoning about the intentions of the author rather difficult. In this case, my instinct is that 3.2.x are likely to be safe. Here are the recommended version pins in the strict scheme:

```
install_requires =
    psutil ~= 5.6
    click ~= 7.0
    adafruit-circuitpython-dht ~= 3.2.0 ; 'arm' in platform_machine
```

Which pinning scheme to use

Each scheme has advantages and disadvantages; each has been in fashion at some points of Python's lifetime and not others. At the time of writing, the loose style is in fashion, and I tend to agree with that. If you're writing a very large application that is distributed as multiple packages, then you may find the strict style more appropriate for your needs, but using the strict scheme means more frequent testing of versions and releasing new patch releases that only update the version pins of upstream dependencies.

I would not recommend using the strict scheme unless you had a compelling reason to; the advent of environment management tools like Pipenv allows for end-users to manage their dependency version set with ease. Set version pins that prevent the installation of versions that you *know* will not work, but leave it up to end users to deal with future versions.

Uploading a version

We now have a complete 1.0.0 version of the `apd.sensors` package, so it's time to upload it to our custom index server. I will also be uploading this to PyPI, as this will allow for real-world uses of this code, as well as making it easier to follow along with some later examples in this book. I am also making sure to upload it to PyPI as I want to be sure that people following the examples in this book get the correct code that I'm distributing and therefore need to ensure that the name is reserved on PyPI.

Note   You should not attempt to upload your version of this package to PyPI, under the name `apd.sensors` or any other name. It is acceptable to fork someone else's package to add features or fix bugs, assuming the license permits it and you've made something generally useful, but you should not upload packages you've created just for personal learning. `https://test.pypi.org/` is a good server to use for learning about distribution tools. It is specifically for trying things out, and data is regularly deleted.

I will be using the tool twine to upload to PyPI. Twine is the preferred method to upload packages and can be installed with `pipenv install --dev twine`. You may alternatively consider installing twine in the same way as you installed Pipenv, as it's a generally useful package for all Python developers. In this case, it would be `pip install --user twine`.

We now need to build the distributions that we're planning on installing. This is done with `pipenv run python setup.py sdist bdist_wheel`. This command generates a source distribution and a wheel distribution. It is considered best practice to upload a source distribution as well as a wheel, even in cases where the wheel should be universal. This ensures interoperability with different python versions.

We now have two files in the dist directory, `apd.sensors-1.0.0.tar.gz` and `apd.sensors-1.0.0-py3-none-any.whl`. The tag on the wheel indicates that it is a Python 3–compatible wheel that does not specify a Python ABI[14] requirement and works on any operating system.

Twine includes a basic linter to ensure that the generated distributions will not have any rendering errors when displayed on PyPI. You can do this with the `twine check` command, as shown:

```
> pipenv run twine check dist\*
Checking distribution dist\apd.sensors-1.0.0-py3-none-any.whl: Passed
Checking distribution dist\apd.sensors-1.0.0.tar.gz: Passed
```

These files could then be uploaded to PyPI, if appropriate. The command to do so is

```
> pipenv run twine upload dist\*
```

You will be prompted for authentication information during this process (you can sign up for an account at `https://pypi.org`). Once this process has been completed, you will not be able to overwrite the distributions; any changes will require you to increment the patch version, even if they're only minor.[15]

---

[14]Application Binary Interface, a specification for how compiled components interact. Python's ABI can differ based on things like the amount of memory allocated for strings.

[15]In fact, I quickly uploaded 1.0.1 to replace 1.0.0 due to accidentally uploading a distribution with broken metadata while writing this chapter. This is the kind of mistake that `twine check` aims to prevent.

Configuring twine

There are a few configuration options for twine that you may find useful. For one, if you install the library `keyring`, you can configure twine to remember your credentials in your operating system's credential manager, such as macOS's Keyring, Windows' Windows Credential Locker, or KDE's KWallet. If you're using a supported operating system, you can then store your credentials using

```
> keyring set https://upload.pypi.org/legacy/ your-username
```

You can also set these values in plain text if your risk appetite allows for this. If so, you would set them in the `~/.pypirc` file, which is also used to configure custom index server data.

```
[distutils]
index-servers =
  pypi
  rpi4

[pypi]
username:MatthewWilkes

[rpi4]
repository: http://rpi4:8080
username: MatthewWilkes
password: hunter2
```

You will then be able to upload the files to your local repository server, just like with PyPI. To do this, you will need to specify the target index you're aiming for, in this case, `rpi4`:

```
> pipenv run twine upload -r rpi4 dist\*
```

You can use twine to upload any package to your local index server, including the wheels we generated earlier, as follows:

```
> pipenv lock -r requirements.txt
> pipenv run pip wheel -r requirements.txt -w wheels
> pipenv run twine upload --skip-existing -r rpi4 wheels\*
```

If you've built your own wheels and uploaded them to your index server, you will need to re-run `pipenv lock` to make sure that the new hashes are recorded as valid install options.

Summary

For all but the simplest of Python projects, I recommend you package the code using setuptools. The declarative format has significant advantages over the older `setup.py` format and is widely supported. Using the packaging system is very useful, even for small proof-of-concept style projects as it helps avoid bugs relating to Python code being in the right location to be imported.

For commercial environments, I would strongly recommend setting up a private index server using pypiserver and protecting this through the use of the built-in authentication mechanisms, as well as IP filtering if appropriate for your system. I also recommend mirroring your dependencies into the private index server, potentially as wheel files built on your infrastructure.

Additional resources

The landscape of packaging tools changes very quickly, but if you're interested in this topic, I'd recommend reading through the following links and trying out some of the other tools:

> There are many Python specification documents explaining decisions and technical details of the improvements to the packaging system. If you're interested in these, the following are the most relevant: `www.python.org/dev/peps/pep-0508/` (conditional dependency specifications), `www.python.org/dev/peps/pep-0517/` (pluggable build systems), `www.python.org/dev/peps/pep-0518/` (dependencies on build systems), `www.python.org/dev/peps/pep-0420` (namespace packages), and `www.python.org/dev/peps/pep-0427/` (Wheels).

> Poetry, an alternative to setuptools and Pipenv with very different goals, is worth investigating. Its dependency resolution scheme in particular is excellent: `https://python-poetry.org/`.

Flit (`https://flit.readthedocs.io/en/latest/`) is an alternative to setuptools and twine that is especially well suited to small projects. It is a very good fit for stand-alone tools without many dependencies, where you want to avoid some of the complexity of setuptools.

The setuptools documentation has a lot of information about legacy configuration, but `https://setuptools.readthedocs.io/en/latest/setuptools.html#configuring-setup-using-setup-cfg-files` in particular has a detailed explanation of the different keys to use in `setup.cfg` files.

Detailed information on the Markdown format can be found at `www.markdownguide.org/`.

Guides to writing more extensive documentation in reStructuredText can be found at `www.sphinx-doc.org/`.

CHAPTER 4

From script to framework

The package we've created so far has a relatively basic script interface and no extensibility. The majority of applications do not need a way to be extended; it is often easier to package all optional code together rather than go to the trouble of maintaining plugins that are distributed apart from the main codebase. However, it can be very appealing to use a plugin architecture to manage (for example) optional features of an application.

If your direct users are other programmers, then it might be a good idea to provide a plugin architecture to make their jobs easier. This is often the case for open source frameworks, where external developers may create additional features, either for their own use or through consulting agreements for their clients. If you're working on an open source project and are unsure if you should use a plugin architecture, I'd err on the side of including it. People will extend your code either way; it's easier to make sense of bug reports that include well-defined plugins than it is for forks of your software that add additional features.

The users of our sensor tool aren't necessarily programmers; they're people that want to get information on a given system. However, it's possible that they'll want custom information for their particular use case, in which case they may well engage a programmer to add a new feature.

We're already well on our way to being able to offer a plugin architecture; we have a well-defined class that describes the behavior of our sensors in the form of our `Sensor[type]` generic base class. Aside from a well-defined interface, we need a way of enumerating the sensors that we have available to us. We do this in the `show_sensors` function, which hard-codes all the sensors in the file. This works perfectly well for applications that don't need a plugin architecture, where all the sensors are written by the same developers and distributed as a single group. It fails as soon as we expect third parties to be writing custom sensors.

147

© Matthew Wilkes 2020
M. Wilkes, *Advanced Python Development*, https://doi.org/10.1007/978-1-4842-5793-7_4

Writing a sensor plugin

For a moment, let's think about what we'd want from this tool as a user. As well as the temperature and humidity sensors that many people might use, there are a few things I'd like to monitor that very few other people would find useful. One of them is the output of my roof-mounted solar panels. I have a script to pull readings over Bluetooth from my inverter, which uses an existing open source command-line tool to do the hard work of collecting and interpreting the data. I'd like to be able to incorporate this into my data collection.

As integration with a specific brand and model of solar panel inverter is not a useful component for most people, I am not going to integrate it into the core apd.sensors package. Instead, I'll create a stand-alone plugin, as users might for their custom logic.

If I envisioned this being a generally useful sensor, I might be tempted to add this sensor to the same file as the existing ones and list it alongside the others in show_sensors. This would mean that every other user of the software would see the following as part of the script's output:

```
> pipenv run sensors
...
```
Solar panel cumulative output
Unknown

Solar panel output isn't a useful addition for the vast majority of people; it's better as an optional component that users can install if needed. I wouldn't even run this on all of the Raspberry Pi nodes that I have set up, as only one is connected to the solar panel inverter.

If you are building a server monitoring setup with this code, you likely need a few different sets of plugins. While you may have CPU and RAM usage figures on all machines, there are application-specific metrics for some server roles, for example, job queue length for machines that handle asynchronous tasks, the number of blocked hosts for a web application firewall server, or connection statistics for a database server.

There are two broad approaches as to how to deal with the fact that this requires an outside tool. Firstly, I could create a Python distribution that includes the C code for the tool that I require. I would then have to arrange for that to be compiled and linked when my Python package is installed. I'd need to include error handling for problems with this tool not being installable and document its requirements. Once it's installed, I could use that binary using either its existing script interface or directly with Python's support for calling native code.

Alternatively, I could document that my sensor only works if that tool is installed and make the code assume that it is present. This massively simplifies the process for me, the developer, but makes installation harder for end-users. As I don't envision this being generally useful, this is by far the most appealing choice. There is no sense in building something perfect over something good enough, especially when you have very few users.

I choose the path of assuming that the existing tool is in place, and my code will not return a result if that program is missing. The standard library function `subprocess.check_output(...)` is very useful for this, as it makes it simple to call another process, wait for it to finish, and read both its output status and what was printed.

Developing the plugin

Developing this sensor is another great opportunity to use Jupyter notebooks for prototyping. We need a remote environment on a Raspberry Pi server, as discussed in Chapter 1, with the `apd.sensors` package installed into it. This allows us to connect through our local Jupyter instance and be able to import the Sensor base class from the version of `apd.sensors` installed on the server.

We can then begin prototyping, starting off with a Jupyter cell that only gets the data out of the inverter and another underneath that formats it as we'd like, as shown in Listing 4-1.

Listing 4-1. Prototype for extracting solar power information

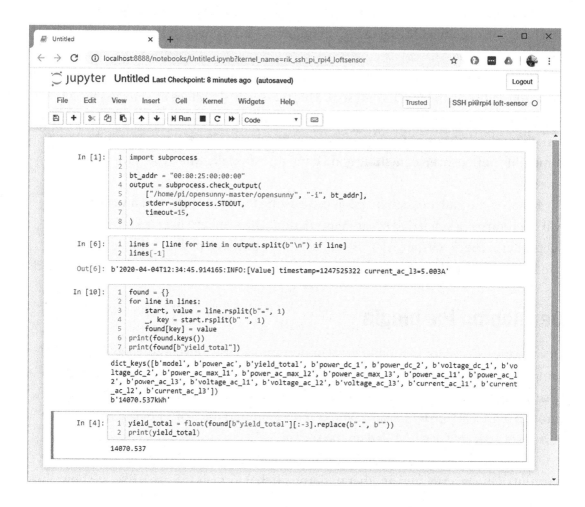

We can then build that up to contain a cell with the whole sensor subclass in and then "kick the tires" by checking that `str(SolarCumulativeOutput)` and similar function calls behave as expected. You may also like to take this opportunity to write some test bodies in Jupyter cells. There are a few projects that attempt to integrate pytest directly in jupyter, such as ipytest, but very few of your tests should need to be run on the target host. Any that do require specific host hardware should be marked with `@pytest.mark.skipif(...)` decorators when converted to standard Python files. You should only write enough testing code in the notebook to make sure you've not made an error in the raw data collection.

The relevant cell of the prototyping can be brought into a `sensor.py` file, as shown in Listing 4-2.

Listing 4-2. apd/sunnyboy_solar/sensor.py

```python
import typing as t
import subprocess
import sys

from apd.sensors.sensors import Sensor

bt_addr = "00:80:25:00:00:00"

class SolarCumulativeOutput(Sensor[t.Optional[float]]):
    title = "Solar panel cumulative output"

    def value(self) -> t.Optional[float]:
        try:
            output: bytes = subprocess.check_output(
                ["opensunny", "-i", bt_addr],
                stderr=subprocess.STDOUT,
                timeout=15,
            )
        except subprocess.CalledProcessError:
            return None

        lines = [line for line in output.split(b"\n") if line]
        found = {}
        # Data format: datetime:INFO:[value] timestamp=0000 key=value
        for line in lines:
            start, value = line.rsplit(b"=", 1)
            _, key = start.rsplit(b" ", 1)
            found[key] = value

        try:
            yield_total = float(found[b"yield_total"][:-3].replace(b".", b""))
        except (ValueError, IndexError):
            return None
        return yield_total

    @classmethod
    def format(cls, value: t.Optional[float]) -> str:
```

```
    if value is None:
        return "Unknown"
    return "{} kWh".format(value / 1000)
```

Even for this one-shot sensor, I'd strongly recommend creating a package, following the same approach as in Chapter 3. A package makes it easy to distribute the sensor code to our servers and to keep them up to date. You could write a single package that contains multiple custom sensors if you'd like to reduce the overhead involved, but don't be tempted to work around the packaging system and just have free-floating Python files.

Once we've written our sensor, we include the relevant details in its `setup.cfg` and the same `setup.py` from our `apd.sensors` package and build and can publish a distribution to our local index server. Alternatively, if we were not entirely confident that we'd covered all the edge cases during development, we might choose to install an editable checkout from version control on the server in question. That would allow us to run its tests and potentially make tweaks without having to round-trip code from a local machine to the remote host.

Adding a new command option

We've just created a new package that includes a single sensor, but we don't have any way of viewing its data from the command-line tool that we created in the previous chapter. That tool has a few built-in sensors and iterates over them when generating its output. We need to modify the script so that it can also show the values of sensors in other Python files.

To begin with, we can add a new option to `apd.sensors` that loads a sensor by its Python import location. That is, given the name of the sensor and the module it's defined in, it would load that sensor and display its results. This is inspired by the `--develop` option in the pre-commit script for loading a hook by its path, for ease of testing.

With this option in place, we will be able to specify that we want the value of our solar power sensor instead of the built-in sensors, meaning we don't have to write a special command to handle this sensor specifically.

Subcommands

We currently have a `show_sensors` function that includes the sensors to show as a hard-coded list. In this case, we'd want to do the same processing but change the way the list is generated to accept command-line arguments. There are two broad approaches that we could take, either we could create subcommands or we could add command-line flags.

Subcommands might not be a term you've heard before, but you've certainly used them. Tools like Git make heavy use of subcommands, where the git command on its own has no meaning. In fact, the commands `git`, `git --help`, and `git help` are synonyms: they all print a usage guide to the terminal. The more common invocations of git, such as `git add`, `git clone`, and `git commit`, are all examples of subcommands. The Git process does not have a single function that implements all the behaviors of the program; it uses subcommands to group similar functionality together. Some git commands even use multiple levels of subcommand, such as `git bisect start`.[1]

We could adopt this approach by moving the existing `show_sensors(...)` function to be a subcommand called `show` and add a new `develop` subcommand.

Click provides infrastructure called parameters for this purpose; you can add options and/or arguments to functions, which are exposed as part of the command-line interface. You should think of *arguments* as always being present, even though the end-user may not specify a value for them. If the user doesn't supply a value, then a default value would be used. Arguments are the core bits of data that a function operates on.

On the other hand, *options* are flags that are not always passed. They can change the behavior merely by being present, or they can contain optional values similar to arguments.

---

[1] git bisect is one of the single most useful functions of git, it deserves to be much more widely known than it is. If you're trying to find where a problem was introduced, it will automate performing a binary search on your history. For example, if you have written a new test for a bug that was introduced after version `1.0` and before `1.2` and you want to find the exact commit that introduced it, you could run

```
> git bisect start
> git bisect bad 1.2
> git bisect good 1.0
> pipenv run git bisect run pytest tests/test_new_bug.py
```

This subcommand uses `@click.argument` to specify that some data is passed as a required parameter on the command line. The `metavar=` parameter of `@argument` is the placeholder for the value to be displayed to users when they use `--help`.

```
@click.argument("sensor_path", required=True, metavar="path")
```

In the following example, I haven't yet included an implementation of `get_sensor_by_path(...)`; it can just return a hard-coded instance of the solar power sensor for now. We will provide an implementation later; for now, we're focusing on whether we should use subcommands or not. The following is an example of creating subcommands with click:

```
@click.group()
def sensors() -> None:
    return

@sensors.command(help="Displays the values of the sensors")
def show() -> None:
    sensors = get_sensors()
    for sensor in sensors:
        click.secho(sensor.title, bold=True)
        click.echo(str(sensor))
        click.echo("")

@sensors.command(help="Displays the values of a specific sensor in"
"development")
@click.argument("sensor_path", required=True, metavar="path")
def develop(sensor_path) -> None:
    sensor = get_sensor_by_path(sensor_path)

    click.secho(sensor.title, bold=True)
    click.echo(str(sensor))
    click.echo("")

if __name__ == "__main__":
    sensors()
```

Here, the entrypoint into the system is no longer a show_sensors() command, it is a sensors() group. The show_sensors() function has been renamed to show() and is now declared with @sensors.command rather than @click.command. The change in the command decorator is what connects this command to the group named sensors.

The console_scripts entrypoint would also have to be changed to match this refactoring:

```
[options.entry_points]
console_scripts =
  sensors = apd.sensors.sensors:sensors
```

Tip   Just like when we first added the console_scripts declaration, this change only takes effect during the installation of the package. You can force this by running pipenv install -e . which is useful when you're experimenting with different approaches. Once you've incremented the version number in __init__.py and re-run pipenv lock, Pipenv notices this change and automatically reinstalls the package. You can take advantage of this and set a version number like 1.1.0dev1. The dev marker lets you increment the version number without any risk of using a version number that you later use for a real release.

I would recommend incrementing the VERSION attribute to a dev release for features such as this unless there are only a small number of developers working on the code and they have no barriers to communication (such as timezone differences).

Once these changes have been made, it is possible to execute the subcommand to show the value of the in-development sensor we have. As I created an apd.sunnyboy_solar package that contains a sensor.py file and a SolarCumulativeOutput class, the string that represents my sensor is apd.sunnyboy_solar.sensor:SolarCumulativeOutput.[2] I can check the output with the following command:

---

[2]Of course, the function to resolve a sensor by path is only a placeholder right now, so the value doesn't really matter.

```
> pipenv run sensors develop apd.sunnyboy_solar.
sensor:SolarCumulativeOutput
```
Solar panel cumulative output
```
14070.867 kWh
```

However, the transition to subcommands does mean that the command `pipenv run sensors` no longer behaves as it did previously. To get the data we expect for the preset sensors, we now need to run `pipenv run sensors show`. Because of this change, users cannot safely upgrade from an old version to a new one without changing the way they interact with the software. The upshot of this is that we need a large bump to the version number to communicate this change's importance to our users.

If we consider the principles of the semantic versioning policy, we are considering a change that adds a feature and breaks backward compatibility. Breaking backward compatibility implies we should change the major version number, making any release of the software with this new subcommand layout be version `2.0.0`. Some developers may find this unintuitive, as there is not a large *conceptual* change between versions `1.0.0` and `2.0.0`. However, this is often borne out of a desire to avoid large major version numbers from a sense of aesthetics. I would strongly advise you don't shy away from incrementing version numbers when there is a backward compatible change, as it really does help users reason about what upgrades are safe to apply.

Command options

The other way of looking at this feature is that displaying a single sensor's output is fundamentally the same task as displaying the output of all sensors, albeit with some different preferences. This is the core of the decision you need to make when deciding between subcommands and options: is the feature you're adding another logical feature of the application, or is it a different behavior for an existing feature?

There is no hard-and-fast rule for how to differentiate the two; in our case, there are arguments to be made each way. In my opinion, changing either the sensors that are being read or the format of the output are all arguments to the same underlying "show" function. My implementation uses the "option" approach, but this is a subtle difference that depends very much on how you view the tool that you're creating.

To use the option approach, we need to add a `@click.option` line to the existing `show_sensors(...)` function that represents the path to the sensor that we should use instead of the hard-coded sensor list.

In our case, we would add an option called --develop which is not required and then use an if statement to decide if we should load the sensor referred to by the develop option or if we should use our hard-coded list as usual.

```
@click.command(help="Displays the values of the sensors")
@click.option(
    "--develop", required=False, metavar="path",
    help="Load a sensor by Python path"
)
def show_sensors(develop: str) -> None:
    sensors: Iterable[Sensor[Any]]
    if develop:
        sensors = [get_sensor_by_path(develop)]
    else:
        sensors = get_sensors()
    for sensor in sensors:
        click.secho(sensor.title, bold=True)
        click.echo(str(sensor))
        click.echo("")
    return
```

This behaves very similarly to the subcommand approach with the default syntax being unchanged and the new code path being available with

```
> pipenv run sensors --develop=apd.sunnyboy_solar.
sensor:SolarCumulativeOutput
Solar panel cumulative output
14070.867 kW
```

Error handling

The program we've written has, thus far, not had a real implementation of get_sensor_by_path(...), which is vital for it to be usable in the real world. We could write a naïve function that implements this, for example:

Unsafe version of get_sensor_by_path

```python
def get_sensor_by_path(sensor_path: str) -> Any:
    module_name, sensor_name = sensor_path.split(":")
    module = importlib.import_module(module_name)
    return getattr(module, sensor_name)()
```

This implementation has some significant flaws. Firstly, we are assuming that sensor_path always contains a colon. If this isn't true, a ValueError is raised for insufficient values to unpack on the first line. Then, the next line could raise an ImportError and the third line an AttributeError. Those errors would be shown to the user as tracebacks, which is not very user-friendly. The more useful error messages we want to offer to the user, the more conditions we need to add.

That isn't the biggest problem with this implementation, in any case. On the final line of this function, we want to instantiate the sensor that the user has selected, but we don't *know* that it's a sensor subclass. If the user ran pipenv run sensors --develop=sys:exit, then the command would call sys.exit() and immediately terminate. If they ran pipenv run sensors --develop=http.server:test, then the command would block and an unconfigured HTTP server would start up listening on port 8000 on all addresses.

These aren't serious security vulnerabilities, as anyone who could run the sensor script could presumably run Python themselves and invoke these functions themselves. However, there is no good reason to allow users to do things that are clearly wrong and *potentially* damaging. It's essential to consider the safety of such code every time you write it, as the trade-offs are always different.

The following implementation of get_sensor_by_path(...) traps all the common errors that could be caused by bad user input and reraises as a RuntimeError[3] with the appropriate user message.

Implementation of get_sensor_by_path that optionally raises RuntimeError

```python
def get_sensor_by_path(sensor_path: str) -> Sensor[Any]:
    try:
        module_name, sensor_name = sensor_path.split(":")
```

---

[3]ValueError would be more appropriate here, but I'm raising RuntimeError to be confident that only the errors I explicitly raise will be captured as user-facing messages. We'll return to this choice in Chapter 11.

```
except ValueError:
    raise RuntimeError("Sensor path must be in the format "
    "dotted.path.to.module:ClassName")

try:
    module = importlib.import_module(module_name)
except ImportError:
    raise RuntimeError(f"Could not import module {module_name}")

try:
    sensor_class = getattr(module, sensor_name)
except AttributeError:
    raise RuntimeError(f"Could not find attribute {sensor_name} in "
    f"{module_name}")

if (isinstance(sensor_class, type) and issubclass(sensor_class, Sensor)
and sensor_class != Sensor):
    return sensor_class()
else:
    raise RuntimeError(f"Detected object {sensor_class!r} is not "
    f"recognised as a Sensor type")
```

AUTOMATIC TYPE INFERENCE

It's worth paying attention to the type annotations of both versions of this function. The first version had no check to see if the specified component was a sensor, so we declared it as returning Any.

If we create the following test code in src/apd/sensors/mypyexample.py and then run *it* through the mypy type checker, we see that it can't identify the type of sensor:

```
import importlib

module = importlib.import_module("apd.sensors.sensors")
class_ = getattr(module, "PythonVersion")
sensor = class_()
reveal_type(sensor)
```

159

Result

```
mypyexample.py:6: note: Revealed type is 'Any'
```

The parser cannot tell what type the class in the class_ variable is, as it would need to execute the particular code in import_module and getattr(...) to find what object is returned. In the preceding example, both of these are hard-coded, but if one or both of these strings were supplied by user input, then it would be impossible without knowing what the user input would be in advance. Therefore, as far as mypy is concerned, class_ and sensor can be any type.

However, if we guard the line that instantiates class_ with some checks to determine if class_ is a type, and if that type is a subclass of Sensor, then mypy understands the situation well enough[4] to detect that sensor is an instance of Sensor[Any].

```
import importlib

from .sensors import Sensor

module = importlib.import_module("apd.sensors.sensors")
class_ = getattr(module, "PythonVersion")
if isinstance(class_, type) and issubclass(class_, Sensor):
    sensor = class_()
    reveal_type(sensor)
```

---

[4]At the time of writing, mypy still has some minor issues with understanding namespace packages. This is why the revealed type is sensors.sensors.Sensor[Any] without the leading apd. and why I put this trivial example in the src/apd/sensors directory. This is unlikely to present a problem in real-world development, but adding the following to setup.cfg can help work around this problem for local development:

```
[mypy]
namespace_packages = True
mypy_path = src
```

This explicitly enables looking for namespace packages and declares that the directory src should be in the search path. You can then whitelist missing modules with package-specific config sections to ensure that only modules that you know have no type information are excluded from processing, as follows:

```
[mypy-psutil]
ignore_missing_imports = True
```

Result

```
mypyexample.py:6: note: Revealed type is 'sensors.sensors.Sensor[Any]'
```

It is possible to force an instance to be considered as Sensor[Any] manually by using typing.cast(Sensor[Any], sensor), but this is rarely necessary and can potentially mask some errors.

The calling function can then trap any RuntimeError that we generate and display a user-suitable error message by coercing the exception to a string:

```
if sensor_path:
    try:
        sensors = [get_sensor_by_path(sensor_path)]
    except RuntimeError as error:
        click.secho(str(error), fg="red", bold=True, err=True)
        sys.exit(ReturnCodes.BAD_SENSOR_PATH)
```

This prints the value of the RuntimeError in bold red text to the standard error stream and then exits the script with a known exit code. Exit codes are a handy feature of console scripts in Unix-like environments. It allows for scripted calling of the program that can handle error cases without having to parse the resultant errors.

We should use an enumeration to store the valid codes. This is a special base class for classes that contain only a mapping from a name to an integer that includes some useful features like custom string representations that can be useful when debugging.

```
class ReturnCodes(enum.IntEnum):
    OK = 0
    BAD_SENSOR_PATH = 17
```

Many tools use low numbers and numbers approximately equal to 255 to define their own internal errors, so picking an offset of 16 makes it unlikely that our return codes would conflict with any others that our tools raise. In particular, we should not use 1 as anything but a general failure code. I have picked 17 as the exit code to represent errors where the arguments passed to the program mean that parsing could not succeed.

Off-loading parsing to Click with argument types

Click supports decoding the values passed in as parameters automatically. For some argument types, this makes intuitive sense; it is easier to declare that a parameter is a number (or a boolean value, etc.) than always to pass on a string and have the command parse the value itself.

There are built-in types in Click that can be used to improve the usability of command-line tools. The simple types `click.STRING`, `click.INT`, `click.FLOAT`, and `click.BOOL` do relatively straightforward parsing of their input values, converting the norms of command-line invocations to Python values. For example, `click.FLOAT` calls `float(...)` on the input, and `click.BOOL` checks the input against a short list of known values that mean `True` or `False`, such as y/n, t/f, 1/0, and so on. It is possible to specify these types by using the Python type (i.e., `str`, `int`, `float`, `bool`) directly as a shorthand, and if no type is specified, Click attempts to guess the type.

There are some more involved types, such as `click.IntRange` which applies validation on top of `click.INT` and `click.Tuple(...)` which allows for specifying the type of options that take multiple options. For example, if you were working on a program that accepts locations, you might have a `--coordinate` argument which would be defined as follows:

```
@click.option(
    "--coordinate",
    nargs=2,
    metavar="LAT LON",
    help="Specify a latitude and longitude according to the WGS84 \
    coordinate system",
    type=click.Tuple((click.FloatRange(-90, 90), click.FloatRange(-180, 180))),
)
```

Using these types ensures that data passed to your functions is valid and that end-users get useful error messages. It also significantly reduces the amount of parsing and validation logic you have to write. This can be especially useful with the most complex of all the types Click offers, `click.File`. This type allows you to specify that an open file reference should be passed to the function and closed properly after the function has finished executing. It also allows for specifying - to mean that the standard input and standard output streams should be used instead of files on the drive, which is a feature that many command-line tools offer and usually has to be added as a special case.

Perhaps the most surprisingly useful type is `click.Choice`, which takes a tuple of strings to check the value against. For example, `click.Choice(("red", "green", "blue"), case_sensitive=False)` provides a type validator that only accepts the strings "red", "green", and "blue". Additionally, if your user has enabled autocomplete for your program, then these values can be suggested automatically if a user hits tab during this argument.

Custom click argument types

New types can be added to Click's parsing system, which allows for programs that need to do the same command-line parsing regularly to split this out into a single reusable function and trust the framework to invoke it.

In our case, we only have one place where we expect a reference to a Python class to be passed as an argument so there is no practical reason to implement Python class as a type that functions can expect. It's *relatively* rare for this to be the right approach, but it's certainly possible that you'll need to do this for a project in future.

The following is a parser for Python class:

```
from click.types import ParamType

class PythonClassParameterType(ParamType):
    name = "pythonclass"

    def __init__(self, superclass=type):
        self.superclass = superclass

    def get_sensor_by_path(self, sensor_path: str, fail: Callable[[str],
    None]) -> Any:
        try:
            module_name, sensor_name = sensor_path.split(":")
        except ValueError:
            return fail(
                "Class path must be in the format dotted.path."
                "to.module:ClassName"
            )
        try:
            module = importlib.import_module(module_name)
```

```
        except ImportError:
            return fail(f"Could not import module {module_name}")
        try:
            sensor_class = getattr(module, sensor_name)
        except AttributeError:
            return fail(f"Could not find attribute {sensor_name} in "
            f"{module_name}")
        if (
            isinstance(sensor_class, type)
            and issubclass(sensor_class, self.superclass)
            and sensor_class != self.superclass
        ):
            return sensor_class
        else:
            return fail(
                f"Detected object {sensor_class!r} is not recognised as a "
                f"{self.superclass} type"
            )

    def convert(self, value, param, ctx):
        fail = functools.partial(self.fail, param=param, ctx=ctx)
        return self.get_sensor_by_path(value, fail)

    def __repr__(self):
        return "PythonClass"

# A PythonClassParameterType that only accepts sensors
SensorClassParameter = PythonClassParameterType(Sensor)
```

And here is the updated option call to use built-in parser:

```
@click.option(
    "--develop",
    required=False,
    metavar="path",
    help="Load a sensor by Python path",
    type=SensorClassParameter,
)
```

```
EXERCISE 4-1: ADDING AUTOCOMPLETE SUPPORT
```

I mentioned `click.Choice` earlier in this chapter, which provides support for autocompleting the values of certain options. It is possible to provide a callback for any option parameter to allow custom autocompletion.

It isn't feasible to write a perfect autocomplete implementation for the `--develop` flag, as it involves autocompleting Python module names. It would be too difficult to scan the environment to determine all possibilities.

However, it is much easier to write an autocomplete implementation that completes the class part once the module has been entered. There is an example of one such implementation in the accompanying code for this chapter; try writing one yourself before looking at it.

The method signature for the autocomplete method is

```
def AutocompleteSensorPath(
    ctx: click.core.Context, args: list, incomplete: str
) -> t.List[t.Tuple[str, str]]:
```

The autocompletion method is enabled for an option by adding `autocompletion=Autocomp leteSensorPath` as an argument.

When testing this, you may need to drop into a shell within the virtual environment and manually enable autocompletion for the sensors executable. For example, to enable autocomplete for the bash shell, you'd use

```
> pipenv shell
> eval "$(_SENSORS_COMPLETE=source_bash sensors)"
```

You need to manually enable autocompletion because autocomplete configuration is usually handled by a package installer and varies wildly between operating systems. The `_SENSORS_COMPLETE=source_bash` environment variable tells click to generate a bash autocomplete configuration instead of the normal handling. In the preceding example, this is processed immediately using eval, but you could also save the result in a file and then include that in your shell's profile. You should check what the recommended approach is for your particular operating system and shell combination.

In addition, the `:` character may cause some shells to abort autocompletion. In this case, enclose the argument to `--develop` in quotation marks and try again.

Canned options

Finally, some uses of options are more common than others. The most common option that people want in their program is --help to display information about how a command is to be invoked. Click automatically adds this option to all commands unless you specify add_help_option=False in the @click.command(...) call. You can manually add help options using the @click.help_option(...) decorator function, for example, if you need to support different languages:

```
@click.command(help="Displays the values of the sensors")
@click.help_option("--hilfe")
def show_sensors(develop: str) -> int:
    ...
```

Another frequently desired function is --version, which prints the version of the command that is installed on the user's computer. Like --help, this is implemented internally as an option with is_flag=True and is_eager=True, as well as having a specialized callback method. Options that have is_flag set do not have an explicit value attached, they are either present or not, which is represented by their value being either True or False.

The is_eager parameter marks an option as being important to parse early on in the process of parsing the command-line options. It allows the --help and --version commands to implement their logic before the other arguments to the function have been parsed, which helps the program to feel quick and responsive.

The version parameter is applied using the @click.version_option(...) decorator. The decorator takes the options prog_name to specify the name of the current application and version to specify the current version number. These are both optional: if prog_name is not set, then the name the program was invoked with is used. If the version parameter is omitted, then the currently installed version is looked up from the Python environment. As such, it's usual *not* to need to override either of these values. The standard way to add this option is therefore to add the decorator: @click.version_option().

For some operations, such as deletions, you may want to get explicit confirmation from the user before continuing. This can be implemented with `@click.confirmation_option(prompt="Are you sure you want to delete all records?")`. The `prompt=` option is optional: if it is omitted, the default prompt of "Do you want to continue?" is used. Users can also skip the prompt by passing the command-line flag `--yes`.

Finally, there is a `@click.password_option` decorator, which prompts the user for a password immediately after the application starts. This defaults to asking the user for their password and to then confirm it, as though a password is being set, but the confirmation step can be disabled with `confirmation_prompt=False`. The password itself is not shown in the terminal, preventing it from being read by people near the computer at the time. If you use this option, you should ensure that the underlying command takes a `password=` option, so you have access to the password the user entered.

Allowing third-party sensor plugins

Now that we've upgraded the command-line tool to allow for testing our external sensor and we've completed an implementation that returns useful data, we have covered the rarer of two use cases: helping developers write new plugins. The more common case is that of end-users – people who have installed a plugin sensor and want it to "just work." It would not be appropriate to have these users need to specify Python paths on every command-line invocation. We need a way of dynamically generating the list of available sensors.

There are two broad approaches that we can take to this problem: autodetection and configuration. Autodetection involves sensors registering themselves with the command-line tool in such a way that a list of all installed sensors is available at runtime. Alternatively, configuration relies on users maintaining a file that points to what sensors they want to install, which is then parsed at runtime.

Like most decisions between two approaches that we've made so far, there are strengths and weaknesses of both methods, and the trick is in picking the right one for your particular use case, as shown in Table 4-1.

Table 4-1. *Comparison of configuration and autodetection of sensor types*

Comparison	Configuration	Autodetection
Ease of installation	Install package and edit configuration file	Install package
Reorder plugins	Possible	Not possible
Override built-in plugin with a new implementation	Possible	Not possible
Exclude installed plugin	Possible	Not possible
Plugins can have parameters	Possible	Not possible
User-friendliness	Requires that users be comfortable editing configuration files	No additional steps are required

Using a configuration-based system allows for a lot more control over the details of the plugin system. It is very well suited for plugin architectures that are likely to be used by developers or systems integrators as it allows them to configure the exact environment they want and to store this in version control. An example of this is the Django apps system. Apps are installed into the local environment but do not affect the website until they have been added to the `settings.py` file, at which point they can have plugin-specific settings added.

This approach is appropriate for Django and other systems where a customized deployment is created by mixing and matching third-party code and specially developed software. It is common to want to use a subset of the features offered by apps that have been installed, for example, by omitting some middleware options or setting up different URL schemes. This complexity stands in stark contrast to systems like WordPress, where installation of a plugin is intended to be well within the capabilities of nontechnical users. In this case, installing the plugin is sufficient itself, and more complex configuration is handled by the application rather than a central configuration file.

The autodetection method is significantly easier for nontechnical end-users, as they do not need to edit configuration files. It also makes the system less sensitive to typographical errors. For our use case, it's unlikely that we would need to disable plugins, as users can ignore any data they don't require. The ordering of plugins is similarly unimportant.

Overriding plugins with a new implementation may seem useful at first glance, but it would mean that collected values might have slightly different meanings depending on which version is used. For example, we might want to add a "Temperature" sensor that returns the system temperature rather than the ambient temperature. For some use cases, these might be interchangeable, but it's best to keep the distinction in the data. We can always draw an equivalence when analyzing the data if required.

The one feature that a configuration-based system has that would be useful for this program is the ability to pass configuration values through to the sensors themselves. So far we have three sensors that would very much benefit from configuration: the temperature and humidity sensors are hard-coded to expect the sensor to be on IO pin D4 of the system they're running on, and the solar panel sensor is hard-coded to a specific Bluetooth hardware address.

Both of these are acceptable for private plugins that we don't expect to work for other people (such as the solar panel monitor), but the temperature and humidity sensors are a more general-purpose sensor that we would expect a range of users to be interested in installing. The temperature and humidity sensors need to have minimal configuration options for end-users.

Plugin detection using fixed names

It would be possible to write a plugin architecture that detects sensors defined in a file that's importable by virtue of it being in the current working directory. This approach uses Python's source code parsing as the parsing system for the configuration files. For example, we could create a custom_sensors.py file and import any sensors that we want to use in that file.

```
def get_sensors() -> t.Iterable[Sensor[t.Any]]:
    try:
        import custom_sensors
    except ImportError:
        discovered = []
    else:
        discovered = [
            attribute
            for attribute in vars(custom_sensors).values()
            if isinstance(attribute, type)
            and issubclass(attribute, Sensor)
        ]
    return discovered
```

The vars(custom_sensors) function here is the most unusual part of the code. It returns a dictionary of all things defined in that module where the keys are the variable names and the values the contents of the variable.

Note   The vars(...) function is helpful when debugging. If you have a variable obj and call vars(obj), you get a dictionary of the data set on that object.[5] The related function dir(obj) returns a list of all attribute names resolvable on that instance. If you want to learn about an object during a debugging session, these are both very useful.

Using Python as the configuration has the advantage of being very simple, but writing a custom Python file is a very technical approach that most users wouldn't like to use. Users would have to manually copy the sensor code into this file (or import it from elsewhere) and manage any dependencies themselves. I cannot recommend this as a plugin architecture system for any circumstance, but the idea of having a python file be importable through being in a working directory is *sometimes* useful as a means of configuration, as we will see toward the end of this book.

Plugin detection using entrypoints

For our use case, I think that the ease of use is the most important consideration, so we should adopt an approach that does not rely on configuration files for plugin detection. Python has a feature for implementing this type of autodetection that we briefly mentioned in a previous chapter. It's called *entrypoints*. The entrypoint feature was what we used to declare that a function should be exposed as a console script (in fact, that is by far the most common use of the feature), but any Python code can use the entrypoint system for its own plugins.

A Python package can declare that it provides entrypoints, but as they're a feature of the packaging tools, entrypoints cannot be set up from anywhere but a Python package's metadata. When a Python distribution is created, much of the metadata is split out into files in a metadata directory. This is distributed along with the actual code. This parsed version of the metadata is what is scanned when code requests the registered values for

---

[5]This works on almost all objects, but a few highly optimized objects don't support it. Specifically, it works for objects defined in Python code that don't have a __slots__ attribute.

an entrypoint. If a package provides entrypoints, then they can be enumerated as soon as the package is installed, making for a very effective way for code to discover plugins across packages.

Entrypoints are registered in a two-level namespace. The outer name is the entrypoint group, which is a simple string identifier. For the automatic generation of command-line tools, this group name is `console_scripts` (and, less commonly, `gui_scripts` for graphical tools). These group names do not have to be preregistered, so your packages can provide entrypoints that other software may use. If your end-user does not have that software installed, then they are ignored. The group name can be any string, which can then be used to query all the things referred to by the entrypoint.

You can find what entrypoint groups are in use in your Python installation using the `pkg_resources` module. This isn't something you ever need to do in code, as evidenced by the fact that there isn't an easy API for it, but it is interesting to look at when learning about the feature and how other Python tools use it. The following is a one-line program[6] (excluding imports and formatting for ease of reading) used to list the entrypoint types in use in a Python environment:

---

[6]This program is an example of flattening lists (or, in this case, sets) in Python. This is *my* preferred way of doing this, using a list comprehension to create a list of sets and then the reduce function, which is equivalent to

```
set.union(set.union(set.union(x[0], x[1]), x[2]), x[3])
```

for a four-item list called x.

Another way of approaching this is to create an empty set and update it inside a for loop over the entries, like

```
groups = set()
for package in pkg_resources.working_set: groups.update(set(
package.get_entry_map(group=None).keys())))
```

or using the `itertools` module, with

```
set(itertools.chain.from_iterable(package.get_entry_map(group=None).keys() for
package in pkg_resources.working_set))
```

Any of these are appropriate; you should use whichever feels more natural to you. There is one other style which is sometimes recommended; in my opinion it is significantly harder to read and should be avoided. That is a list (or set) comprehension where two or more loops form a single comprehension, read from left to right. It would look like this:

```
{group for package in pkg_resources.working_set for group in
package.get_entry_map(group=None).keys()}
```

171

```
>>> functools.reduce(
...     set.union,
...     [
...         set(package.get_entry_map(group=None).keys())
...         for package in pkg_resources.working_set
...     ],
... )
...
{'nbconvert.exporters', 'egg_info.writers', 'gui_scripts', 'pygments.
lexers', 'console_scripts', 'babel.extractors', 'setuptools.installation',
'distutils.setup_keywords', 'distutils.commands'}
```

The preceding example shows that there are nine different groups of entrypoints in use on my computer. Most of these are involved in Python package management, but three are other plugin systems installed on my computer. nbconvert.exporters is part of the Jupyter suite of tools; in the first chapter, we used nbconvert to convert our notebook to a standard Python script. That converter was found by checking this entrypoint, meaning that it would be possible for us to write our own exporters if desired. pygments.lexers is part of the pygments code formatting library; these entrypoints allow for new languages to be supported by pygments, and babel.extractors are entrypoints to help the i18n tool babel find translatable strings in different types of source code.

The second layer of namespacing is the name of the individual entrypoint. These must be unique within a group and are not inherently meaningful. You can search for a particular entrypoint name with iter_entry_points(group, name), but it's more common to get all entrypoints within a group, with iter_entry_points(group).

All this means that we need to decide on a standard string to use as the entrypoint group name and have plugins declare that they provide entrypoints in this group. We must also update our core code to ensure that all the plugins are declared as such. We will use the string apd.sensors.sensor as that is meaningful and unlikely to conflict with things other developers might do. The setup.cfg file of apd.sensors would have the entrypoints section modified as follows:

```
[options.entry_points]
console_scripts =
  sensors = apd.sensors.cli:show_sensors
```

```
apd.sensors.sensor =
  PythonVersion = apd.sensors.sensors:PythonVersion
  IPAddresses = apd.sensors.sensors:IPAddresses
  CPULoad = apd.sensors.sensors:CPULoad
  RAMAvailable = apd.sensors.sensors:RAMAvailable
  ACStatus = apd.sensors.sensors:ACStatus
  Temperature = apd.sensors.sensors:Temperature
  RelativeHumidity = apd.sensors.sensors:RelativeHumidity
```

The apd.sunnyboy_solar package use the same entrypoint group name to add its one plugin to the set of known plugins, by declaring the following entrypoints section in its setup.cfg:

```
[options.entry_points]
apd.sensors.sensor =
  SolarCumulativeOutput = apd.sunnyboy_solar.sensor:SolarCumulativeOutput
```

The only change we'd need to make to the code to use entrypoints instead of hard-coding the sensors is to rewrite the get_sensors method, as follows:

```
def get_sensors() -> t.Iterable[Sensor[t.Any]]:
    sensors = []
    for sensor_class in pkg_resources.iter_entry_points(
    "apd.sensors.sensor"):
        class_ = sensor_class.load()
        sensors.append(t.cast(Sensor[t.Any], class_()))
    return sensors
```

The cast here is not strictly necessary. We could also use the isinstance(...) guarding[7] that we looked at for the --develop option; however in this case, we're willing to trust that plugin authors only create entrypoints that refer to valid sensors. Previously we were relying on command-line invocations, where the chance of errors is rather higher. The effect of this is that we're telling the typing framework that anything we get from loading an apd_sensors entrypoint and calling the result is a valid sensor.

---

[7]That is, isinstance(sensor_class, type) and issubclass(sensor_class, Sensor) and sensor_class != Sensor

Like with the `console_scripts` entrypoints, we need to reinstall both of these packages to make sure that the entrypoints are processed. For real releases of the script, we would increment the minor version number as we've introduced a new feature that doesn't break backward compatibility, but as we're working with a development installation, we would re-run `pipenv install -e .` to force the installation.

Configuration files

The alternative approach, which we dismissed earlier, was to write a configuration file. Python's standard library supports parsing ini files, which are relatively easy for users to edit. Alternatively, a configuration format like YAML or TOML may make parsing easier, but editing would be less familiar for users.

Generally speaking, I would recommend using the ini format for configuration due to the benefits of its familiarity to end-users.[8] We also need to decide where to keep the ini files; they could be in a working directory, perhaps explicitly included as a command-line argument if appropriate, or in a well-known default directory for the current operating system.

Wherever we decide to store the files, we would create a new argument to the command line that accepts the location of a configuration file to use; only the default behavior would differ. We would also need to create a function that reads the configuration file and instantiates the sensors using any relevant configuration data.

The `configparser` module in the standard library has a simple interface for loading ini formatted data from one or more files, so this is what we would use to load the configuration values. We'll define our ini format as having a `[config]` section that contains a `plugins=` value. The items in the `plugins` value point at new sections, each of which defines a sensor with its (optional) configuration values. The following is a basic `config.cfg` file for `apd.sensors`:

```
[config]
plugins =
    PythonVersion
    IPAddress
```

---

[8]TOML is close enough to ini format that it would also be a good choice.

```
[PythonVersion]
plugin = apd.sensors.sensors:PythonVersion

[IPAddress]
plugin = apd.sensors.sensors:IPAddresses
```

This shows some of the power of a configuration system, as this configuration file only loads two of the sensors, which greatly speeds up execution time. Less obvious is the fact that the sensor configuration blocks do not need to have the same name as the sensor classes from which they're derived, for example, IPAddress vs. IPAddresses. The same sensor class can be listed multiple times in this way, making it possible to have a configuration that defines multiple instances of the same sensor with different parameters, and collects data from each.[9] A sensor could also be removed from the plugins line to disable it temporarily without needing to delete its configuration.

The parser for this config file maps the plugins line of the [config] section to the key config.plugins. Our code must check this value, extract the names, and then iterate over the sections to which it refers. It's a good idea to keep the parsing and the sensor instantiation as independent functions, as this dramatically improves the testability of each. The testability would be slightly better if reading the config and parsing it were distinct functions, but as configparser provides this functionality, it makes sense to reduce the amount of file handling code we need to write ourselves and leave that to configparser.

Like the previous --develop helper functions, we would catch any relevant errors here and reraise as RuntimeError with a user-friendly message. These would then be raised to end-users as an error message and with a new return code to represent a problem with the config file:

```
def parse_config_file(
    path: t.Union[str, t.Iterable[str]]
) -> t.Dict[str, t.Dict[str, str]]:
    parser = configparser.ConfigParser()
    parser.read(path, encoding="utf-8")
```

---

[9]For this to be useful, there would also need to be support code to allow picking a human-readable name for the different instances.

```
    try:
        plugin_names = [
            name for name in parser.get("config", "plugins").split() if name
        ]
    except configparser.NoSectionError:
        raise RuntimeError(f"Could not find [config] section in file")
    except configparser.NoOptionError:
        raise RuntimeError(f"Could not find plugins line in [config] section")
    plugin_data = {}
    for plugin_name in plugin_names:
        try:
            plugin_data[plugin_name] = dict(parser.items(plugin_name))
        except configparser.NoSectionError:
            raise RuntimeError(f"Could not find [{plugin_name}] section "
            f"in file")
    return plugin_data

def get_sensors(path: t.Iterable[str]) -> t.Iterable[Sensor[t.Any]]:
    sensors = []
    for plugin_name, sensor_data in parse_config_file(path).items():
        try:
            class_path = sensor_data.pop("plugin")
        except TypeError:
            raise RuntimeError(
                f"Could not find plugin= line in [{plugin_name}] section"
            )
        sensors.append(get_sensor_by_path(class_path, **sensor_data))
    return sensors
```

The get_sensors(...) function would take an iterable of strings which are the possible paths to config files. A new --config parameter can be added to the show_sensors command that defaults to "config.cfg" to collect the value of path that will be passed to get_sensors(...).

```
@click.option(
    "--config",
    required=False,
    metavar="config_path",
    help="Load the specified configuration file",
)
```

Each sensor that needs a configuration variable must now accept it as a parameter to the __init__(...) function for the sensor class. This function defines the behavior for creating instances of the class and is where you would handle arguments to the class instantiation. The Temperature sensor would store the variables it needs in the __init__(...) function and then refer back to them in the value(...) function. The following is a partial listing of Temperature sensor that accepts configuration parameters:

```
class Temperature(Sensor[Optional[float]]):
    title = "Ambient Temperature"

    def __init__(self, board="DHT22", pin="D4"):
        self.board = board
        self.pin = pin

    def value(self) -> Optional[float]:
        try:
            import adafruit_dht
            import board

        except (ImportError, NotImplementedError):
            return None
         try:
            sensor_type = getattr(adafruit_dht, self.board)
            pin = getattr(board, self.pin)
            return sensor_type(pin).temperature
        except RuntimeError:
            return None
```

For some applications, you may want to provide more standardized loading of configuration files, in which case we can take advantage of the fact that configparser can handle a list of potential paths to pass in all possible config file locations.[10] A simple way of doing this would be to include /etc/apd.sensors/config.cfg and ~/.apd_sensors/config.cfg in the code, but this would not work on Windows. The Python package installer pip follows the configuration pattern. It has a very sophisticated code path for determining where config files could be, correctly implementing the expected locations for a range of platforms. As pip is MIT licensed, which is compatible with apd.sensors's license, we can make use of those functions to make the sensors command feel more like a well-behaved citizen of those different operating system ecosystems. An example of this is included in the accompanying code for this chapter.

Of course, changing the way that plugins are loaded has a knock-on effect for the tests of apd.sensors, meaning that some new fixtures and patches are required to support the substantive changes in cli.py. This does also allow us to be more flexible in our tests, by including configuration files that set up dummy sensors that are only ever used to test the infrastructure of the program.

Environment variables

A final way that we could approach the need to configure a small number of sensors is to make use of environment variables. These are variables that are made available to programs by the system, often containing information like library paths. We can write the few sensors that need configuration to look in the environment variables for their configuration. In this case, we wouldn't need any loading of configuration files. We could use the autodetect style of sensor discovery and put the value extraction in the __init__ functions. Environment variables are exposed like a dictionary on the attribute os.environ, so the equivalent to the preceding implementation of Temperature that uses the environment would be

```
def __init__(self):
    self.board = os.environ.get("APD_SENSORS_TEMPERATURE_BOARD", "DHT22")
    self.pin = os.environ.get("APD_SENSORS_TEMPERATURE_PIN", "D4")
```

---

[10]Configuration in files that are listed later will overwrite conflicting configuration from files listed earlier. The ordering should therefore always be from system to user to instance-specific configuration.

These could be set on the command line; however, the easiest way to define them when using pipenv is to use the "dotenv" standard, that is, creating a file called .env in the root of your pipenv installation that contains the relevant definitions. The pipenv run command loads this file and sets any variables defined every time a program is run. In this case, the file would look something like

.env

```
APD_SENSORS_TEMPERATURE_BOARD=DHT22
APD_SENSORS_TEMPERATURE_PIN=D4
```

Managing environment variables can be difficult on some platforms. This .env file paradigm allows us to treat them like a minimal configuration file, which makes them a good choice for *very* minimal configuration. There is a similar trade-off to the one we looked at for command-line parameters; we are choosing a simpler solution that offers no automatic parsing for configuration, rather than the more involved parsing for arguments, because unlike the argument parsing, these decisions have a substantial effect on the usability of the program.

Approach for apd.sensors vs. similar programs

While there are arguments for using a comprehensive configuration filesystem, for my particular use case, I want something that works out of the box with minimal effort from end-users. People following along who are thinking of, say, server status aggregation may find themselves coming down on the other side of this decision. It very much depends on the user interface that you want to offer, with it being possible to write more and more complex code to support your exact desires.

For example, some tools that make use of the subcommand style of command invocation actually define a config command to assist users in managing their config files, rather than having them edit them directly. The version control software git is an example of this, where any user-facing setting can be set using the `git config` command, specifying which of various configuration files should be read.

For apd.sensors, at this stage, the path of least resistance is to use entrypoints to enumerate the plugins and environment variables to configure them, disregarding any possibility to ignore installed plugins or reorder them.

Summary

Much of the rest of this chapter has covered general software engineering topics, such as configuration file management and command-line tool user experience. The tools available to us in Python offer a lot of flexibility in these regards, so we can focus on making the best decision for our users, rather than being pushed toward an approach by limitations of the software.

The plugin system requirement is where Python really shines, however. The tool we're building is somewhat unusual, in that it's designed to allow other code to extend it. Although it's common for developer frameworks to use plugin systems, most software that you write is a stand-alone application. This makes it all the more surprising that Python's entrypoint system is so good. It is a fantastic way of defining simple plugin interfaces; it deserves to be more well known.

The overall approach that we've taken with the software during the course of this chapter is to opt for the simplest user interface that we can offer to users. We have looked at alternatives that we may choose to introduce in future, but have decided that the features they offer are not important at this stage.

Our command-line tool is effectively complete. We have a working plugin interface that allows for configuration of individual sensor parameters and for application-specific sensors to be installed. The program is a stand-alone Python application that can be installed on the various computers we want to monitor. The best way of doing this is to use a new `Pipfile`, as the one we have been using so far is intended to build a development environment of the code.

The new `Pipfile` will use a released version of `apd.sensors` and the private distribution server we created to house releases. We can create this on a Raspberry Pi and then distribute the `Pipfile` and `Pipfile.lock` to all other Raspberry Pis that we want to install on.

Production deployment Pipfile

```
[[source]]
name = "pypi"
url = "https://pypi.org/simple"
verify_ssl = true
```

```
[[source]]
name = "piwheels"
url = "https://piwheels.org/simple"
verify_ssl = true

[[source]]
name = "rpi"
url = "http://rpi4:8080/simple"
verify_ssl = false

[packages]
apd-sensors = "*"

[requires]
python_version = "3.8"
```

Additional resources

As this chapter has focused on decision-making more than features of Python, there are not many new pieces of software introduced in this chapter. The following online resources provide some additional detail on approaches that were not relevant to our use case, as well as some help with advanced use of command-line scripts on different operating systems:

The Python Packaging Authority documentation has a section on enumerating plugins using other methods, such as finding modules that match a given name. If you're interested in other ways of discovering code, take a look at `https://packaging.python.org/guides/creating-and-discovering-plugins/`.

The TOML language specification document may be of interest if you're looking to write a configuration file–based system. `https://github.com/toml-lang/toml`. A Python implementation is available at `https://pypi.org/project/toml/`.

Developers using Windows may find the following Microsoft page describing how to manage environment variables in PowerShell to be useful: `https://docs.microsoft.com/en-us/powershell/module/microsoft.powershell.core/about/about_environment_variables` (Linux and macOS users have it easier with `NAME=value` and `echo $NAME`).

Some more information on setting up autocomplete for your click-based programs can be found in the Click documentation, at `https://click.palletsprojects.com/en/7.x/bashcomplete`.

CHAPTER 5

Alternative interfaces

We have a command-line tool that reports the results of various data collection functions on a server, but being able to connect to a server and run a command-line tool to check their current state isn't a sustainable way to monitor a lot of data collection systems. We don't want to have to note down the results from multiple command-line tool invocations and analyze them by hand. It would be better to be able to collect the information automatically, as well as be able to analyze the raw values, rather than the formatted result that we show to users.

Rather than write a program that connects over SSH to each server in turn and invokes the command-line tool, we can create a simple HTTP-based web server that returns the value of the sensors in response to an API call. For this, we'll have to create a new interface to the same sensors.

Web microservices

There has been a trend in the last few years toward creating web applications by loosely coupling many services, each of which performs a specific task. This architecture trades the convenience of a unified codebase for the flexibility to evolve each component independently. Some web frameworks are better suited to this kind of problem than others – with some being created specifically to work in this niche.

There are lots of Python web frameworks, like Django, Pyramid, Flask, and Bottle, any of which would work as a basis for an API server. Both Django and Pyramid are excellent choices for complex web applications, offering many built-in features like translation, session management, and database transaction management. Others, like Flask and Bottle, are much more minimal. They have a small set of dependencies and excel as bases for microservices.

We need a very simple API server, without any interface designed for humans. There's no need for HTML templating, navigation systems, or CSS and Javascript management. Web frameworks designed for microservices are perfect for very small API servers.

© Matthew Wilkes 2020
M. Wilkes, *Advanced Python Development*, https://doi.org/10.1007/978-1-4842-5793-7_5

WSGI

All Python web frameworks use a standard for creating applications that are served over HTTP, called the Web Server Gateway Interface, or WSGI. WSGI is a simple API that we can use directly to write functions that are exposed to the Web.

A WSGI application is a Python callable that takes two arguments. The first is a dictionary that represents the environment (which contains the various HTTP headers and server information such as the remote address of the client), and the second is a start_response(...) function, which expects a HTTP status code as a string and an iterable of response headers, as 2-tuples of strings.

The Python standard library includes a simple WSGI server for trying out WSGI applications. It's not good enough to be used for production code, but it's handy for development. It is imported from the wsgiref.simple_server module, where the make_server(...) context manager takes the host and port bind parameters as well as a function to serve. The resulting context object has a serve_forever() method to run the HTTP server until interrupted with <CTRL+c> and a handle_request() method to respond to a single request. Using the wsgiref server to run a demo, Hello World website is demonstrated in Listing 5-1.

Listing 5-1. Hello world WSGI app

```python
import wsgiref.simple_server

def hello_world(environ, start_response):
    headers = [
        ("Content-type", "text/plain; charset=utf-8"),
        ("Content-Security-Policy", "default-src 'none';"),
    ]
    start_response("200 OK", headers)
    return [b"hello  world", ]

if __name__ == "__main__":
    with wsgiref.simple_server.make_server("", 8000, hello_world) as
    server:
        server.serve_forever()
```

The start_response(...) function is specific to whatever WSGI-compatible server is responsible to handling incoming connections, but it always behaves the same way.

The hello_world(...) function will work equally well if it's served on Python's built-in testing web server, a specialized production-quality web server like Gunicorn or even a PaaS provider like Heroku. There are no server-specific imports or function calls involved in hello_world(...); it is all entirely generic.

The return value for this function is the body of the response, which perhaps counterintuitively, is an iterable of byte strings, rather than a single byte string. If we open http://localhost:8000 in a web browser, we see "hello world", as shown in Figure 5-1.

Figure 5-1. *Browser view of hello world application*

Using a generator function allows the server to begin passing some data to the client before everything has been generated, by yielding partial data before computing the rest. If we switch from plain text to HTML,[1] we can see the effect of this by introducing some intentional delays, such as in Listing 5-2.

Listing 5-2. Generator-based hello world WSGI app

```
import time
import wsgiref.simple_server

def hello_world(environ, start_response):
    headers = [
        ("Content-type", "text/html; charset=utf-8"),
        ("Content-Security-Policy", "default-src 'none';"),
    ]
```

---

[1]Many browsers will only render plain text data as a whole, but will render partial HTML responses while waiting for the rest.

```
    start_response("200 OK", headers)
    yield b"<html><body>"
    for i in range(20):
        yield b"<p>hello world</p>"
        time.sleep(1)
    yield b"</body></html>"

if __name__ == "__main__":
    with wsgiref.simple_server.make_server("", 8000, hello_world) as
    server:
        server.serve_forever()
```

When we open `http://localhost:8000` in a browser, we now see the hello world messages appearing as new lines once per second. This is useful for large responses, in terms of throughput, and also to reduce memory usage on the server. For example, if we had written a WSGI application that transmits every line of a 500MB log file, then iterating over the lines and yielding them one by one would mean that no more than one line is in memory at once, and that data is sent as soon as the file begins to be read. If we had to return a single string, then the entire file would have to be read into memory, then passed to the server for transmission as a whole.

We could use this same approach to make a WSGI endpoint that iterates over the sensors and `yields` the information about each sensor in turn. However, a single JSON object is easier to parse as an API response, so it's better to create a dictionary of sensor title to value and serialize that as a whole. Now is a good time to add typing information to this function, so that we can take advantage of mypy's type hinting for flagging errors. The resulting server is Listing 5-3, which we should save as `src/apd/sensors/wsgi.py`.

Listing 5-3. Basic WSGI server to show sensor data

```
import json
import typing as t
import wsgiref.simple_server

from apd.sensors.cli import get_sensors

if t.TYPE_CHECKING:
    # Use the exact definition of StartResponse, if possible
    from wsgiref.types import StartResponse
```

```python
else:
    StartResponse = t.Callable

def sensor_values(
    environ: t.Dict[str, str], start_response: StartResponse
) -> t.List[bytes]:
    headers = [
        ("Content-type", "application/json; charset=utf-8"),
        ("Content-Security-Policy", "default-src 'none';"),
    ]
    start_response("200 OK", headers)
    data = {}
    for sensor in get_sensors():
        data[sensor.title] = sensor.value()
    encoded = json.dumps(data).encode("utf-8")
    return [encoded]

if __name__ == "__main__":
    with wsgiref.simple_server.make_server("", 8000, sensor_values) as server:
        server.handle_request()
```

We can test this by starting the server on our development machine using

```
> pipenv run python -m apd.sensors.wsgi
```

Accessing this web server and passing it through the jq JSON formatter[2] result in the following output:

```json
{
  "AC Connected": false,
  "CPU Usage": 0.098,
  "IP Addresses": [
    [
      "AF_INET6",
      "fe80::xxxx:xxxx:xxxx:fa5"
    ],
```

---

[2]curl http://localhost:8000/ | jq on a Linux or macOS system with the relevant programs installed. You could equally open this URL in a browser and view the data there.

```
    [
      "AF_INET6",
      "2001:xxxx:xxxx:xxxx:xxxx:xxxx:xxxx:1b9b"
    ],
    [
      "AF_INET6",
      "2001:xxxx:xxxx:xxxx:xxxx:xxxx:xxxx:fa5"
    ],
    [
      "AF_INET",
      "192.168.1.246"
    ]
  ],
  "Python Version": [
    3,
    8,
    0,
    "final",
    0
  ],
  "RAM Available": 716476416,
  "Relative Humidity": null,
  "Ambient Temperature": null,
  "Solar panel cumulative output": null
}
```

Note   We have checked t.TYPE_CHECKING and conditionally imported something. Some names can only be imported in mypy, not normal Python. This happens when there are helper variables defined in a .pyi file rather than integrating type hints directly in the .py file. The StartResponse variable is one of these; it represents the type of the standard start_response(...) function, which isn't needed by the actual definition of the wsgiref server, just the type hints. This block lets us import the correct value when type checking, but in other situations, we fall back to the less specific t.Callable, as the type hint is not important outside of type checking runs.

Of course, we should write a test to make sure that the endpoint works as expected. As we've not yet written any code to handle error cases, there aren't many tests we can usefully write, but an analogue of the high-level functional test of the CLI in test_sensors.py is appropriate.

As the WSGI interface is a Python API, it's possible to write functional tests for them by calling the sensor_values(...) function with placeholder values for the environ and start_response parameters. The package WebTest provides a way of wrapping a WSGI function and interacting with it using an API that behaves like a high-level HTTP API, making for much easier test writing. After installing WebTest, we can add the test in Listing 5-4 to the tests/ directory and run it.

```
> pipenv install --dev webtest
```

Listing 5-4. Functional test for wsgi service

```python
import pytest

from webtest import TestApp

from apd.sensors.wsgi import sensor_values
from apd.sensors.sensors import PythonVersion

@pytest.fixture
def subject():
    return sensor_values

@pytest.fixture
def api_server(subject):
    return TestApp(subject)

@pytest.mark.functional
def test_sensor_values_returned_as_json(api_server):
    json_response = api_server.get("/sensors/").json
    python_version = PythonVersion().value()
```

```
sensor_names = json_response.keys()
assert "Python Version" in sensor_names
assert json_response["Python Version"] == list(python_version)
```

While our WSGI application works, it's far from production quality. This is where microframeworks are useful; they let us move from single endpoint web applications with no error checking into reliable, production-quality web applications.

API design

Before we go any further, we should plan the API we want to offer. We want to be able to retrieve all of the sensor values, but it may be useful to get a single specific value, as the extraction of the sensor values may take some time. We also need to decide on the authentication for this API, as it will no longer be protected by virtue of only being available to people who can log in to the relevant server.

Most APIs don't use a traditional username and password login system; rather, they use a single API key as their credentials. The considerations for picking an authorization system are the same whether our users are people, identified by a username and password, or other programs, identified by an API key.

There are three broad approaches to user authorization.[3] A flat permission structure is popular for simple applications, where a user only needs to be logged in to access all the functionality of the site. This method is commonly used in simple Django applications. If a user is logged in and the `is_staff` attribute is set on the user object, they have access to the administrator features of the website.

The second option is demonstrated by the full authorization system in Django. It works on a groups and permissions system. Users can have permissions assigned to them, either directly or through their membership of a group. These permissions are granular but relatively global. If a user has, for example, the "Edit users" permission, they would be able to edit any user.

Finally, the most complex system involves permissions that have flexible relationships between both users and data. In this case, users are not assigned a permission directly, but rather permissions are assigned to a user or group in the context

---

[3]Authorization as opposed to authentication. *Authorization* is the process of determining if a given person is permitted to do something; *authentication* is the process of determining if a user is the person they claim to be. These are often shortened to authn and authz (which may confuse people used to the British spelling, authorisation).

of a piece of data in the site. In this case, we might see that in the context of a given user, the "Edit users" permission is assigned to the whole administrators group and the individual user in question.

Figure 5-2 shows the decision tree that I recommend using to determine which of the three approaches is the best fit for your use case.

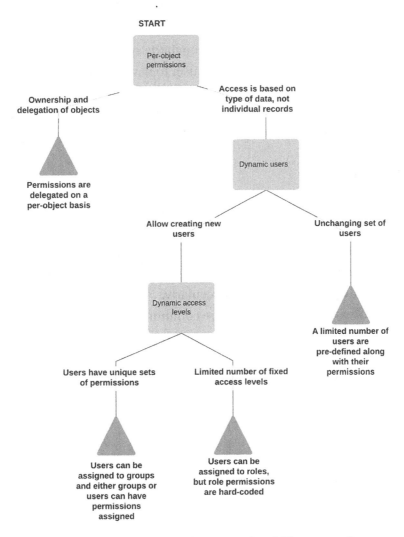

Figure 5-2. *Decision tree for choosing between the different authz approaches*

Our API will be read-only; the only function that we need to guard is the ability to read the sensor values. To answer the first question, we need to decide if we want to grant API access to different sets of sensors depending on the identity of the requesting user. Are some users allowed to see the Python version but not the Temperature? Our only use case for this API is to collect the information from multiple sources and store it centrally, meaning we only ever want to load all sensor values and we want to do so with a minimum of HTTP requests. An authorization solution that treats all users the same is the most appropriate. The objective of this access control is not to differentiate between users with different permission levels; all we care about is that the user is valid or not.

Therefore, we take the right-hand branch at the first question. The next decision is if we need to be able to create new users through the system or if we can define user credentials in advance. We only need a single user to have access to the information, so we don't need to add new users as we go.

The result of this is that we have the authentication system on the far right; user accounts are defined in advance as a property of the deployment.

Authentication

The authentication framework we choose should also match how we expect to interact with the API server. The form of authentication that users are most familiar with is a dedicated login page which provides a session credential, usually in the form of a cookie. Cookies have a limited lifespan, although that could be a very long time, which allows the user to avoid actively reauthenticating regularly.

The alternative, which is somewhat more common among APIs, is that each request could contain the authentication information, either as a dedicated HTTP header or through the use of the HTTP Basic and Digest auth features.

As we intend for our API to be accessed by an automated process and the login information is not expected to change, an API key style authentication system fits our needs.

Flask

The *Flask* microframework was inspired by an April Fool's joke: a microframework called *denied* that was distributed as a single file with a very simple interface. The author, Armin Ronacher, wrote a 160-line framework that emphasized marketing over advanced features. Perhaps unsurprisingly for a time when most web frameworks focused on large, fully featured applications, many people were actually interested in a simple interface for web programming. A year later, *Flask* was born, a high-quality web framework that aimed to satisfy the people who were so interested in *denied*.

Flask provides for generating HTML using the Jinja2 templating language, managing request and response headers, managing URL routing, and generating errors when needed. This flexibility makes it much easier to simplify the function we wrote earlier to remove some of the implementation details, as well as to extend the interface to offer more features.

Before we can start writing our Flask-based web server, we need to add Flask to the dependencies of our project. We'll take a different approach to what we've done in the past and add this as an "extra". Extras are optional dependency sets for Python packages which a user can select at install time. Users who only want the command-line tool would run `pipenv install apd.sensors`, whereas users who also want the API access would run `pipenv install apd.sensors[webapp]`.

setup.cfg section to define the webapp extra

```
[options.extras_require]
webapp = flask
```

The choice to make the CLI dependencies a core requirement and the API server optional is completely arbitrary; it's entirely possible for developers to require an extra for both features or to include them both as default dependencies.

Tip   You should decide on what dependencies are installed by default and which are extras based on the needs of your users. If you suspect some users may not want to use an entirely self-contained feature, especially if it has a large dependency set, then it is a good candidate for an extra.

Bear in mind that trying to import a module that has imports from packages specified in `extras_require` can result in an import error. If you have a command-line script in such a module, you should catch import errors and return a useful error on the command line. An `ImportError` traceback is not an appropriate error to show to users who try to run a CLI tool without specifying that they wanted the CLI dependencies at install time.

Once we've added the webapp extra declaration, we can declare our environment as needing that extra, using `pipenv install -e .[webapp]`. This causes flask to be added to the set of dependencies and installed into the environment. A flask executable is installed, which can be accessed with `pipenv run flask`, but the important thing for us is that we are able to import the Flask application code.

The equivalent Flask app to the basic sensor listing WSGI application we created is very similar (Listing 5-5), which demonstrates how little Flask interposes between the web server and the programmer. The key to this is the `@app.route(...)` decorator call. We'll look at decorators in the next section, but for now it's enough to know that a decorator manipulates a function or class whose definition it directly precedes. In this case, the `@app.route("/sensors/")` defines that the following function is the implementation responsible for `http://localhost:8000/sensors/`.

Listing 5-5. Minimal example of sensor API server in Flask

```
import json
import typing as t
import wsgiref.simple_server

from flask import Flask

from apd.sensors.cli import get_sensors

app = Flask(__name__)

@app.route("/sensors/")
def sensor_values() -> t.Tuple[t.Dict[str, t.Any], int, t.Dict[str, str]]:
    headers = {"Content-Security-Policy": "default-src 'none'"}
    data = {}
    for sensor in get_sensors():
        data[sensor.title] = sensor.value()
    return data, 200, headers

if __name__ == "__main__":
    with wsgiref.simple_server.make_server("", 8000, app) as server:
        server.serve_forever()
```

If we weren't setting any explicit header values, we could simplify the `sensor_values()` function even further, returning just the dictionary of data.[4] Flask automatically handles

---

[4]Flask provides type annotations, so some errors in defining this function would be caught by mypy. For example, if you want to provide a status, it must be an integer. Returning `t.Tuple[t.Dict, str]` would result in a type checking error.

194

converting dictionaries returned by view functions to their JSON representation, as well as encoding the string and setting the appropriate Content-Type header.

The biggest difference that this WSGI endpoint has over the basic one we created by hand is that this one returns different things depending on URL. Our original implementation did not check for a particular URL and always returned the values of the sensors. The new implementation will return 404 for any URL except `/sensors/` (and `/sensors`, which will be redirected to `/sensors/`).

To test this new Flask version, we need to import the name app rather than `sensor_values()`, as `sensor_values()` has become an implementation detail and app is the actual WSGI endpoint. Also, if we hadn't done so before, we would have to make sure that we made a GET request to the correct URL.

DISPATCHING FUNCTIONS ON THE WEB

In Chapter 2, we discussed the concept of dynamic dispatch, where functions are looked up through the class they're called on at runtime. So, the `@app.route(...)` decorator we're using has an implicit first argument of app, allowing the decorator to register the function being decorated as a known route on the app object.

WSGI applications have the same function called with the same environ and request types, no matter what the request. It's up to that function to determine what code is responsible for responding to that request.

The app object has a set of registered view functions to pick between. These are usually annotated with conditions, such as a specific regular expression to match for URLs; whether the request was a GET, a POST, a DELETE, and so on; and even complex conditions like permission lookups or Accept headers.

It's the responsibility of the framework to determine which of the user-supplied functions should be called for a given web request. As this allows single functions to be mapped to URLs, this makes the process of writing code for the Web easier to manage than the WSGI default of a single function that does all the work.

The Pyramid web framework takes this to an extreme with its predicate system, allowing any arbitrary conditions to be associated with a view function. It allows for different functions to be responsible for a given URL based on any arbitrary condition and is a very powerful feature.

Python decorators

Before we're able to call this API production-ready, we need to implement the access control that we discussed. We can implement this by using a decorator, just as Flask annotates a function with the URL pattern it is associated with using the route decorator.

A decorator is a Python function that takes a single callable or class as an argument and returns the same type of argument which it was passed.[5] The decorator pattern allows users to write custom function prologues or epilogues – code which is run before or after the main body of the function. You have no access to the function's internal variables, just the inputs and outputs, but this is enough to add additional error checking on the inputs or transformations on the output. In addition, some decorator function code runs at the time the function is defined, which can be used to set up metadata (such as URL routing) at the time the application starts.

It is possible to accomplish many of the things that decorators do by calling a utility function at the start or end of the function body; decorators are very much a convenience feature. Python developers generally prefer to write decorators as they are seen as more idiomatic of the language, but they also have a few real advantages.

Using a utility function to do the work of a decorator means that the function being manipulated needs to have some conditional logic added to handle the various utility function results. Table 5-1 shows an example of a utility function and a decorator to make a function return 0 if any of its arguments are negative. The has_negative_arguments(...) function determines if the case we're looking to disallow applies, but the code to handle that case has to be added to the power(...) function itself.

---

[5]Technically, any value can be returned, but it is very confusing to end users to return something that doesn't have a compatible call signature.

Table 5-1. *A helper function and a decorator approach to validating arguments*

Helper function approach	Decorator approach

```
def has_negative_arguments(*args):
    for arg in args:
        if arg < 0:
            return True
    return False

def power(x, y):
    if has_negative_arguments(x, y):
        return 0
    return x ** y
```

```
def disallow_negative(func):
    def inner(*args):
        for arg in args:
            if arg < 0:
                return 0
        return func(*args)
    return inner

@disallow_negative
def power(x, y):
    return x ** y
```

The decorator approach places the condition inside the decorator, along with the test. This approach means the decorator is entirely self-contained; functions that want to use it are not required to include any logic beyond that needed for their own implementation.

There is no difference in behavior between the two implementations; however, the decorator version moves all the complexity to the decorator definition itself, leaving the user function free. Generally, decorators are used by multiple functions, so this pattern allows for clean, easily understood code.

Closures

Decorators rely on a language feature called closures, which are a somewhat complex consequence of variable scoping. In Python, when a function uses internal variables, those variables are only available by name inside that function: although their value may be returned, the binding of the internal name of that variable is lost when execution passes from the function.

```
def example(x, y):
    a = x + y
    b = x * y
    c = b * a
    print(f"a: {a}, b: {b}, c: {c}")
    return c
```

```
>>> result = example(1, 2)
a: 3, b: 2, c: 6
>>> print(result)
6
```

During the execution of the example(...) function, the variables x and y are the parameters that were passed to the function. The variables a, b, and c get defined progressively as the execution continues. Once execution passes back through the return function to the containing scope, all these variable associations are lost. Only the *value* that was once associated with c is kept, which is then stored in the result variable of the containing scope.

However, if we'd defined a function within this function and returned that, then that inner function must still have access to all the variables it needs to execute. The interpreter will not disassociate these variables as long as they're still required. Any variables defined in the outer function scope that are used by the inner function will pass their associations down into this new function,[6] and the variables stay available to that inner function, but not any other functions. This inner function is called a *closure*.

```
def example(x, y):
    a = x + y
    b = x * y
    c = b * a
    print(f"a: {a}, b: {b}, c: {c}")
    def get_value_of_c():
        print(f"Returning c: {c}")
        return c
    return get_value_of_c

>>> getter = example(1, 2)
a: 3, b: 2, c: 6
```

---

[6]The associations of this function are stored as attributes on the function and its code object. The names of the values are stored as inner_function.__code__.co_freevars and their values are stored as cell objects on inner_function.__closure__, which themselves have a cell_contents attribute. The name "freevars" refers to "free variables" – variables that are used in a scope but not defined in it. You never need to look at these for anything other than curiosity about how the Python interpreter works.

```
>>> print(getter)
<function example.<locals>.get_value_of_c at 0x034F96F0>
>>> print(getter())
Returning c: 6
6
```

In this example, the variable c is associated with the get_value_of_c() function, so that it can be returned when the function is called. When we call the get_value_of_c() function, it has access to the variable c from the example, but not the variables a or b as it doesn't use them.

Modifying variables in parent scopes

It's possible to go even further than this and write complex sets of functions that operate on variables in their containing scope, potentially changing their values. I can't think of any time I've needed this functionality, but it is helpful to understand how the variable scoping works.

To achieve this, we need to use the **nonlocal** keyword. While Python can infer that a variable should be pulled from the containing scope if its value is used, it cannot infer if setting a variable is an attempt to modify the outer variable or create a new one. The assumption would be that you were creating a new variable that shadowed the outer one,[7] in just the same way that functions could shadow names available in their module's global scope.

Toy example of a pair of functions that operate on a variable they share through closures.

```
def private_variable():
    value = None
    def set(new_value):
        nonlocal value
        value = new_value
    def get():
        return value
    return set, get
```

---

[7]*Shadowing* is the name given to defining a new variable with the same name as something else that's accessible. For example, list = [1, 2,3] shadows the built-in list type, making it impossible to use list(...) in that scope.

```
>>> a_set, a_get = private_variable()
>>> b_set, b_get = private_variable()

>>> print(a_get, a_set)
<function private_variable.<locals>.get at 0x034F98E8>
<function private_variable.<locals>.set at 0x034F9660>
>>> print(b_get, b_set)
<function private_variable.<locals>.get at 0x034F9858>
<function private_variable.<locals>.set at 0x034F97C8>

>>> a_set(10)
>>> print(f"a={a_get()} b={b_get()}")
a=10 b=None

>>> b_set(4)
>>> print(f"a={a_get()} b={b_get()}")
a=10 b=4
```

This demonstrates that it's possible to write a function that contains a function and that inner function can use data defined in the outer function. Decorators take this one step further, by having the data that's shared between the outer and inner functions be a third function, the one being extended.

Basic decorators

The simplest possible decorator function is one that has no effect on the function that it is decorating. This is demonstrated as Listing 5-6. In this example, the function outer() takes a user function as the argument func= and returns a function called inner(...) as its result. This makes @outer a decorator function whose behavior is defined by inner(...). The function inner is a closure, so it has access to the func= argument of the outer(...) function. This variable is the original function, so inner(...) can call it with the same arguments it received and return its result to delegate to the function being decorated.

Listing 5-6. A decorator that does nothing but prints the variables it uses internally

```
def outer(func):
    print(f"Decorating {func}")
    def inner(*args, **kwargs):
        print(f"Calling {func}(*{args}, **{kwargs})")
        value = func(*args, **kwargs)
        print(f"Returning {value}")
        return value
    return inner

@outer
def add_five(num):
    return num+5
```

The line Decorating <function add_five at 0x034F9930> is printed as soon as this code is interpreted. If it's stored as a module, it would be shown as soon as the module is imported. This demonstrates that the contents of the outer(...) function in a decorator are run when a function is parsed, not when it's executed.

If we use this in an interactive session, we can see that the add_five(...) function has been replaced by inner, but it still works the same way, albeit with the additional printing.

```
>>> print(add_five)
<function outer.<locals>.inner at 0x034F9A50>
>>> add_five(1)
Calling <function add_five at 0x034F9930>(*(1,), **{})
Returning 6
6
```

The inner function uses *args, **kwargs as its arguments to accept any number of arguments and passes them on to func. The decorator we've written here does not change the arguments, so the function signatures of inner and func need to be compatible. If inner(...) defined arguments that were different to func's, then this decorator couldn't be used.

Tip   Often the wrapper function needs to *access* at least one argument that's passed to the inner function, but pass them through unchanged. In this case I'd recommend trying to match the function arguments precisely, rather than trying to extract the value from *args or **kwargs. This avoids any bugs introduced in finding the right value from args or kwargs.

Sometimes we want to create a decorator that manipulates the arguments, for example, to fill in one or more arguments without the caller needing to pass them or to drop one or more arguments that the underlying function doesn't expect. In this way, decorators can be used to change a function signature. Being able to change the signature allows us to write decorators to simplify an API for programmers while still matching a more complex signature for other parts of the application.

For example, the sorted(...) standard library function used to have an optional cmp= argument as well as a key= argument. The cmp= argument was removed in Python 3, so old code being ported to Python 3 sometimes needs to be updated.

The two approaches are quite different; it's not easy to convert code written as a cmp function to an equivalent key function. The functools module in the standard library includes a cmp_to_key function that can be used as a decorator and performs this conversion.

Decorators with arguments

There is one more common form of decorators, one which adds yet *another* nested function to the mix. This form is by far the most confusing to see written out but is a logical consequence of the code that we've seen so far. This last form is a decorator that takes immediate arguments.

The syntax for using a decorator is adding @decorator on the line above a function or a class, which is equivalent to adding the line function = decorator(function) after the function has been defined.

When using a decorator that takes arguments, the format for supplying those arguments is @decorator(arg), which could be rewritten as function = decorator(arg)(function). That is, the decorator function is no longer decorator(...) itself, but the return value of decorator(arg). An example is shown as Listing 5-7.

Listing 5-7. A simple decorator that takes an argument

```
def add_integer_to_all_arguments(offset):
    def decorator(func):
        def inner(*args):
            args = [arg + offset for arg in args]
            return func(*args)
        return inner
    return decorator

@add_integer_to_all_arguments(10)
def power(x, y):
    return x ** y

@add_integer_to_all_arguments(3)
def add(x, y):
    return x + y
```

These decorated functions have an offset added to all arguments, but the offset is different in each case as the decorator's parameter defines the offset.

```
>>> print(power)
<function add_integer_to_all_arguments.<locals>.decorator.<locals>.inner at
0x00B0CBB8>
>>> power(0, 0)
10000000000
>>> print(add)
<function add_integer_to_all_arguments.<locals>.decorator.<locals>.inner at
0x00B0CC48>
>>> add(0,0)
6
```

Tip   There is a decorator that helps with the writing of user-friendly decorators. Decorating the inner function with `@functools.wraps(func)` ensures that if a user tries to view the documentation, help, or even the name of the decorated function, they see the same information as an undecorated version of that same function.

If we had used this decorator on the `inner(...)` function earlier, the terminal session would have looked as follows:

```
>>> print(power)
<function power at 0x00B0CCD8>
>>> power(0, 0)
10000000000
>>> print(add)
<function add at 0x00B0CB70>
>>> add(0,0)
6
```

Nesting three functions can be a difficult thing to keep straight in your head, especially as there are two levels of closure, one providing the `offset` variable and the other providing `func`. This syntax is the kind of confusing nested logic that is generally a good idea to avoid. On the rare occasions that such a decorator is needed, it's quite common for developers to remind themselves of the correct syntax by consulting documentation.

An alternative to triple-nested functions is to use a class-based decorator (Listing 5-8), which looks a lot more like standard Python, so it is easier to understand from a glance. This works because a class defines an `__init__(...)` function to accept parameters on instantiation and can provide a `__call__(...)` method to allow the class to be called directly, like a function. It follows the same pattern as the private variable example earlier in this chapter; it's bad practice to use a closure just to store a variable for a long period before a function uses it. A class instance is a better fit for this.

Listing 5-8. A class-based version of an offset decorator

```
class add_integer_to_all_arguments:
    def __init__(self, offset):
        self.offset = offset

    def __call__(self, func):
        def inner(*args):
            args = [arg + self.offset for arg in args]
            return func(*args)
        return inner
```

The class-based decorator and the multiply-nested function–based decorators are functionally equivalent; but I find the class-based approach to be more natural and easier to remember.

Decorator-based security

Now we've looked at how decorators work; we can apply this to checking for authorized API access in our functions. Flask view functions do not expect arguments; the HTTP request data is stored on a global variable, so the decorator that we write doesn't need to process any arguments. We don't have to worry about matching the arguments to the function as very few Flask view functions take arguments.

We do need to ensure that the return value of the function is allowed by the type annotations, though. Flask supports quite a few different ways of returning a response from a view function. The body of a response can be returned as a string or as a dictionary in the case of a JSON response. The function can return either the body or a (body, status) tuple, or (body, headers), or (body, status, headers), and many more. This flexibility makes typing more complex.[8]

A typed decorator for a flask view that doesn't do anything is shown as Listing 5-9. This is a generic function, in the same way that we defined Sensor to be a generic class. The decorator @outer takes as an argument a function that needs no arguments and returns *something*. The return value of the decorator is a function that takes no arguments and returns the same thing as the argument function.

---

[8]These are still a matter of personal taste; use them if you find them useful. As this function isn't part of a public API, there is no additional benefit to users of the code, just those maintaining it.

Listing 5-9. A decorator for a flask function

```
import functools
import typing as t

ViewFuncReturn = t.TypeVar("ViewFuncReturn")

def outer(func: t.Callable[[], ViewFuncReturn]) -> t.Callable[[],
ViewFuncReturn]:

    @functools.wraps(func)
    def wrapped() -> ViewFuncReturn:
        return func()

    return wrapped
```

The ViewFuncReturn type variable is the placeholder for the return value of the
function being decorated. If that function is declared to return a string, then the
dictionary would be seen as equivalent to

```
def outer(func: t.Callable[[], str]) -> t.Callable[[], str]:

    @functools.wraps(func)
    def wrapped() -> str:
        return func()

    return wrapped
```

If the same function were decorating a view that returned a tuple of (dict, int),
then the decorator would match that instead.

We want to create a decorator that checks for the user being authenticated. The
code for this is given as Listing 5-10. If the user is authenticated, we want to use the
function as normal. If they aren't, then the decorator should return an error value. The
appropriate error would be a JSON document with the error details and the status 403
Forbidden. Therefore, the wrapper function must be declared to return either whatever
the underlying function would return or t.Tuple[t.Dict[str, str], int].

Listing 5-10. Authentication decorator for flask API methods

```python
from hmac import compare_digest
import functools
import os
import typing as t

import flask

ViewFuncReturn = t.TypeVar("ViewFuncReturn")
ErrorReturn = t.Tuple[t.Dict[str, str], int]  # The type of response we
# generate as an error

def require_api_key(
    func: t.Callable[[], ViewFuncReturn]
) -> t.Callable[[], t.Union[ViewFuncReturn, ErrorReturn]]:
    """ Check for the valid API key and return an error if missing. """

    api_key = os.environ.get["APD_SENSORS_API_KEY"]

    @functools.wraps(func)
    def wrapped(*args, **kwargs) -> t.Union[ViewFuncReturn, ErrorReturn]:
        """ Extract the API key from the inbound request and return an
        error if no match """

        headers = flask.request.headers
        supplied_key = headers.get("X-API-Key", "")

        if not compare_digest(api_key, supplied_key):
            return {"error": "Supply API key in X-API-Key header"}, 403

        # Return the value of the underlying view
        return func(*args, **kwargs)

    return wrapped
```

The upshot of this is that the require_api_key decorator changes the function it decorates to return either the *same* type of data that func returns[9] *or* a tuple containing a string-to-string dictionary and an integer.

---

[9]Note, this doesn't guarantee that it's the same data, just the same type.

The way the function implements the permission check is as follows. To start with, we extract the API key we're looking for from the environment, under the name APD_SENSORS_API_KEY. There is no fallback to a default value here, and this part of the decorator code is executed at startup, so if the API key isn't set, the program fails with a KeyError.

Next, there is the function definition that wraps the original func() function, called wrapped(). This wrapping function is what's defined as returning either ViewFuncReturn or ErrorReturn.

EXERCISE 5-1: TYPING

The type definitions in this section are very complex; it can be hard to understand what is happening. I recommend you try writing some simple functions and checking them with mypy to get an intuitive understanding of what's happening here.

You could start with the base program in Listing 5-11 and experiment with changing the type of the hello() function, the ErrorReturn type and whether or not the hello function has the @result_or_number decorator. This may be an easier start, as the return types are much simpler than those of the actual Flask functions.

Listing 5-11. Sample file for experimenting with decorator typing

```python
import functools
import random
import typing as t

ViewFuncReturn = t.TypeVar("ViewFuncReturn")
ErrorReturn = int

def result_or_number(
    func: t.Callable[[], ViewFuncReturn]        •
) -> t.Callable[[], t.Union[ViewFuncReturn, ErrorReturn]]:

    @functools.wraps(func)
    def wrapped() -> t.Union[ViewFuncReturn, ErrorReturn]:

        pass_through = random.choice([True, False])
        if pass_through:
            return func()
```

```
        else:
            return random.randint(0, 100)

    return wrapped

@result_or_number
def hello() -> str:
    return "Hello!"

if t.TYPE_CHECKING:
    reveal_type(hello)
else:
    print(hello())
```

The body of this wrapped function is where the actual work takes place. The supplied API key is read from the flask request headers, which are accessed as global state within the flask framework, hence why there is no request argument involved in these functions. The key supplied by the request is read from the X-API-Key header, with a default value of an empty string if no header is supplied.

The empty string default is there because in the next line a call to compare_digest is used to compare the received and expected API keys. This is a string comparison function that is suitable for comparing authentication strings of known lengths, such as HMAC digests.[10] There is a theoretical chance that using standard comparison could leak information about the correct API key through how long it takes the error to be returned, so it's best practice to use a constant-time comparison. This compare_digest function can still leak information about the length of the secret string. Although that is not a serious concern in this case, it's such a simple problem to fix that there's no reason not to use a secure comparison function.

Finally, depending on the result of the compare_digest function, we either delegate to the original function or return the stock error response.

Sensor endpoint code

```
@app.route("/sensors/")
@require_api_key
def sensor_values() -> t.Tuple[t.Dict[str, t.Any], int, t.Dict[str, str]]:
```

---

[10]HMAC digests are a cryptographic hash used for authenticating data against a shared secret key. They are almost impossible to forge, so they are often used in authentication systems.

```
    headers = {"Content-Security-Policy": "default-src 'none'"}
    data = {}
    for sensor in get_sensors():
        data[sensor.title] = sensor.value()
    return data, 200, headers
```

Here, the sensor view function we created earlier is decorated with our new @require_api_key decorator, and API key checks will happen automatically. It is important to note that the decorators here are ordered; they are applied from bottom to top, where the output of the bottom decorator becomes the input to the one above.

```
def sensor_values():
    ...
sensor_values = app.route("/sensors/")(require_api_key(sensor_values))
```

The app.route(...) decorator is what associates the function with the flask URL routing system. It's the function it decorates that is associated with the URL; the function isn't looked up at runtime. While this difference might sound academic, it means that only decorators *below* the app.route(...) decorator will be applied to the function that is available on the Web.

If these decorators were applied in the opposite order, there would be no API key validation on this view. This is where we return to functional testing; calling the function directly from a unittest does not find it through the flask view registry and could make the programmer think that the view was correctly protected. It is important to test security features end to end, not just in isolation.

Testing the view function

We already have a basic test to see if the sensor data is returned over an API request using the WebTest framework, but we've broken this test by adding the API key validator. If no API key is set in your environment and you run pipenv run pytest, then the test fails with a KeyError. If you have set an API key in your local environment, then it fails with a Forbidden error.

We've made a slight error in judgment in our decorator function when it comes to testability. As mentioned, the expected API key is loaded at import time, which has the nice side effect of causing an error on startup if the API key isn't set. However, import time data loading can make testing code harder. We want to run tests with a known

API key setup, but to do this, we need to ensure that the key is set into the environment before the *first* time the module containing the view functions is imported.

Flask provides a config attribute on the application that can be used to store configuration data, which is a much more sensible place to store the expected API key than within a decorator closure. This way, the configuration data can still be loaded when the web server starts, or the test framework can provide it for any test-specific configuration.

Flask assumes configuration data is loaded from a Python file, which might tempt us to change the configuration system of the apd.sensors package to the same pattern, but as we only need to add one configuration variable, we'll stick to the existing environment variable pattern here.

The best approach is to create a setup function that populates the Flask configuration with information from the environment. The check for the API key configuration variable happens here explicitly, as we've had to remove the check for os.environ inside the decorator to support testing. An explicit check is usually easier to understand than an implicit requirement causing a KeyError, which should help reassure us that this is a better approach. Without an explicit check here, the API key would not be checked until the first time a protected view was loaded.

Setup function

```
REQUIRED_CONFIG_KEYS = {"APD_SENSORS_API_KEY"}

def set_up_config(environ: t.Optional[t.Dict[str, str]] = None) -> flask.
Flask:
    if environ is None:
        environ = dict(os.environ)
    missing_keys = REQUIRED_CONFIG_KEYS - environ.keys()
    if missing_keys:
        raise ValueError("Missing config variables: {}".format(",
        ".join(missing_keys)))
    app.config.from_mapping(environ)
    return app
```

Note   The REQUIRED_CONFIG_KEYS variable here is set to a set literal, not a dict literal. Set literals look very similar to dictionary literals, as do set comprehensions and dictionary comprehensions. The difference is the lack of :value.

The test setup can then be modified to call this setup function with the appropriate testing configuration values. We create a new fixture to provide the testing API key, which can be hard-coded or random,[11] then change the subject fixture to depend on this API key fixture and pass its value in as explicit settings.

```
import pytest
from webtest import TestApp

from apd.sensors.wsgi import app, set_up_config
from apd.sensors.sensors import PythonVersion

@pytest.fixture
def api_key():
    return "Test API Key"

@pytest.fixture
def subject(api_key):
    set_up_config({"APD_SENSORS_API_KEY": api_key})
    return app

@pytest.fixture
def api_server(subject):
    return TestApp(subject)
```

The individual tests will either need to depend on the api_key fixture if they're testing the behavior of authorized access or to use the expect_errors option of the WebTest framework to allow checking of error responses, rather than needing to surround the get request with a try/except block.

Example tests for the API endpoint

```
@pytest.mark.functional
def test_sensor_values_fails_on_missing_api_key(api_server):
    response = api_server.get("/sensors/", expect_errors=True)
    assert response.status_code == 403
    assert response.json["error"] == "Supply API key in X-API-Key header"
```

---

[11]If the API key were generated randomly, we'd also have to ensure that the subject fixture gets the same value as the individual test methods. This is done in pytest with fixture scoping and is explained in Chapter 11 of this book.

```
@pytest.mark.functional
def test_sensor_values_returned_as_json(api_server, api_key):
    value = api_server.get("/sensors/", headers={"X-API-Key": api_key}).json
    python_version = PythonVersion().value()

    sensor_names = value.keys()
    assert "Python Version" in sensor_names
    assert value["Python Version"] == list(python_version)
```

These tests verify that the API server is working as intended, so at this stage, it's safe to cut a new release of the apd.sensors package, one that documents this new API server so that we can install it on our Raspberry Pi servers.

The new release adds a new feature without breaking backward compatibility, which once again means we increment the minor version number, making the first release that supports web API access 1.3.0.

Deployment

We now have a working API endpoint that we can serve locally as a test using python -m apd.sensors.wsgi, or we can serve it through a production-quality WSGI server such as *Waitress*. To do this, we'd need to install Waitress and give it a reference to the WSGI app we want to run. Many other WSGI servers are available, such as mod_wsgi, which has tight integration with Apache; Gunicorn, which is a stand-alone application with good control over performance; Circus and Chaussette, which include process management and fine-grained control over workers; and uWSGI, which has a reputation for good performance.

We are using Waitress, as it has a simple interface and is implemented in pure Python with no compiled extensions, so it is installable on a wide range of operating systems.

```
> pipenv install waitress
> pipenv run waitress-serve --call apd.sensors.wsgi:set_up_config
```

The API web service is served by default on port 8080, but it can be configured with any port or a UNIX socket. If it is intended to be run on a machine that is accessible over the Internet rather than on a local network, you should consider setting up a TLS termination reverse proxy such as apache, nginx, or HAProxy for your deployments. The modern Web is encrypted by default, and users expect to access services over a secure connection only. Luckily, there are multiple ways to obtain a free TLS certificate for your domains. LetsEncrypt and AWS Certificate Manager are perhaps the most common.

In the preceding example, the apd.sensors.wsgi:set_up_config is being addressed with the same dotted path and then colon syntax that we used in our command-line argument and for defining entrypoints. I've pointed it to the set_up_config(...) function, which is not itself a WSGI callable. This is possible thanks to the --call option, which means that the target is not a WSGI application but is a WSGI application *factory*: a callable that returns a configured WSGI application.

Our flask application is instantiated at module scope; we could refer to it directly with pipenv run waitress-serve apd.sensors.wsgi:app, but this would not work as expected as the configuration variables would not have been set. By returning the module-scope app object from our set_up_config function, we make it act like a factory and ensure that the configuration variables are loaded.

The set_up_config(...) function modifies globally scoped values like app, rather than returning a stand-alone application, so it is not a true factory. However, as its signature is the same and we only need one app at a time, we can abuse the feature.

It's also common for users to write a custom wsgi.py file that sets up their WSGI application, potentially wrapping it in any *middlewares* that provide extra functionality. If we were to do this for this API server, it would look like

wsgi.py

```
from apd.sensors.wsgi import set_up_config
app = set_up_config()
```

Starting the server

```
> pipenv run waitress-serve wsgi:app
```

Extending software as a third party

Nothing that we have done in this chapter involves changing the API of the apd.sensors package, so the API server we created in the core package could equally have been created by someone other than the core maintainer of the software. Anyone could have written a WSGI server to expose sensor values and created a new package, say apd.apiserver, that loaded the sensors and provided an API endpoint to query their values.

Note   The following section, up to the "Fixing the serialization problem in our code" heading, will consider the experience that other developers would have trying to extend our code and the tools they could use. After this, we will return to improvements we can make ourselves.

However, there are times when we do need to change the interface to extend a piece of software. If we look back at our `Temperature` sensor, we made a decision early on that made JSON serialization trivial. The value function returns a float, which represents the temperature in degrees centigrade. JSON can serialize integers, strings, lists, and dictionaries, but it cannot serialize datetimes or custom objects. There is a package called pint that has dedicated representations of physical constants which we might have chosen to use instead,[12] in which case the value of the temperature sensor would not have been serializable.

Pint doesn't declare support type annotations, as its use of metaclasses and on-the-fly construction of types from data files make it hard to provide a useful set of types to expose to end-users. The developer of pint has understandably chosen to focus on flexibility for end-users in terms of being able to control the sets of units, rather than optimizing for type checking.

Sensor that uses pint values as its return type

```
import os
from typing import Optional, Any

import pint

ureg = pint.UnitRegistry()
```

---

[12]In fact, if I hadn't been writing the code with the idea that I'd soon be adding JSON support, I would have done so. I often use Pint and the Python REPL or Jupyter as a calculator for lengths, areas, and electrical values, such as calculating the correct resistor to use in a circuit:

```
>>> import pint
>>> ureg = pint.UnitRegistry()
>>> Vs = 3.3 * ureg.volt
>>> Vf = 1.85 * ureg.volt
>>> I = 20 * ureg.milliamp
>>> R = (Vs - Vf) / I
>>> print(R.to(ureg.ohm))
72.49999999999999 ohm
```

```python
class Temperature(Sensor[Optional[Any]]):
    title = "Ambient Temperature"

    def __init__(self, board=None, pin=None):
        self.board = os.environ.get("APD_SENSORS_TEMPERATURE_BOARD", "DHT22")
        self.pin = os.environ.get("APD_SENSORS_TEMPERATURE_PIN", "D4")

    def value(self) -> Optional[Any]:
        try:
            import adafruit_dht
            import board
            sensor_type = getattr(adafruit_dht, self.board)
            pin = getattr(board, self.pin)
        except (ImportError, NotImplementedError, AttributeError):
            # No DHT library results in an ImportError.
            # Running on an unknown platform results in a
            # NotImplementedError when getting the pin
            return None
        try:
            return ureg.Quantity(sensor_type(pin).temperature, ureg.celsius)
        except RuntimeError:
            return None

    @classmethod
    def format(cls, value: Optional[Any]) -> str:
        if value is None:
            return "Unknown"
        else:
            return "{:.3~P} ({:.3~P})".format(value, value.to(ureg.fahrenheit))

    def __str__(self) -> str:
        return self.format(self.value())
```

As pint does not declare support for type checking, these functions are defined as returning Any, meaning they cannot be easily type-checked. We also need to add pint to setup.cfg as an ignored module when it comes to searching for type definitions to silence the warnings that it cannot be found:

Code to add to setup.cfg

```
[mypy-pint]
ignore_missing_imports = True
```

METACLASSES

I mentioned earlier that Pint uses metaclasses and on-the-fly type construction. These are somewhat related techniques: they are both ways of customizing the behavior of classes themselves, not just their instances. In pint, these methods are used to add an additional hook, `after_init(...)`, which is automatically called after the `__init__(...)` function and to create unlimited numbers of subclasses of some built-in types that reference different class variables.

Some readers of this book will be expecting expansive discussion on the use of metaclasses, seeing them as the epitome of an advanced Python feature. I have decided to omit them as this book is aimed at explaining features that a professional Python programmer would benefit from being able to employ.

I have *never* had cause to create a metaclass in all my time as a Python developer or to explicitly use one in a class that I'm writing. I do use them implicitly through base classes regularly. While only a tiny proportion of Python developers ever need to create a metaclass, most developers interact with metaclasses without ever knowing.

The Python standard library module enum and the ORM SQLAlchemy are the best examples of good metaclass use that I know of. Both make extensive use of metaclasses, but the skill of their respective developers has kept a very intuitive interface, at the expense of the readability of their own implementations. If you're doing metaclasses right, the users will never even know they're there.

Most advice on metaclasses says that you do not need to use metaclasses unless you know that you need them. This is somewhat circular, so refer to Figure 5-3 for the decision tree I would use when deciding if I need to use metaclasses.

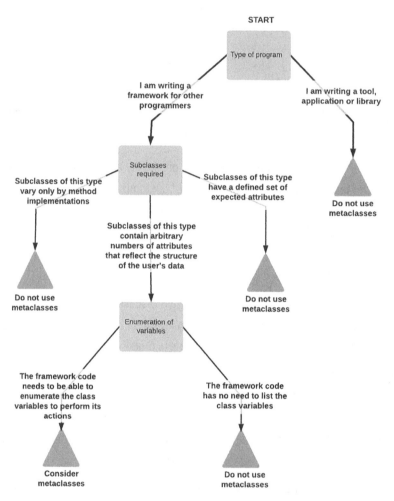

Figure 5-3. *Decision tree for deciding whether to use metaclasses*

This is not exhaustive, just my opinion as to when to consider metaclasses. There may be other situations where they are the appropriate solution, but in general, I would consider them **only** for declaratively exposing the structure of user data to a framework. Most other uses of metaclasses can be expressed more intuitively as standard Python. It's my strong recommendation to prioritize writing code that is understandable at a glance over *clever* code.

The first substantive difference between the float and pint-based implementations comes in the value() function, which takes the floating-point representation of the temperature and marks it as a Quantity of degrees Celsius. In the same way that dynamic dispatch allows the addition of integers and strings to behave differently, it allows the developer to forget about the exact type of temperature units being used and treat all temperatures the same.

Imagine for a moment that we also had a single temperature sensor that was connected to a smart home thermostat which could return its temperature only in degrees Fahrenheit. It's quite possible that we would want to display the difference between each of our temperature sensors and this central sensor. If we were using floating-point units, we would have to either normalize all the temperature sensors to the same unit system at the time the data is collected or else use external knowledge that some readings are using a different temperature scale when doing reporting. Pint allows us to seamlessly work with numbers from different measurement systems without needing explicit conversion.

We can see this used in the `format(...)` method,, where instead of calling a custom class method to convert Celsius to Fahrenheit, we use a conversion feature of pint itself. `cls.celsius_to_fahrenheit(value)` becomes `value.to(ureg.fahrenheit)`, thereby splitting the logic into collection and formatting. In the original form, the format method requires that its value is degrees Celsius; in the latter form, it can defer to the value itself to know what conversion is required if any.

{:.3~P} FORMAT SPECIFICATION

The `"{}".format(value)` style formatting in Python allows for the type of the value function to define its own formatting specification. There is no `.3~P` specification built-in to Python: this is supplied by Pint.

The `__format__(self, spec)` method allows classes to define their own formatting rules. Pint provides L, H, and P formatters for LaTeX, HTML, and PrettyPrint, respectively, with an optional ~ to use abbreviated unit names and the standard float formatting options to specify the magnitude portion.

Any class you write can provide these too, so our sensors could have defined a `__format__(...)` method to provide different formatting options if it was relevant. In general, this feature is only useful for projects like Pint that provide complex data storage classes for the use of other programmers.

All of these advantages come at a price, however. When we try to access the JSON API, we see a HTTP error 500 page, and in the logs of the web server, we get a traceback ending in

```
TypeError: Object of type Quantity is not JSON serializable
```

In our desire to make the value() method more flexible, we've broken an implicit assumption that we made in the flask application: that the result of that value() function can be JSON serialized. At no point did we write in the documentation of any previous versions that the value method may only return types that are JSON serializable. There's no guarantee that other users of our software haven't done something similar using the plugin architecture, so without realizing it, we've broken the semantic versioning policy.

We should have created a new pair of methods to convert between the value the sensor returns and a JSON-serializable representation, making the Sensor class look like

Updated Sensor type to include JSON serialization

```python
class Sensor(Generic[T_value]):
    title: str

    def value(self) -> T_value:
        raise NotImplementedError

    @classmethod
    def format(cls, value: T_value) -> str:
        raise NotImplementedError

    def __str__(self) -> str:
        return self.format(self.value())

    @classmethod
    def to_json_compatible(cls, value: T_value) -> t.Any:
        return json.dumps(value)

    @classmethod
    def from_json_compatible(cls, json_version: t.Any) -> T_value:
        return json.loads(value)
```

The pair of to_json_compatible(...) and from_json_compatible(...) methods are responsible for converting a value to a representation that can be serialized and back again. They are class methods because, like format(...), they operate on values without needing an active sensor of that type to be available. These methods push the user toward returning a JSON structure, which fits in well with our API output.

This update to API could be made as part of the standard `Sensor` class, or a subclass could be created (such as `SerializableSensor`[13]) which allows users to choose to implement only the older variant of the sensor API if they so choose.

However, at the start of this section, we decided to consider what would happen if we'd created this API server as a third-party piece of software, with no access to change the form of the `Sensor` type. As such, we cannot simply decide to change the Sensor interface: if we were in this situation in real life, it would be in a package we don't control, and other people would be implementing that interface.

Agreeing on an ad hoc signature with peers

As a developer looking to extend an interface in code you don't maintain, the first thing to decide is what functions you feel are missing from the interface as defined by the originator of the software. As an end-user, you can add whatever functions you like to your subclasses, but you cannot easily dictate to the other authors of classes that they should implement the same functions.

When deciding which functions to add to an interface, you should choose functions that other developers are likely to consider useful. If you pick functions that are both easy to implement and generally useful, it is much more likely that other class authors would choose to implement them. If you pick very specific methods, then they might decide that it's not worth the effort.

As such, `to_json_compatible(...)` and `from_json_compatible(...)`, despite being what we'd pick as the maintainer of the software, might be seen as too specific by other developers. I think a pair of `serialize(...)` and `deserialize(...)` methods would be more likely to be implemented.

We could write our flask function to iterate over the sensors and use the `serialize(...)` method if possible, falling back to the value otherwise. We can assume that a sensor's `serialize(...)` method does not raise any exceptions when passed valid data, but we know that not all sensors will have this method and `json.dumps(...)` will fail with some sensor data, so we also need to fall back through three methods for serializing the value.

---

[13]Like *authorization*, the word serialize is traditionally spelled using US English conventions in APIs, so with a z rather than an s.

First, we get the value from the sensor and pass it to the serialize(...) method. If this fails with an AttributeError, then there is likely no serialize(...) method, so try again with json.dumps(...). If this fails with a TypeError, then we cannot serialize this sensor and should return a placeholder.

An example of how to progressively support a serialize(...) method:

```
for sensor in get_sensors():
    raw_value = sensor.value()
    try:
        value = {"serialized": sensor.serialize(raw_value)}
    except AttributeError:
        try:
            value = {"serialized": json.dumps(raw_value)}
        except TypeError:
            value = {"error": f"Cannot serialize value {raw_value}"}
    data[sensor.title] = value
```

This will allow all existing sensors to continue to operate without any code changes so long as their value is JSON serializable, returning an error if not. Any sensor that implements a serialize(...) method will have the result of that method returned instead.

This case of two nested try/except statements is somewhat ugly but functional. In other programming languages, you might implement the same logic by checking for the existence of a serialize(...) method, rather than trying to call it. In Python, it's preferred to try and invoke methods and catch errors than to check if they are present; however, there are times when checking is the best option.

The preceding example still has a potential failure mode. It's quite possible that someone has implemented a serialize() method but no deserialize(...) method, due to the requirements of some other popular consumer of the sensor API. In this case, we'd still be better off using the value() method, as we'd have no guarantee of being able to get the true value back to analyze. In this case, we have to check for the presence of both methods, rather than just trying to use the one we need right now.

```
for sensor in get_sensors():
    raw_value = sensor.value()
    if hasattr(sensor, "serialize") and hasattr(sensor, "deserialize"):
        value = {"serialized": sensor.serialize(raw_value)}
```

```
else:
    try:
        value = {"serialized": json.dumps(raw_value)}
    except TypeError:
        value = {"error": f"Cannot serialize value {raw_value}"}
data[sensor.title] = value
```

Of course, there are potentially more complex sets of methods and variables that your code might want to look for to determine if a particular set of features is present or not. You might be tempted to consolidate this introspection as a function, say does_sensor_support_serialization(sensor: Sensor[Any]) -> bool, and use that as the condition instead. This is made even more tempting the more times the code path diverges between the two cases.

Python has a feature called abstract base classes (or ABCs) that can be used to make this kind of class introspection feel more natural in a Python context. One type of class introspection that *is* regularly used is checking if an object is an instance of a particular class or its subclasses; ABCs allow you to replace more complex introspection of classes with isinstance(...) calls.

Abstract base classes

Abstract base classes are a special type of class; they cannot be instantiated directly, but they can be used as a parent class for your code. They can also "claim" other classes so that they are considered to be subclasses, either by having them be explicitly registered as a virtual subclass or by writing a function that examines a class to decide if it should be considered a subclass.

ABCs are another Python feature that people often think of as being particularly advanced because they've not had cause to use them before. It makes sense that most developers won't have used ABCs, as they are especially useful for cases where regular object-oriented software engineering practices are not practical. A cohesive, unified codebase does not generally have cause to use ABCs, but a sprawling application based on multiple pieces of software may find that ABCs are just the right amount of magic, allowing for application code that minimizes the impact of technical debt.

The approach that ABCs take is to override the logic of isinstance(...) and issubclass(...). The normal definition of issubclass(...) in Python is that a class (A) is a subclass of another (B) if the class definition lists B as a parent or if any of the classes it lists are themselves a subclass of B. ABCs have two additional checks: issubclass(A, B) will return True if A is a subclass of B, if B.register(A) was called at any point before the issubclass check, or if B.__subclasshook__(A) returns True.

Additionally, the more familiar isinstance(...) function works similarly, but with an instance of a class rather than the class itself. Most Python developers consider isinstance(...) to be a natural line of code to write in some situations but would balk at checking for specific sets of methods, preferring instead to use duck typing, even at the cost of readability.

This is where ABCs are most useful; they allow complex class introspection to be performed in a way that feels natural to developers casually reading the code and is highly maintainable to those who are familiar with it.

Note   Any class inherits from the abc.ABC class[14] follows the special class rules of ABCs, including the ability to customize isinstance(...) behavior, but strictly speaking, a class is only an *abstract* base class if it has at least one abstract method, defined with the @abc.abstractmethod decorator.

It would be useful for us to create an abstract base class for our serialization behavior, to avoid explicitly having to check for the two relevant methods in our flask route. SerializableSensor defines the methods we require for serialization and deserialization as abstract methods.[15]

```
class SerializableSensor(ABC):

    @classmethod
    @abstractmethod
    def deserialize(cls, value):
        pass
```

---

[14]As will any that's defined as class MyClass(metaclass=abc.ABCMeta), but I don't think this approach is as clear. Python uses metaclasses to implement ABCs as it needs to be able to introspect the methods that have been defined to decide if a class can be instantiated.

[15]Abstract methods are the other useful feature of ABCs. They prevent any class that has ABC in its superclasses from being instantiated. They must be overridden by a subclass or that class will fail to instantiate. Python developers will often create methods that raise NotImplementedError to communicate that a method must be overridden, but this approach makes bugs easier to find by moving the error to when the object is instantiated, rather than when the method is first used.

```
@classmethod
@abstractmethod
def serialize(cls, value):
    pass
```

We can then use that, either by subclassing this ABC or by registering an implementation. The two approaches are shown in Table 5-2.

Table 5-2. *An example of two ways of creating an ExampleSensor that is considered a subclass of SerializableSensor*

Subclassing method	Registration method[16]
| ```python
class ExampleSensor(
    Sensor[bool],
    SerializableSensor
):
    def value(self) -> bool:
        return True

    @classmethod
    def format(cls, value: bool
    ) -> str:
        return "{}".format(value)

    @classmethod
    def serialize(cls, value: bool
    ) -> str:
        return "1" if value else "0"

    @classmethod
    def deserialize(cls, serialized:
    str) -> bool:
        return bool(int(serialized))
``` | ```python
class ExampleSensor(Sensor[bool]):

    def value(self) -> bool:
        return True

    @classmethod
    def format(cls, value: bool) -> str:
        return "{}".format(value)

    @classmethod
    def serialize(cls, value: bool
    ) -> str:
        return "1" if value else "0"

    @classmethod
    def deserialize(cls, serialized:
    str) -> bool:
        return bool(int(serialized))

SerializableSensor.register(
ExampleSensor)
``` |

---

[16]The registration function, `SerializableSensor.register(other_class)`, takes the class to be registered as a single argument and returns that same class, meaning it meets the definition of a class decorator. You can therefore alternatively write this as a `@SerializableSensor.register` line directly before the class definition.

There are advantages and disadvantages to each approach. For the subclass method, the parent class provides helper functions or default implementations of serialize(...) and deserialize(...). For the registration method, classes that happen to implement the correct methods can be marked as subclasses without having to modify them. This is especially useful when those classes are not in code you control, such as classes in a dependency. You don't need to pick between using either the subclassing or registration methods; you can subclass from an ABC and still register other classes as virtual subclasses.

Finally, the last possible method is the subclass hook, where no explicit registration is required. To achieve this, we add a new method to the SerializableSensor class, which contains the logic for determining if a class is a SerializableSensor or not. The __subclasshook__ class method takes a single argument, the class to introspect.

It can return True or False to specify if the passed class is indeed an instance of the ABC or NotImplemented to defer to the normal Python behavior. The NotImplemented option is essential, as __subclasshook__ is invoked not just for SerializableSensor but for any classes that declare it as a superclass. Returning NotImplemented avoids having to reimplement the default Python logic for those cases.[17]

```
@classmethod
def __subclasshook__(cls, C):
    if cls is SerializableSensor:
        has_abstract_methods = [hasattr(C, name) for name in {"value",
        "serialize", "deserialize"}]
        return all(has_abstract_methods)
    return NotImplemented
```

ABCs also support type annotations, so the final version of the ABC should include appropriate annotations to allow for static typing of any class that inherits directly from the base. We'll add the value(...) function to the list of abstract methods in the base class. We can also set up the SerializableSensor base class as generic which must take a subtype that's compatible with the subtype of the sensor it's paired with. This allows us to ensure at a static typing level that the serialize method supports the same types as the value(...) function:

---

[17]To demonstrate why this is important, imagine we use SerializableSensor as the base class for our Temperature sensor. We want isinstance(obj, SerializableSensor) to use the subclass hook, but we only want isinstance(obj, Temperature) to return true if obj is an instance of the Temperature sensor, not anything with the required methods to be a SerializableSensor.

```python
from abc import ABC, abstractmethod
import typing as t

T_value = t.TypeVar("T_value")

class SerializableSensor(ABC, t.Generic[T_value]):

    title: str

    @abstractmethod
    def value(self) -> T_value:
        pass

    @classmethod
    @abstractmethod
    def serialize(cls, value: T_value) -> str:
        pass

    @classmethod
    @abstractmethod
    def deserialize(cls, serialized: str) -> T_value:
        pass

    @classmethod
    def __subclasshook__(cls, C: t.Type[t.Any]) -> t.Union[bool,
    "NotImplemented"]:
        if cls is SerializableSensor:
            has_abstract_methods = [hasattr(C, name) for name in {"value",
            "serialize", "deserialize"}]
            return all(has_abstract_methods)
        return NotImplemented
```

Fallback strategies

Using ABCs cleans up the if statement that switches between the Sensor being able to handle serializing its own value and needing to use the fallback implementation, but it doesn't help us with implementing the fallback logic as it stands.

Any of the various serialization methods we could pick between (including JSON) provide a pair of serialization and deserialization functions, often called dumps(...) and loads(...). We can provide mixin[18] classes for our users to use if they desire.

An example of a JSON fallback mixin class

```
class JSONSerializedSensor(SerializableSensor[t.Any]):

    @classmethod
    def serialize(cls, value: t.Any) -> str:
        try:
            return json.dumps(value)
        except TypeError:
            return json.dumps(None)

    @classmethod
    def deserialize(cls, serialized: str) -> t.Any:
        return json.loads(serialized)
```

This class inherits from SerializableSensor, so it follows the special class handling rules of ABCs. The SerializableSensor class declares that value, serialize, and deserialize methods are required, but we've only defined two of these methods. That means the JSONSerializedSensor is still considered an abstract base class so it cannot be instantiated. If you tried to instantiate this class, the following TypeError would be raised:

```
TypeError: Can't instantiate abstract class JSONSerializedSensor with
abstract methods value
```

Adapter pattern

The JSONSerializedSensor superclass provides a way to add the JSON serialization methods to our own classes, but it doesn't help if we have other sensors installed, as we can't just edit them to use the superclass.

---

[18]A mixin class is a name for a superclass that provides a few related methods for authors of classes to inherit from. Most of the time that you see a class with multiple superclasses, it's because some of them are mixins.

The classic approach to this problem is called the adapter pattern and is one of the better-known of the famous *Gang of Four* software engineering patterns. An adapter is an object that wraps another to provide a different interface. In this case, we can create an adapter for a given sensor by storing an instance of that sensor as an attribute of instances of the wrapper:

Example of an adapter from ExampleSensor to SerializableSensor using JSONSerializedSensor

```
class SerializableExample(JSONSerializedSensor):

    def __init__(self):
        self.wrapped = ExampleSensor()
        self.title = self.wrapped.title

    def value(self) -> bool:
        return self.wrapped.value()
```

The `serialize(...)` and `deserialize(...)` methods are coming from the `JSONSerializedSensor` that we already developed, so this adapter pattern allows us to use the implementation from the mixin as our fallback strategy. The same would be true of any other partial implementation of the `SerializedSensor` protocol, potentially using different serializers.

Rather than creating a fallback sensor type for each class, we can create them dynamically. These dynamic wrapped sensors must assume the underlying value type is Any, as we have no specific guarantee of what the type of sensor we will pass to it.

```
def get_wrapped_sensor(sensor_class: Sensor[t.Any]) -> SerializableSensor:
    class Fallback(JSONSerializedSensor):

        def __init__(self):
            self.wrapped = sensor_class()
            self.title = self.wrapped.title

        def value(self) -> t.Any:
            return self.wrapped.value()

    return Fallback
```

The code we use to iterate over the sensors and get their values can now be changed to instantiate this wrapper if the sensor isn't serializable:

```python
for sensor in get_sensors():
    raw_value = sensor.value()
    sensor_class = type(sensor)
    if not issubclass(sensor, SerializableSensor):
        sensor_class = get_wrapped_sensor(sensor_class)

    value = {"serialized": sensor_class.serialize(raw_value)}
    data[sensor.title] = value
```

Dynamic class generation

This method does not map precisely to a classic design pattern, partially because it is not possible in compiled languages. This method defines a new class on the fly which subclasses both the original Sensor class and the serialization mixin, creating a new class with the behavior of both. This only works reliably if there is no overlap in method definitions between the two class implementations. Still, it has the advantage that the derived class can be treated as though it's a sensor that implements serialization directly, as the format(...) and __str__() methods are still present, rather than being hidden by a wrapper.

Many Python developers find this a difficult choice to make, as the adapter pattern is simpler and more explicit, whereas the dynamic class generation approach relies on the language's behavior to resolve methods in a way that is not transparent to the end-user, but the dynamic class generation approach appears simpler to the casual observer.

Function to merge the JSON serializer implementation into an arbitrary sensor

```python
def get_merged_sensor(sensor_class: Sensor[t.Any]) -> SerializableSensor:
    class Fallback(sensor_class, JSONSerializedSensor):
        pass

    return Fallback
```

This sensor class can then be used anywhere that sensors are expected, as well as anywhere that expects Serializable sensors are needed. For example, we could provide a get_serializable_sensors() method that copies the implementation of get_sensors() but switches out any nonserializable sensors.

```
def get_sensors() -> t.Iterable[Sensor[t.Any]]:
    sensors = []
    for sensor_class in pkg_resources.iter_entry_points("apd.sensors.sensors"):
        class_ = sensor_class.load()
        if not issubclass(class_, SerializableSensor):
            class _ = get_merged_sensor(class_)
        sensors.append(t.cast(Sensor[t.Any], class_()))
    return sensors
```

Other serialization formats

All of our preceding examples use the JSON protocol, so any class that doesn't provide explicit serialization *and* isn't compatible with JSON serializable still would not work. For this, we'd need to use a more generic serializer, such as pickle.

Warning   You will often see warnings that pickle should not be used on untrusted data as it is not safe. This is vital, as crafted pickle variables can result in arbitrary code execution. If a sensor were somehow compromised or malicious and returned the serialized value `c__builtin__\neval\n(` `V__import__("webbrowser").open("https://advancedpython.dev/` `pickles")\ntR.`, then when the API consumer tried to deserialize it, this book's website would open on the API consumer's computer.

I don't think it's appropriate to use pickles in this case, as there are a small number of sensor types and they return relatively simple data. The following discussion is included because serialization is a common problem, and pickles are often suggested.

In general, it's better to put in the extra engineering effort to avoid using pickles, but if you find yourself in a situation where you need them, you should ensure that at a minimum you use HMAC to authenticate them, as demonstrated in Table 5-3.

Table 5-3. *Example functions for signing and verifying a pickle*

Signing a pickle

```
import hashlib
import hmac
import pickle

secret = bytearray([
0xb2,0x56,0xc4,0x88,0x09,0xa0,0x8a,0x1e,
0x28,0xe3,0xa3,0x25,0xe9,0x2b,0x98,0x6f,
0x13,0x60,0xfb,0x26,0x06,0x9b,0x9d,0x6f,
0x3a,0x01,0x2c,0x3f,0x9d,0x9f,0x72,0xcd
])

untrusted_pickle = pickle.dumps(2)
digest = hmac.digest(
    secret,
    untrusted_pickle,
    hashlib.sha256
)
signed_pickle = digest + b":" + untrusted_pickle
```

Verifying a signature

```
import hashlib
import hmac
import pickle

secret = bytearray([
0xb2,0x56,0xc4,0x88,0x09,0xa0,0x8a,0x1e,
0x28,0xe3,0xa3,0x25,0xe9,0x2b,0x98,0x6f,
0x13,0x60,0xfb,0x26,0x06,0x9b,0x9d,0x6f,
0x3a,0x01,0x2c,0x3f,0x9d,0x9f,0x72,0xcd
])

digest, untrusted = received_pickle.split(
    b":", 1
)

expected_digest = hmac.digest(
    secret,
    untrusted,
    hashlib.sha256
)

if not hmac.compare_digest(digest, expected_digest):
    raise ValueError("Bad Signature")
else:
    value = pickle.loads(untrusted)
```

This scheme is symmetric; anyone who can verify a pickle can also create a valid signature for an arbitrary pickle, but it is usually sufficient for closed systems. As it's symmetric, it's very important to keep the secret from becoming publicly known. The secret is usually stored in a configuration file or environment variable so that it can be different for each user of the code. More complex signatures using asymmetric keys are possible but are rarely worth the engineering effort over creating a defined JSON (or other) schema to deserialize data safely.

Bringing it all together

In our parallel world where we are attempting to retrofit a WSGI server into the existing Sensor ecosystem, we now have all the code we need (Listing 5-12). The bulk of the web server code is the same as it was for our real, integrated Flask application; the only significant change in the web server code is the addition of an if statement and matching else clause in the sensor_values() view, adding a total of three lines to the view code. We have successfully encapsulated the class introspection and fallback logic into the supporting code, which can be split out into a utilities Python file and left to work its magic.

Listing 5-12. A possible implementation of WSGI server and fallback encoding in a third-party piece of code

```python
from abc import ABC, abstractmethod
import typing as t
import json

import flask

from apd.sensors.sensors import Sensor
from apd.sensors.cli import get_sensors
from apd.sensors.wsgi import require_api_key, set_up_config

app = flask.Flask(__name__)

T_value = t.TypeVar("T_value")

class SerializableSensor(ABC, t.Generic[T_value]):

    title: str
```

```
    @abstractmethod
    def value(self) -> T_value:
        pass

    @classmethod
    @abstractmethod
    def serialize(cls, value: T_value) -> str:
        pass

    @classmethod
    @abstractmethod
    def deserialize(cls, serialized: str) -> T_value:
        pass

    @classmethod
    def __subclasshook__(cls, C: t.Type[t.Any]) -> t.Union[bool,
    "NotImplemented"]:
        if cls is SerializableSensor:
            has_abstract_methods = [
                hasattr(C, name) for name in {"value", "serialize", "deserialize"}
            ]
            return all(has_abstract_methods)
        return NotImplemented

class JSONSerializedSensor(SerializableSensor[t.Any]):
    @classmethod
    def serialize(cls, value: t.Any) -> str:
        try:
            return json.dumps(value)
        except TypeError:
            return json.dumps(None)

    @classmethod
    def deserialize(cls, serialized: str) -> t.Any:
        return json.loads(serialized)

class JSONWrappedSensor(JSONSerializedSensor):
    def __init__(self, sensor: Sensor[t.Any]):
        self.wrapped = sensor
        self.title = sensor.title
```

```
    def value(self) -> t.Any:
        return self.wrapped.value()

def get_serializable_sensors() -> t.Iterable[SerializableSensor[t.Any]]:
    sensors = get_sensors()
    found = []
    for sensor in sensors:
        if isinstance(sensor, SerializableSensor):
            found.append(sensor)
        else:
            found.append(JSONWrappedSensor(sensor))
    return found

@app.route("/sensors/")
@require_api_key
def sensor_values() -> t.Tuple[t.Dict[str, t.Any], int, t.Dict[str, str]]:
    headers = {"Content-Security-Policy": "default-src 'none'"}
    data = {}
    for sensor in get_serializable_sensors():
        data[sensor.title] = sensor.serialize(sensor.value())
    return data, 200, headers

if __name__ == "__main__":
    import wsgiref.simple_server

    set_up_config(None, app)

    with wsgiref.simple_server.make_server("", 8000, app) as server:
        server.serve_forever()
```

Fixing the serialization problem in our code

The diversion into how we would approach this problem in third-party code aside,
we should also solve this issue in the mainline codebase of apd.sensors. When we
were looking to do this as a third-party tool, we had a strong incentive to pick function
signatures that would be generally useful, so plumped for a specific serialize and
deserialize method, which other consumers might use (for example) for logging to a

file. Now we're back to our role as the maintainer of the software we have more flexibility in deciding what the interface should be. We still want the code to be easy to implement, but we have a much stronger authority to dictate the functions that we think are best.

I very much believe that restricting ourselves to using only JSON API here is beneficial, as it makes the raw data easier to understand. If our interface had a serialize(...), then we would have no guarantee that the output would be something human readable. Therefore, instead of creating serialize(...) and deserialize(...) functions, I'll create functions that reduce the value to something that is JSON serializable and rebuild it from such values.

We can define these on the Sensor base class with whatever default implementation we want. There's currently no guarantee that any given sensor is compatible with the JSON serialization, so the default implementation must be to raise an exception.

Additional methods to add to Sensor base class

```
@classmethod
def to_json_compatible(cls, value: T_value) -> Any:
    raise NotImplementedError

@classmethod
def from_json_compatible(cls, json_version: Any) -> T_value:
    raise NotImplementedError
```

We now need to provide implementations of this pair of methods for each of our existing sensors. There are three different code paths that need to be updated. The first is for the majority of sensors that are already JSON compatible. For this, we can create a new mixin class:

```
class JSONSensor(Sensor[T_value]):
    @classmethod
    def to_json_compatible(cls, value: T_value) -> t.Any:
        return value

    @classmethod
    def from_json_compatible(cls, json_version: t.Any) -> T_value:
        return cast(JSONT_value, json_version)
```

TYPING OF JSON VALUES

There is no easy way of representing that something is JSON compatible in a Python type hint as the definition of JSON compatible is inherently recursive. A list is JSON compatible only if all its elements are, for example. We *could* try to approximate a definition of JSON-compatible type more and more closely by limiting the type of the JSON to a maximum level of recursion, such as

```python
from typing import *

JSON_0 = Union[str, int, float, bool, None]
JSON_1 = Union[Dict[str, JSON_0], List[JSON_0], JSON_0]
JSON_2 = Union[Dict[str, JSON_1], List[JSON_1], JSON_1]
JSON_3 = Union[Dict[str, JSON_2], List[JSON_2], JSON_2]
JSON_4 = Union[Dict[str, JSON_3], List[JSON_3], JSON_3]
JSON_5 = Union[Dict[str, JSON_4], List[JSON_4], JSON_4]
JSON_like = JSON_5
```

The T_value generic reference we used for Sensor can be any type, but we would want our JSONSensor superclass to only work with JSON-compatible types, so a different TypeVar with a bind parameter would be needed:

```python
JSONT_value = TypeVar("JSONT_value", bound=JSON_like)
```

This exercise in working around the type checker is counterproductive, in my opinion. Typing is there to help developers, not to make them jump through hoops. If something is difficult to express as a static type hint, then you should make it clear with documentation and comments instead. You should trust that developers will do the right thing. As such, I will be using Any as the type hint to represent JSON-compatible Python objects.

Most of the sensors that we've written can use JSONSensor transparently; however, the PythonVersion sensor has a very strange type. It uses a custom class that cannot be instantiated directly. This implementation detail of Python isn't important, but we need to change the sensors slightly in order to be able to convert back from JSON to something that behaves like the actual value.

```python
from typing import NamedTuple

version_info_type = NamedTuple(
    "version_info_type",
    [
        ("major", int),
        ("minor", int),
        ("micro", int),
        ("releaselevel", str),
        ("serial", int),
    ],
)

class PythonVersion(JSONSensor[version_info_type]):
    title = "Python Version"

    def value(self) -> version_info_type:
        return version_info_type(*sys.version_info)

    @classmethod
    def format(cls, value: version_info_type) -> str:
        if value.micro == 0 and value.releaselevel == "alpha":
            return "{0.major}.{0.minor}.{0.micro}a{0.serial}".format(value)
        return "{0.major}.{0.minor}".format(value)
```

This uses a typed named tuple to emulate the real sys.version_info, as otherwise we wouldn't be able to implement from_json_compatible(...) to return the exact same value as value().

Finally, the temperature and solar power sensors both use physical quantities as their value type, so they will use pint's unit system for their value and need a custom pair of JSON methods.

JSON method pair for temperature

```python
class Temperature(Sensor[Optional[Any]]):
    ...
    @classmethod
    def to_json_compatible(cls, value: Optional[Any]) -> Any:
```

```
    if value is not None:
        return {"magnitude": value.magnitude, "unit": str(value.units)}
    else:
        return None

@classmethod
def from_json_compatible(cls, json_version: Any) -> Optional[Any]:
    if json_version:
        return ureg.Quantity(json_version["magnitude"],
        ureg[json_version["unit"]])
    else:
        return None
```

We've gained a fair amount of support code for the sensors while creating this version of the software; it's time to move that out of the way of the implementations of the sensors, to make the codebase easier to navigate.

Tidying up

The sensors.py file currently has two base classes and some actual sensors. It's clearer only to have the sensors listed in this file, so I will move the support code to base.py.

It would also be a good idea to make the JSON API use the same keys as the sensor entrypoints. This would make it a lot easier to deserialize data, as we could easily look up the sensor class that defined it. To this end, a new name attribute is added. The full definition of the Sensor base class is shown as Listing 5-13.

Listing 5-13. Definition of the sensor base class from base.py

```
import typing as t

T_value = t.TypeVar("T_value")

class Sensor(t.Generic[T_value]):
    name: str
    title: str

    def value(self) -> T_value:
        raise NotImplementedError
```

```python
    @classmethod
    def format(cls, value: T_value) -> str:
        raise NotImplementedError

    def __str__(self) -> str:
        return self.format(self.value())

    @classmethod
    def to_json_compatible(cls, value: T_value) -> t.Any:
        raise NotImplementedError()

    @classmethod
    def from_json_compatible(cls, json_version: t.Any) -> T_value:
        raise NotImplementedError()

class JSONSensor(Sensor[T_value]):
    @classmethod
    def to_json_compatible(cls, value: T_value) -> t.Any:
        return value

    @classmethod
    def from_json_compatible(cls, json_version: t.Any) -> T_value:
        return t.cast(T_value, json_version)
```

Versioning APIs

As part of these changes, we have changed the behavior of the API, although in a minimal way. The only user-facing difference is that API values are keyed by the sensor ID now, rather than the human-readable name. We need to create a new user-facing version of the API, as it behaves differently to past versions.

New API versions are usually made by providing the different API on a slightly different URL, containing the version number. We could change the API in place, but anybody that depended on the API would suddenly start seeing a different behavior. This likely isn't a problem for personal projects, but APIs that are available to the public or within a company are likely to have users that you can't discuss changes with beforehand.

Tip   Having the ability to support old API versions doesn't mean that you are required to support them. It's entirely possible that you might have /v/1.0 and /v/1.1, but later decide to release /v/2.0 which is very different from the other two. In this case, you might decide to remove the older API versions entirely. Having the version number in the URL does not force you to maintain support for older versions, but if you do not scope your API endpoints by version, it is tough to maintain an older version if you later choose to.

When versioning an API, you need to make decisions about how you will handle bugs. In general, there are two strategies. Either you can leave bugs in place, insisting that people upgrade to the newest version of the API, or you can fix bugs in unobtrusive ways. Leaving bugs in place is a more common solution, as fixing them is significantly more work. Security bugs in old API versions should **always** be fixed, though.

The changes we've made in this chapter were to handle serializing the temperature and humidity sensors now that we've changed them to use pint. The original API returned these values in degrees Celsius; the new one returns a dictionary that includes the temperature system.

In the version of the code that accompanies this chapter, I have applied a fix to prevent any sensor that cannot be JSON serialized from appearing in the v1.0 API output by catching TypeError and skipping the sensor if needed. This means that the temperature and humidity sensors will no longer appear there, only in the v2 API. Whether or not to spend the extra time and effort adding a special case for pint objects in the v1.0 API very much depends on the needs of your users.

To facilitate hosting multiple versions of the API, we'll move the views to a new file named for the version of the API and register them against a flask.Blueprint instance for that API version, instead of directly against the flask.Flask object. Flask blueprints are groups of related URLs that can be added to an application. Using a blueprint allows us to write view code that works within a subpath of the main website without having to modify all the individual URLs to include the API version number:

v10.py

```
version = flask.Blueprint(__name__, __name__)

@version.route("/sensors/")
@require_api_key
```

```
def sensor_values() -> t.Tuple[t.Dict[str, t.Any], int, t.Dict[str, str]]:
    ...
```

__init__.py

```
app = flask.Flask(__name__)
app.register_blueprint(v10.version, url_prefix="/v/1.0")
```

The file structure of the wsgi directory will have a different file for every API version, which currently is `v10.py` and `v20.py`, as well as some support code such as the authentication functions.

```
src/apd/sensors/wsgi/
├── __init__.py
├── base.py
├── serve.py
├── v10.py
└── v20.py
```

Here I've given the API a simple version number, but many public APIs use calendar versioning as their version number. This can be more user-friendly, but it really is a matter of personal preference.

Testability

When supporting multiple versions of the API, we will also need to test them all. Even if you decide that it's not important for old versions to work correctly, you will still need to ensure that there are no security problems introduced in the old versions of the API.

I approach this by having a class for each version of the API. This allows for setting up fixtures to avoid having to have each test specify which API version it is targeting. For example, we already have a test to check if a missing API key causes a HTTP forbidden error when accessing the sensors. It's written as

```
@pytest.mark.functional
def test_sensor_values_fails_on_missing_api_key(self, api_server):
    response = api_server.get("/sensors/", expect_errors=True)
    assert response.status_code == 403
    assert response.json["error"] == "Supply API key in X-API-Key header"
```

This test assumes that api_server is a WebTest application that has the API mounted at the root. This was fine when we were not namespacing API versions, but it would appear that we'd have to write this test for /v/1.0/sensors and /v/2.0/sensors. Having a support class for each API version means that we can mount that version's blueprint at the root of a Flask app, rather than testing against the composite app that has the blueprints mounted on different prefixes.

Test class that treats /v/1.0 as the root

```
from apd.sensors.wsgi import v10

class Testv10API:
    @pytest.fixture
    def subject(self, api_key):
        app = flask.Flask("testapp")
        app.register_blueprint(v10.version)
        set_up_config({"APD_SENSORS_API_KEY": api_key}, to_configure=app)
        return app

    @pytest.fixture
    def api_server(self, subject):
        return TestApp(subject)
```

The TestV20API class does the same but uses v20.version instead of v10.version, making the tests in each class see the appropriate API version at the root of their HTTP namespace. The preceding missing API key test can then be factored out into a mixin class, along with any other tests that work the same across different versions of the API. For us, this will be the two tests that handle API authentication.

```
class CommonTests:
    @pytest.mark.functional
    def test_sensor_values_fails_on_missing_api_key(self, api_server):
        response = api_server.get("/sensors/", expect_errors=True)
        assert response.status_code == 403
        assert response.json["error"] == "Supply API key in X-API-Key header"
```

```
@pytest.mark.functional
def test_sensor_values_require_correct_api_key(self, api_server):
    response = api_server.get(
        "/sensors/", headers={"X-API-Key": "wrong_key"}, expect_errors=True
    )
    assert response.status_code == 403
    assert response.json["error"] == "Supply API key in X-API-Key header"
```

As the test class name does not start with Test, the pytest runner does not see these as independent tests, which is good as they rely on a fixture called api_server, which is not defined. However, when we add CommonTests as a base class of both TestV10API and TestV20API, these test functions are inherited by both classes. Only test classes that start with the word Test are examined by pytest, so the CommonTests class is never executed in isolation. The methods it contains are inherited by the version-specific classes, which have the appropriate fixtures to support them.

Summary

We've covered a lot in this chapter, introducing web APIs with Flask and covering how we'd go about extending the Sensor interface to work around the limits of JSON serialization. The ecosystem of Python web development is vast, and many books dive into a small aspect of this world alone.

Although we do need a HTTP API to complete our sensor aggregation program, it isn't fundamentally a web application. I would encourage anyone interested in learning about Python on the Web to try out some popular frameworks (such as Django, Pyramid, and Flask) and learn their strengths and weaknesses. Django is rightly praised as a good framework for all-round web development, but the minimal style of Flask and the expressivity of Pyramid make them valuable tools to be aware of when picking a platform.

We've also covered practicalities of extending a class definition, both as the original author of the system and as a third party using abstract base classes. Finally, we also covered many common recipes for Python code, such as HMAC for message authentication and decorators for extending function behaviors.

The Sensor API has been changed in a way that breaks backward compatibility, so the version number of the package has been updated to 2.0.0, and the documentation now explains how the API can be accessed. In the next chapter, we will start work on collating the information in a central source using this new HTTP API.

Additional resources

The following resources provide some additional information on the topics that we've covered and are worth reading if you have a particular interest in web programming:

> The WSGI specification is a Python-specific standard for web applications. A lot of background information can be found at `http://wsgi.org`.

> The full documentation for the Flask web framework is at `https://flask.palletsprojects.com/`.

> I recommend looking at `www.djangoproject.com/` and `https://trypyramid.com/` as other Python web frameworks of particular note.

> The Pint library that I used for physical units has examples and advanced usage information available at `https://pint.readthedocs.io/`.

> The JWT project (`https://jwt.io/`) details a more involved way to use HMAC for authentication and has many examples and sample code.

> Some production-quality WSGI servers are `https://gunicorn.org/`, `https://modwsgi.readthedocs.io/en/develop/`, and `https://pypi.org/project/waitress/`.

> Information on the WSGI app testing library WebTest is at `https://docs.pylonsproject.org/projects/webtest/`.

CHAPTER 6

Aggregation process

Now that we have a robust codebase for gathering data from a computer and reporting it over a HTTP interface, it's time to start logging and analyzing this data. We need to create a central aggregation process that connects to each of the sensors and pulls the data down. Such a process would allow us to observe correlations between different sensors at the same time as well as trends over time.

To begin with, we'll need to create a new Python package. It doesn't make sense for us to distribute all the code for the aggregation process along with the data collection code; we expect many more deployments of the sensor than of the aggregation process.

It's rare for programmers to start a new project from nothing and to write all the boilerplate themselves. Much more common is to use a template, either explicitly or by copying another project and removing its functionality. It's much easier to get started from a piece of code that exists but does nothing than it is from an empty directory.

Cookiecutter

While you can create new projects from a template just by copying the directory, there are tools that make the process easier. Although copying a template directory and modifying it seems simple, it often involves renaming files and directories from "skeleton" or "example" to match the name of the project that you're creating. Tools like cookiecutter automate this process by allowing you to create templates that use variables provided when first creating a project.

247

© Matthew Wilkes 2020
M. Wilkes, *Advanced Python Development*, https://doi.org/10.1007/978-1-4842-5793-7_6

I recommend using cookiecutter to create new projects. It would be a global development tool for us, rather than a project-specific tool. We should install it into the system Python environment,[1] as we did with Pipenv.

```
> pip install --user cookiecutter
```

There are many preexisting cookiecutter templates; some provide templates for generic Python packages, others have templates for more complicated things. There are specialized templates for things as diverse as hybrid Python/rust packages, Python-based smartphone applications, and Python web applications.

You do not need to install cookiecutter templates; in fact, you cannot. A template can only be referenced as either a path to a local copy of the template or as a remote specification for git (as in, what you would usually pass to git clone[2]). When you specify a remote template, cookiecutter automatically downloads and uses that template. If you've already used that template previously, you'll be prompted to replace it with the freshly downloaded version.

Tip   If you have a template that you use regularly, I recommend keeping a local checkout of it. Don't forget to update it regularly, in case fixes have been applied in the git repository, but as well as a small speed improvement, this allows you to generate code when not connected to the Internet.

If you find yourself without a network connection but didn't maintain a local checkout, cookiecutter may have a cache from a past invocation at ~/.cookiecutter/

---

[1]Cookiecutter does have quite a few dependencies. Of all the tools we've installed system-wide so far, this is the one I'd be most tempted to isolate. You could use pipenv to create an environment just for cookiecutter and add the bin/ (or, on Windows, Scripts/) directory associated with the environment (run pipenv --venv to find this) to your system path. You may also need to do this if your system Python environment is a very old version.

[2]There are also helpers for popular Git hosting platforms, such as GitHub.
For example, gh:MatthewWilkes/cookiecutter-simplepackage will reference
the cookiecutter-simplepackage repository on my GitHub account.

Creating a new template

We could use these templates as the basis for our aggregation process, but none of them exactly match the decisions we made in the earlier chapters. Instead, I'll create a new template that captures this book's recommendations for a minimal Python package. You can adapt this to match your preferences or create new templates to automate boilerplate code creation specific to your work.

Note   If you want to use the template as I describe here, there's no need for you to make your own version. My template can be used with `cookiecutter gh:MatthewWilkes/cookiecutter-simplepackage`. This section explains the process of creating your own custom templates.

We'll create a new git repository to hold the template. The first thing we need to add is a `cookiecutter.json` file, shown in Listing 6-1. This file defines the variables we're going to ask the user for and their defaults. Most of these are simple strings, in which case the user is prompted to enter a value or press enter to accept the default value, displayed in parentheses. They can also contain variable substitutions from earlier entries (which can, in turn, be Python expressions) by surrounding the Python expression in braces, in which case the result of these substitutions is used as the default. Finally, they can be a list, in which case the user is presented with a list of options and asked to pick one, with the first item being the default.

Listing 6-1. cookiecutter.json

```
{
    "full_name": "Advanced Python Development reader",
    "email": "example@advancedpython.dev",
    "project_name": "Example project",
    "project_slug": "{{ cookiecutter.project_name.lower().replace(' ',
    '_').replace('-', '_') }}",
    "project_short_description": "An example project.",
    "version": "1.0.0",
    "open_source_license": ["BSD", "GPL", "Not open source"]
}
```

We also need to create a directory that contains the templates we're going to create. We can also use braces to include user-supplied values in filenames, so this should be called {{ cookiecutter.project_slug }} to create a directory whose name is the same as the project_slug value. We could use any value from cookiecutter.json; however, the project slug is the best choice. This directory will become the root of the new project's git repository, so its name should match the expected repository name.

From here, we can create the various files that we want to include in every project of this type, such as the build files (setup.py, setup.cfg), the documentation (README.md, CHANGES.md, LICENCE), and the test/ and src/ directories.

There is a complication, however. The template includes a {{ cookiecutter.project_slug }}/ directory inside src/, which works fine for any packages that don't contain a . in their slug, but if we were creating apd.sensors, we'd see a discrepancy between what the cookiecutter generates and what we want (Figure 6-1).

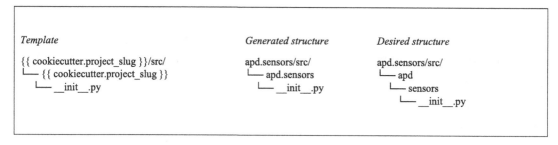

Figure 6-1. *A comparison of the folder structure we have vs. what we need*

We need this additional level in the directory structure because apd is a namespace package. When we first created apd.sensors, we decided that apd would be a namespace, which allows us to create multiple packages within the namespace on the condition that no code is placed directly in the namespace packages, only the standard packages they contain.

We need some custom behavior here, above and beyond what is possible with a template alone.[3] We need to recognize where there is a . in a slug and, in that case, split the slug and create nested directories for each of the parts. Cookiecutter supports this requirement through the use of a post-generation hook. In the root of the template, we

---

[3]It *is* possible to achieve this with just a template, but only if the template is specific to the number of nested namespace packages in use.

can add a hooks directory with a `post_gen_project.py` file. *Pre-generation hooks*, stored as hooks/`pre_gen_project.py`, are used to manipulate and validate user input before generation starts; *post-generation hooks*, stored as hooks/`post_gen_project.py`, are used to manipulate the generated output.

The hooks are Python files which are executed directly at the appropriate stage of generation. They do not need to provide any importable functions; the code can be at the module level. Cookiecutter first interprets this file as a template, and any variables are substituted before it executes the hook code. This behavior allows data to be inserted using variables directly into the hook's code (such as in Listing 6-2), rather than the more usual approach of using an API to retrieve the data.

Listing 6-2. hooks/post_gen_project.py

```python
import os

package_name = "{{ cookiecutter.project_slug }}"
*namespaces, base_name = package_name.split(".")

if namespaces:
    # We need to create the namespace directories and rename the inner directory
    directory = "src"
    # Find the directory the template created: src/example.with.namespaces
    existing_inner_directory = os.path.join("src", package_name)

    # Create directories for namespaces: src/example/with/
    innermost_namespace_directory = os.path.join("src", *namespaces)
    os.mkdir(innermost_namespace_directory)

    # Rename the inner directory to the last component
    # and move it into the namespace directory
    os.rename(
        existing_inner_directory,
        os.path.join(innermost_namespace_directory, base_name)
    )
```

Note   The *namespaces, base_name = package_name.split(".")
line is an example of extended unpacking. It has a similar meaning to *args in
function definitions; the base_name variable contains the last item split from
package_name, and any previous ones are stored as a list called namespaces. If
there are no . characters in package_name, then base_name would be equal to
package_name and namespaces would be an empty list.

Using the cookiecutter template I've created here can be done with the GitHub
helper, as I've stored the code in GitHub. It is also available in the accompanying code for
this chapter. The cookiecutter invocation is as follows, with gh: being the GitHub helper
prefix:

```
> cookiecutter gh:MatthewWilkes/cookiecutter-simplepackage
```

Or, you can test invocations with your local, working copy with

```
> cookiecutter ./cookiecutter-simplepackage
```

Creating the aggregation package

We can now use the cookiecutter template to create a package for the aggregation
process, called apd.aggregation. Change to the parent directory of the apd.code
directory, but there's no need to create a directory for the aggregation process as our
cookiecutter template does this. We invoke the cookiecutter generator and fill in the
details we want and then can initialize a new git repository in that directory with the
generated files added in the first commit.

Console session from generating apd.aggregation

```
> cookiecutter gh:MatthewWilkes/cookiecutter-simplepackage
full_name [Advanced Python Development reader]: Matthew Wilkes
email [example@advancedpython.dev]: matt@advancedpython.dev
project_name [Example project]: APD Sensor aggregator
project_slug [apd_sensor_aggregator]: apd.aggregation
```

```
project_short_description [An example project.]: A programme that queries
apd.sensor endpoints and aggregates their results.
version [1.0.0]:
Select license:
1 - BSD
2 - MIT
3 - Not open source
Choose from 1, 2, 3 (1, 2, 3) [1]:
> cd apd.aggregation
> git init
Initialized empty Git repository in /apd.aggregation/.git/
> git add .
> git commit -m "Generated from skeleton"
```

The next step is to start creating utility functions and accompanying tests to gather the data. As part of this, we must make some decisions about what exactly the responsibilities of the aggregation process are and what features it provides.

The full list of features we would want from our aggregation process is as follows. We won't necessarily build all of these features in the course of this book, but we need to ensure that we have a design that doesn't rule any of them out.

- Gather value of a sensor from all endpoints on demand

- Record value of a sensor automatically at a specific time interval

- Recall data of a sensor recorded at a particular point in time for one or more endpoints

- Recall data of a sensor at a range of times for one or more endpoints

- Find times where sensor values match some condition (such as within a range, maximum, minimum), either across all time or in a time range

- Support all sensor types, without needing modifications to the server to store their data

  - It's fine to require the sensor be installed on the server to analyze it, but not to retrieve data.

- Must be possible to export and import compatible data, both for data portability and backup purposes

- Must be possible to delete data by time or endpoint[4]

Database types

The first thing we need to do is decide how the data should be stored in this application. There are lots of databases available, which cover a wide variety of feature sets. Developers very often choose a particular database according to the current fashion, rather than a dispassionate analysis of the pros and cons. Figure 6-2 is a decision tree that encapsulates the broad questions I ask myself when deciding what style of database to use. This only helps you find a broad category of database, not a particular piece of software, as the feature sets vary massively. Still, I believe it is helpful to ask these questions when deciding on a type of database.

---

[4]The export and deletion options are especially important for any deployment where sensors are colocated with members of the public, such as the use of noise sensors in homes around Amsterdam to monitor airplane noise in 2004. It's important that we build our software in a way that respects the privacy of our users and the public.

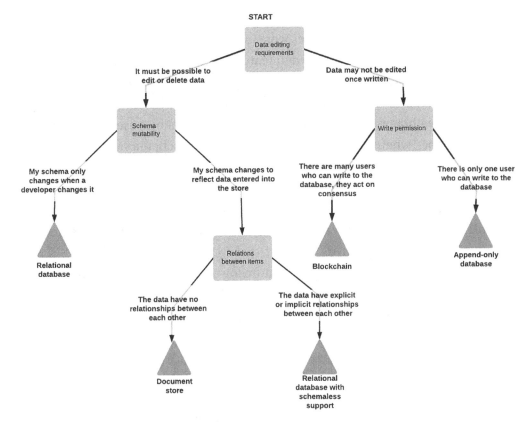

Figure 6-2. *Decision tree for picking a class of database*

The first question I ask myself is to rule out a few special cases of database technology. These are valuable technologies, and in their particular niche, they are excellent, but they are relatively infrequency required. These are append-only databases – where, once something is written, it can't be (easily) removed or edited. This kind of database is a perfect match for logs, such as transaction logs or audit logs. The primary difference between a blockchain and an append-only database is trust; while both prevent editing or deleting data in the typical case, a standard append-only database can be edited by manipulating the underlying storage files. A blockchain is slightly different; it allows a group of people jointly to act as the maintainer. Data can only be edited or removed if at least 50% of the users agree. Any users that don't agree can keep the old data and leave the group. At the time of writing, blockchains are the fashionable database *du jour*, but they are inappropriate for almost all applications.

Much more useful are the database types to the left of the diagram. They are the SQL and NoSQL databases. NoSQL databases were fashionable in the early 2010s. Relational databases have since adopted some of their features as extensions and additional data types. The use of SQL or not isn't the critical way of distinguishing between these database types, but rather if they are *schemaless* or not. This difference is similar to Python with and without type hints; a schemaless database allows users to add data of any arbitrary shape,[5] whereas a database that has a defined schema validates data to ensure it meets the expectations of the database author. A schemaless database might appear to be more appealing, but it can make querying or migrating data much more difficult. If there are no guarantees over what columns are present and their types, it's possible to store data that appears to be correct but presents problems later in development.

For example, imagine we have a temperature log table which stores the time a temperature value is logged, the sensor that logged this temperature, and the value. The value would likely be declared to be a decimal number, but what would happen if a sensor provided a string like "21.2c" instead of 21.2? In a schema-enforcing database, this would raise an error, and the data would fail to insert. In a schemaless database, the insert would succeed but attempts to aggregate the data (such as calculating the mean) fail if one of these incorrectly formatted entries is present in the retrieved data set. As with Python's type hinting, this doesn't protect against all errors, just a type of error. A value of 70.2 would be accepted as it's a valid number, even though a human can tell that it is a measurement in degrees Fahrenheit rather than Celsius.

The final thing we need to consider is how we're going to be querying the data. Querying support is the hardest of these three questions to generalize, as there are significant differences within classes of database. People often describe relational databases as being better for querying and NoSQL databases as being more reliant on a natural key, like a path in an object store or a key in a key/value store. However, this is an oversimplification. For example, SQLite is a relational database, but it has a relatively minimal set of indexing options compared to alternatives such as PostgreSQL; and Elasticsearch is a NoSQL database designed for flexibility in indexing and search.

---

[5]When people talk about the shape of data, they mean the structure of the data types. For example, {"foo": 2} is the same shape as {"bar": 99}, but different to ["foo", 2] and {"foo": "2"}.

Our example

In our case, we find it very difficult to decide a single type for the value of a sensor, other than the fact that all values are JSON serializable. We want to be able to access the internals of this type, for example, the magnitude of a temperature value or the length of a list of IP addresses. If we were to build this with standard relational database constructs, we'd struggle to represent these options in a future-proof way. We'd have to write the database structure with foreknowledge of the different types of value that could be returned.

A better fit for us is to use a schemaless database, letting the JSON representation of the sensor returned from the API be the data that's stored. We have a guarantee that we can restore this data accurately (assuming we have the same version of the sensor code), and there is no difficulty in finding a way of representing it.

This question has taken us to the lowest of the decision points on our decision tree; we now need to consider the relationships between items in the database. A single sensor value is related to other values by virtue of being generated by the same sensor type, by being retrieved from the same endpoint, as well as by being retrieved at the same time. That is, sensor values are related through sensor name, endpoint URL, and creation time. These multiple dimensions of relationship should steer us toward a database with rich indexing and query support, as it would help us to find related data. We would also want to look to a database with good querying support as we want to be able to find records from their values, not just the sensor and time.

These requirements lead us to the *relational databases with schemaless support* option. That is, we should strongly consider a database that is relational at its core but supports types that implement schemaless behavior. A good example of this is PostgreSQL and its JSONB type. JSONB is used to store data in a JSON format[6] and allows indexes to be created that work on its internal structure.

```
CREATE TABLE sensor_values(
    id SERIAL PRIMARY KEY,
    sensor_name TEXT NOT NULL,
```

---

[6]There are two JSON formats, JSON and JSONB. JSONB parses the JSON when data is loaded, but JSON is slightly more forgiving. If you need to store JSON that contains duplicate keys, meaningful whitespace, or meaningful ordering of keys, you should use the JSON type rather than JSONB. If you are not intending to search within the JSON data, then the overhead from using JSONB may not be worth it.

```
    collected_at TIMESTAMP
    data JSONB
)
```

This format balances some of the advantages of fixed-schema databases, in that it's partially fixed. The name and collected_at fields are fixed columns, but the remaining data field is a schemaless field. In theory, we could store JSON or any other serialization format as a TEXT column in this table, but using the JSONB field allows us to write queries and indexes that introspect this value.

Object-relational mappers

It's entirely possible to write SQL code directly as Python, but it's relatively rare for people to do this. Databases are complex beasts, and SQL is infamous for being vulnerable to injection attacks. It's not possible to completely abstract away the peculiarities of individual databases, but tools do exist that take care of table creation, column mapping, and SQL generation.

The most popular of these in the Python world is SQLAlchemy, written by Michael Bayer and others. SQLAlchemy is a very flexible object-relational mapper; it handles the translation between SQL statements and native Python objects, and it does so in an extensible way. Another commonly used ORM is the Django ORM, which is less flexible but offers an interface which requires less knowledge of how databases work. In general, you'll only be using the Django ORM if you're working on a Django project, and otherwise, SQLAlchemy is the most appropriate ORM.

Note   SQLAlchemy does not ship with type hints; however, there is a mypy plugin called *sqlmypy* that provides hints for SQLAlchemy and teaches mypy to understand the types implied by column definitions. I would recommend using this on SQLAlchemy-based projects where you are using type checking. The code accompanying this chapter makes use of this plugin.

To begin with, we need to install SQLAlchemy and a database driver. We need to add SQLAlchemy and psycopg2 to the install_requires section in setup.cfg and trigger these dependencies to be reevaluated using pipenv install -e . on the command line.

There are two ways of describing a database structure with SQLAlchemy, the classic and declarative styles. In the classic style, you instantiate Table objects and associate them with your existing classes. In the declarative style, you use a particular base class (which brings in a metaclass), then you define the columns directly on the user-facing class. In most cases, the Python style of the declarative method makes it the natural choice.

The same table as earlier, in SQLAlchemy declarative style

```
import sqlalchemy
from sqlalchemy.ext.declarative import declarative_base
from sqlalchemy.dialects.postgresql import JSONB, TIMESTAMP

Base = declarative_base()

class DataPoint(Base):
    __tablename__ = 'sensor_values'
    id = sqlalchemy.Column(sqlalchemy.Integer, primary_key=True)
    sensor_name = sqlalchemy.Column(sqlalchemy.String)
    collected_at = sqlalchemy.Column(TIMESTAMP)
    data = sqlalchemy.Column(JSONB)
```

You can then write queries using Python code which will automatically create the appropriate SQL. The create_engine(...) function is used to create a database connection from a connection string. The setting echo=True can be passed, allowing you to see the generated SQL. The next step is to use sessionmaker(...) to create a function that allows you to start a new session and transaction and then finally to create a session for the database connection, as follows:

```
>>> engine = sqlalchemy.create_engine("postgresql+psycopg2://apd@localhost/
apd", echo=True)
>>> sm = sessionmaker(engine)
>>> Session = sm()
>>> Session.query(DataPoint).filter(DataPoint.sensor_name ==
"temperature").all()
INFO sqlalchemy.engine.base.Engine SELECT sensor_values.id AS
sensor_values_id, sensor_values.sensor_name AS sensor_values_sensor_name,
sensor_values.collected_at AS sensor_values_collected_at, sensor_values.data
AS sensor_values_data
```

```
FROM sensor_values
WHERE sensor_values.sensor_name = %(sensor_name_1)s
INFO sqlalchemy.engine.base.Engine {'sensor_name_1': 'temperature'}
[]
```

COLUMN OBJECTS AND DESCRIPTORS

The column objects we've used on our class behave in an unusual way. When we access a column from the class, such as DataPoint.sensor_name, we get a special object that represents the column itself. These objects intercept many Python operations and return placeholders that represent the operation. Without this interception, DataPoint.sensor_name == "temperature" would be evaluated and the filter(...) function would be equivalent to Session.query(DataPoint).filter(False).all().

DataPoint.sensor_name=="temperature" returns a BinaryExpression object. This object is opaque, but the SQL template (excluding the constant values) can be previewed with str(...):

```
>>> str((DataPoint.sensor_name=="temperature"))
                          'sensor_values.sensor_name = :sensor_name_1'
```

The implied database type of an expression is stored on the type attribute of the result of the expression. In the case of comparisons, it is always Boolean.

When the same expression is performed on an instance of the DataPoint type, it retains none of the SQL-specific behaviors; the expression evaluates the actual data of the object as normal. Any instance of a SQLAlchemy declarative class works as a normal Python object.

As such, developers can use the same expression to represent both a Python condition and a SQL condition.

This is possible because the object referred to by DataPoint.sensor_name is a *descriptor*. A descriptor is an object that has some combination of the methods __get__(self, instance, owner), __set__(self, instance, value), and __delete__(self, instance).

Descriptors allow for custom behavior of instance attributes, allowing for arbitrary values to be returned when the value is accessed on a class or an instance, as well as customizing what happens when the value is set or deleted.

Here is an example of a descriptor that behaves like a normal Python value on an instance but exposes itself on the class:

```python
class ExampleDescriptor:

    def __set_name__(self, instance, name):
        self.name = name

    def __get__(self, instance, owner):
        print(f"{self}.__get__({instance}, {owner})")
        if not instance:
            # We were called on the class available as `owner`
            return self
        else:
            # We were called on the instance called `instance`
            if self.name in instance.__dict__:
                return instance.__dict__[self.name]
            else:
                raise AttributeError(self.name)

    def __set__(self, instance, value):
        print(f"{self}.__set__({instance}, {value})")
        instance.__dict__[self.name] = value

    def __delete__(self, instance):
        print(f"{self}.__delete__({instance}")
        del instance.__dict__[self.name]

class A:
    foo = ExampleDescriptor()
```

The following console session demonstrates the two code paths of the preceding __get__ method, as well as the set and delete functionality.

```python
>>> A.foo
<ExampleDescriptor object at 0x03A93110>.__get__(None, <class 'A'>)
<ExampleDescriptor object at 0x03A93110>
>>> instance = A()
```

```
>>> instance.foo
<ExampleDescriptor object at 0x03A93110>.__get__(<A object at 0x01664090>,
<class 'A'>)
Traceback (most recent call last):
  File "<stdin>", line 1, in <module>
  File ".\exampledescriptor.py", line 16, in
    __get__raise AttributeError(self.name)
AttributeError: foo
>>> instance.foo = 1
<ExampleDescriptor object at 0x03A93110>.__set__(<A object at 0x01664090>, 1)
>>> instance.foo
<ExampleDescriptor object at 0x03A93110>.__get__(<A object at 0x01664090>,
<class 'A'>)
1
>>> del instance.foo
<ExampleDescriptor object at 0x03A93110>.__delete__(<A object at 0x01664090>)
```

Most of the time that you need a descriptor, it's to make an attribute that's the result of a computation. This is better expressed with the @property decorator, which constructs a descriptor behind the scenes. Properties are especially useful in the common case where only the get functionality needs to be customized, but they support custom implementations of setting and deleting too.

```
class A:

    @property
    def foo(self):
        return self._foo

    @foo.setter
    def foo(self, value):
        self._foo = value

    @foo.deleter
    def foo(self):
        del self._foo
```

Some core Python features are implemented as descriptors: they're a very powerful way of hooking into a deep part of the core object logic. Without knowing about them, features like the @property and @classmethod decorators seem like magic that's specifically looked for by the interpreter, rather than something you could program yourself.

That said, I have never yet had cause to write a descriptor, although I've used the @property decorator frequently. If you find yourself copy/pasting your property definitions, you may want to consider consolidating their code into a single descriptor.

Versioning the database

There is a function in SQLAlchemy to create all the various tables, indexes, and constraints that have been defined in this database. This checks the tables and columns that have been defined and generates the matching database structure for them.

Creating all defined database tables using SQLAlchemy

```
engine = sqlalchemy.create_engine(
"postgresql+psycopg2://apd@localhost/apd", echo=True)
Base.metadata.create_all(engine)
```

This function looks great at first, but it's very limited. You will likely add more tables or columns in future or at least more indexes when you've done some performance testing. The create_all(...) function creates all things that do not yet exist, meaning any tables that are changed but did exist previously are not updated if you re-run create_all(...). As such, relying on create_all(...) can result in a database that has all the tables you expect but not all of the columns.

To combat this, people use a SQL migration framework. Alembic is the most popular one for SQLAlchemy. It works by connecting to an instance of the database and generating the actions that would be needed to bring the connected database in sync with the one defined in code. If you're using the Django ORM, there is a built-in migration framework that instead works by analyzing all the past migrations and comparing that analyzed state with the current state of the code.

These frameworks allow us to make changes to the database and trust that they will be propagated to actual deployments, regardless of what versions of the software they've used in the past. If a user skips a version or three, any migrations between those versions will also be run.

To do this, we'll add Alembic to the setup.cfg list of dependencies, then re-run pipenv install -e . to refresh these dependencies and install Alembic. We then use the alembic command-line tool to generate the required files to use Alembic in our package.

```
> pipenv run alembic init src\apd\aggregation\alembic
Creating directory src\apd\aggregation\alembic ...  done
Creating directory src\apd\aggregation\alembic\versions ...  done
Generating alembic.ini ...  done
Generating src\apd\aggregation\alembic\env.py ...  done
Generating src\apd\aggregation\alembic\README ...  done
Generating src\apd\aggregation\alembic\script.py.mako ...  done
Please edit configuration/connection/logging settings in 'alembic.ini'
before proceeding.
```

The majority of the files are created in an alembic/ directory inside the package. We need to put the files here so that they're accessible to people who install the package; files outside of this hierarchy aren't distributed to end-users. The exception is alembic.ini, which provides the logging and database connection configuration. These are different for each end-user and so can't be included as part of the package.

We need to modify the generated alembic.ini file, primarily to change the database URI to match the connection string we're using. We can leave the value of script_location=src/apd/aggregation/alembic if we like, as in this development environment, we're using an editable installation of apd.aggregation, but that path won't be valid for end-users, so we should change it to reference an installed package, and we should include a minimal alembic.ini example in the readme file.

Caution   Alembic scripts generally only apply to user models (dependencies have their own configuration and ini files to migrate their models). Users never have a valid reason to generate new migrations for models included in their dependencies. Django's ORM, on the other hand, processes user models and dependencies at the same time, so if a maintainer releases a broken version of a package, it's possible that end-users might inadvertently create new migrations for it when generating their own migrations. For this reason, it's essential to check that migration files are properly committed and released. When generating new migrations as an end-user, you should sanity-check the files that are created are for your code and not a dependency.

Minimal alembic.ini for end users

```
[alembic]
script_location = apd.aggregation:alembic
sqlalchemy.url = postgresql+psycopg2://apd@localhost/apd
```

We also need to customize the generated code inside the package, starting with the env.py file. This file needs a reference to the metadata object that we looked at earlier when using the create_all(...) function, so it can determine what the state of the models is in code. It also contains functions for connecting to the database and for generating SQL files that represent the migration. These can be edited to allow customizing database connection options to match our project's needs.

We need to change the target_metadata line to use the metadata of our declarative Base class that the models use, as follows:

```
from apd.aggregation.database import Base
target_metadata = Base.metadata
```

Now we can generate a migration to represent the initial state of the database,[7] the one that creates the datapoints table that we created to back the DataPoint class.

```
> pipenv run alembic revision --autogenerate -m "Create datapoints table"
```

The revision command creates a file in the alembic/versions/ directory. The first part of the name is an opaque identifier which is randomly generated, but the second half is based on the message given above. The presence of the --autogenerate flag means that the generated file won't be empty; it contains the migration operations required to match the current state of the code. The file is based on a template, script.py.mako in the alembic/ directory. This template is added automatically by Alembic. Although we can modify it if we want, the default is generally fine. The main reason to change this would be to modify the comments, perhaps with a checklist of things to check when generating a migration.

---

[7]We could generate the initial state with the Base.metadata.create_all(engine) command mentioned at the start of this chapter, but only because the current state is also the initial state. If we made any changes, then create_all(...) would no longer generate the initial state. Putting this in an initial migration means that users can always set up the database by upgrading to the latest version of the database.

After running black on this file and removing comments containing instructions, it looks like this:

alembic/versions/6d2eacd5da3f_create_sensor_values_table.py

```python
"""Create datapoints table

Revision ID: 6d2eacd5da3f
Revises: N/A
Create Date: 2019-09-29 13:43:21.242706

"""
from alembic import op
import sqlalchemy as sa
from sqlalchemy.dialects import postgresql

# revision identifiers, used by Alembic.
revision = "6d2eacd5da3f"
down_revision = None
branch_labels = None
depends_on = None

def upgrade():
    op.create_table(
        "datapoints",
        sa.Column("id", sa.Integer(), nullable=False),
        sa.Column("sensor_name", sa.String(), nullable=True),
        sa.Column("collected_at", postgresql.TIMESTAMP(), nullable=True),
        sa.Column("data", postgresql.JSONB(astext_type=sa.Text()),
        nullable=True),
        sa.PrimaryKeyConstraint("id"),
    )

def downgrade():
    op.drop_table("datapoints")
```

The four module-scope variables are used by Alembic to determine the order in which migrations should be run. These should not be altered. The bodies of the upgrade() and downgrade() functions are what we need to check, to make sure that they're doing all the changes we expect and only the changes we expect. The most common change that's needed is if there is an incorrect change detected, such as the migration altering a column but the target state being equal to the start state. This can happen if a database backup was incorrectly restored, for example.

A less common (but still regularly seen) problem is that sometimes an alembic migration includes import statements which introduce code from a dependency or elsewhere in user code, usually when developers are using a custom column type. In this case, the migration must be altered as it's important that the migration code is entirely freestanding. Any constants should also be copied into the migration file, for this same reason.

If a migration imports external code, then its effects may change over time as that external code changes. Any migrations whose effects aren't wholly deterministic could lead to real-world databases having inconsistent states, depending on which version of the dependency code was available at the time of the migration.

EXAMPLE OF A MIGRATION REPEATABILITY ISSUE

For example, consider the following partial migration code for adding a user table to a piece of software:

```
from example.database import UserStates

def upgrade():
    op.create_table(
        "user",
        sa.Column("id", sa.Integer(), nullable=False),
        sa.Column("username", sa.String(), nullable=False),
        sa.Column("status", sa.Enum(UserStates), nullable=False),
        ...
        sa.PrimaryKeyConstraint("id"),
    )
```

There is a status field which, as an Enum field, can only contain preselected values. If version 1.0.0 of the code defines UserStates = ["valid", "deleted"], then the Enum will be created with those as the valid options. However, version 1.1.0 might add another state, making UserStates = ["new", "valid", "deleted"] to represent users having to verify their accounts before they can log in. Version 1.1.0 would also need to add a migration to add "new" as a valid type to this Enum.

If a user installed version 1.0.0 and ran the migration, then later installed 1.1.0 and re-ran the migration, then the database would be correct. However, if the user only learned about the software after 1.1.0 came out and ran both migrations with 1.1.0 installed, then the initial migration would add all three user states, and the second one would be unable to add a value that's already present.

As developers, we're used to the idea that we shouldn't duplicate code, as it causes maintainability problems, but database migrations are an exception. You should duplicate any code you need in order to ensure that the behavior of the migration doesn't change over time.

Finally, some changes are ambiguous. If we were to change the name of the datapoints table we've created here, it would not be clear to Alembic if this were a name change or the removal of one table and the creation of another that happens to have the same structure. Alembic always errs on the side of drop and recreate, so if a rename is intended, but the migration isn't changed, data loss occurs.

Details on the available operations are available in the Alembic documentation, which provides all the everyday operations you might need. Operation plugins can offer new operation types, especially database-specific operations.

Tip   When you make changes to an upgrade operation, you should also make the equivalent changes to the downgrade operation. If you don't want to support downgrading from a particular version, you should raise an exception rather than leave incorrect autogenerated migration code in place. For nondestructive migrations, allowing downgrade is very helpful as it allows developers to revert their database when switching between feature branches.

With this migration generated and committed into source control, we can run the migrations, which generate this datapoints table for us. Running the migrations is done with the alembic command line, as follows:

```
> alembic upgrade head
```

Other useful alembic commands

There are a few subcommands that Alembic users need on a day-to-day basis. These are listed as follows:

- `alembic current`
    - Shows the version number that the connected database is at.
- `alembic heads`
    - Shows the latest version number in the migration set. If there is more than one listed version, then the migrations need to be merged.
- `alembic merge heads`
    - Creates a new migration that depends on all the revisions listed by alembic heads, ensuring that they are all performed.
- `alembic history`
    - Shows a listing of all migrations known to Alembic.
- `alembic stamp ‹revisionid›`
    - Replace ‹revisionid› with the alphanumeric revision identifier to mark an existing database as being at that version without running any migrations.
- `alembic upgrade ‹revisionid›`
    - Replace ‹revisionid› with the alphanumeric revision identifier to upgrade to. This can be head[8] for the most recent revision. Alembic follows the revision history, running the upgrade method of any migrations that have not been performed.

---

[8]Using heads will also upgrade to the most recent revision, but it will follow any branched paths, rather than requiring they are merged. I recommend not using this functionality and ensuring that you merge any forked migrations instead.

- alembic downgrade **‹revisionid›**

    - Like upgrade, but the target revision is earlier, and the downgrade
      methods are used. In my experience, this works less well across
      merge migrations than a straight migration path, and you should
      be aware that a downgrade isn't the same as an undo. It cannot
      restore data in columns that were dropped.

Loading data

Now we have the data model defined, and we can begin to load in data from the sensors.
We'll do this over HTTP with the excellent *requests* library. There is support for making
HTTP requests built-in to Python, but the requests library has a better user interface.
I recommend using requests over the standard library HTTP support in all situations.
You should only use the standard library's HTTP request support in cases where it's not
practical to use dependencies.

The lowest-level building block we need for pulling data from sensors is a function
that, given the API details for an endpoint, makes a HTTP request to the API, parses the
results, and creates DataPoint class instances for each sensor.

Function that adds datapoints from a server

```python
def get_data_points(server: str, api_key: t.Optional[str]) ->
t.Iterable[DataPoint]:
    if not server.endswith("/"):
        server += "/"
    url = server + "v/2.0/sensors/"
    headers = {}
    if api_key:
        headers["X-API-KEY"] = api_key
    try:
        result = requests.get(url, headers=headers)
    except requests.ConnectionError as e:
        raise ValueError(f"Error connecting to {server}")
    now = datetime.datetime.now()
    if result.ok:
```

```
    for value in result.json()["sensors"]:
        yield DataPoint(
            sensor_name=value["id"], collected_at=now, data=value["value"]
        )
else:
    raise ValueError(
        f"Error loading data from {server}: "
        + result.json().get("error", "Unknown")
    )
```

This function connects to the remote server and returns DataPoint objects for each sensor value present. It can also raise a ValueError representing an error encountered while attempting to read the data and performs some basic checking of the URL provided.

YIELD AND RETURN

I just described the get_data_points() function as *returning* DataPoint objects, but that's not strictly correct. It uses the yield keyword, rather than return. We briefly saw this in Chapter 5 when writing a WSGI application that returns parts of the response with a delay in between.

The yield statement makes this a generator function. A generator is a lazily evaluated iterable of values. It can produce zero or more values or even infinitely many. Generators only generate the items that the caller requests, unlike normal functions which calculate the full return value before the first one is available to the caller.

The easiest way to build a simple generator is with a generator expression, which, if you're familiar with list, set, and dictionary comprehensions, will look like what you'd imagine a tuple comprehension to be.

```
>>> [item for item in range(10)]
[0, 1, 2, 3, 4, 5, 6, 7, 8, 9]
>>> (item for item in range(10))
<generator object <genexpr> at 0x01B58EB0>
```

These generator expressions cannot be indexed like a list, you can only request the next item from them:

```
>>> a=(item for item in range(10))
>>> a[0]
Traceback (most recent call last):
  File "<stdin>", line 1, in <module>
TypeError: 'generator' object is not subscriptable
>>> next(a)
0
>>> next(a)
1
...
>>> next(a)
8
>>> next(a)
9
>>> next(a)
Traceback (most recent call last):
File "<stdin>", line 1, in <module>
StopIteration
```

It is also possible to convert them to lists or tuples using the `list(a)` syntax (so long as they don't contain infinitely many items); however, this takes their state into account. If you've already extracted some or all of the items from the generator, then the result of `list(a)` will only contain those remaining.

Generator functions

The preceding examples are generator expressions, but `get_data_points()` is a generator function. These use the `yield` keyword to specify what the next value should be, and then execution is paused until the user requests a further value. Python remembers the function's state; when the next item is requested, it is resumed from the point of the yield statement.

This can be very useful, as some functions take a long time to generate each subsequent value. The alternative is to make a function where you need to specify the number of items you want to generate, but the generator model allows you to inspect the items as they're returned before deciding if you want more.

Consider the following generator function:

```
def generator() -> t.Iterable[int]:
    print("Stating")
    yield 1
    print("Part way")
    yield 2
    print("Done")
```

Here, print(...) is standing in for more complex code, perhaps connecting to external services or a complex algorithm. If we coerce this generator to a tuple, the prints all happen before we get our result:

```
>>> tuple(generator())
Stating
Part way
Done
(1, 2)
```

However, if we use the items one by one, we can see that the code between yield statements is executed between the values being returned:

```
>>> for num in generator():
...     print(num)
...
Stating
1
Part way
2
Done
```

When to use them

Sometimes it can be unclear if it's best to use a generator or a normal function. Any function that just generates data alone can be a generator function or a standard function, but functions that perform actions on data (such as adding data points to a database) must be sure to *consume* the iterator.

The commonly stated rule of thumb is that such functions should return a value, rather than yield values, but any pattern that causes the full iterator to be evaluated is fine. Another way of doing this is by looping over all the items:

```
def add_to_session(session)
    for item in generator:
        session.add(item)
```

or by converting the generator to a concrete list or tuple type:

```
def add_to_session(session)
    session.add_all(tuple(generator))
```

However, if there were a `yield` statement in the preceding functions, then they would not work as expected. Both of the preceding functions can be called with add_to_session(generator), and all items produced by the generator would be added to the session. The following, if called in the same way, would result in no items being added to the session:

```
def add_to_session(session)
    for item in generator:
        session.add(item)
        yield item
```

If in doubt, use a standard function, rather than a generator function. Either way, make sure you test that your function is behaving as expected.

EXERCISE 6-1: PRACTICE WITH GENERATORS

Write a generator function that provides an infinite supply of data points from a single sensor. You should use `yield` on `DataPoint` instances you construct and wait a second between samplings using the `time.sleep(...)` function.

Once you have written this function, you should loop over its values to see the data come through in bursts as the sensor is queried. You should also try using the standard library's `filter(function, iterable)` function to find only the values of a specific sensor.

An example implementation for this is available in this chapter's accompanying code.

This function is a great start: it provides something we can iterate over that contains DataPoint objects, but we need to create a database connection, add them to a session, and commit that session. To this end, I've defined two helper functions (shown in Listing 6-3), one that, given a database session and server information, gets all the data points from each server and calls session.add(point) to add them to the current database transaction. The second is intended as a stand-alone data collection function. It sets up the session, calls add_data_from_sensors(...), and then commits the session to the database. I have also created another click-based command-line tool that performs these actions, allowing the parameters to be passed on the command line.

Listing 6-3. Helper functions in collect.py

```python
def add_data_from_sensors(
    session: Session, servers: t.Tuple[str], api_key: t.Optional[str]
) -> t.Iterable[DataPoint]:
    points: t.List[DataPoint] = []
    for server in servers:
        for point in get_data_points(server, api_key):
            session.add(point)
            points.append(point)
    return points

def standalone(
    db_uri: str, servers: t.Tuple[str], api_key: t.Optional[str], echo:
    bool = False
) -> None:
    engine = sqlalchemy.create_engine(db_uri, echo=echo)
    sm = sessionmaker(engine)
    Session = sm()
    add_data_from_sensors(Session, servers, api_key)
    Session.commit()
```

Click entrypoint in cli.py

```python
@click.command()
@click.argument("server", nargs=-1)
@click.option(
    "--db",
```

```
    metavar="<CONNECTION_STRING>",
    default="postgresql+psycopg2://localhost/apd",
    help="The connection string to a PostgreSQL database",
    envvar="APD_DB_URI",
)
@click.option("--api-key", metavar="<KEY>", envvar="APD_API_KEY")
@click.option(
    "--tolerate-failures",
    "-f",
    help="If provided, failure to retrieve some sensors' data will not "
    "abort the collection process",
    is_flag=True,
)
@click.option("-v", "--verbose", is_flag=True, help="Enables verbose mode")
def collect_sensor_data(
    db: str, server: t.Tuple[str], api_key: str, tolerate_failures: bool,
    verbose: bool
):
    """This loads data from one or more sensors into the specified database.

    Only PostgreSQL databases are supported, as the column definitions use
    multiple pg specific features. The database must already exist and be
    populated with the required tables.

    The --api-key option is used to specify the access token for the sensors
    being queried.

    You may specify any number of servers, the variable should be the full URL
    to the sensor's HTTP interface, not including the /v/2.0 portion. Multiple
    URLs should be separated with a space.
    """

    if tolerate_failures:
        attempts = [(s,) for s in server]
    else:
        attempts = [server]
    success = True
    for attempt in attempts:
```

```
    try:
        standalone(db, attempt, api_key, echo=verbose)
    except ValueError as e:
        click.secho(str(e), err=True, fg="red")
        success = False
return success
```

This sample uses some more features of click, including the fact that docstrings on click commands are exposed to the end-user as help for the command. The help text adds a lot to the length of the function, but it's less intimidatingly verbose in a code editor with syntax highlighting. This is exposed when a user uses the --help flag, as shown in the following:

```
> pipenv run collect_sensor_data --help
Usage: collect_sensor_data [OPTIONS] [SERVER]...

  This loads data from one or more sensors into the specified database.

  Only PostgreSQL databases are supported, as the column definitions use
  multiple pg specific features. The database must already exist and be
  populated with the required tables.

  The --api-key option is used to specify the access token for the sensors
  being queried.

  You may specify any number of servers, the variable should be the full URL
  to the sensor's HTTP interface, not including the /v/2.0 portion. Multiple
  URLs should be separated with a space.

Options:
  --db <CONNECTION_STRING>  The connection string to a PostgreSQL database
  --api-key <KEY>
  -f, --tolerate-failures   If provided, failure to retrieve some sensors'
                            data will not abort the collection process

  -v, --verbose             Enables verbose mode
  --help                    Show this message and exit.
```

Then, we are using @click.argument for the first time. We use this to collect bare arguments to the function, not options with associated values. The nargs=-1 option to this argument states that we accept any number of arguments, rather than a specific number (usually 1). As such, the command could be invoked as collect_sensor_data http://localhost:8000/ (to collect data from localhost only), as collect_sensor_data http://one:8000/ http://two:8000/ (to collect data from two servers), or even as collect_sensor_data (no data would be collected, but the database connection would be tested implicitly).

The --api-key and --verbose options likely don't need any explanation, but the --tolerate-failures option is one that we might not have considered. Without this option and its support code, we'd run the standalone(...) function with all the sensor locations, but if one failed, the entire script would fail. This option allows the user to specify that in cases where there are multiple servers specified, then any that succeed have their data saved and failing sensors are omitted. The code achieves this by using this option to decide if it should download data from [("http://one:8000/", "http://two:8000/")] or [("http://one:8000/",), ("http://two:8000/",)]. The code for this command passes all the servers to standalone(...) in the normal case, but if --tolerate-failures is added, then there will be one call to standalone(...) for each of the server URLs. This is very much a convenience feature, but it's one I would like if I were using this command myself.

Finally, the support functions are relatively simple. The add_data_from_sensors(...) function wraps the existing get_data_points(...) function and calls session.add(...) on each data point it returns. It then passes these through to the caller as a return value, but as a list rather than a generator. As we're looping over the generators, it ensures that the iterator is fully consumed. Calls to add_data_from_sensors(...) have access to the DataPoint objects, but they are not obliged to iterate over them to consume a generator.

Caution   Developers who enjoy a functional coding style sometimes fall into a trap here. They may be tempted to replace this function with something like map(Session.add, items). The map function creates a generator, so this would need to be consumed to have any effect. Doing so can introduce subtle bugs, such as code that only works when you have a verbose flag enabled, which causes the iterable to be consumed by logging statements.

Do not use `map(...)` if the function you called on the items has any side effects, such as registering the objects with a database session. Always use a loop instead; it's clearer and places no obligations on later code to ensure the generator is consumed.

New technologies

We've touched lightly on some technologies that are very frequently used. I recommend taking the time to understand all of the decisions we made in this chapter regarding their use. To that end, a quick recap of my recommendations is given in the following.

Databases

Pick a database that matches what you need to do with your data, not what is the current vogue. Some databases, like PostgreSQL, are a good default choice precisely because they offer so much flexibility, but flexibility comes at a complexity cost.

Use an ORM and a migration framework if you're using a SQL-based database. In all but extreme edge cases, they serve you better than writing your own custom SQL. Don't be fooled into thinking that the ORM would shield you from knowing about databases, however. It eases the interface, but you'll have a tough time if you try to interact with a database without understanding its needs.

Custom attribute behavior

If you need something that acts like a calculated property, that is, something that behaves like an attribute on an object but actually builds its value from other sources, a @property is the best way to go. The same is true for one-off wrappers of values, where data is modified or reformatted. In this case, a property with a setter should be used.

If you are writing a behavior to be used multiple times in your codebase (and especially if you're building a framework for others to use), a descriptor is usually a better choice. Anything that you can do with a property can be done with a custom descriptor, but you should prefer properties as they're easier to understand at a glance. If you create a behavior, you should be careful to ensure that it does not stray too far from behavior other developers would expect from Python code.

Generators

Generators are appropriate for cases where you want to provide an infinite (or exceedingly long) stream of values to be looped over. They can be used to reduce memory consumption if the user of the generator does not need to keep a record of all previous values. This strength can also be their biggest drawback: code in a generator function is not guaranteed to execute unless you consume the whole generator.

Do not use generators except for in functions where you need to generate a list of items which would only be read once, where the generation is expected to be slow, and where you're not certain that the caller needs to process all of the items.

Summary

We've done a lot in this chapter: we've created a new package, introduced ORMs and migration frameworks, and peeked behind the curtain at some deep magic the Python interpreter uses to determine what happens when you access an attribute of an object. We also have a working aggregation process that pulls data from each of our sensors and stores them for later use.

In the next chapter, we'll dive even further into complex uses of the `yield` functionality when we look at how asynchronous programming can be achieved in Python and when it's an appropriate solution to problems.

Additional resources

I recommend looking into the following resources to learn more about the techniques we've used during this chapter. As always, feel free to read only those which interest you or are relevant to your work.

Julia Evans's *Become a SELECT star* (paid for, samples available at `https://wizardzines.com/zines/sql/`) is a charming explanation of the details of relational databases in a printable format. If you're new to relational databases, this is a great place to start.

The PostgreSQL documentation on JSON types has details about query behavior for extracting information from within a JSON field. It is at `www.postgresql.org/docs/current/datatype-json.html`.

The blogpost `https://www.citusdata.com/blog/2016/07/14/choosing-nosql-hstore-json-jsonb/` has some good tips on how to choose between the two variants of JSON column in PostgreSQL, as well as the older `hstore` type that I haven't covered in this book.

The Python documentation on descriptors has many examples of how descriptors are used to implement features of the standard library: `https://docs.python.org/3/howto/descriptor.html`.

There is an aggregator of Cookiecutter templates at `http://cookiecutter-templates.sebastianruml.name/`.

CHAPTER 7

Parallelization and async

A common problem that developers find themselves faced with is that they have an operation that spends a lot of time waiting for something to happen, as well as other operations which do not depend on the results of that first operation. It can be frustrating to wait for the slow operation to complete when there are other things the program could be doing. This is the fundamental problem that asynchronous programming tries to solve.

This problem becomes most noticeable during IO operations, such as network requests. In our aggregation process, we have a loop which issues HTTP requests to various endpoints, then processes the results. These HTTP requests can take some time to complete, as they often involve examining external sensors and looking at values over a few seconds. If each request takes 3 seconds to complete, then checking 100 sensors would mean waiting for 5 minutes, on top of all the processing time.

The alternative approach is for us to parallelize some aspects of the program. The most natural functions to parallelize are steps that involve waiting for some external system. If only the three waiting steps in Figure 7-1 could be parallelized, there would be significant time savings, as shown in Figure 7-2.

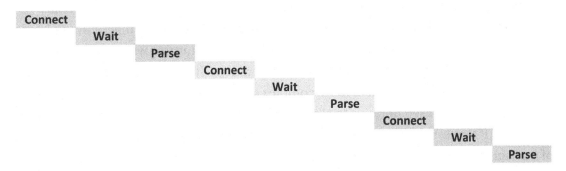

Figure 7-1. *Step-by-step process for connecting to three sensor servers and downloading their data*

© Matthew Wilkes 2020
M. Wilkes, *Advanced Python Development*, https://doi.org/10.1007/978-1-4842-5793-7_7

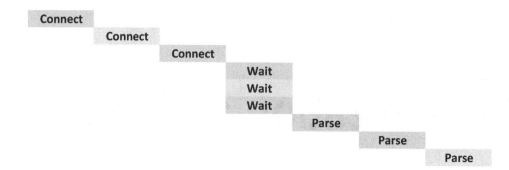

Figure 7-2. *Step-by-step process with parallelized waiting, parsing does not necessarily happen in order*

Of course, computers have practical limits on how many network requests can be outstanding at once. Anyone who has copied files to an external hard drive is familiar with the idea that some storage media are better equipped to process multiple sequential accesses than parallel ones. The best fit for parallel programming is when there is a balance between IO-bound and CPU-bound operations that need to be performed. If there is an emphasis on CPU-bound, the only speed increases possible are by committing more resources. On the other hand, if there is too much IO happening, we may have to limit the number of simultaneous tasks to avoid a backlog of processing tasks building up.

Nonblocking IO

The simplest way to write asynchronous functions in Python, and one that has been possible for a very long time, is to write functions that use nonblocking IO operations. Nonblocking IO operations are variants of the standard IO operations that return as soon as an operation starts, rather than the normal behavior of returning when it completes.

Some libraries may use these for low-level operations, like reading from a socket, but it's rare for them to be used in more complex settings or by most Python developers. There are no widely used libraries to allow developers to take advantage of nonblocking IO for HTTP requests, so I cannot recommend it as a practical solution to the problem of managing simultaneous connections to web servers. Still, it's a technique that was used more in the Python 2 era, and it's interesting to look at as it helps us understand the advantages and disadvantages of more modern solutions.

We'll look at an example implementation here so that we can see the differences in how the code must be structured to take advantage of this. The implementation relies on the `select.select(...)` function of the standard library, which is a wrapper for the `select(2)` system call. When given a list of file-like objects (which includes sockets and subprocess calls), `select` returns the ones that have data ready for reading[1] or blocks until at least one is ready.

`select` represents the key idea of asynchronous code, the idea that we can wait for multiple things in parallel, but with a function that handles blocking until some data is ready. The blocking behavior changes from waiting for each task in turn to waiting for the first of multiple simultaneous requests. It may seem counterintuitive that the key to a nonblocking IO process is a function that blocks, but the intention isn't to remove blocking entirely, it's to move the blocking to when there is nothing else we could be doing.

Blocking is not a bad thing; it's what allows our code to have an easy-to-understand execution flow. If `select(...)` did not block when there were no connections ready, we'd have to introduce a loop to call `select(...)` repeatedly until a connection is ready. Code that blocks immediately is easier to understand, as it never has to handle cases where a variable is a placeholder for a future result that is not yet ready. The select approach sacrifices some of that naïve clarity in our program flow by deferring the blocking until a later point, but it allows us to take advantage of parallelized waiting.

Caution   The following example functions are very optimistic; they are not standards-compliant HTTP functions, and they make many assumptions about how the server behaves. This is intentional; they are here to illustrate an approach, not as a recommendation for code to be used in the real world. It works well enough for instructional and comparison purposes, and that's about it.

An example of a program to make some nonblocking IO HTTP requests is shown as Listing 7-1. The most striking difference between the HTTP handling of our code and this sample is the addition of two additional functions – the ones that perform the HTTP request and response actions. Splitting the logic like this makes this approach unappealing, but it's important to remember that there are equivalents to these functions in the requests package; we're only seeing them here because we're looking at a method for which there is no library to fall back on.

---

[1] It can do other things, like detecting when a file is ready to be written to, but that's not relevant for our needs.

Listing 7-1. Optimistic nonblocking HTTP functions – nbioexample.py

```python
import datetime
import io
import json
import select
import socket
import typing as t
import urllib.parse

import h11

def get_http(uri: str, headers: t.Dict[str, str]) -> socket.socket:
    """Given a URI and a set of headers, make a HTTP request and return the
    underlying socket. If there were a production-quality implementation of
    nonblocking HTTP this function would be replaced with the relevant one
    from that library."""
    parsed = urllib.parse.urlparse(uri)
    if parsed.port:
        port = parsed.port
    else:
        port = 80
    headers["Host"] = parsed.netloc
    sock = socket.socket()
    sock.connect((parsed.hostname, port))
    sock.setblocking(False)

    connection = h11.Connection(h11.CLIENT)
    request = h11.Request(method="GET", target=parsed.path,
    headers=headers.items())

    sock.send(connection.send(request))
    sock.send(connection.send(h11.EndOfMessage()))
    return sock

def read_from_socket(sock: socket.socket) -> str:
    """ If there were a production-quality implementation of nonblocking HTTP
    this function would be replaced with the relevant one to get the body of
```

```
    the response if it was a success or error otherwise. """
    data = sock.recv(1000000)
    connection = h11.Connection(h11.CLIENT)
    connection.receive_data(data)

    response = connection.next_event()
    headers = dict(response.headers)
    body = connection.next_event()
    eom = connection.next_event()

    try:
        if response.status_code == 200:
            return body.data.decode("utf-8")
        else:
            raise ValueError("Bad response")
    finally:
        sock.close()

def show_responses(uris: t.Tuple[str]) -> None:
    sockets = []
    for uri in uris:
        print(f"Making request to {uri}")
        sockets.append(get_http(uri, {}))
    while sockets:
        readable, writable, exceptional = select.select(sockets, [], [])
        print(f"{ len(readable) } socket(s) ready")
        for request in readable:
            print(f"Reading from socket")
            response = read_from_socket(request)
            print(f"Got { len(response) } bytes")
            sockets.remove(request)

if __name__ == "__main__":
    show_responses([
        "http://jsonplaceholder.typicode.com/posts?userId=1",
        "http://jsonplaceholder.typicode.com/posts?userId=5",
        "http://jsonplaceholder.typicode.com/posts?userId=8",
    ])
```

The result of running this file with a Python interpreter would be these three URLs being fetched, then read as their data became available, shown as follows:

```
> pipenv run python .\nbioexample.py
Making request to http://jsonplaceholder.typicode.com/posts?userId=1
Making request to http://jsonplaceholder.typicode.com/posts?userId=5
Making request to http://jsonplaceholder.typicode.com/posts?userId=8
1 socket(s) ready
Reading from socket
Got 27520 bytes
1 socket(s) ready
Reading from socket
Got 3707 bytes
1 socket(s) ready
Reading from socket
Got 2255 bytes
```

The get_http(...) function is what creates the socket. It parses the URL that it has been given and sets up a TCP/IP socket to connect to that server. This does involve some blocking IO, specifically any DNS lookups and socket setup actions, but these are relatively short compared to the time waiting for the body, so I have not attempted to make them nonblocking.

Then, the function sets this socket as *nonblocking* and uses the h11 library to generate a HTTP request. It's entirely possible to generate a HTTP request[2] with string manipulation alone, but this library simplifies our code significantly.

We call the read_from_socket(...) function once there is data available on the socket. It assumes that there are less than 1000000 bytes of data and that represents a complete response,[3] then uses the h11 library to parse this into objects representing the headers and the body of the response. We use that to determine if the request was successful and return either the body of the response or raise a ValueError. The data is decoded as UTF-8 because that's what Flask is generating for us on the other end. It's essential to decode with the correct character set; this can be done by providing a header with the character set defined or by having some other guarantee about what the

---

[2]Assuming you're using HTTP 0.9, 1.0, or 1.1. HTTP 2.0 and higher are binary protocols.

[3]This is a terrible assumption and would cause lots of intermittent bugs. To do this for real, we'd have to build up the response chunk by chunk.

character set is. As we also wrote the server code, we know that we're using Flask's built-in JSON support, which uses Flask's default encoding, which is UTF-8.

Tip   In some situations, you may not know for sure which character encoding is in use. The chardet library analyzes text to suggest the most likely encoding, but this is not foolproof. This library, or fallback like try/except blocks with multiple encodings, is only appropriate when loading data from a source that is not consistent and does not report its encoding. In the majority of cases, you should be able to specify the exact encoding, and you must do this to avoid subtle errors.

Making our code nonblocking

In order to integrate the preceding functions into our codebase, the other functions in our code require some changes, as shown in Listing 7-2. The existing get_data_points(...) function would need to be split into connect_to_server(...) and prepare_datapoints_from_response(...) functions. We thereby expose the socket object to the add_data_from_sensors(...) function, allowing it to use select instead of just looping over each server.

Listing 7-2. Additional glue functions

```python
def connect_to_server(server: str, api_key: t.Optional[str]) ->
socket.socket:
    if not server.endswith("/"):
        server += "/"
    url = server + "v/2.0/sensors/"
    headers = {}
    if api_key:
        headers["X-API-KEY"] = api_key

    return get_http(url, headers=headers)

def prepare_datapoints_from_response(response: str) ->
t.Iterator[DataPoint]:
    now = datetime.datetime.now()
    json_result = json.loads(response)
```

```
    if "sensors" in json_result:
        for value in json_result["sensors"]:
            yield DataPoint(
                sensor_name=value["id"], collected_at=now,
                data=value["value"]
            )
    else:
        raise ValueError(
            f"Error loading data from stream: " + json_result.get("error",
            "Unknown")
        )

def add_data_from_sensors(
    session: Session, servers: t.Tuple[str], api_key: t.Optional[str]
) -> t.Iterable[DataPoint]:
    points: t.List[DataPoint] = []
    sockets = [connect_to_server(server, api_key) for server in servers]
    while sockets:
        readable, writable, exceptional = select.select(sockets, [], [])
        for request in readable:
            # In a production quality implementation there would be
            # handling here for responses that have only partially been
            # received.
            value = read_from_socket(request)
            for point in prepare_datapoints_from_response(value):
                session.add(point)
                points.append(point)
            sockets.remove(request)
    return points
```

It may sound minor, but this is sufficient reason to decide against using this method of making HTTP requests in production code. Without a library to simplify the API here, the cognitive load that is added by using nonblocking sockets is, in my opinion, excessive. The ideal approach would introduce no changes to the program flow, but minimizing the changes helps keep code maintainable. The fact that this implementation leaks the raw sockets into application functions is unacceptable.

Overall, while this approach does reduce waiting time, it requires us to restructure our code significantly, and it only provides savings in the wait step, not in the parsing stage. Nonblocking IO is an interesting technique, but it is only appropriate for exceptional cases and requires significant alterations to program flow as well as abandoning all common libraries to achieve even the most basic outcomes. I don't recommend this approach.

Multithreading and multiprocessing

A much more common approach is to split the workload into multiple threads or processes. Threads allow logical subproblems to be processed at the same time. It's possible whether they are CPU-bound or IO-bound. In this model, it's possible for the parsing of one set of results to happen before the waiting has even started for another, as the entire retrieval process is split into a new thread. Each of the tasks run in parallel, but within a thread everything runs sequentially (as shown in Figure 7-3), with functions blocking as usual.

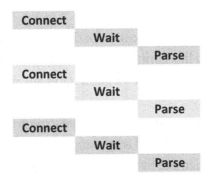

Figure 7-3. *Parallel tasks when using threading or multiple processes*

The code within a thread always executes in order, but when multiple threads are running at once, there is no guarantee that their execution is synchronized in any meaningful way. Even worse than that, there's no guarantee that the execution of code in different threads is aligned to a statement boundary. When two threads access the same variable, there's no guarantee that *either* of the actions are performed first: they can overlap. The internal low-level "bytecode" that Python uses to execute user functions are the building blocks of parallelism in Python, not the statement.

Low-level threads

The lowest-level interface to threads in Python is the threading.Thread object, which effectively wraps a function call into a new thread. A thread's actions can be customized by passing a function as the target= parameter or by subclassing threading.Thread and defining a run() method, as shown in Table 7-1.

Table 7-1. *The two methods of providing the code for a thread to execute*

```
import threading

def helloworld():
    print("Hello world!")

thread = threading.Thread(
    target=helloworld,
    name="helloworld"
)
thread.start()
thread.join()
```

```
import threading

class HelloWorldThread(threading.Thread):
    def run(self):
            print("Hello world!")

thread = HelloWorldThread(name="helloworld")
thread.start()
thread.join()
```

The start() method begins the execution of the thread; the join() method blocks the execution until that thread has completed. The name parameter is mostly useful for debugging performance problems, but it's a good habit always to set a name if you're ever creating threads manually.

Threads do not have a return value, so if they need to return a computed value, that can be tricky. One way of passing a value back is by using a mutable object that it can change in place or, if using the subclass method, by setting an attribute on the thread object.

An attribute on the thread object is a good approach when there is a single, simple return type, such as a boolean success value, or the result of a computation. It's a good fit for when the thread is doing a discrete piece of work.

A mutable object is the best fit when you have multiple threads, each working on a part of a common problem, for example, gathering the sensor data from a set of URLs, with each thread being responsible for one URL. The queue.Queue object is perfect for this purpose.

EXERCISE 7-1: WRITE A WRAPPER TO RETURN VIA A QUEUE

Rather than adjust the function directly, write some code to wrap any arbitrary function and store its results in a queue instead of directly returning, to allow the function to be run cleanly as threads. If you get stuck, look back at Chapter 5 and how to write a decorator that takes arguments.

The function, return_via_queue(...), should be such that the following code works:

```
from __future__ import annotations
...

def add_data_from_sensors(
    session: Session, servers: t.Tuple[str], api_key: t.Optional[str]
) -> t.Iterable[DataPoint]:
    points: t.List[DataPoint] = []
    q: queue.Queue[t.List[DataPoint]] = queue.Queue()
    wrap = return_via_queue(q)
    threads = [
        threading.Thread(target=wrap(get_data_points), args=(server, api_key))
        for server in servers
    ]
    for thread in threads:
        # Start all threads
        thread.start()
    for thread in threads:
        # Wait for all threads to finish
        thread.join()
    while not q.empty():
        # So long as there's a return value in the queue, process one
        # thread's results
        found = q.get_nowait()
        for point in found:
            session.add(point)
            points.append(point)
    return points
```

You must also adjust the get_data_points(...) function to return a list of DataPoint objects, rather than an iterator of them, or to do an equivalent conversion in the wrapper function. This is to ensure that all the data is processed in the thread before it returns its data to the main thread. As generators don't produce their values until the values are requested, we need to ensure that the requesting happens within the thread.

An example implementation of the wrapper method and a simple threaded version of this program is available in the code samples for this chapter.

Note on   future   imports

Statements like from __future__ import example are ways of enabling features that will be part of a future version of Python. They must be at the very top of a Python file, with no other statements before them.

In this case, the line q: queue.Queue[t.List[DataPoint]] = queue.Queue() is the problem. The queue.Queue object in the standard library is not a generic type in Python 3.8, so it cannot accept a type definition of the type of objects it contains. This omission is tracked as bug 33315 in Python, where there is justified reluctance to either add a new typing.Queue type or to adjust the built-in type.

Despite this, mypy treats queue.Queue as a generic type; it's just the Python interpreter that does not. There are two ways of fixing this, either by using a string-based type hint so that the Python interpreter doesn't try to evaluate queue.Queue[...] and fail

```
q: "queue.Queue[t.List[DataPoint]]" = queue.Queue()
```

or by using the annotations option from __future__, which enables the type annotation parsing logic planned for Python 4. This logic prevents Python from parsing annotations at runtime and is the approach taken in the preceding sample.

This low level of threading is not at all user-friendly. As we've seen in the preceding exercise, it is possible to write a wrapper code that makes functions work unchanged in a threaded environment. It would also be possible to write a wrapper for the threading.Thread object that automatically wraps the function being called and automatically retrieves the result from an internal queue and returns it to the programmer seamlessly.

Luckily, we don't have to write such a feature in production code; there's a helper built-in to the Python standard library: concurrent.futures.ThreadPoolExecutor.

The ThreadPoolExecutor manages the number of threads in use, allowing the programmer to limit the number of threads that execute at once.

The equivalent invocation of a single hello world thread using a ThreadPoolExecutor would be

```python
from concurrent.futures import ThreadPoolExecutor

def helloworld():
    print("Hello world!")

with ThreadPoolExecutor() as pool:
    pool.submit(helloworld)
```

Here, we see a context manager that defines the period where the pool of threads is active. As no max_threads argument is passed to the executor, Python picks an amount of threads based on the number of CPUs available on the computer running the program.

Once inside this context manager, the program submits function calls to the thread pool. The pool.submit(...) function can be called any number of times to schedule additional tasks, the result of which is a Future object representing that task. Futures will be very familiar to developers who have worked with modern JavaScript; they are objects that represent a value (or an error) that will be present at some point in the future. The result() method returns whatever value the function that was submitted returned. If that function raised an exception, then the same exception will be raised when the result() method is called.

```python
from concurrent.futures import ThreadPoolExecutor

def calculate():
    return 2**16

with ThreadPoolExecutor() as pool:
    task = pool.submit(calculate)

>>> print(task.result())
65536
```

Caution   If you don't access the result() method of a future, then any exceptions it raises are never propagated to the main thread. This can make debugging difficult, so it's best to ensure you always access the result, even if you never assign it to a variable.

If `result()` is called within the `with` block, execution blocks until the relevant task has completed. When the `with` block ends, execution blocks until *all* scheduled tasks have completed, so calls to the result method after the `with` block ends always return immediately.

Bytecode

In order to understand some of the limits of threading in Python, we need to look behind the curtain of how the interpreter loads and runs code. In this section, Python code may be shown annotated with the underlying bytecode used by the interpreter. This bytecode is an implementation detail and is stored in `.pyc` files. It encodes the behavior of the program at the lowest level. Interpreting a complex language like Python is not a trivial task, so the Python interpreter caches its interpretation of code as a series of many simple operations.

When people talk about Python, they generally are talking about CPython, the implementation of Python in the C programming language. CPython is the *reference* implementation, in that it's intended to be what people refer to when seeing how Python does things. There are other implementations, the most popular of which is PyPy, an implementation of Python that is written in a specially designed, Python-like language rather than C.[4] Both CPython and PyPy cache their interpretation of Python code as Python bytecode.

Two other implementations of Python are worth mentioning: Jython and IronPython. Both of these also cache their interpretation as bytecode, but crucially they use a different bytecode. Jython uses the same bytecode format as Java, and IronPython uses the same bytecode format as .NET. For this chapter, when we talk about bytecode, we're talking about Python bytecode, as we're looking at it in the context of how threads are implemented in CPython.

Generally speaking, you won't have to worry about bytecode, but an awareness of its role is useful for writing multithreaded code. The samples given in the following were generated using the `dis` module[5] in the standard library. The function `dis.dis(func)`

---

[4]One reason to use PyPy is that it has a JIT compiler, making some code run faster. Compatibility with CPython isn't 100%, mainly due to how compiled extensions are handled, but the performance of your programs may be very different under PyPy. It might be worth trying it, to see if your programs work, and if they're faster or slower.

[5]Short for disassemble.

shows the bytecode for a given function, assuming that it's written in Python, rather than a C extension. For example, the sorted(...) function is implemented in C and therefore has no bytecode to show.

To demonstrate this, let's look at a function with its disassembly (Listing 7-3). The function has been annotated with the disassembly results from dis.dis(increment), which shows the line number within the file, the bytecode offset of the instruction within the function, the instruction name, and any instruction parameters as their raw values with the Python representation in parentheses.

Listing 7-3. A simple function to increment a global variable

```
num = 0

def increment():
    global num
    num += 1            # 5  0    LOAD_GLOBAL              0 (num)
                        #     2    LOAD_CONST               1 (1)
                        #     4    INPLACE_ADD
                        #     6    STORE_GLOBAL             0 (num)

    return None         # 10 8    LOAD_CONST               0 (None)
                        #    10    RETURN_VALUE
```

The line num += 1 looks like an atomic operation,[6] but the bytecode reveals that the underlying interpreter runs four operations to complete it. We don't care what these four instructions are, just the fact that we cannot trust our intuition on what operations are atomic and which are not.

If we were to run this increment function 100 times in succession, the result stored to num would be 100, which makes logical sense. If this function were to be executed in a pair of threads, there would be no guarantee that the final result would be 100. In this case, the correct result is only found so long as no thread ever executes the LOAD_GLOBAL bytecode step while another is running the LOAD_CONST, IN_PLACE_ADD, or STORE_GLOBAL steps. Python does not guarantee this, so the preceding code is not *thread-safe*.

---

[6]An operation that is done in one step that cannot be split up.

There is overhead to starting a thread, and the computer will be running multiple processes at the same time. The two threads could happen to run sequentially, despite having two threads available, or they could both start at the same time, or there could be an offset between the start times. The way the executions can overlap is represented in Figure 7-4.

Figure 7-4.   *Possible arrangements of two threads executing num += 1 at once. Only the leftmost and rightmost examples produce the correct result*

The GIL

That is somewhat simplified, however. CPython has a feature called the GIL, or Global Interpreter Lock, which is used to make thread-safety easier.[7] This lock means that only one thread can be executing Python code at once. That's not enough to solve our problem, however, because the granularity of the GIL is at the level of bytecode, so although no two bytecode instructions execute simultaneously, the interpreter can still switch between each path, causing overlap. As such, Figure 7-5 shows a more accurate representation of how the threads can overlap.

---

[7]Some implementations of Python, especially those that run on an underlying virtual machine like Jython, do not implement the GIL as the VM offers the same guarantee. The overall effect is the same, but the specific details of bytecode and switching are different.

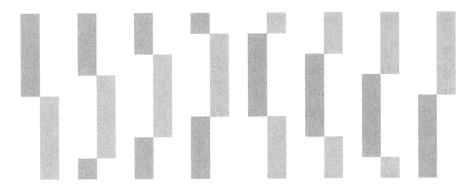

Figure 7-5. *Possible arrangements of num += 1 execution with the GIL active. Only the leftmost and rightmost produce the correct result*

It might appear that the GIL removes the benefit of threading without guaranteeing the correct result, but it's not as bad as it immediately appears. We will deal with the benefits of this shortly, but first, we should address this negating the advantages of threading. It's not strictly true that no two bytecode instructions can run at once.

Bytecode instructions are much simpler than lines of Python, allowing the interpreter to reason about what actions it is taking at any given point. It can, therefore, allow multiple threads to execute when it's safe to do so, such as during a network connection or when waiting for data to be read from a file.

Specifically, not everything the Python interpreter does requires the GIL to be held. It must be held at the start and end of a bytecode instruction, but it can be released internally. Waiting for a socket to have data available for reading is one of the things that can be done without holding the GIL. During a bytecode instruction where an IO operation is happening, the GIL can be released, and the interpreter can simultaneously execute any code that does not require the GIL to be held, so long as it's in a different thread. Once the IO operation finishes, it must wait to regain the GIL from whichever thread took it, before execution can continue.

In situations like this, where the code never has to wait for an IO function to complete, Python interrupts the threads at set intervals to schedule the others fairly. By default, this is approximately every 0.005 seconds which happens to be a long enough period that our example works as hoped on my computer. If we manually tell the interpreter to switch threads more frequently, using the `sys.setswitchinterval(...)` function, we start to see failures.

Code for testing thread-safety at different switch intervals

```
if __name__ == "__main__":
    import concurrent.futures
    import sys
    for si in [0.005, 0.0000005, 0.0000000005]:
        sys.setswitchinterval(si)
        results = []
        for attempt in range(100):
            with concurrent.futures.ThreadPoolExecutor(max_workers=2) as pool:
                for i in range(100):
                    pool.submit(increment)
            results.append(num)
            num = 0
        correct = [a for a in results if a == 100]
        pct = len(correct) / len(results)
        print(f"{pct:.1%} correct at sys.setswitchinterval({si:.10f})")
```

On my computer, the result of running this is

```
100.0% correct at sys.setswitchinterval(0.0050000000)
71.0% correct at sys.setswitchinterval(0.0000005000)
84.0% correct at sys.setswitchinterval(0.0000000005)
```

The default behavior being 100% correct in my test doesn't mean that it solves the problem. 0.005 is a well-chosen interval that results in a lower chance of errors for most people. The fact that a function happens to work when you test it does not mean that it's guaranteed to always work on every machine. The trade-off to introducing threads is that you gain relatively simple concurrency but without strong guarantees about shared state.

Locks and deadlocks

By enforcing a rule that bytecode instructions do not overlap, they're guaranteed to be atomic. There is no risk of two STORE bytecode instructions for the same value happening simultaneously, as no two bytecode instructions can run truly simultaneously. It may be that the implementation of an instruction voluntarily releases the GIL and waits to reobtain it for sections of its implementation, but that is not the same as any two arbitrary instructions happening in parallel. This atomicity is used by Python to build thread-safe types and synchronization tools.

If you need to share state between threads, you must manually protect this state with locks. Locks are objects that allow you to prevent your code from running at the same time as other code that it would interfere with. If two concurrent threads both try to acquire the lock, only one will succeed. Any other threads that try to acquire the lock will be blocked until the first thread has released it. This is possible because the locks are implemented in C code, meaning their execution takes place as one bytecode step. All the work of waiting for a lock to become available and acquiring it is performed in response to a single bytecode instruction, making it atomic.

Code protected by a lock can still be interrupted, but no conflicting code will be run during these interruptions. Threads can still be interrupted while they hold a lock. If the thread that they are interrupted in favor of attempts to take that same lock, it will fail to do so and will pause execution. In an environment with two threads, this means execution would pass straight back to the first function. If more than one thread is active, it may pass to other threads first, but the same inability to take the first thread's lock applies.

Increment function with locking

```
import threading

numlock = threading.Lock()
num = 0

def increment():
    global num
    with numlock:
        num += 1
    return None
```

In this version of the function, the lock called numlock is used to guard the actions that read/write the num value. This context manager causes the lock to be acquired before execution passes to the body and to be released before the first line after the body. Although we've added some overhead here, it is minimal, and it guarantees that the result of the code is correct, regardless of any user settings or different Python interpreter versions.

Result of testing with a lock surrounding num += 1

```
100.0% correct at sys.setswitchinterval(0.0050000000)
100.0% correct at sys.setswitchinterval(0.0000005000)
100.0% correct at sys.setswitchinterval(0.0000000005)
```

This code results in the correct result being found no matter what the switching interval is, as the four bytecode instructions that make up num += 1 are guaranteed to be executed as one block. There is an additional locking bytecode instruction before and after each block of four, as shown in Figure 7-6.

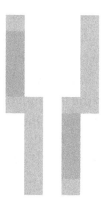

Figure 7-6. *Possible arrangements of num += 1 on two threads with explicit locking shown at the start and end*

From the perspective of the two threads being used in the thread pool, the with numlock: line may block execution, or it may not. Neither thread needs to do anything special to handle the two cases (acquiring the lock immediately or waiting for a turn), and therefore this is a relatively minimal change to the control flow.

The difficulty comes in ensuring that required locks are in place and that no contradictions exist. If a programmer defines two locks and uses them simultaneously, it's possible to create a situation where the program becomes *deadlocked*.

Deadlocks

Consider a situation where we are incrementing two numbers in one thread and decrementing them in another, resulting in the following functions:

```
num = 0
other = 0

def increment():
    global num
    global other
    num += 1
    other += 1
    return None

def decrement():
    global num
    global other
    other -= 1
    num -= 1
    return None
```

The program suffers from the same problem that we had previously; if we schedule these functions in a ThreadPoolExecutor, then the result may be incorrect. We might think to apply the same locking pattern that fixed this previously, adding an otherlock lock to complement the numlock lock that we already created, but the potential for deadlocks lurks in this code. There are three ways we could arrange the locks in these functions (shown in Table 7-2), one of which can cause deadlocks.

Table 7-2. *Three locking approaches for simultaneously updating two variables*

Minimizing locked code(resistant to deadlocks)	Using locks in a consistent order (resistant to deadlocks)	Using locks in an inconsistent order (**causes deadlocks**)
| ```
num = 0
other = 0

numlock = \
threading.Lock()
otherlock = \
threading.Lock()

def increment():
    global num
    global other
    with numlock:
        num += 1
    with otherlock:
        other += 1
    return None

def decrement():
    global num
    global other
    with otherlock:
        other -= 1
    with numlock:
        num -= 1
    return None
``` | ```
num = 0
other = 0

numlock = threading.Lock()
otherlock = \
threading.Lock()

def increment():
    global num
    global other
    with numlock, otherlock:
        num += 1
        cother += 1
    return None

def decrement():
    global num
    global other
    with numlock, otherlock:
        other -= 1
        num -= 1
    return None
``` | ```
num = 0
other = 0

numlock = \
threading.Lock()
otherlock = \
threading.Lock()

def increment():
    global num
    global other
    with numlock, otherlock:
        num += 1
        other += 1
    return None

def decrement():
    global num
    global other
    with otherlock, numlock:
        other -= 1
        num -= 1
    return None
``` |

The best option is to ensure that we never hold both locks simultaneously. This makes them truly independent, so there is no risk of deadlock. In this pattern, threads never wait to acquire a lock until they've already released the previous lock they held.

The middle implementation uses both locks at once. This is less good, as it's holding locks for longer than they are needed, but sometimes it's unavoidable for code to need to lock two variables. Although both of the preceding functions can be written to use only one lock at a time, consider the case of a function that exchanges the values:
```

```
def switch():
    global num
    global other
    with numlock, otherlock:
        num, other = other, num
    return None
```

This function requires that neither num nor other is being used by another thread while it's executing, so it needs to keep both numbers locked. Locks are acquired in the same order in the increment() and decrement() (and switch()) functions, so each one tries to acquire numlock before otherlock. If both threads were synchronized in their execution, they would both try to acquire numlock at the same time and one would block. No deadlocks would occur.

The final example shows an implementation where the ordering of the locks in the decrement() function has been inverted. This is very difficult indeed to notice but has the effect of causing deadlocks. It's possible for a thread running this third version of increment() to acquire the numlock lock at the same time that a thread running decrement acquires the otherlock lock. Now both threads are waiting to acquire the lock they don't have, and neither can release their lock until after they've acquired the missing one. **This causes the program to hang indefinitely.**

There are a few ways to avoid this problem. As this is a logical assertion about the structure of your code, the natural tool would be to a static checker to ensure that your code never inverts the order in which locks are acquired. Unfortunately, I do not know of any existing implementation of this check for Python code.

The most straightforward alternative is to use a single lock to cover both variables rather than to lock them individually. Although this is superficially attractive, it does not scale well as the number of objects that need protecting grows. A single lock object would prevent any work being done to the num variable while another thread works on the other variable. Sharing locks across independent functions greatly increases the amount of blocking involved in your code, which can serve to negate the advantages brought by threading.

You might be tempted to abandon the with numlock: method of acquiring a lock and calling the lock's acquire() method directly. While this allows you to specify a timeout and an error handler in case the lock was not acquired within the timeout, I would not recommend it. The change makes the code's logic harder to follow with the introduction of an error handler, and the only appropriate response to detecting a deadlock in this manner is to raise an exception. This slows down the program because of the timeouts and doesn't solve the problem. This approach may be useful when debugging locally, to allow you to examine the state during a deadlock, but it should not be considered for production code.

My recommendation would be that you should use all these approaches to preventing deadlocks. Firstly, you should use the minimum amount of locks necessary to make your program thread-safe. If you do need multiple locks, you should minimize the time that they're held for, releasing them as soon as the shared state has been manipulated. Finally, you should define an ordering of your locks and always use this ordering when acquiring locks. The easiest method to do this is always to acquire locks alphabetically. Ensuring a fixed ordering of locks still requires manual checking of your code, but each use of locks can be checked against your rule independently rather than against all other uses.

Avoiding global state

It's not always possible to avoid global state, but in many situations, it is. Generally speaking, it's possible to schedule two functions to run in parallel if neither function depends on the values of shared variables.[8] Imagine that instead of 100 calls to `increment()` and 100 calls to `decrement()`, we were scheduling 100 calls to `increment()` and 1 to a function called `save_number_to_database()`. There is no guarantee how many times `increment()` will have completed before `save_number_to_database()` is called. The number saved could be anywhere between 0 and 100, which is clearly not useful. These functions don't make sense to be run in parallel because they both depend on the value of a shared variable.

There are a couple of main ways that shared data can interrelate. Shared data can be used to collate data across multiple threads, or it can be used to pass data between multiple threads.

Collating data

Our two `increment()` and `decrement()` functions are only simple demonstrations. They manipulate their shared state by adding or subtracting one, but normally functions run in parallel would do a more complex manipulation. For example, in `apd.aggregation`, the shared state is the set of sensor results we have, and each thread adds more results to that set.

---

[8]Except for variable types that are designed for thread-safety, such as queues.

With both of these examples, we can split the work of deciding what the manipulation should be and applying the manipulation. As it's only the stage where we apply the manipulation that requires access to shared state, this allows us to do any calculations or IO operations in parallel. Each thread would then return the result and then merge the results together at the end, as shown in Listing 7-4.

Listing 7-4. Example of using task result to store intended changes

```
import concurrent.futures
import threading

def increment():
    return 1

def decrement():
    return -1

def onehundred():
    tasks = []
    with concurrent.futures.ThreadPoolExecutor() as pool:
        for i in range(100):
            tasks.append(pool.submit(increment))
            tasks.append(pool.submit(decrement))
    number = 0
    for task in tasks:
        number += task.result()
    return number

if __name__ == "__main__":
    print(onehundred())
```

Passing data

The examples we've covered so far all involve the main thread delegating work to subthreads, but it's common for new tasks to be discovered during the processing of the data from earlier tasks. For example, most APIs paginate data, so if we had a thread to fetch URLs and a thread to parse the responses, we need to be able to pass initial URLs to the fetch thread from the main thread and also to pass newly discovered URLs from the parse thread to the fetch thread.

When passing data between two (or more) threads, we need to use queues, either `queue.Queue` or the variant `queue.LifoQueue`. These implement FIFO and LIFO[9] queues, respectively. While we previously used `Queue` only as a convenient, thread-safe data holder, now we'll be using it as intended.

Queues have four primary methods.[10] The `get()` and `put()` methods are self-explanatory, except to say that if the queue is empty, then the `get()` method blocks, and if the queue has a maximum length set and is full, then the `put()` method blocks. In addition, there is a `task_done()` method, which is used to tell the queue that an item has been successfully processed, and a `join()` method, which blocks until all items have been successfully processed. The `join()` method is usually called by the thread that adds the items to the queue, to allow it to wait until all work has been completed.

Because the `get()` method blocks if the queue is currently empty, it's not possible to use this method in nonthreaded code. It does, however, make them perfect for threaded code where there is a need to wait until the thread producing data has made it available.

Tip   It's not always clear in advance how many items will be stored in a queue. If `get()` is called after the last item has been retrieved, then it will block indefinitely. This can be avoided by providing a timeout parameter to get, in which case it will block for the given amount of seconds before raising a `queue.Empty` exception. A better approach is to send a sentinel value, like None. The code can then detect this value and know that it no longer needs to retrieve new values.

If we were building a threaded program to get information from the GitHub public API, we'd need to be able to retrieve URLs and parse their results. It would be nice to be able to do parsing while URLs are being fetched, so we would split the code between fetching and parsing functions.

Listing 7-5 shows an example of such a program, where multiple GitHub repos can have their commits retrieved in parallel. It uses three queues, one for the input to the fetch thread, one for the output of fetch and input of parse, and one for the output of parse.

---

[9]*Last In, First Out* and *First In, First Out*.

[10]They also have some methods for introspecting the state of the queue, such as `empty()`, `full()`, and `qsize()`. It's possible that the underlying queue will change between checking the state and the next instruction, though. These methods are only really useful when you have additional guarantees about the state of the program, so you know the queue won't be changing.

Listing 7-5. Threaded API client

```python
from concurrent.futures import ThreadPoolExecutor
import queue
import requests
import textwrap

def print_column(text, column):
    wrapped = textwrap.fill(text, 45)
    indent_level = 50 * column
    indented = textwrap.indent(wrapped, " " * indent_level)
    print(indented)

def fetch(urls, responses, parsed):
    while True:
        url = urls.get()
        if url is None:
            print_column("Got instruction to finish", 0)
            return
        print_column(f"Getting {url}", 0)
        response = requests.get(url)
        print_column(f"Storing {response} from {url}", 0)
        responses.put(response)
        urls.task_done()

def parse(urls, responses, parsed):
    # Wait for the initial URLs to be processed
    print_column("Waiting for url fetch thread", 1)
    urls.join()

    while not responses.empty():
        response = responses.get()
        print_column(f"Starting processing of {response}", 1)

        if response.ok:
            data = response.json()
            for commit in data:
                parsed.put(commit)
```

```python
            links = response.headers["link"].split(",")
            for link in links:
                if "next" in link:
                    url = link.split(";")[0].strip("<>")
                    print_column(f"Discovered new url: {url}", 1)
                    urls.put(url)

        responses.task_done()
        if responses.empty():
            # We have no responses left, so the loop will
            # end. Wait for all queued urls to be fetched
            # before continuing
            print_column("Waiting for url fetch thread", 1)
            urls.join()

    # We reach this point if there are no responses to process
    # after waiting for the fetch thread to catch up. Tell the
    # fetch thread that it can stop now, then exit this thread.
    print_column("Sending instruction to finish", 1)
    urls.put(None)

def get_commit_info(repos):
    urls = queue.Queue()
    responses = queue.Queue()
    parsed = queue.Queue()

    for (username, repo) in repos:
        urls.put(f"https://api.github.com/repos/{username}/{repo}/commits")

    with ThreadPoolExecutor() as pool:
        fetcher = pool.submit(fetch, urls, responses, parsed)
        parser = pool.submit(parse, urls, responses, parsed)
    print(f"{parsed.qsize()} commits found")

if __name__ == "__main__":
    get_commit_info(
        [("MatthewWilkes", "apd.sensors"), ("MatthewWilkes", "apd.aggregation")]
    )
```

Running this code results in a two-column output, consisting of the messages from each thread. The full output is too long to include here, but a small section is given in the following as a demonstration:

```
Getting https://api.github.com/repos/MatthewW
ilkes/apd.aggregation/commits
Storing <Response [200]> from https://api.git
hub.com/repos/MatthewWilkes/apd.aggregation/c
ommits
                                        Starting processing of
                                        <Response [200]>
                                        Discovered new url:
                                        https://api.github.com/
                                        repositories/188280485/
                                        commits?page=2
                                        Starting processing of
                                        <Response [200]>
Getting https://api.github.com/repositories/1
88280485/commits?page=2
                                        Discovered new url:
                                        https://api.github.com/
                                        repositories/222268232/
                                        commits?page=2
```

By examining the logged messages from each of the threads, we can view how their work is scheduled in parallel. Firstly, the main thread sets up the necessary queues and subthreads, then waits for all the threads to finish. As soon as the two subthreads start, the fetch thread starts working on the URLs passed by the main thread, and the parse thread quickly pauses while waiting for responses to parse.

The parse thread uses urls.join() when there is no work for it, so whenever it runs out of work, it waits until the fetch thread has caught up with all the work that it was sent. This is visible in Figure 7-7, as the parse lines always resume after the fetch lines are complete.

The fetch thread doesn't use the join() method of any of the queues, it uses get() to block until there is some work to do. As such, the fetch thread can be seen resuming while the parse thread is still executing. Finally, the parse thread sends a sentinel value to the fetch thread to end, and when both exits the thread pool context manager in the main thread exits and execution returns to the main thread.

311

Main thread

Fetch

Parse

Figure 7-7. *Diagram of the timing of the three threads in Listing 7-5*

Other synchronization primitives

The synchronization we used with queues in the preceding example is more complex than the lock behavior we used earlier. In fact, there are a variety of other synchronization primitives available in the standard library. These allow you to build more complex thread-safe coordination behaviors.

Reentrant locks

The Lock object is very handy, but it's not the only system used for synchronizing code across threads. Perhaps the most important of the others is the reentrant lock, which is available as threading.RLock. A reentrant lock is one that can be acquired more than once, so long as the acquisitions are nested.

Listing 7-6. An example of nested locking using RLocks

```
from concurrent.futures import ThreadPoolExecutor
import threading

num = 0

numlock = threading.RLock()

def fiddle_with_num():
    global num
    with numlock:
        if num == 4:
            num = -50

def increment():
    global num
    with numlock:
        num += 1
        fiddle_with_num()
```

```
if __name__ == "__main__":
    with ThreadPoolExecutor() as pool:
        for i in range(8):
            pool.submit(increment)
    print(num)
```

The advantage conferred here is that functions that depend on a lock being held can call others that also depend on the same lock being held, without the second blocking until the first releases it. That greatly simplifies creating APIs that use locks.

Example output from Listing 7-6

```
> python .\listing7-06-reentrantlocks.py
-46
```

Conditions

Unlike the locks that we've used so far, conditions declare that a variable is ready, not that it is busy. Queues use conditions internally to implement the blocking behavior of get(), put(...), and join(). Conditions allow for more complex behaviors than a lock being acquired.

Conditions are a way of telling other threads that it's time to check for data, which must be stored independently. Threads that are waiting for data call the condition's wait_for(...) function inside a context manager, whereas threads that are supplying data call the notify() method. There is no rule that a thread can't do both at different times; however, if all threads are waiting for data and none are sending, it's possible to introduce a deadlock.

For example, when calling the get(...) method of a queue, the code immediately acquires the queue's single lock through its internal not_empty condition, then checks to see if the internal storage of the queue has any data available. If it does, then an item is returned and the lock is released. Keeping the lock for this time ensures that no other users can retrieve that item at the same time, so there is no risk of duplication. If, however, there is no data in the internal storage, then the not_empty.wait() method is called. This releases the single lock, allowing other threads to manipulate the queue, and does not reacquire the lock and return until the condition is *notified* that a new item has been added.

There is a variant of the notify() method called notify_all(). The standard notify() method only wakes one thread that's waiting on the condition, whereas notify_all() wakes all threads waiting. It's always safe to use notify_all() in place of notify(), but notify() saves waking up multiple threads when it's expected that only one will be unblocked.

A condition alone is only enough to send a single bit of information: that data has been made available. To actually retrieve the data, we must store it in some fashion, like the internal storage of the queue.

The example in Listing 7-7 creates two threads, each pulling a number from a shared data list and then pushing the number modulo 2 to a shared results list. The code uses two conditions to achieve this, one to ensure there is data available to be processed and one to determine when the threads should be shut down.

Listing 7-7. An example program using conditions

```
from concurrent.futures import ThreadPoolExecutor
import sys
import time
import threading

data = []
results = []
running = True
data_available = threading.Condition()
work_complete = threading.Condition()

def has_data():
    """ Return true if there is data in the data list """
    return bool(data)

def num_complete(n):
    """"Return a function that checks if the results list has the length
    specified by n"""

    def finished():
        return len(results) >= n

    return finished
```

```python
def calculate():
    while running:
        with data_available:
            # Acquire the data_available lock and wait for has_data
            print("Waiting for data")
            data_available.wait_for(has_data)
            time.sleep(1)
            i = data.pop()
        with work_complete:
            if i % 2:
                results.append(1)
            else:
                results.append(0)
            # Acquire the work_complete lock and wake listeners
            work_complete.notify_all()

if __name__ == "__main__":
    with ThreadPoolExecutor() as pool:
        # Schedule two worker functions
        workers = [pool.submit(calculate), pool.submit(calculate)]

        for i in range(200):
            with data_available:
                data.append(i)
                # After adding each piece of data wake the data_available lock
                data_available.notify()
        print("200 items submitted")

        with work_complete:
            # Wait for at least 5 items to be complete through the
            # work_complete lock
            work_complete.wait_for(num_complete(5))

        for worker in workers:
            # Set a shared variable causing the threads to end their work
            running = False
        print("Stopping workers")

    print(f"{len(results)} items processed")
```

Example output from Listing 7-7

```
> python .\listing7-07-conditions.py
Waiting for data
Waiting for data
200 items submitted
Waiting for data
Waiting for data
Waiting for data
Stopping workers
Waiting for data
Waiting for data
7 items processed
```

Barriers

Barriers are the most conceptually simple synchronization objects in Python. A barrier is created with a known number of *parties*. When a thread calls `wait()`, it blocks until there are the same number of threads waiting as the number of parties to the barrier. That is, `threading.Barrier(2)` blocks the first time `wait()` is called, but the second call returns immediately and releases the first blocking call.

Barriers are useful when multiple threads are working on aspects of a single problem, as they can prevent a backlog of work building up. A barrier allows you to ensure that a group of threads only run as quickly as the slowest member of the group.

A timeout can be included in the initial creation of the barrier or any `wait()` call. If any wait call takes longer than its timeout, then all waiting threads raise a `BrokenBarrierException`, as will any subsequent threads that try to wait for that barrier.

The example in Listing 7-8 demonstrates synchronizing a group of five threads that each wait a random amount of time so that they all continue execution once the last is ready.

Listing 7-8. Example of using a barrier

```
from concurrent.futures import ThreadPoolExecutor
import random
import time
import threading
```

```
barrier = threading.Barrier(5)

def wait_random():
    thread_id = threading.get_ident()
    to_wait = random.randint(1, 10)
    print(f"Thread {thread_id:5d}: Waiting {to_wait:2d} seconds")
    start_time = time.time()
    time.sleep(to_wait)
    i = barrier.wait()
    end_time = time.time()
    elapsed = end_time - start_time
    print(
        f"Thread {thread_id:5d}: Resumed in position {i} after "
        f"{elapsed:3.3f} seconds"
    )

if __name__ == "__main__":
    with ThreadPoolExecutor() as pool:
        # Schedule two worker functions
        for i in range(5):
            pool.submit(wait_random)
```

Example output from Listing 7-8

```
> python .\listing7-08-barriers.py
Thread 21812: Waiting  8 seconds
Thread 17744: Waiting  2 seconds
Thread 13064: Waiting  4 seconds
Thread 14064: Waiting  6 seconds
Thread 22444: Waiting  4 seconds
Thread 21812: Resumed in position 4 after 8.008 seconds
Thread 17744: Resumed in position 0 after 8.006 seconds
Thread 22444: Resumed in position 2 after 7.999 seconds
Thread 13064: Resumed in position 1 after 8.000 seconds
Thread 14064: Resumed in position 3 after 7.999 seconds
```

Event

Events are another simple synchronization method. Any number of threads can call the `wait()` method on an event, which blocks until the event is triggered. An event can be triggered at any time by calling the `set()` method, which wakes all threads waiting for the event. Any subsequent calls to the `wait()` method return immediately.

As with barriers, events are very useful for ensuring that multiple threads stay synchronized, rather than some racing ahead. Events differ in that they have a single thread that makes the decision for when the group can continue, so they are a good fit for programs where a thread is dedicated to managing the others.

The event method can also be reset using the `clear()` method, so any more future calls to `wait()` will block. An event's current state can be examined with the `is_set()` method. The example in Listing 7-9 uses an event to synchronize a group of threads with one master thread, such that they all wait at least as long as the master, but no longer.

Listing 7-9. Example of using events to set a minimum wait time

```
from concurrent.futures import ThreadPoolExecutor
import random
import time
import threading

event = threading.Event()

def wait_random(master):
    thread_id = threading.get_ident()
    to_wait = random.randint(1, 10)
    print(f"Thread {thread_id:5d}: Waiting {to_wait:2d} seconds "
    f"(Master: {master})")
    start_time = time.time()
    time.sleep(to_wait)
    if master:
        event.set()
    else:
        event.wait()
    end_time = time.time()
    elapsed = end_time - start_time
```

```
    print(
        f"Thread {thread_id:5d}: Resumed after {elapsed:3.3f} seconds"
    )

if __name__ == "__main__":
    with ThreadPoolExecutor() as pool:
        # Schedule two worker functions
        for i in range(4):
            pool.submit(wait_random, False)
        pool.submit(wait_random, True)
```

Example console output of Listing 7-9

```
> python .\listing7-09-events.py
Thread 19624: Waiting  9 seconds (Master: False)
Thread  1036: Waiting  1 seconds (Master: False)
Thread  6372: Waiting 10 seconds (Master: False)
Thread 16992: Waiting  1 seconds (Master: False)
Thread 22100: Waiting  6 seconds (Master: True)
Thread 22100: Resumed after 6.003 seconds
Thread 16992: Resumed after 6.005 seconds
Thread  1036: Resumed after 6.013 seconds     '
Thread 19624: Resumed after 9.002 seconds
Thread  6372: Resumed after 10.012 seconds
```

Semaphore

Finally, semaphores are conceptually more complex but are a very old concept and so are common to many languages. A semaphore is similar to a lock, but it can be acquired by multiple threads simultaneously. When a semaphore is created, it must be given a value. The value is the number of times that it can be acquired simultaneously.

Semaphores are very useful for ensuring that operations that rely on a scarce resource (such as ones that use a lot of memory or open network connections) are not run in parallel above a certain threshold. For example, Listing 7-10 demonstrates five threads that wait a random amount of time, but where only three can wait at one time.

Listing 7-10. Example of using semaphores to ensure only one thread waits at once

```python
from concurrent.futures import ThreadPoolExecutor
import random
import time
import threading

semaphore = threading.Semaphore(3)

def wait_random():
    thread_id = threading.get_ident()
    to_wait = random.randint(1, 10)
    with semaphore:
        print(f"Thread {thread_id:5d}: Waiting {to_wait:2d} seconds")
        start_time = time.time()
        time.sleep(to_wait)

        end_time = time.time()
        elapsed = end_time - start_time
        print(
            f"Thread {thread_id:5d}: Resumed after {elapsed:3.3f} seconds"
        )

if __name__ == "__main__":
    with ThreadPoolExecutor() as pool:
        # Schedule two worker functions
        for i in range(5):
            pool.submit(wait_random)
```

Example console output of Listing 7-10

```
> python .\listing7-10-semaphore.py
Thread 10000: Waiting 10 seconds
Thread 24556: Waiting  1 seconds
Thread 15032: Waiting  6 seconds
Thread 24556: Resumed after 1.019 seconds
Thread 11352: Waiting  8 seconds
Thread 15032: Resumed after 6.001 seconds
```

```
Thread  6268: Waiting  4 seconds
Thread 11352: Resumed after 8.001 seconds
Thread 10000: Resumed after 10.014 seconds
Thread  6268: Resumed after 4.015 seconds
```

ProcessPoolExecutors

Just as we've looked at the use of ThreadPoolExecutor to delegate the execution of code to different threads, which causes us to fall foul of the GIL's restrictions, we can use the ProcessPoolExecutor to run code in multiple processes if we're willing to abandon all shared state.

When executing code in a process pool, any state that was available at the start is available to the subprocesses. However, there is no coordination between the two. Data can only be passed back to the controlling process as the return value of the tasks submitted to the pool. No changes to global variables are reflected in any way.

Although multiple independent Python processes are not bound by the same one-at-a-time execution method imposed by the GIL, they also have significant overheads. For IO-bound tasks (i.e., tasks that spend most of their time waiting and therefore not holding the GIL), a process pool is generally slower than a thread pool.

On the other hand, tasks that involve large amounts of computation are well suited to being delegated to a subprocess, especially long-running ones where the overhead of the setup is lessened compared to the savings of parallel execution.

Making our code multithreaded

The function that we want to parallelize is get_data_points(...); the functions that implement the command line and database connections do not significantly change when dealing with 1 or 500 sensors; there is no particular reason to split its work out into threads. Keeping this work in the main thread makes it easier to handle errors and report on progress, so we rewrite the add_data_from_sensors(...) function only.

Implementation of add_data_from_sensors that uses ThreadPoolExecutor

```python
def add_data_from_sensors(
    session: Session, servers: t.Tuple[str], api_key: t.Optional[str]
) -> t.List[DataPoint]:
    threads: t.List[Future] = []
```

```
    points: t.List[DataPoint] = []
    with ThreadPoolExecutor() as pool:
        for server in servers:
            points_future = pool.submit(get_data_points, server, api_key)
            threads.append(points_future)
        for points_future in threads:
            points += handle_result(points_future, session)
    return points

def handle_result(execution: Future, session: Session) ->
t.List[DataPoint]:
    points: t.List[DataPoint] = []
    result = execution.result()
    for point in result:
        session.add(point)
        points.append(point)
    return points
```

As we will submit all our jobs to the ThreadPoolExecutor before the first time that we call a result() method, they will all be queued up for simultaneous execution in threads. It's the result() method and the end of the with block that triggers blocking; submitting jobs does not cause the program to block, even if you submit more jobs than can be processed simultaneously.

This method is much less intrusive to the program flow than either the raw threaded approach or the nonblocking IO approaches, but it does still involve changing the execution flow to handle the fact that these functions are now working with Future objects rather than the data directly.

AsyncIO

AsyncIO is the elephant in the room when talking about Python concurrency, thanks mainly to the fact that it's one of the flagship features of Python 3. It is a language feature that allows for something that works like the nonblocking IO example but with a somewhat similar API to the ThreadPoolExecutor. The API isn't precisely the same, but the underlying concept of submitting tasks and being able to block to wait for their results is shared between the two.

Asyncio code is cooperatively multitasked. That is, code is never interrupted to allow another function to execute; the switching only occurs when a function blocks. This change makes it easier to reason about how code will behave, as there's no chance of a simple statement like `num += 1` being interrupted.

There are two new keywords that you often see when working with asyncio, the `async` and `await` keywords. The `async` keyword marks certain control flow blocks (specifically, `def`, `for`, and `with`) as using the asyncio flow, rather than the standard flow. The meanings of these blocks are still the same as in standard, synchronous Python, but the underlying code paths can be quite different.

The equivalent of the `ThreadPoolExecutor` itself is the event loop. When executing asynchronous code, an event loop object is responsible for keeping track of all the tasks to be executed and coordinating passing their return values back to the calling code.

There is a strict separation between code intended to be called from a synchronous context and an asynchronous one. If you accidentally call async code from synchronous contexts, you'll find yourself with coroutine objects rather than the data types you're expecting, and if you call synchronous code from an async context, you can inadvertently introduce blocking IO that causes performance problems.

To enforce this separation, and to allow API authors optionally to support both synchronous and asynchronous uses of their objects, the `async` modifier is added to `for` and `with` to specify that you're using the async-compatible implementation. These variants *cannot* be used in a synchronous context or on objects that do not have an asynchronous implementation (such as tuples or lists, in the case of `async for`).

async def

We can define new coroutines in the same way that we define functions. However, the `def` keyword becomes `async def`. These coroutines return values like any other. As such, we can implement the same behavior from Listing 7-3 in an asyncio method, as shown in Listing 7-11.

Listing 7-11. Example of concurrent increment and decrement coroutines

```python
import asyncio

async def increment():
    return 1
```

```
async def decrement():
    return -1

async def onehundred():
    num = 0
    for i in range(100):
        num += await increment()
        num += await decrement()
    return num

if __name__ == "__main__":
    asyncio.run(onehundred())
```

This behaves in the same way: two coroutines are run, their values are retrieved, and the num variable is adjusted according to the result of those functions. The main difference is that instead of these coroutines being submitted to a thread pool, the onehundred() async function is passed to the event loop to run, and that function is responsible for calling the other coroutines that do the work.

When we call a function that is defined as asynchronous, we receive a coroutine object as the result, rather than having the function execute.

```
async def hello_world():
    return "hello world"
```

```
>>> hello_world()
<coroutine object hello_world at 0x03DEDED0>
```

The asyncio.run(...) function is the main entrypoint for asynchronous code. It blocks until the passed function, and all other functions which that function schedules, are complete. The upshot is that only one coroutine at a time can be initiated by synchronous code.

await

The await keyword is the trigger for blocking until an asynchronous function has completed. However, this only blocks the current asynchronous call stack. You can have multiple asynchronous functions executing at once, in which case another function is executed while waiting for the result.

The await keyword is equivalent to the Future.result() method in the ThreadPoolExecutor example: it transforms an *awaitable* object into its result. It can appear wherever an asynchronous function call is used; it's equally valid to write any of the three variants of printing the result of a function shown in Figure 7-8.

```
data = get_data()          data = await get_data()         print(await get_data())
print(await data)          print(data)
```

Figure 7-8. *Three equivalent uses of the await keyword*

Once await has been used, the underlying awaitable is consumed. It is not possible to write

```
data = get_data()
if await data:
    print(await data)
```

An awaitable object is an object that implements the __await__() method. This is an implementation detail; you won't need to write an __await__() method. Instead, you will use a variety of different built-in objects that provide it for you. For example, any coroutines defined using async def have an __await__() method.

Aside from coroutines, the other common awaitable is Task, which can be created from a coroutine with the asyncio.create_task(...) function. The normal usage is that one function is called with asyncio.run(...) and that function schedules further functions with asyncio.create_task(...).

```
async def example():
    task = asyncio.create_task(hello_world())
    print(task)
    print(hasattr(task, "__await__"))
    return await task
```

```
>>> asyncio.run(example())
```

```
<Task pending coro=<hello_world() running at <stdin>:1>>
True
'hello world'
```

A task is a coroutine that has been scheduled for parallel execution. When you `await` a coroutine, you cause it to be scheduled for execution, then immediately block waiting for its result. The `create_task(...)` function allows you to schedule a task *before* you need its result. If you have multiple operations to perform, each of which performs some blocking IO, but you `await` the coroutines directly, then one won't be scheduled until the previous is complete. Scheduling the coroutines as tasks first allows them to run in parallel, as demonstrated by Table 7-3.

Table 7-3. *Comparison of tasks and bare coroutines for parallel waiting*

Awaiting coroutines directly	Converting to tasks first
| ```python
import asyncio
import time

async def slow():
    start = time.time()
    await asyncio.sleep(1)
    await asyncio.sleep(1)
    await asyncio.sleep(1)
    end = time.time()
    print(end - start)

>>> asyncio.run(slow())
3.0392887592315674
``` | ```python
import asyncio
import time

async def slow():
    start = time.time()
    first = asyncio.create_task(asyncio.sleep(1))
    second = asyncio.create_task(asyncio.sleep(1))
    third = asyncio.create_task(asyncio.sleep(1))
    await first
    await second
    await third
    end = time.time()
    print(end - start)

>>> asyncio.run(slow())
1.0060641765594482
``` |

There are some useful convenience functions to handle scheduling tasks based on coroutines, most notably `asyncio.gather(...)`. This method takes any number of awaitable objects, schedules them as tasks, awaits them all, and returns an awaitable of a tuple of their return values in the same order that their coroutines/tasks were originally given in.

This is very useful for when multiple awaitables should be run in parallel:

```python
async def slow():
    start = time.time()
    await asyncio.gather(
        asyncio.sleep(1),
```

```
        asyncio.sleep(1),
        asyncio.sleep(1)
    )
    end = time.time()
    print(end - start)
>>> asyncio.run(slow())
1.0132906436920166
```

async for

The async for construct allows iterating over an object where the iterator *itself* is defined by asynchronous code. It is not correct to use async for on synchronous iterators that are merely being used in an asynchronous context or that happen to contain awaitables.

None of the common data types we've used are asynchronous iterators. If you have a tuple or a list, then you use the standard for loop, regardless of what they contain or if they're being used in synchronous or asynchronous code.

This section contains examples of three different approaches to looping in an asynchronous function. Type hinting is especially useful here, as the data types here are subtly different, and it makes it clear which types each function expects.

Listing 7-12 demonstrates an **iterable of awaitables**. It contains two asynchronous functions: one coroutine that returns a number[11] and one adds up the contents of an iterable of awaitables. That is, the add_all(...) function expects a standard iterable of coroutines (or tasks) from number(...). The numbers() function is synchronous; it returns a standard list containing two invocations of number(...).

Listing 7-12. Looping over a list of awaitables

```
import asyncio
import typing as t

async def number(num: int) -> int:
    return num
```

---

[11]This is a contrived example, as there's no reason to write a function that returns only its own argument, especially in an asynchronous way, but if we imagine that rather than returning the input, this is making a call to a web service that returns the data, this is more defensible. This is a trade-off between a useful function and something that's more easily understood.

```
def numbers() -> t.Iterable[t.Awaitable[int]]:
    return [number(2), number(3)]

async def add_all(numbers: t.Iterable[t.Awaitable[int]]) -> int:
    total = 0
    for num in numbers:
        total += await num
    return total

if __name__ == "__main__":
    to_add = numbers()
    result = asyncio.run(add_all(to_add))
    print(result)
```

In the add_all(...) function, the loop is a standard for loop, as it's iterating over a list. The contents of the list are the result of number(2) and number(3), so these two calls need to be awaited to retrieve their respective results.

Another way of writing this is to invert the relationship between the iterable and the awaitable. That is, instead of a list of awaitables of ints, pass an **awaitable of a list of ints**. Here, numbers() is defined as a coroutine, and it returns a list of integers.

Listing 7-13. Awaiting a list of integers

```
import asyncio
import typing as t

async def number(num: int) -> int:
    return num

async def numbers() -> t.Iterable[int]:
    return [await number(2), await number(3)]

async def add_all(nums: t.Awaitable[t.Iterable[int]]) -> int:
    total = 0
    for num in await nums:
        total += num
    return total

if __name__ == "__main__":
    to_add = numbers()
```

```
result = asyncio.run(add_all(to_add))
print(result)
```

The numbers() coroutine is now responsible for awaiting the individual number(...) coroutines. We still use a standard for loop, but now instead of awaiting the contents of the for loop, we await the value we're looping over.

With both approaches, the first number(...) call is awaited before the second, but with the first approach, control passes back to the add_all(...) function between the two. In the second, control is only passed back after all numbers have been awaited individually and assembled into a list. With the first method, each number(...) coroutine is processed as it's needed, but with the second all processing of the number(...) calls happens before the first value is used.

The third way of approaching this involves using async for. To do this, we convert the numbers() coroutine from Listing 7-13 to a generator function, resulting in the code in Listing 7-14. This is the same approach as used in synchronous Python code to avoid high memory usage, with the same trade-off that the value can only be iterated over once.

Listing 7-14. Asynchronous generator

```
import asyncio
import typing as t

async def number(num: int) -> int:
    return num

async def numbers() -> t.AsyncIterator[int]:
    yield await number(2)
    yield await number(3)

async def add_all(nums: t.AsyncIterator[int]) -> int:
    total = 0
    async for num in nums:
        total += num
    return total

if __name__ == "__main__":
    to_add = numbers()
    result = asyncio.run(add_all(to_add))
    print(result)
```

329

We still need the await keywords in the numbers() method as we want to iterate over the results of the number(...) method, not over placeholders for the results. Like the second version, this hides the details of awaiting the individual number(...) calls from the sum(...) function, instead of trusting the iterator to manage it. However, it also retains the property of the first that each number(...) call is only evaluated when it's needed: they're not all processed in advance.

For an object to support being iterated over with for, it must implement an __iter__ method that returns an iterator. An iterator is an object that implements both an __iter__ method (that returns itself) and a __next__ method for advancing the iterator. An object that implements __iter__ but not __next__ is not an *iterator* but an *iterable*. Iterables can be iterated over; iterators are also aware of their current state.

Equally, an object that implements an asynchronous method __aiter__ is an AsyncIterable. If __aiter__ returns self and it also provides an __anext__ asynchronous method, it's an AsyncIterator.

A single object can implement all four methods to support both synchronous and asynchronous iterations. This is only relevant if you're implementing a class that can behave as an iterable, either synchronous or asynchronous. The easiest way to create an async iterable is using the yield construct from an async function, and that's enough for most use cases.

In all of the preceding examples, we're using coroutines directly. As the functions specify they work on typing.Awaitable, we can be sure that the same code would work if we passed tasks rather than coroutines. The second example, where we are awaiting a list, is equivalent to using the built-in asyncio.gather(...) function. Both return an awaitable of an iterable of results. As such, this may be the method that you'll see most often, albeit expressed as shown in Listing 7-15.

Listing 7-15. Using gather to process tasks in parallel

```
import asyncio
import typing as t

async def number(num: int) -> int:
    return num

async def numbers() -> t.Iterable[int]:
    return await asyncio.gather(
```

```
        number(2),
        number(3)
    )
async def add_all(nums: t.Awaitable[t.Iterable[int]]) -> int:
    total = 0
    for num in await nums:
        total += num
    return total

if __name__ == "__main__":
    to_add = numbers()
    result = asyncio.run(add_all(to_add))
    print(result)
```

async with

The with statement also has an async counterpart, async with, which is used to facilitate the writing of context managers that depend on asynchronous code. It's quite common to see this in asynchronous code, as many IO operations involve setup and teardown phases.

In the same way that async for uses __aiter__ rather than __iter__, asynchronous context managers define the __aenter__ and __aexit__ methods to replace __enter__ and __exit__. Once again, objects can choose to implement all four to work in both contexts, if appropriate.

When using synchronous context managers in an asynchronous function, there's a potential for blocking IO to happen before the first line and after the last line of the body. Using async with and a compatible context manager allows for the event loop to schedule some other asynchronous code during that blocking IO period.

We will cover using and creating context managers in more detail over the next two chapters, but both are equivalent to try/finally constructions, but standard context managers use synchronous code in their enter and exit methods, whereas async context managers use asynchronous code.

Async locking primitives

Although asynchronous code is less vulnerable to concurrency safety issues than threads are, it is still possible to write asynchronous code that has concurrency bugs. The switching model being based on awaiting a result rather than threads being interrupted prevents most accidental bugs, but it's no guarantee of correctness.

For example, in Listing 7-16 we have an asyncio version of the increment example from when we looked at threads. This has an `await` within the `num +=` line and introduces an `offset()` coroutine to return the 1 that will be added to num. This `offset()` function also uses `asyncio.sleep(0)` to block for a fraction of a second, which simulates the behavior of a blocking IO request.

Listing 7-16. Example of an unsafe asynchronous program

```
import asyncio
import random

num = 0

async def offset():
    await asyncio.sleep(0)
    return 1

async def increment():
    global num
    num += await offset()

async def onehundred():
    tasks = []
    for i in range(100):
        tasks.append(increment())
    await asyncio.gather(*tasks)
    return num

if __name__ == "__main__":
    print(asyncio.run(onehundred()))
```

Although this program should print 100, it may print any number as low as 1, depending on the decisions the event loop makes about scheduling tasks. To prevent this, we need to either move the await offset() call to not be part of the += construction or lock the num variable.

AsyncIO provides direct equivalents of Lock, Event, Condition, and Semaphore from the threading library. These variants use asynchronous versions of the same API, so we can fix the event function as shown in Listing 7-17.

Listing 7-17. Example of asynchronous locking

```
import asyncio
import random

num = 0

async def offset():
    await asyncio.sleep(0)
    return 1

async def increment(numlock):
    global num
    async with numlock:
        num += await offset()

async def onehundred():
    tasks = []
    numlock = asyncio.Lock()

    for i in range(100):
        tasks.append(increment(numlock))
    await asyncio.gather(*tasks)
    return num

if __name__ == "__main__":
    print(asyncio.run(onehundred()))
```

Perhaps the biggest difference between threaded and async versions of synchronization primitives is that async primitives cannot be defined at the global scope. More accurately, they can only be instantiated from within a running coroutine as they must register themselves with the current event loop.

Working with synchronous libraries

The code we've written so far relies on us having an entirely asynchronous stack of libraries and functions to call from our async code. If we introduce some synchronous code, then we block all our tasks while executing it. We can demonstrate this using the time.sleep(...) method to block for a set amount of time. Earlier we used asyncio.sleep(...) to model a long-running async-aware task; mixing these lets us look at the performance of such a mixed system:

```
import asyncio
import time

async def synchronous_task():
    time.sleep(1)

async def slow():
    start = time.time()
    await asyncio.gather(
        asyncio.sleep(1),
        asyncio.sleep(1),
        synchronous_task(),
        asyncio.sleep(1)
    )
    end = time.time()
    print(end - start)

>>> asyncio.run(slow())
2.006387243270874
```

In this case, our three asynchronous tasks all take 1 second and are processed in parallel. The blocking task also takes 1 second but is processed in series, meaning the total time taken is 2 seconds. To ensure that all four functions run in parallel, we can use the loop.run_in_executor(...) function. This allocates a ThreadPoolExecutor (or another executor of your choice) and runs specified tasks in that context rather than in the main thread.

```
import asyncio
import time
```

```python
async def synchronous_task():
    loop = asyncio.get_running_loop()
    await loop.run_in_executor(None, time.sleep, 1)

async def slow():
    start = time.time()
    await asyncio.gather(
        asyncio.sleep(1),
        asyncio.sleep(1),
        synchronous_task(),
        asyncio.sleep(1)
    )
    end = time.time()
    print(end - start)
>>> asyncio.run(slow())
1.0059468746185303
```

The run_in_executor(...) function works by switching out the problem to one that is easily made asynchronous. Instead of trying to turn arbitrary Python functions from synchronous into asynchronous, finding the right places to yield control back to the event loop, getting woken up at the correct time, and so on, it uses a thread (or a process) to execute the code. Threads and processes are inherently suitable to asynchronous control by virtue of being an operating system construct. This reduces the scope of what needs to be made compatible with the asyncio system to starting a thread and waiting for it to be complete.

Making our code asynchronous

The first step in making our code work in an asynchronous context is to pick a function to act as the first in the chain of asynchronous functions. We want to keep the synchronous and asynchronous code separate, so we need to pick something that's high enough in the call stack that all things that need to be asynchronous are (perhaps indirectly) called by this function.

In our code, the get_data_points(...) function is the only one that we want to run in an asynchronous context. It is called by add_data_from_sensors(...), which is itself called by standalone(...), which is called by collect_sensor_data(...) in turn. Any of these four functions can be the argument to asyncio.run(...).

The collect_sensor_data(...) function is the click entrypoint, so it cannot be an asynchronous function. The get_data_points(...) function needs to be called multiple times, so it is a better fit for a coroutine than the main entrypoint into the asynchronous flow. This leaves standalone(...) and add_data_from_sensors(...).

The standalone(...) function does the setup for the database already; it is a good place to do the event loop setup too. Therefore, we need to make the add_data_from_sensors(...) an async function and adjust how it is called from standalone(...).

```
def standalone(
    db_uri: str, servers: t.Tuple[str], api_key: t.Optional[str], echo:
    bool = False
) -> None:
    engine = create_engine(db_uri, echo=echo)
    sm = sessionmaker(engine)
    Session = sm()
    asyncio.run(add_data_from_sensors(Session, servers, api_key))
    Session.commit()
```

We now need to change our implementations of the lower-level functions to not call any blocking synchronous code. Currently, we are making our HTTP calls using the requests library, which is a blocking, synchronous library.

As an alternative, we'll switch to the aiohttp module to make our HTTP requests. Aiohttp is a natively asynchronous HTTP library that supports both client and server applications. The interface is not as refined as that of requests, but it is quite usable.

The biggest difference in API is that HTTP requests involve many context managers, as follows:

```
async with aiohttp.ClientSession() as http:
    async with http.get(url) as request:
        result = await request.json()
```

As the name suggests, a ClientSession represents the idea of a session with a shared cookie state and HTTP header configuration. Within this, requests are made with asynchronous context managers like get. The result of the context manager is an object which has methods that can be awaited to retrieve the contents of the response.

The preceding construction, which is admittedly much more verbose than the equivalent using requests, allows for many places where the execution flow could be yielded to work around blocking IO. The obvious one is the await line, which relinquishes control while waiting for the response to be retrieved and parsed as JSON. Less obvious is the entry and exit of the http.get(...) context manager, which can set up socket connections, allowing things like DNS resolution not to block execution. It's also possible for the execution flow to be yielded when entering and exiting a ClientSession.

All this is to say that while the preceding construction is more verbose than the same code using requests, it does allow for transparently setting up and tearing down of shared resources relating to the HTTP session and is doing so in a way that does not significantly slow the process.

In our add_data_from_sensors(...) function, we need to handle the fact that this session object is now required, preferably in a way that shares the client session between our multiple requests. We also need to keep a record of the request coroutine calls, so we can schedule them in parallel and retrieve their data.

```
async def add_data_from_sensors(
    session: Session, servers: t.Tuple[str], api_key: t.Optional[str]
) -> t.List[DataPoint]:
    todo: t.List[t.Awaitable[t.List[DataPoint]]] = []
    points: t.List[DataPoint] = []
    async with aiohttp.ClientSession() as http:
        for server in servers:
            todo.append(get_data_points(server, api_key, http))
        for a in await asyncio.gather(*todo):
            points += await handle_result(a, session)
    return points
```

In this function, we define two variables, a list of awaitables that each return a list of DataPoint objects, as well as a list of DataPoint objects that we fill as we process the awaitables. Then, we set up the ClientSession and iterate over the servers, adding an invocation of get_data_points(...) for each server. At this stage, these are coroutines as they are not scheduled as a task. We could await them in turn, but this would have the effect of making each request happen sequentially. Instead, we use asyncio.gather(...) to schedule them as tasks and allow us to iterate over the results, which are each a list of DataPoint objects.

Next, we need to add the data to the database. We're using SQLAlchemy here, which is a synchronous library. For production-quality code, we'd need to ensure that there is no chance of blocking here. The following implementation does not guarantee that the session.add(...) method can block due to the data being synchronized with the database session.

A placeholder for handle_result that should not be used in production code

```
async def handle_result(result: t.List[DataPoint], session: Session) ->
t.List[DataPoint]:
    for point in result:
        session.add(point)
    return result
```

We will look at methods for dealing with database integration in a parallel execution context in the next chapter, but this is good enough for a prototype.

Finally, we need to do the actual work of getting the data. The method is greatly different to the synchronous version, except that it also requires the ClientSession to be passed in, and some minor changes must be made to accommodate the difference in HTTP request API.

Implementation of get_data_points using aiohttp

```
async def get_data_points(server: str, api_key: t.Optional[str], http:
aiohttp.ClientSession) -> t.List[DataPoint]:
    if not server.endswith("/"):
        server += "/"
    url = server + "v/2.0/sensors/"
    headers = {}
    if api_key:
        headers["X-API-KEY"] = api_key
    async with http.get(url) as request:
        result = await request.json()
        ok = request.status == 200
    now = datetime.datetime.now()
    if ok:
        points = []
        for value in result["sensors"]:
```

```
        points.append(
            DataPoint(
                sensor_name=value["id"], collected_at=now,
                data=value["value"]
            )
        )
    return points
else:
    raise ValueError(
        f"Error loading data from {server}: "
        + result.json().get("error", "Unknown")
    )
```

This method makes many different choices when compared to a multithreaded or a multiprocess model. A multiprocess model allows for true concurrent processing, and a multithreaded approach can achieve some very minor performance gains thanks to the less restrictive guarantees about switching, but asynchronous code has a much more natural interface, in my opinion.

The key disadvantage of the asyncio approach is that the advantages can only be truly realized with asynchronous libraries. Other libraries can still be used by combining asyncio and threaded approaches, which is made easy by the good integration between these two methods, but there is a significant refactoring requirement to converting existing code to an asynchronous approach and, equally, a significant learning curve in becoming accustomed to writing asynchronous code in the first place.

Comparison

There are implementations of all four approaches in the code accompanying this chapter, so it's possible for us to run a simple benchmark to compare their speeds. Benchmarking a proposed optimization in this way is always difficult; it's hard to get real numbers from anything but a real-world test, so the following should be taken with a pinch of salt.

These numbers were generated by extracting data from the same sensor multiple times in a single invocation. Aside from the other load on the machine timing these invocations, the numbers are unrealistic because they do not involve looking up connection information for many different targets and because the server returning the requested data is limited in the number of simultaneous requests that it can service.

As you can see from Figure 7-9, the threaded and asyncio approaches are almost indistinguishable in terms of time taken. The nonblocking IO method that we rejected due to its complexity is also comparable. A multiprocess approach is noticeably slower, but similar to the other three approaches. The standard, synchronous approach behaves similarly with only one or two sensors to collect data from, but the larger result sets quickly become pathological, taking an order of magnitude longer than the concurrent approaches.

The information we should take from this is that this workload is well suited to parallelization. The fact that asyncio is as much as 20% faster in our benchmark does not necessarily equate to it being a faster technology, just faster in this particular test. Future changes to the codebase, as well as different testing conditions, could easily change the relationship between the technologies.

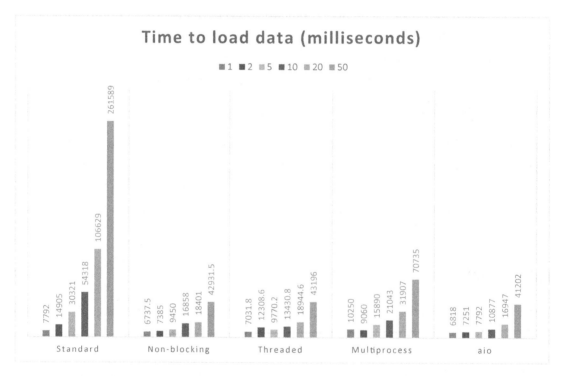

Figure 7-9. *Time taken to load data from 1, 2, 5, 10, 20, or 50 HTTP APIs, using different parallelization methods*

Making a choice

There are two pernicious falsehoods about asyncio circulating in the Python community at the time of writing. The first is that asyncio has "won" at concurrency. The second is that it's bad and should not be used. It should come as no surprise that the truth lies somewhere in the middle. Asyncio is brilliant for network clients that are largely IO-bound but isn't a panacea.

When deciding between the different approaches, the first question to ask yourself is if your code is spending most of its time waiting for IO or if it's spending most of its time processing data. A task that waits for a short while and then does a lot of calculation is not a great fit for asyncio as it can parallelize the waiting but not the execution, leaving a backlog of CPU-bound tasks to perform. Equally, it's not a natural fit for a thread pool, as the GIL prevents the various threads running truly in parallel. A multiprocess deployment has higher overheads but is able to take advantage of true parallelization in CPU-bound code.

If the task does spend more time waiting than executing code, it's likely that asyncio or a thread-based parallelization approach will be the best choice. As a rule of thumb, I recommend preferring asyncio for applications that call out to servers but do not wait for network requests themselves, and combinations of process and thread pools for applications that do accept inbound connections.[12] A decision tree representing this is given as Figure 7-10.

---

[12]With apologies to my friends Nathan and Ramon who maintain the Guillotina project, a specialist framework for very high-performance REST APIs in Python, who will advocate strongly for the benefits of asyncio in server code.

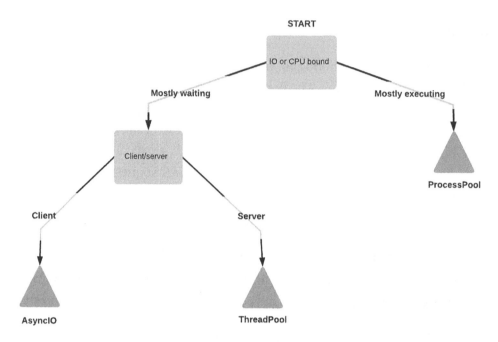

Figure 7-10. *Decision tree for parallelization methods in client/server applications*

This is not a hard rule; there are too many exceptions to list, and you should consider the details of your application and test your assumptions, but in general, I prefer the robust and predictable behavior of preemptive multitasking[13] for a server application.

Our sensor API endpoints are entirely standard Python, but are run through the waitress WSGI server. The WSGI server makes the concurrency decision for us, with `waitress-serve` instantiating a four-thread thread pool to handle inbound requests.

The collector process involves a large amount of waiting in every invocation and is entirely client side, so using asyncio to implement its concurrent behaviors is a good fit.

---

[13]*Preemptive multitasking* is when a central authority can interrupt tasks to give another task a chance to execute. In this case, the Python GIL enforces this with its switch interval. The alternative, *cooperative multitasking*, is the idea that tasks must voluntarily give up control to their peers. This is the basis of the name coroutine and also the reason that bugs in Windows 3.1 applications could inadvertently freeze the system so easily.

Summary

In this chapter, we've looked at the two most common types of parallelization, threading and asyncio, as well as other methods that are less widely used. Concurrency is a difficult topic, and we've not finished covering the things that you can achieve with asyncio, but we will be leaving threads behind at this point.

Asynchronous programming is a very powerful tool, one that all Python programmers should be aware of, but the trade-offs of threads and asyncio are very different, and generally speaking, only one will be useful in any given program.

If you need to write a program that relies on concurrency in Python, I strongly recommend experimenting with the different approaches to find which matches your problem best. I also would encourage you to make sure you understand the uses of all the synchronization primitives we've used in this chapter, as appropriate use of locks can make the difference between a program that's slow and hard to understand and a program that's fast and intuitively written.

Additional resources

The following links contain some useful background information on topics that I've covered in this chapter, as well as some other, less common approaches:

> The HTTP zine by Julia Evans gives a good explanation of the internals of the HTTP protocol and the differences between versions: `https://wizardzines.com/zines/http/`.

> Greenlets are a precursor to native coroutines in Python, which may be of use to people who need to use very old versions of Python: `https://greenlet.readthedocs.io/en/latest/`.

> Similarly, `https://github.com/stackless-dev/stackless/wiki` covers Stackless Python, which is a variant of Python intended to offer better performance when running many small operations in parallel. Greenlets are derived from the stackless project.

> Just as ThreadPools are backed by threads, ProcessPools are backed by processes. Information on Python's lower-level process management functionality is at `https://docs.python.org/3/library/multiprocessing.html`.

The slides for David Beazley's excellent presentation "Understanding the GIL" are available at `www.dabeaz.com/GIL/`. Although some minor details have changed in the ten years since it was written (such as the concept of "ticks"), the overall description is still very accurate and worth a read.

Information on the PyPy implementation of Python can be found at `www.pypy.org/`.

CHAPTER 8

Advanced asyncio

Now that we've decided that asyncio is an appropriate technology to use for our aggregation process, we need to ensure that the code we're working from is production-quality. So far we've omitted any tests in the apd.aggregation codebase; it's time to address that problem, as well as the problem of the blocking database integration that we mentioned in passing in the previous chapter.

Testing async code

We can use the existing tools we've been using to test our async code, but we need to make some minor adjustments to set up the async environment. One way to do this would be to modify individual test functions to invoke `asyncio.run(...)` over a wrapper function. This ensures that the testing system is entirely synchronous, but for each individual test, an event loop is set up, a coroutine scheduled, and execution blocked until it's complete.

We can achieve this by writing an asynchronous function which contains any async setup and teardown; then any synchronous setup, teardown, and assertions are added to the main test function.

```python
def test_get_data_points_fails_with_bad_api_key(self, http_server):
    async def wrapped():
        async with aiohttp.ClientSession() as http:
            return await collect.get_data_points(http_server, "incorrect", http)

    with pytest.raises(
        ValueError,
        match=f"Error loading data from {http_server}: Supply API key in "
        f"X-API-Key header",
    ):
        asyncio.run(wrapped())
```

© Matthew Wilkes 2020
M. Wilkes, *Advanced Python Development*, https://doi.org/10.1007/978-1-4842-5793-7_8

The preceding example uses a `http_server` fixture which returns the URL to an API server, then creates a coroutine that sets up an aiohttp session and calls `get_data_points(...)`, the method under test. There's a big sacrifice in clarity involved here: the code is out of order. The asynchronous code is listed first, followed by the assertions, and then the synchronous code. Normally, we mix code and assertions more freely according to the flow of the program. Although we could move some of the assertion work into the asynchronous part of the test, there would always be additional code to set up the async environment for the inner function.

An alternative is to use a pytest plugin to handle the wrapping automatically. `pytest-asyncio` does this, making it possible to mix standard test methods with test coroutines. Any coroutine that's marked as being an asyncio test using the pytest marking system is executed in an async environment, with all the work of wrapping it happening transparently in the plugin.

Using a plugin allows for a much clearer execution flow, without any boilerplate code to bridge the gap between synchronous and asynchronous code, as shown in the following:

```
@pytest.mark.asyncio
async def test_get_data_points_fails_with_bad_api_key(self, http_server):
    with pytest.raises(
        ValueError,
        match=f"Error loading data from {http_server}: Supply API key "
        f"in X-API-Key header",
    ):
        async with aiohttp.ClientSession() as http:
            await collect.get_data_points(http_server, "incorrect", http)
```

Caution   We've introduced a dependency here, albeit one that only applies when running tests. We haven't been listing test dependencies in `setup.cfg`, choosing only to include them in the Pipfile as development dependencies. As such, we can install this dependency with

```
pipenv install --dev pytest-asyncio
```

This is fine in most cases, but in larger codebases you may need to test combinations of components and versions rather than having a single Pipfile. It's possible to list the test dependencies in `setup.cfg`, to avoid duplication. To do this, create a new `[options.extras_require]` line called "test" and list the test dependencies there. There is a legacy setuptools feature called tests_require that you may sometimes see, but I always recommend an extra instead, as it provides more explicit control over if test dependencies are installed.

Testing our code

The ability to write asynchronous test functions is a great start, but we also need to set up some fixtures to give the aggregation code sensor endpoints to interrogate. There are two approaches to this; we could either provide mock data as part of the aggregation tests or have the aggregation tests depend on the server code and start a real, albeit temporary, server.

Neither option is a particularly appealing prospect; they each have significant downsides. If we write our tests to check against a known HTTP response, then this would need to update this every time that the underlying API changes. Hopefully, this won't happen often, but blobs of opaque JSON are hard for people to reason about when reading the test code.

Often, tests that manipulate large pieces of data are written by copying the input data, running the test, and then using the output data to write an `assert` statement. This is a somewhat dangerous practice, as it makes the test about ensuring that nothing has changed, rather than checking that a specific thing is correct.

The alternative, running the back-end server and connecting to that, is more a realistic approach and avoids raw JSON in tests, but it adds a dependency on the server code to the tests. Consequently, all tests require a socket connection to be created, as well as adding overhead in server setup and teardown.

The dilemma is the same problem we faced in Chapter 5, where we had to decide between testing the command-line interface's output and the functions of sensors directly. Once we recognize this, it's much easier to decide what to do. A functional test provides a broad basis for checking that things are working as expected, but faster, specialized tests are more pleasant to develop with. Critically, having both helps us to differentiate test failures between when there has been a change to the underlying platform and when the faster tests are modeling the real behavior poorly.

As such, I'll add the same marker to declare these tests as functional tests. In Chapter 5, we did this with @pytest.mark.functional on individual test methods, as well as a pytest.ini file that defined the functional marker. As all of our functional tests for this package are in a module that won't contain any nonfunctional tests, we can mark the entire module instead. Classes or modules can have a marker by setting the pytestmark module variable to reference the marker, as follows:

```
import pytest

pytestmark = [pytest.mark.functional]
```

Test servers and pytest fixtures with teardown

The first thing we need to do for our test setup is to instantiate a test server. The server needs to be providing a HTTP socket, as we're testing code that makes HTTP requests. We need a server that listens on a port that we can specify so that we can avoid port collisions with other software; we may need more than one of these servers running at once, to test that data can be aggregated from multiple endpoints.

In our original apd.sensors package, we created a set_up_config(...) function that took configuration values and an optional app parameter, then applied those config variables to the app. If app wasn't supplied, then the default app (which sets up the various API versions on known URLs) is used.

To create multiple flask apps with different configs, we need to be able to create flask apps that are functionally equivalent to the default one, which for the purposes of our tests means they must have the v2.0 API served on /v/2.0. We can create a new get_independent_flask_app(...) function that does this, by duplicating some of the code from apd.sensors, as shown in Listing 8-1.

Listing 8-1. Helper functions and a fixture to run a HTTP server

```
from concurrent.futures import ThreadPoolExecutor
import typing as t
import wsgiref.simple_server

import flask
import pytest
```

```
from apd.sensors.wsgi import v20
from apd.sensors.wsgi import set_up_config

def get_independent_flask_app(name: str) -> flask.Flask:
    """ Create a new flask app with the v20 API blueprint loaded, so
    multiple copies
    of the app can be run in parallel without conflicting configuration """
    app = flask.Flask(name)
    app.register_blueprint(v20.version, url_prefix="/v/2.0")
    return app

def run_server_in_thread(name: str, config: t.Dict[str, t.Any], port: int)
-> t.Iterator[str]:
    # Create a new flask app and load in required code, to prevent config
    # conflicts
    app = get_independent_flask_app(name)
    flask_app = set_up_config(config, app)
    server = wsgiref.simple_server.make_server("localhost", port, flask_app)

    with ThreadPoolExecutor() as pool:
        pool.submit(server.serve_forever)
        yield f"http://localhost:{port}/"
        server.shutdown()

@pytest.fixture(scope="session")
def http_server() -> t.Iterator[str]:
    yield from run_server_in_thread(
        "standard", {"APD_SENSORS_API_KEY": "testing"}, 12081
    )
```

This function lets us create flask apps that have independent configurations, but all include the v2.0 API on the correct URL. The run_server_in_thread(...) utility function is a higher-level one, to create a flask app, configure it, and make it serve requests.

Note   There is some disagreement over if it's worthwhile to add type definitions to test methods. I find that PyTest's lack of typing support removes most of the utility, but it depends a lot on your codebase. If you've got good coverage of types, you may find it worthwhile. Personally, I recommend type-checking utility functions, adding return type annotations to test methods and fixtures. This is normally enough to ensure that your test helpers are type-checked when used, but I recommend being more pragmatic about typing for test methods and I often skip this.

To service requests, we'll use the wsgiref server from the standard library. We've previously used its `serve_forever()` function to handle requests as part of testing the `apd.sensors` HTTP server. This does almost exactly what we want, in that it takes a WSGI application and makes it available over HTTP; but it does so in a blocking way. Once we call `serve_forever()`, the server normally runs until the user interrupts it with <CTRL+c>. This is not what we want for a test fixture, so we need to off-load this to run concurrently.

A threaded execution model is perfect for this: we can spawn a new thread to handle the `serve_forever()` call and interrupt it once we're done with the server. Unlike previous fixtures that we've written, we don't just want to create a value and pass it to the test method, we want to do the setup, pass a value, and then do teardown to clear up the thread that we've created.

Pytest fixtures that do setup and teardown use the `yield` keyword instead of `return`, effectively making the fixture a single-item generator. Anything before the `yield` keyword is executed as normal, and the value yielded is what's given to test functions as an argument. Anything after the `yield` is only executed once the fixture is torn down. By default, fixtures are torn down at the end of each test. We can change the scope to be `"session"` to mean that the fixture should only be set up and torn down once per pytest invocation, rather than after every test.

This construction allows the `server.shutdown()` call and the cleanup of the thread pool to happen after the last test that needs `http_server` has completed.

Note   The shutdown method is an implementation detail of the WSGIServer from the standard library, but it's a critical one. Once our test method has finished executing, we want to shut down the thread serving requests. If we don't do this, then the test program will hang waiting for the threads to finish, but the threads will never terminate in normal operation. The shutdown method manipulates an internal flag that the wsgiref server checks every 500 milliseconds. If it's set, the `serve_forever()` call returns and therefore causes the thread to exit.

Anything running in a thread must be shut down explicitly before the process can complete.[1] In this case, we're lucky that the API was designed with this in mind, but if you're working with other APIs that don't offer a shutdown function, you may have to create your own shared variable and check that in the function that you submit to the pool. It is not possible to force a thread to stop from the outside; your threads must be written to cease when no longer needed.

The utility function allows us to create multiple such test servers, differing only by configuration, and pass their addresses to test methods. We can create as many fixtures as we like, passing different data to each. For example, a fixture to set up a server that uses a different API key and will therefore reject requests is given as follows:

```
@pytest.fixture(scope="session")
def bad_api_key_http_server():
    yield from run_server_in_thread(
        "alternate", {"APD_SENSORS_API_KEY": "penny"}, 12082
    )
```

The final thing to mention here is the `yield from` construction in the fixtures themselves. A `yield from` expression is very useful when building generators. When given an iterable, it yields over value, then passes execution to the next line. This allows writing iterators that defer to another iterator as part of a more complex implementation,

---

[1] A thread can be marked as a "daemon" thread using `thread_obj.daemon = True` before starting it. This will allow the process to end with the thread still running, but this can cause the thread to terminate mid-action. It's usually better to use a sentinel value to allow all threads to shut down cleanly.

for example, one that appends additional items to the start and end of an existing iterator. It can also be used to chain multiple iterators together, although the itertools.chain function in the standard library may be clearer for this purpose.[2]

```
def additional(base_iterator):
    yield "Start"
    yield from base_iterator
    yield "End"
```

Pytest treats fixtures that yield their value differently to those that return their value, so although we don't want to manipulate the iterator we're wrapping, we need to iterate over it and yield the single value so that pytest understands that this fixture has setup and teardown. Pytest determines this by introspecting the fixture function and checking if it is a generator function.[3] If the wrapper function body were to be return run_server_in_thread(...), then, although the actual result of calling the function would be the same, the function itself wouldn't be considered a generator function. It would be a function that returns a generator.

Introspecting the function allows for fixtures that intentionally return generators, such as the following example which returns a generator with a single value. If this fixture were to be used in a test function, then the function would be given the generator itself, not its single value.

```
@pytest.fixture
def single_item_iterator():
    def gen_func():
        yield "An item"
    return gen_func()
```

Fixture scoping

By default, all fixtures are scoped at the test level, meaning the fixture code is run once for every test that depends on them. Our fixtures that create a new HTTP server are scoped at the session level, meaning they are only run once and the value is shared by all tests.

---

[2]itertools.chain(*iterators) returns a single iterator that contains the items from each, in turn.

[3]This is done with the inspect.isgeneratorfunction(...) function in the standard library.

Fixtures can use other fixtures as a way of sharing setup code between multiple fixtures and tests. For example, in the future, we may have many more required configuration values as part of the server setup for apd.sensors. In this case, we wouldn't want to repeat them all for every HTTP server being set up; we would want to put the default configuration in a fixture, as shown in Listing 8-2. This way, it can be read by both HTTP server fixtures and any tests that need the config values.

Listing 8-2. Changes to the fixtures to support a common config fixture

```
import copy

@pytest.fixture(scope="session")
def config_defaults():
    return {
        "APD_SENSORS_API_KEY": "testing",
        "APD_SOME_VALUE": "example",
        "APD_OTHER_THING": "off"
    }

@pytest.fixture(scope="session")
def http_server(config_defaults) -> t.Iterator[str]:
    config = copy.copy(config_defaults)
    yield from run_server_in_thread("standard", config, 12081)

@pytest.fixture(scope="session")
def bad_api_key_http_server(config_defaults) -> t.Iterator[str]:
    config = copy.copy(config_defaults)
    config["APD_SENSORS_API_KEY"] = "penny"
    yield from run_server_in_thread(
        "alternate", config, 12082
    )
```

This hypothetical config_defaults fixture has scope="session" set because it too runs at the session scoping level. However, this is a logical consequence of the fact that it is used by session-scoped fixtures, not a free choice. If the config_defaults fixture had a narrower scope, then there would be a contradiction. Should it be set up and torn down according to the narrow scope or after the session-scoped items that depend on it are torn down?

Our example might appear harmless, but if the fixture returns dynamic values, or sets up some resource, then the behavior needs to be consistent. As such, any attempt to use a fixture that has a narrower scope than the fixture that's using it causes pytest to fail with scope mismatch errors, such as those in the following:

```
ScopeMismatch: You tried to access the 'function' scoped fixture
'config_defaults' with a 'session' scoped request object, involved factories
tests\test_http_get.py:57:  def http_server(config_defaults)
tests\test_http_get.py:49:  def config_defaults()
```

There are several scopes available to developers; these are (from narrowest to widest) `function`, `class`, `module`, `package`,[4] and `session`. The default is function, and any fixture that defines an explicit scope must only depend on fixtures that use scopes that use that scope or a wider one. For example, any class-scoped fixture can depend on class, module, package, or session fixtures, but not function-scoped fixtures.

Somewhat confusingly, there is a second type of scoping that applies to fixtures, their *discoverability*. This is defined by where in the codebase a fixture is defined. It determines which functions can use the fixture but has no effect on how invocations of the fixture are shared between tests.

The HTTP server fixtures we created earlier are specified as being in the *session* scope, but they're defined in a test module, which makes their discoverability equivalent to *module* scope. There are three possible discoverability scopes, equivalent to class, module, and package. Fixtures defined in the `conftest.py` module are available to all tests in a codebase; ones defined in a test module are available to all tests in that module; and ones defined as a method of a test class are available to all tests in that class.

It's very common for a discovery scope to differ from the defined scope, especially as the default scope for a fixture is function, which has no equivalent discoverability scope. If the discoverability is wider than the declared scope, then the fixture could be set up, used, and torn down multiple times throughout the test process. If it's the same, then the fixture will be set up, used, and then torn down immediately afterward. Finally, if a test's declared scope is wider than its discoverability, then it won't be torn down until some later point in the test run, potentially a long time after it was no longer needed. These three possibilities are demonstrated in Table 8-1.

---

[4]The package fixture scope is currently experimental and may be removed in a future version of pytest. The scopes I use most often are (in order) function, session, class, and module. I have not yet had cause to use the package scope.

Table 8-1. *The effects of the 15 different combinations of scope*

	scope=function	scope=class	scope=module	scope=package	scope=session
Defined in a class	Multiple invocations	One invocation	Delayed teardown	Delayed teardown	Delayed teardown
Defined in module	Multiple invocations	Multiple invocations	One invocation	Delayed teardown	Delayed teardown
Defined in conftest.py	Multiple invocations	Multiple invocations	Multiple invocations	One invocation	Delayed teardown

If multiple fixtures of the same name exist, then the one with the narrowest discovery scope is used for each test. That is, a fixture defined in `conftest.py` is available to all tests, but if a module has a fixture of the same name, then that one is used instead for tests within the module. The same is true if a class has a fixture of the same name.

Caution   This overriding is only about discovery; there is no effect on the lifetime of the fixture and its teardown behavior. If you have a fixture that sets up and tears down a resource, like our HTTP servers, and you override that for a class, then it's possible for other versions of the same fixture to have been set up and not yet torn down.[5] Any time that you define a fixture where the narrowest override used and the widest declared scope used are listed in Table 8-1 as "Delayed teardown, you *must* ensure that your fixtures do not try to hold the same resources, such as TCP/IP sockets.

We do have a mismatch in our code: our HTTP server fixture is defined in a test module but uses the session scope, so it can suffer from delayed teardown. We could fix this by moving the fixtures to `conftest.py` or by changing the declared scope to `module`. We need to decide if we want our fixture to be coterminous with the test run and available to any test to use or if we want it to be available only to the `test_http_get.py` test module and to be torn down once those tests have been executed.

---

[5]If you want to see this for yourself, you can add `print(...)` calls to your fixtures and run pytest with the `-s` switch, to prevent the capture of stdout. Be aware, however, that pytest doesn't guarantee the order that it decides to run tests in, so this is more useful for debugging a problem than verifying that no problems can occur.

As we don't intend to create an extensive test suite of functional tests that would require the use of this fixture, I'll leave it in the test module and reduce the scope to match.

Mocking objects for easier unit testing

To write unit tests of our code, we need to find an alternative to starting a server for the aiohttp library to connect to. If we were using the requests library to make the HTTP request, we'd likely use the *responses* testing tool, which patches parts of requests' internals to allow specific URLs to be overridden.

If our implementation of get_data_points(...) were to be synchronous, we'd register the URL we wanted to override with responses and ensure that the package was activated for the test method. Test functions using responses, such as the hypothetical one shown as follows, don't suffer from mocking introducing excessive complexity at the cost of readability.

```
@responses.activate
def test_get_data_points(self, mut, data) -> None:
    responses.add(responses.GET, 'http://localhost/v/2.0/sensors/',
            json=data, status=200)
    datapoints = mut("http://localhost", "")
    assert len(datapoints) == len(data["sensors"])
    for sensor in data["sensors"]:
        assert sensor["value] in (datapoint.data for datapoint in
        datapoints)
        assert sensor["id"] in (datapoint.sensor_name for datapoint in
        datapoints)
```

We want to be able to do something similar for the aiohttp library, but we have a slight advantage in that our function expects a http client object to be passed to get_data_points(...) function. We can write a mock version of the ClientSession object that acts enough like the real one to allow us to inject fake data, without having to patch the real implementation like responses does.

For simple objects, we often use the unittest.mock functionality built-in to the standard library. Mocking allows us to instantiate objects and define what the results of various operations would be. The object we need has a get(...) method, which returns a context manager. This context manager's enter method returns a response object, which has a status attribute and a json() coroutine, which is a relatively complex set of requirements. Listing 8-3 demonstrates a fixture to build this object using unittest.mock.

Listing 8-3. Using unittest's mocking to mock a complex object

```python
from unittest.mock import Mock, MagicMock, AsyncMock

import pytest

@pytest.fixture
def data() -> t.Any:
    return {
        "sensors": [
            {
                "human_readable": "3.7",
                "id": "PythonVersion",
                "title": "Python Version",
                "value": [3, 7, 2, "final", 0],
            },
            {
                "human_readable": "Not connected",
                "id": "ACStatus",
                "title": "AC Connected",
                "value": False,
            },
        ]
    }

@pytest.fixture
def mockclient(data):
    client = MagicMock()
    response = Mock()
    response.json = AsyncMock(return_value=data)
    response.status = 200
    client.get.return_value.__aenter__ = AsyncMock(return_value=response)
    return client
```

This object isn't very easy to reason about: the code in `mockclient` is quite dense, and it relies on understanding the differences between the different types of mock class available, as well as the implementation of context managers. You cannot tell at a glance how to use this object from the test fixture.

We could have written this same functionality by creating custom classes that mirror the functionality of the real classes we want to replace, as shown in Listing 8-4. This approach results in significantly longer code, so some developers prefer the generic mocking method mentioned earlier.

Listing 8-4. Manually mocking a complex object

```python
import contextlib
from dataclasses import dataclass
import typing as t

import pytest

@pytest.fixture
def data() -> t.Any:
    return {
        "sensors": [
            {
                "human_readable": "3.7",
                "id": "PythonVersion",
                "title": "Python Version",
                "value": [3, 7, 2, "final", 0],
            },
            {
                "human_readable": "Not connected",
                "id": "ACStatus",
                "title": "AC Connected",
                "value": False,
            },
        ]
    }
```

```python
@dataclass
class FakeAIOHttpClient:
    data: t.Any

    @contextlib.asynccontextmanager
    async def get(self, url: str, headers: t.Optional[t.Dict[str,
    str]]=None) -> FakeAIOHttpResponse:
        yield FakeAIOHttpResponse(json_data=self.data, status=200)

@dataclass
class FakeAIOHttpResponse:
    json_data: t.Any
    status: int

    async def json(self) -> t.Any:
        return self.json_data

@pytest.fixture
def mockclient(data) -> FakeAIOHttpClient:
    return FakeAIOHttpClient(data)
```

The setup using this method is approximately twice as long, but it's much easier to tell at a glance what the objects involved are. The difference between these two approaches is very much one of personal preference. Personally, I prefer the second method in most circumstances, as I feel that it has some concrete advantages.

The unittest.mock method creates mocks for all attribute accesses. This can introduce subtle testing bugs, as code can start to depend on a new attribute and that will be mocked out by default. For example, if we wrote some code that used if response.cookies:, then the first method of mocking would always evaluate that to True in mock sessions, but the second would raise an AttributeError. I usually prefer to know that my mocks are incomplete through exceptions, rather than incorrect behavior.

Then, the former method is more difficult to use when writing mocks that include branching logic. They're a good fit for making assertions on what code path was followed, but less good for returning different data according to the circumstance. For example, if we wanted a mock session that could return different data for different URLs, the changes to the custom objects are relatively clear. The equivalent changes when using mock objects are much more complex.

Mocks with branching logic

To introduce per-url mocked responses using the Fake* objects, only the
FakeAIOHttpClient class and its invocation in mockclient need to be altered, and those
changes are very much standard Python logic.

```
@dataclass
class FakeAIOHttpClient:
    responses: t.Dict[str, str]

    @contextlib.asynccontextmanager
    async def get(self, url: str, headers: t.Optional[t.Dict[str,
    str]]=None) -> FakeAIOHttpResponse:
        if url in self.responses:
            yield FakeAIOHttpResponse(json_data=self.responses[url],
            status=200)
        else:
            yield FakeAIOHttpResponse(json_data=None, status=404)
```

However, an equivalent change to the unittest-based mock system requires
significantly more support code and for some work to be refactored to be more similar to
our custom mocking approach.

```
def FakeAIOHTTPClient(response_data):
    client = Mock()
    def find_response(url):
        get_request = MagicMock()
        response = Mock()
        if url in response_data:
            response.json = AsyncMock(return_value=response_data[url])()
            response.status = 200
        else:
            response.json = AsyncMock(return_value=None)()
            response.status = 404
        get_request.__aenter__ = AsyncMock(return_value=response)
        return get_request
    client.get = find_response
    return client
```

```
@pytest.fixture
def mockclient(data):
    return FakeAIOHTTPClient({
        "http://localhost/v/2.0/sensors/": data
    })
```

Data classes

You may have noticed the @dataclass decorator on the preceding classes, as they're not something we've used yet. Data classes are a Python feature that was introduced in the 3.7 release. They are roughly equivalent to the named tuple feature that was widely used in older version of Python; they're a way of defining containers for data that minimizes the amount of boilerplate required.

Normally, when defining a class to store data, we must define an __init__(...) method to take arguments (potentially with defaults) which are then set as instance attributes. Each field name appears three times, once in the argument list and once on either side of the assignment operation, for example, the following variant of our fake response object, which just stores two pieces of data:

```
class FakeAIOHttpResponse:
    def __init__(self, body: str, status: int):
        self.body = body
        self.status = status
```

This class structure is quite familiar to many Python developers, because we often need to create ways of storing structured data that uses attribute access to retrieve fields. The collections.namedtuple(...) function is a way of doing this in a declarative way:

```
import collections
```

```
FakeAIOHttpResponse = collections.namedtuple("FakeAIOHttpResponse",
["body", "status"])
```

Aside from reducing the need to declare classes that contain nothing but boilerplate code, this has the advantage of ensuring that a useful text representation of the object is returned and that comparison operators like == and != behave as expected. Our original class mentioned earlier doesn't compare the values on the class, so FakeAIOHttpResponse("", 200) == FakeAIOHttpResponse("", 200) evaluates as False with the class version and True with the namedtuple version.

361

A named tuple is a specialized type of tuple; the items can be accessed either using attribute access with the field name or item access with the index. That is, for an instance of FakeAIOHttpResponse, x.body == x[0]. Finally, they provide an _asdict() utility method, which returns a dictionary containing the same data as the named tuple instance.

The biggest downside of named tuples is that they cannot easily have methods added to them. It is possible to subclass named tuples and add methods that way, but I wouldn't recommend it due to the poor readability involved.

```
class FakeAIOHttpResponse(collections.namedtuple("", ["body", "status"])):
    async def json(self) -> t.Any:
        return json.loads(self.body)
```

This is where data classes shine. A class can be made into a dataclass by using the @dataclasses.dataclass decorator on the class definition. Fields are defined using the typing syntax, optionally with a default value. The dataclass decorator is responsible for converting these class variables into custom __init__(...), __repr__(), __eq__(...), and other methods.

```
@dataclass
class FakeAIOHttpResponse:
    body: str
    status: int = 200

    async def json(self) -> t.Any:
        return json.loads(self.body)
```

Tip   Sometimes you'll want to add other code to the __init__ method, beyond just storing values. You can do this with data classes by defining a __post_init__ method, which will be called after the boilerplate in __init__ is complete.

Although data classes offer many of the same features as named tuples, they are not entirely compatible with the API that named tuples provide. They do not implement item access,[6] and conversion to both dictionaries and tuples is done with `dataclasses.asdict(...)` and `dataclasses.astuple(...)` functions, rather than methods on the class itself.

Another advantage of data classes over named tuples, albeit one that we're not using here, is that they are mutable. It is possible to change the value of attributes of a data class object after it has been instantiated. The same is not true of named tuples. This feature is optional; classes defined with `@dataclass(frozen=True)` do not support attributes being changed after instantiation. Making a data class frozen has the advantage of also it *hashable*, meaning it can be stored as part of a set or the keys of a dict.

Caution   Although dataclasses that are frozen don't allow their values to be *replaced*, if one of the values is mutable, it's possible for this field to be changed in place. I don't recommend using the `frozen=True` option if you're using lists, sets, or dictionaries (for example) as value types.

There are a few other options that can be passed to the `@dataclass` decorator: `eq=False` suppresses the generation of an equality function so that instances that are the same values do not compare equal. Alternatively, passing `order=True` additionally generates rich comparison fields, where the ordering of the objects is the same as a tuple of their values, in order.

It is possible to specify per-field metadata for some advanced use cases. For example, we might want the repr of a response to look like `FakeAIOHttpResponse(url='http://localhost', status=200)`, that is, adding a URL item and omitting the body from the repr. We can do this by using a `field` object, as opposed to the standard method of writing a custom `__repr__()` method. A comparison of the two approaches is shown in Table 8-2.

---

[6]`response['body']` would not work.

Table 8-2. *Comparison of custom repr behavior with and without the dataclass helper*

Using a field(...) to customize the default repr	Using a custom __repr__

<pre>from dataclasses import
dataclass, field
 	
@dataclass
class FakeAIOHttpResponse:
    url: str
    body: str = field(repr=False)
    status: int = 200
 	
    async def json(self) -> t.Any:
        return json.loads(self.body)</pre>
	<pre>from dataclasses import dataclass
	
	@dataclass
	class FakeAIOHttpResponse:
	    url: str
	    body: str
	    status: int = 200
	
	    def __repr__(self):
	        name = type(self).__name__
	        url = self.url
	        status = self.status
	        return f"{name}({url=}, {status=})"
	
	    async def json(self) -> t.Any:
	        return json.loads(self.body)</pre>

The field(...) method has the advantage of being significantly shorter, albeit slightly less intuitive. The __repr__() method allows full control, at the expense of needing to reimplement the default behavior.

There is a situation where the field method is mandatory: to support fields whose default is a mutable object, such as a list or a dict. This is for the same reason that it's recommended not to use mutable objects as the default values for functions, as them being modified in place can cause data to bleed through across instances.

Field objects accept a default_factory parameter, which is a callable that generates the default for each instance. This can be a user-specified function or a class constructor that takes no arguments.

```
options: t.List[str] = field(default_factory=list)
```

contextlib

In the same way that we used yield to split the setup and teardown sections of a pytest fixture, we can use the decorators from contextlib in the standard library to create context managers without having to implement __enter__() and __exit__(...) method pairs explicitly.

The @contextlib.contextmanager decorator is the easiest way to create a context manager, especially the trivially simple ones we are working with here. The most common use of a context manager is to create some resource and make sure that it's cleaned up correctly afterward. Table 8-3 shows that if we were making a context manager that behaved the same way as our HTTP server fixture from earlier, the code would be almost identical.

Table 8-3. *Comparison of a pytest fixture with teardown and a context manager*

Pytest fixture to create a HTTP server	Context manager to create a HTTP server
```import pytest```	```import contextlib```

```@pytest.fixture(scope="module")```
```def http_server():```
    ```yield from run_server_in_thread(```
        ```"standard", {```
            ```"APD_SENSORS_API_KEY":```
            ```"testing"```
        ```}, 12081```
    ```)```
	```@contextlib.contextmanager```
	```def http_server():```
	    ```yield from run_server_in_thread(```
	        ```"standard", {```
	            ```"APD_SENSORS_API_KEY":```
	            ```"testing"```
	        ```}, 12081```
	    ```)```

More complex context managers, such as ones that need to handle exceptions happening within the code they wrap, need to treat the yield statement as the one that potentially raises an exception. The yield statement should therefore usually be within either a try/finally block or a with block to ensure that any resources are torn down correctly.

The get(...) method on FakeAIOHttpClient is an asynchronous context manager rather than a standard context manager. The @contextlib.contextmanager decorator creates __enter__() and __exit__(...) methods from a generator method; what we need is a decorator to create __aenter__() and __aexit__(...) coroutines from a generator coroutine. This is available as the @contextlib.asynccontextmanager decorator.

Test methods

Now that we have fixtures in place to support the faster integration testing of our code, we can begin writing the actual test functions. Firstly, we can verify the behavior of the get_data_points(...) method without the overhead of the HTTP server.[7] Then we can add tests for add_data_from_sensors(...) method that defers to get_data_points(...). Finally, we need tests to ensure that the database portion of the application is working correctly, which we still need to modify to remove blocking behavior.

The test methods shown in Listing 8-5 use a combination of the techniques we've used so far. The test for get_data_points(...) uses the mockclient made using custom objects. It is the first in a planned group of tests that all depend on the accurate behavior of the HTTP library. On the other hand, the add_data_from_sensors tests use a unittest.mock.Mock() object to mock the database session, as we only need to assert that certain methods were called when we expected.

The patch_aiohttp() fixture uses a combination of the two approaches, as well as the setup and teardown functionality of fixtures. The unittest.mock.patch(...) context manager takes a location of a Python object and replaces it with a mock so long as the context manager is active. As the add_data_from_sensors(...) method doesn't take a ClientSession as an argument, we can't pass our custom mock to it. This allows us to graft our custom mock method onto the aiohttp library, to be returned whenever our code under test creates a ClientSession, just like responses does with the requests library.

Listing 8-5. The various approaches of test methods for apd.aggregation

```python
from unittest.mock import patch, Mock, AsyncMock

import pytest

import apd.aggregation.collect

class TestGetDataPoints:
    @pytest.fixture
    def mut(self):
        return apd.aggregation.collect.get_data_points
```

---

[7]It's important to stress that these test functions are meant to complement the functional test suite, not replace it. Our test runs won't be faster unless we exclude functional tests.

```
    @pytest.mark.asyncio
    async def test_get_data_points(
        self, mut, mockclient: FakeAIOHttpClient, data
    ) -> None:
        datapoints = await mut("http://localhost", "", mockclient)

        assert len(datapoints) == len(data["sensors"])
        for sensor in data["sensors"]:
            assert sensor["value"] in (datapoint.data for datapoint in
            datapoints)
            assert sensor["id"] in (datapoint.sensor_name for datapoint in
            datapoints)

class TestAddDataFromSensors:
    @pytest.fixture
    def mut(self):
        return apd.aggregation.collect.add_data_from_sensors

    @pytest.fixture(autouse=True)
    def patch_aiohttp(self, mockclient):
        # Ensure all tests in this class use the mockclient
        with patch("aiohttp.ClientSession") as ClientSession:
            ClientSession.return_value.__aenter__ = AsyncMock(
            return_value=mockclient)
            yield ClientSession

    @pytest.fixture
    def db_session(self):
        return Mock()

    @pytest.mark.asyncio
    async def test_datapoints_are_added_to_the_session(self, mut,
    db_session) -> None:
        # The only times data should be added to the session are when
        # running the MUT
        assert db_session.add.call_count == 0
        datapoints = await mut(db_session, ["http://localhost"], "")
        assert db_session.add.call_count == len(datapoints)
```

The resulting tests are not overly complex and cover the same general functionality as the functional tests. They provide a base for future tests, with the functional tests providing a fallback that lets us be confident that our tests have useful assertions. The integration tests here are all *positive*, confirming that the normal case works. We do not yet have any that confirm that unusual or edge cases are handled correctly, but they're a good starting point.

Asynchronous databases

So far, we've been using the SQLAlchemy ORM to handle all interactions between the database and Python code, as it allows many of the peculiarities of databases to be put aside in favor of normal-looking Python code. Unfortunately, the SQLAlchemy ORM is not suitable for use in a purely asynchronous environment. SQLAlchemy doesn't guarantee that SQL queries only run in response to `session.query(...)` calls; queries can also run when accessing attributes on objects, not to mention insert and transaction management queries. All of these calls can block execution, severely impacting the performance of an asyncio application.

This doesn't mean that the SQLAlchemy ORM is slower when running in an asynchronous context; the blocking is usually minimal and still exists in synchronous uses of SQLAlchemy. Rather, it means that using the SQLAlchemy ORM in async code can cause degradation of performance back down to the same level as synchronous code, negating much of the benefit of using asyncio.

If we are willing to sacrifice the ORM component of SQLAlchemy, and use it only as a SQL statement generator and interface, the risk of unintentional queries won't occur. This is a real loss, the biggest we've considered so far in relation to making our code asynchronous, as the SQLAlchemy ORM is such a well-designed library.

There is no perfect solution to database connectivity at the time of writing; however, I feel that the statement generation approach is a good compromise. As long as you're not writing an asynchronous server application and can tolerate the risk of performance degradation, you should consider the pragmatic approach of using the ORM and just making every effort to avoid calling blocking code in the main thread.

Classic SQLAlchemy style

We'll use the statement generation approach in our example. We can't continue to use the declarative_base based class we created previously, as that could inadvertently trigger SQL queries. Using the "classic" style (i.e., explicit table objects that are not derived directly from a Python class that they represent) and not configuring up the ORM to link the table and our Python objects lets us safely use DataPoint objects without triggering implicit queries. An implementation of our existing table is given in Listing 8-6.

This approach means that we will not be dealing with our custom objects directly in the database layer, we'll be working with tables and will be responsible for translating between our objects and the SQLAlchemy API. However, we've only changed how we're representing the database, not the database structure, so we don't need to create any migrations for this change.

Listing 8-6. The "classic" style, with independent table and data classes

```python
from dataclasses import dataclass, field
import datetime
import typing as t

import sqlalchemy
from sqlalchemy.dialects.postgresql import JSONB, TIMESTAMP
from sqlalchemy.schema import Table

metadata = sqlalchemy.MetaData()

datapoint_table = Table(
    "sensor_values",
    metadata,
    sqlalchemy.Column("id", sqlalchemy.Integer, primary_key=True),
    sqlalchemy.Column("sensor_name", sqlalchemy.String),
    sqlalchemy.Column("collected_at", TIMESTAMP),
    sqlalchemy.Column("data", JSONB),
)
```

```
@dataclass
class DataPoint:
    sensor_name: str
    data: t.Dict[str, t.Any]
    id: int = None
    collected_at: datetime.datetime = field(
    default_factory=datetime.datetime.now)
```

Before we do anything else, we should update our `alembic/env.py` script, as that needs a reference to the `metadata` object in order to generate migrations. Previously, it imported `Base`, then accessed `Base.metadata`; we must change those lines to use our new metadata object, `apd.aggregation.database.metadata`.

We can no longer create database records by instantiating a `DataPoint` object and adding it to the session; instead, we make insert calls directly to the `datapoint_table` structure.

```
stmt = datapoint_table.insert().values(
    sensor_name="ACStatus",
    collected_at=datetime.datetime(2020,4,1,12,00,00),
    data=False
)
session.execute(stmt)
```

The `stmt` object is an instance of `Insert` from SQLAlchemy. This object represents the structure of the SQL statement to be executed; it isn't a string that is passed directly to the database. While it is possible to view a string that represents the statement, we need to specify what kind of database it's intended for, in order to get accurate results. That is done internally by SQLAlchemy, through a `stmt.compile(dialect=...)` method call based on the connection information. Different databases have slightly different variations of the SQL standard and ways to specify interpolated values; the compilation step is what applies database-specific syntax. All of the variants separate the values being passed from the structure of the SQL as part of the work to prevent SQL injection vulnerabilities.

Uncompiled

```
INSERT INTO datapoints (sensor_name, collected_at, data) VALUES
(:sensor_name, :collected_at, :data)
{'sensor_name': 'ACStatus', 'collected_at': datetime.datetime(2020, 4, 1,
12, 0), 'data': False}
```

mssql

```
INSERT INTO datapoints (sensor_name, collected_at, data) VALUES
(:sensor_name, :collected_at, :data)
{'sensor_name': 'ACStatus', 'collected_at': datetime.datetime(2020, 4, 1,
12, 0), 'data': False}
```

mysql

```
INSERT INTO datapoints (sensor_name, collected_at, data) VALUES (%s, %s, %s)
['ACStatus', datetime.datetime(2020, 4, 1, 12, 0), False]
```

Postgresql

```
INSERT INTO datapoints (id, sensor_name, collected_at, data) VALUES (%(id)
s, %(sensor_name)s, %(collected_at)s, %(data)s)
{'id': None, 'sensor_name': 'ACStatus', 'collected_at': datetime.
datetime(2020, 4, 1, 12, 0), 'data': False}
```

sqlite

```
INSERT INTO datapoints (sensor_name, collected_at, data) VALUES (?, ?, ?)
['ACStatus', datetime.datetime(2020, 4, 1, 12, 0), False]
```

We don't need to look at these strings for any reason other than curiosity, nor do we need to compile the insert statement manually. The session we've set up through SQLAlchemy processes an Insert object directly when executing it using session.execute(stmt).

This execute(...) method is what sends the statement to the database and waits for a response. It is this Python statement that can block, for example, if there is a SQL lock that needs to be waited for. The session.commit() call can also cause blocking, as this is where the previous insert commands are finalized. In short, with this approach, we need to make sure that any calls involving the session always happen in a different thread.

The ability to ignore the details of SQL generation and just call table.insert().values(...) demonstrates some of the advantages we're retaining by using SQLAlchemy, even in this more limited fashion. We can make this slightly better still, by writing utility functions that convert between the two data types. We might initially be tempted to use **dataclasses.asdict(...) to generate the body of the values(...) call, but that would include id=None. We don't want to set the id to be None in our SQL insert, we want to omit it from the arguments list so that the database sets it. To make this easier, we'll create a function on the data class (Listing 8-7) that calls asdict(self) but which only includes the id if it's been explicitly set.

Listing 8-7. Implementation of DataPoint class with a helper method for database queries

```
from dataclasses import dataclass, field, asdict
import datetime
import typing as t

@dataclass
class DataPoint:
    sensor_name: str
    data: t.Dict[str, t.Any]
    id: int = None
    collected_at: datetime.datetime = field(
    default_factory=datetime.datetime.now)

    def _asdict(self):
        data = asdict(self)
        if data["id"] is None:
            del data["id"]
        return data
```

Using run_in_executor

We discussed the run_in_executor(...) function briefly in the previous chapter, with the example of allowing time.sleep(1) to run in parallel with asyncio.sleep(1) rather than sequentially. That was a rather contrived example, but moving database calls to a new thread is a perfect fit for this.

Caution   The run_in_executor(...) method is not interchangeable with the with ThreadPoolExecutor() construction we used earlier. Both delegate work to a thread; the pool executor construction sets up a pool, submits work, and then waits for all work to finish, whereas the run_in_executor(...) approach creates a long-running pool and allows you to submit tasks and await their value from asynchronous code.

Many of the asyncio helper functions that we've used so far, such as asyncio.gather(...), asyncio.create_task(...), and asyncio.Lock(), automatically detect the current asyncio event loop. The run_in_executor(...) function is a bit different; it's only available as a method on the event loop instance. We need to get the current event loop ourselves with asyncio.get_running_loop() and then use that to submit functions to be run in an executor. I would recommend submitting one synchronous task that does all the work you need, rather than submitting individual tasks for each low-level call and glueing them together with asyncio logic, for example, creating a handle_result(...) function (Listing 8-8) that generates insert queries for a group of objects, rather than one function call for each object to be inserted.

Listing 8-8. Database integration function for adding data points

```
def handle_result(result: t.List[DataPoint], session: Session) ->
t.List[DataPoint]:
    for point in result:
        insert = datapoint_table.insert().values(**point._asdict())
        sql_result = session.execute(insert)
        point.id = sql_result.inserted_primary_key[0]
    return result
```

```
async def add_data_from_sensors(
    session: Session, servers: t.Tuple[str], api_key: t.Optional[str]
) -> t.List[DataPoint]:
    tasks: t.List[t.Awaitable[t.List[DataPoint]]] = []
    points: t.List[DataPoint] = []
    async with aiohttp.ClientSession() as http:
        tasks = [get_data_points(server, api_key, http) for server in servers]
        for results in await asyncio.gather(*tasks):
            points += results
    loop = asyncio.get_running_loop()
    await loop.run_in_executor(None, handle_result, points, session)
    return points
```

The arguments to `loop.run_in_executor` are (`executor, callable, *args`), where executor must be either an instance of `ThreadPoolExecutor` or `None` (to use the default executor, creating it if necessary).

Tip   If you're adapting lots of synchronous tasks, I'd recommend managing the thread pools directly. This will allow you to set their number of workers and therefore the number of simultaneous tasks they'll execute. This will also allow you to more effectively reason about what code can be executing simultaneously, when deciding what locking needs to be added to make the code thread-safe.

The `callable` function will be invoked as a task in that executor with the positional arguments specified in `*args`. You cannot specify keyword arguments to the callable as part of this API.

The best way to use a function that requires keyword arguments is by using the `functools.partial(...)` function. It transforms one function into another that takes fewer arguments. If we were to wrap the `handle_result(...)` function in a partial, as shown in the following, then the following function calls would be equivalent:

```
>>> only_points = functools.partial(handle_result, session=Session)
>>> only_session = functools.partial(handle_result, points=points)
>>> no_args = functools.partial(handle_result, points=points,
session=Session)
```

```
>>> handle_result(points=points, session=Session)
[DataPoint(...), DataPoint(...)]

>>> only_points(points=points)
[DataPoint(...), DataPoint(...)]

>>> only_session(session=Session)
[DataPoint(...), DataPoint(...)]

>>> no_args()
[DataPoint(...), DataPoint(...)]
```

Aside from APIs like run_in_executor(...) which do not support keyword arguments, it's sometimes useful to be able to pass functions around with some of their arguments set but not others, for example, to remove the need to pass database sessions or web requests into every function.

DJANGO'S ORM

Many Python developers who work with the Web will work with Django at some point in their career and may wonder what the equivalent process is for interacting with the Django ORM from asynchronous code, such as from channels.

My recommendation for Django would be to use the ORM as normal, but only from synchronous functions. You can call synchronous functions with the utility method @channels.db.database_sync_to_async, which can be used as a decorator on the synchronous functions to make them awaitable. This decorator delegates to run_in_executor(...) with an explicit thread pool, but also performs some Django-specific database connection management.

```
from channels.db import database_sync_to_async

@database_sync_to_async
def handle_result(result: t.List[t.Dict[str, t.Any]]) -> t.List[DataPoint]:
    points: t.List[DataPoints] = []
    for data in result:
        point = DataPoint(**data)
        point.save()
        points.append(point)
    return points
```

The preceding code would be an example of how a hypothetical `handle_result(...)` might look if it were to be used from the context of a Django channel. As Django strongly encourages performing all data-gathering operations in advance, before rendering a response, this is a suboptimal but workable solution.

Querying data

It's a simple matter to query data and receive Python objects when using SQLAlchemy's ORM. Still, as we're only using the query building and execution parts of SQLAlchemy, this is a little more complex. In ORM-enabled SQLAlchemy, we'd find all `DataPoint` entries for the PythonVersion sensor with

```
db_session.query(DataPoint).filter(DataPoint.sensor_name=="PythonVersion")
```

But we need to use the table object instead and reference its columns from the c attribute, as follows:

```
db_session.query(datapoint_table).filter(
datapoint_table.c.sensor_name=="PythonVersion")
```

The objects we get back are not `DataPoint` objects, but SQLAlchemy's own internal named tuple implementation called lightweight named tuples. These are returned for any query where there is no class mapper set up.

These internal named tuples offer an `_asdict()` method, so the best way of converting a `result` object to a `DataPoint` object is `DataPoint(**result._asdict())`. Unfortunately, these objects are generated dynamically and considered an implementation detail of SQLAlchemy. As such, we can't use these objects in type definitions for our functions. Once we've added a helper method for converting named tuples to DataClasses, our final code is the same as Listing 8-9.

Listing 8-9. Final implementation of DataPoint class that supports manual object mapping to SQLAlchemy

```
from dataclasses import dataclass, field, asdict
import datetime
import typing as t
```

```python
@dataclass
class DataPoint:
    sensor_name: str
    data: t.Dict[str, t.Any]
    id: int = None
    collected_at: datetime.datetime = field(
    default_factory=datetime.datetime.now)

    @classmethod
    def from_sql_result(cls, result):
        return cls(**result._asdict())

    def _asdict(self):
        data = asdict(self)
        if data["id"] is None:
            del data["id"]
        return data
```

We can now make queries using SQLAlchemy that return our objects but without the resulting objects having any direct connection to the database that could cause unexpected queries to be issued.

```python
results = map(
    DataPoint.from_sql_result,
    db_session.query(datapoint_table).filter(
    datapoint_table.c.sensor_name=="PythonVersion")
)
```

We can also use this approach when writing tests, making them almost as clear as the same code using the ORM style.

```python
@pytest.mark.asyncio
async def test_datapoints_can_be_mapped_back_to_DataPoints(
    self, mut, db_session, table, model
) -> None:
    datapoints = await mut(db_session, ["http://localhost"], "")
    db_points = [
```

```
        model.from_sql_result(result) for result in
        db_session.query(table)
    ]
    assert db_points == datapoints
```

Tip   If you're using the Pandas data analysis framework, DataFrame objects provide dedicated methods for loading and storing information from SQLAlchemy queries. These `read_sql(...)` and `to_sql(...)` methods are very useful when loading large data sets.

Avoiding complex queries

It's common to see people build very complex queries in an ORM, such as queries that involve multiple joins,[8] conditions, and subqueries. There are a couple of tricks that we can use to make for easier-to-understand code that represents complex conditions. For SQLAlchemy, that is the `@hybrid_property` feature, whereas for Django the equivalent is custom lookups and transforms.

In Chapter 6 we looked at how SQLAlchemy changes the behavior of class attributes in mapped classes so that columns can represent the value of a field or the SQL to represent the column, depending on whether the attribute access was made on an instance of the class or the class itself. Hybrid properties allow the same approach to be extended to your custom logic.

The benefit here is in reorganizing code, so to demonstrate where it can be useful, we first need a feature requirement that would benefit from refactoring. It's quite possible that we'll want to look at a summary of how common values were on a given day. The query to show the names of sensors, their distinct values, and how many times the value was seen for all entries that happened today can be represented in SQLAlchemy as the very long query:

---

[8]Sometimes even joins involving the same table multiple times, which can result in particularly confusing code.

```
value_counts = (
    db_session.query(
        datapoint_table.c.sensor_name,
        datapoint_table.c.data,
        sqlalchemy.func.count(datapoint_table.c.id)
    )
    .filter(
        sqlalchemy.cast(datapoint_table.c.collected_at, DATE)
        == sqlalchemy.func.current_date()
    )
    .group_by(datapoint_table.c.sensor_name, datapoint_table.c.data)
)
```

There are a couple of problems with this. Firstly, the name and data columns appear twice, as we want to group by them but we also need to be able to see which result is connected to which grouping, so they must also appear in the output columns. Secondly, the filter we've got is complex, both to read and to execute. Reading is difficult because it involves multiple calls to SQLAlchemy functions, rather than simple comparisons. Execution is difficult because we're modifying the collected_at attribute with a cast, which would invalidate any indexes on this column (if we'd set any up yet).

Note   I've used sqlalchemy.func.current_date() to represent the current date. Any functions available in the database can be accessed by name through sqlalchemy.func. This was purely a stylistic choice; it's no faster or slower to use datetime.date.today() or anything else that is interpreted by the database as a date.

The easiest way to see how PostgreSQL interprets a query is to open a database shell and run the query there with EXPLAIN ANALYZE modifiers.[9] The output format is rather complicated, but there are many resources for PostgreSQL that go into depth on how to read them and optimization methods.

For now, our objective is to create a query that is both easy to read and not unnecessarily slow. To start with, let's move the common columns into variables to cut down on repetition.

```python
headers = datapoint_table.c.sensor_name, datapoint_table.c.data
value_counts = (
    db_session.query(*headers, sqlalchemy.func.count(datapoint_table.c.id))
    .filter(
        sqlalchemy.cast(datapoint_table.c.collected_at, DATE)
        == sqlalchemy.func.current_date()
    )
    .group_by(*headers)
)
```

---

[9]This can be tricky if your query involves lots of parameters. There is a function in the sqlalchemy-utils package called analyze that will perform the analysis, but it also parses the results rather than displaying the standard format. The following (rather complex) one-liner, when placed in your .pdbrc file, will let you run EXPLAIN ANALYZE queries from a pdb prompt:

```
alias explain_analyze !_compiled=(%1).selectable.compile();_rows=(%2).
execute("EXPLAIN ANALYZE "+ str(_compiled), params=_compiled.params);
print("\n".join(str(_row[0]) for _row in _rows)) and used as follows:
```

```
(Pdb) explain_analyze example_query db_session
GroupAggregate    (cost=25.61..25.63  rows=1  width=72)  (actual  time=0.022..0.022
rows=0 loops=1)
  Group Key: sensor_name, data
  -> Sort  (cost=25.61..25.62 rows=1 width=68) (actual time=0.022..0.022 rows=0 loops=1)
        Sort Key: data
        Sort Method: quicksort  Memory: 25kB
        -> Seq Scan on sensor_values  (cost=0.00..25.60 rows=1 width=68)
        (actual time=0.018..0.018 rows=0 loops=1)
            Filter: (((sensor_name)::text = 'ACStatus'::text) AND
            ((collected_at)::date = CURRENT_DATE))
Planning Time: 1.867 ms
Execution Time: 0.063 ms
```

I've included this in the project .pdbrc starting from this chapter, so it will be available to you if you're following along with the accompanying code.

This leaves the filter section as the bottleneck, both for speed and for readability. The next step I'd propose is adding some indexes to the underlying table, on the collected_at and sensor_name fields. We do this by adding index=True to the fields on the table and generating a new alembic revision, as shown in the following:

```
datapoint_table = Table(
    "datapoints",
    metadata,
    sqlalchemy.Column("id", sqlalchemy.Integer, primary_key=True),
    sqlalchemy.Column("sensor_name", sqlalchemy.String, index=True),
    sqlalchemy.Column("collected_at", TIMESTAMP, index=True),
    sqlalchemy.Column("data", JSONB),
)

> pipenv run alembic revision --autogenerate -m "Add indexes to datapoints"
> pipenv run alembic upgrade head
```

Unfortunately, this isn't enough to make a difference to our execution plan, as we're manipulating the collected_at column as part of the comparison. This invalidates the index, as the results of the CAST() function are not one of the operations that can be cached by the index. It is possible to create a function in your database that returns the date for a given timestamp and to index on the result of that function, but that approach wouldn't make our code any easier to read.

Instead, I would recommend factoring this condition out into an attribute of the class using @hybrid_property. We could replicate the same condition, but this would only make the code easier to read, not more efficient to execute. An advantage of factoring this condition out is that the balance between readability and efficiency changes: we can afford to have a more efficient but less readable condition if it's hidden behind a utility function with a useful name, rather than scattered throughout the codebase.

The @hybrid_property decorator works similarly to the standard @property decorator, except that it has optional expression=, update_expression=, and comparator= attributes. An expression is a class method that returns a *selectable* (i.e., something that represents a value to SQLAlchemy), such as CAST(datapoint_table.c.collected_at, DATE). An update_expression is a class method that takes a value and returns a list of 2-tuples of columns and new values for them, acting as the inverse of expression to allow for updating the column. These two allow for facades to columns that act the same way as native columns. Hybrid properties are often used for things like full name, to concatenate first and last names.[10] It's common for only the `expression` to be implemented, without an `update_expression`. In this case, the property is read-only.

The `comparator` property is a bit different: it can't be used in combination with either the `expression` or `update_expression` features, but it allows for more complex cases to be implemented, where both halves of the comparison operator can be customized before being sent to the database. A common use of this is for lowercasing email addresses or usernames, to try and make them case insensitive.[11]

The reason that comparators and expressions are not compatible is that the `expression` feature is implemented by using a default comparator called the `ExprComparator`, so we can't provide our own comparator without it overriding the code that handles `expression`. As we want to use both features, we can subclass the `ExprComparator` to use the ability it has to delegate to the expression but also override the implementation of the comparator functions.

We can create a `@hybrid_property` that casts the datetime to a date but also uses a custom comparator to take advantage of some database-specific optimizations. Postgres treats dates as being equivalent to a datetime where the time component is midnight. Rather than ensuring that both sides of the comparison are dates, we can ensure that the right-hand side is midnight or later on the date specified and before midnight on the following day. We can achieve this by ensuring that the right-hand side of the comparison is a date and adding 1 to it to find the following day. This allows us to make two comparisons using the index to achieve the same result as one comparison that doesn't use the index. The updated DataPoint implementation is given in Listing 8-10.

---

[10]This is commonly used, but please don't do it. Not everyone has both first and last names; there's no universal way of splitting a full name into constituent names, and there's no way to join constituent names into a full name. See also "Falsehoods Programmers Believe About Names" (and the related articles, ... *time*, ... *addresses*, ... *maps*, ... *gender*, etc.). It is as incumbent on us as engineers to point out these flaws as it was for us to point out the flaws with two digit dates in the 1990s.

[11]These comparators will only work when being queried from SQLAlchemy; they do not change the behavior of unique constraints in the database. You will need to ensure that these constraints are correct too, such as by specifying them as

```
Index("unique_username_idx", func.lower(user_table.c.username), unique=True)
```

Listing 8-10. DataPoint table and model, with transparent optimized comparator for dates

```python
from __future__ import annotations

from dataclasses import dataclass, field, asdict
import datetime
import typing as t

import sqlalchemy
from sqlalchemy.dialects.postgresql import JSONB, DATE, TIMESTAMP
from sqlalchemy.ext.hybrid import ExprComparator, hybrid_property
from sqlalchemy.orm import sessionmaker
from sqlalchemy.schema import Table

metadata = sqlalchemy.MetaData()

datapoint_table = Table(
    "sensor_values",
    metadata,
    sqlalchemy.Column("id", sqlalchemy.Integer, primary_key=True),
    sqlalchemy.Column("sensor_name", sqlalchemy.String, index=True),
    sqlalchemy.Column("collected_at", TIMESTAMP, index=True),
    sqlalchemy.Column("data", JSONB),
)

class DateEqualComparator(ExprComparator):

    def __init__(self, fallback_expression, raw_expression):
        # Do not try and find update expression from parent
        super().__init__(None, fallback_expression, None)
        self.raw_expression = raw_expression

    def __eq__(self, other):
        """ Returns True iff on the same day as other """
        other_date = sqlalchemy.cast(other, DATE)
        return sqlalchemy.and_(
            self.raw_expression >= other_date,
            self.raw_expression < other_date + 1,
        )
```

```python
    def operate(self, op, *other, **kwargs):
        other = [sqlalchemy.cast(date, DATE) for date in other]
        return op(self.expression, *other, **kwargs)

    def reverse_operate(self, op, other, **kwargs):
        other = [sqlalchemy.cast(date, DATE) for date in other]
        return op(other, self.expression, **kwargs)

@dataclass
class DataPoint:
    sensor_name: str
    data: t.Dict[str, t.Any]
    id: t.Optional[int] = None
    collected_at: datetime.datetime = field(
    default_factory=datetime.datetime.now)

    @classmethod
    def from_sql_result(cls, result) -> DataPoint:
        return cls(**result._asdict())

    def _asdict(self) -> t.Dict[str, t.Any]:
        data = asdict(self)
        if data["id"] is None:
            del data["id"]
        return data

    @hybrid_property
    def collected_on_date(self):
        return self.collected_at.date()

    @collected_on_date.comparator
    def collected_on_date(cls):
        return DateEqualComparator(
            cls,
            sqlalchemy.cast(datapoint_table.c.collected_at, DATE),
            datapoint_table.c.collected_at,
        )
```

The ExprComparator type takes three arguments to its constructor, the model class, the expression, and the hybrid property that it's part of. The class= and hybrid_property= arguments in __init__(...) are used to implement the update behavior, but as we don't need this feature, we'll simplify the interface and pass None to these parameters. The expression parameter is the one we want to use for queries and for any comparisons (unless otherwise stated). In the __init__(...) function, we add a new parameter for the underlying column so that we can access the raw data in our custom comparison functions.

The operate(...) and reverse_operate(...) functions are what implement the various comparisons. They allow for manipulation of parameters on both sides of the comparison, which we need to ensure that the thing being compared to is CAST() to a DATE in PostgreSQL. The __eq__(...) method is our custom equality checker, where we implement a more efficient version of checking if both sides are the same date, as described earlier.

The effect of all this is that we can seamlessly compare two datetime values and get the correct result. Both sides are CAST() to DATE unless it's an equality check (the one we were trying to optimize), in which case only the argument is CAST() to a DATE, allowing the column on the left-hand side to make use of indexes. The possible Python expressions, the SQL or Python they're translated into, and whether an index can be used are shown in Table 8-4.

Table 8-4. *Summary of effects of each operation on the hybrid property*

Python expression	Evaluation result	Index used
DataPoint.collected_on_ date	CAST(sensor_values. collected_at AS DATE)	No
DataPoint(...).collected_ on_date	datetime.date(2020, 4, 1)	N/A(Evaluated in Python)
DataPoint.collected_on_ date == other_date	sensor_values.collected_ at >= CAST(%(param_1) s AS DATE) AND sensor_ values.collected_at < CAST(%(param_1)s AS DATE) + %(param_2)s	Yes (collected_at only, not the right-hand side)

(continued)

Table 8-4. (*continued*)

Python expression	Evaluation result	Index used
DataPoint.collected_on_date < other_date	CAST(sensor_values.collected_at AS DATE) < CAST(%(param_1)s AS DATE)	No
DataPoint(...).collected_on_date == other_date	datetime.date(2020, 4, 1) == other_date	N/A (Evaluated in Python)
DataPoint(...).collected_on_date < other_date	datetime.date(2020, 4, 1) < other_date	N/A (Evaluated in Python)

With this `collected_on_date` expression and comparator, we can simplify the query code significantly. Using this as the condition is much easier to understand when reading the code, and we've made sure that efficient SQL is being generated that makes use of the indexes.

```
headers = table.c.sensor_name, table.c.data
value_counts = (
    db_session.query(*headers, sqlalchemy.func.count(table.c.id))
    .filter(
        model.collected_on_date == sqlalchemy.func.current_date()
    )
    .group_by(*headers)
)
```

DJANGO'S ORM (REDUX)

Django's ORM handles this type of problem differently, but equivalent functionality does exist. A brief explanation of how to approach this (for people already familiar with Django) is given in this subsection. Check the additional resources at the end of this chapter for more details.

Django doesn't have an equivalent to @hybrid_property or to storing arbitrary SQL constructions in variables. Code is factored out into reusable components using lookups and transforms.

These are referenced in queries in a similar way to joins, so if the preceding code were a Django model, we would be able to filter by date collected using

```
DataPoints.objects.filter(collected_at__date=datetime.date.today())
```

This uses the built-in `date` transform on datetime fields, which casts the datetime to a date. A transformer is defined with a `lookup_name` attribute to specify the name it's available as and an `output_field` attribute to specify the type it creates. It can have a `function` attribute (if it maps directly to a single-argument database function), or it can define a custom `as_sql(...)` method.

A lookup works similarly to a transformer, but it cannot be chained and therefore does not have an output type. It provides a `lookup_name` attribute and an `as_sql(...)` method, to generate the relevant SQL. These can also be accessed by __name, with the lookup named `exact` being the default if no other is specified.

Both transformers and lookups need to be registered to be used. They can be registered against a field type or against another transformer. If they're registered on a field, they'll always be available on any expression that has that type, but if they're registered against a transformer, they'll only be valid if they immediately follow the transformer.We can build a custom equality check by defining a custom `exact` lookup on the `TruncDate` transformer used in `collected_at__date`, as shown in Listing 8-11. This would apply whenever we use `datetimefield__date`, but not when using native date columns.

Listing 8-11. Implementation of a date comparison in Django's ORM

```
from django.db import models
from django.db.models.functions.datetime import TruncDate

@TruncDate.register_lookup
class DateExact(models.Lookup):
    lookup_name = 'exact'

    def as_sql(self, compiler, connection):
        # self.lhs (left-hand-side of the comparison) is always TruncDate, we
        # want its argument
        underlying_dt = self.lhs.lhs
        # Instead, we want to wrap the rhs with TruncDate
        other_date = TruncDate(self.rhs)
        # Compile both sides
```

```
lhs, lhs_params = compiler.compile(underlying_dt)
rhs, rhs_params = compiler.compile(other_date)
params = lhs_params + rhs_params + lhs_params + rhs_params
# Return ((lhs >= rhs) AND (lhs < rhs+1)) - compatible with
# postgresql only!
return '%s >= %s AND %s < (%s + 1)' % (lhs, rhs, lhs, rhs), params
```

As with the SQLAlchemy version, this allows for an efficient, custom lookup when using collected_at__date=datetime.date.today(), but falls back to the less efficient cast behavior for collected_at__date__le==datetime.date.today() and other comparisons.

Querying against views

It's possible that a query that is difficult to represent with the ORM is needed in many places throughout the codebase. This is slightly more common when using the Django ORM due to how joins are specified, but it does happen when using SQLAlchemy. A typical example is when correlating multiple rows within a table, especially by date or geographical location, rather than a relation to a row in another table. For example, a database that stores users and travel plans and wants to query what pairs of users are near to each other on a given date is hard to represent in an ORM.

In such cases, you may find it easier to create database views and make your queries against them. It won't change the performance characteristics,[12] but does allow for the complex queries to be treated like a table, significantly simplifying the Python side of the equation.

SQLAlchemy supports tables derived from views, so we could use the query we created earlier and transform it into a view, and then map that back into SQLAlchemy as a table. We could create the view manually in the database console, but I'd recommend creating a new alembic revision to issue the CREATE VIEW statement, so that it can be deployed across instances more easily. Create the alembic revision without the --autogenerate flag, and modify the resulting file, as shown in Listing 8-12.

---

[12]Unless postgresql's MATERIALIZED VIEW feature, which caches its results until explicitly refreshed.

Listing 8-12. New migration to add a view with raw SQL

```python
"""Add daily summary view

Revision ID: 6962f8455a6d
Revises: 4b2df8a6e1ce
Create Date: 2019-12-03 11:50:24.403402

"""
from alembic import op

# revision identifiers, used by Alembic.
revision = "6962f8455a6d"
down_revision = "4b2df8a6e1ce"
branch_labels = None
depends_on = None

def upgrade():
    create_view = """
    CREATE VIEW daily_summary AS
      SELECT
        datapoints.sensor_name AS sensor_name,
        datapoints.data AS data,
        count(datapoints.id) AS count
    FROM datapoints
    WHERE
        datapoints.collected_at >= CAST(CURRENT_DATE AS DATE)
        AND
        datapoints.collected_at < CAST(CURRENT_DATE AS DATE) + 1
    GROUP BY
        datapoints.sensor_name,
        datapoints.data;
    """
    op.execute(create_view)

def downgrade():
    op.execute("""DROP VIEW daily_summary""")
```

We can now create a table object to reference this view, allowing us to generate queries in SQLAlchemy:

```
daily_summary_view = Table(
    "daily_summary",
    metadata,
    sqlalchemy.Column("sensor_name", sqlalchemy.String),
    sqlalchemy.Column("data", JSONB),
    sqlalchemy.Column("count", sqlalchemy.Integer),
    info={"is_view": True},
)
```

The info line allows us to set arbitrary metadata. In this case, the is_view metadata is used in the env.py file to configure alembic to ignore tables with this marker when autogenerating revisions. Without this, alembic would try to create matching tables which would conflict with our views. The env.py file needs to be modified to include the function given in Listing 8-13, and the two context.configure(...) function calls must have include_object=include_object added to the arguments.

Listing 8-13. Changes to env.py to enable Table objects to represent views

```
from logging.config import fileConfig

from sqlalchemy import engine_from_config
from sqlalchemy import pool
from alembic import context

from apd.aggregation.database import metadata as target_metadata

def include_object(object, name, type_, reflected, compare_to):
    if object.info.get("is_view", False):
        return False
    return True

def run_migrations_online():
    connectable = engine_from_config(
        config.get_section(config.config_ini_section),
```

```
        prefix="sqlalchemy.",
        poolclass=pool.NullPool,
    )

    with connectable.connect() as connection:
        context.configure(
            connection=connection,
            target_metadata=target_metadata,
            include_object=include_object,
        )

        with context.begin_transaction():
            context.run_migrations()
```

With the preceding changes, it's possible to simplify the summary SQL statement down to db_session.query(daily_summary_view) while executing the same SQL statements. This change to using views should be carefully considered each time you use it. It's usually not clearer to use a view over a SQL statement, but it's an underused technique that I recommend you bear in mind for the more complex queries.

Alternatives

The partial use of SQLAlchemy is what I would recommend for interacting with SQL databases in an asynchronous context, but it's far from perfect. There are some alternative approaches that may be appropriate depending on your use case.

There are some async-native ORMs being developed, such as *Tortoise ORM*. It is built to support asyncio from its foundations, so it does not suffer from the same potential blocking problems that SQLAlchemy suffers from. It is currently a young project, so while it's an interesting approach that I will be keeping my eye on, I cannot recommend it for production code at this time.

Another approach is to drop down to a lower level of database integration using a tool like *asyncpg*. This allows for fully asynchronous interaction with the database, without resorting to off-loading work to threads. The downside is that there is no built-in SQL generator, so it's significantly less user-friendly, and you are more likely to make mistakes. Some simple applications that need particularly fast database connections do use this approach, but it's not one that I'd recommend in the general case.

Finally, there is the pragmatic approach to the risk of SQLAlchemy causing blocking queries that I alluded to earlier in this chapter. Sometimes, the best solution is to accept the risk, because the benefits of using SQLAlchemy more naturally outweigh the consequences of performance losses. This would be absolutely unacceptable in a server-side application, where blocking and slowdown can cause severe degradation of performance for clients, but in a client application where asyncio is being used to improve performance of code that would otherwise be single-threaded, there's very little downside to just using SQLAlchemy with a best-effort approach to running blocking code in executors.

Global variables in asynchronous code

Especially in web development, it's common to find yourself in a situation where you *always* need access to a particular object, meaning that all of your functions need to take this object as a parameter. This is often the request object, which represents the HTTP request that the server is currently handling. It's also common for there to be a configuration object, and in our asynchronous code, we've found ourselves adding a `ClientSession` object to many of our function signatures, rather than instantiating a new one for every HTTP request.

All these are examples of places where the idea of global variables is appealing. Django and Flask both provide a globally scoped way of accessing the configuration (`django.settings` and `flask.current_app.config`), and Flask additionally provides the request through `flask.request`.

You often hear people criticize code that uses global variables, saying that it's evidence that your application hasn't been designed properly. I take a more pragmatic view: objects that are potentially needed by almost every function *shouldn't* exist, but sometimes they do. They should, therefore, be available globally, to prevent them from polluting the function signatures of the entire system.

Let's make our `ClientSession` object one of these globally available items using Python's `contextvars` feature. Context variables are an evolution of the idea of thread-local variables: variables that are globally scoped but can have different values for different simultaneous code. A thread-local variable, created through `threading.Local()`, allows arbitrary data to be stored and retrieved through attribute access, but only within one thread. Any other simultaneous threads will not see the data stored by the other threads; each thread can have its value for that variable.

Our code is not threaded; it uses asynchronous function calls to introduce concurrency, so a thread-local variable would always show the same data to all concurrent tasks. This is where context variables are useful; they provide the same scoping of values with arbitrary scopes, rather than limiting the scope to always being the current thread.

Context variables are defined with the `contextvars.ContextVar(...)` constructor which takes the name of the variable as an argument.

```
from contextvars import ContextVar
import aiohttp

http_session_var: ContextVar[aiohttp.ClientSession] = ContextVar("http_session")
```

The `ContextVar` object doesn't store the value directly; it silently delegates to a context object. You can manually instantiate context objects and execute a function using that context, but there is no need to do this with asynchronous code.[13] Whenever a coroutine is scheduled as a task, a new context is allocated, with values copied from the parent task's context.

Values can be set for a `ContextVar` using the `set(...)` method and retrieved with the `get()` method. If a piece of code tries to call `get()` on a context variable that has not been set in the current context, a LookupError is raised. The necessary modifications are shown as Table 8-5.

Table 8-5. *Changes to get_data_points(...) so the HTTP client is passed as a context variable rather than a parameter*

| ```python
http = http_session_var.get()
to_get = http.get(url,
headers=headers)
async with to_get as request:
    result = await request.json()
    ok = request.status == 200
``` | ```python
async with aiohttp.ClientSession() as http:
        http_session_var.set(http)
        tasks = [
            get_data_points(server, api_key)
            for server in servers
        ]
``` |

---

[13]For synchronous code, a new context can be created and a function invoked that uses that context with

```
context = contextvars.copy_context()
context.run(your_callable)
```

It's also possible to temporarily override the value for a context variable, using the return value of set(...). This isn't usually necessary, but if you do need to change a variable within a coroutine and then change it back again, then this is the preferred pattern:

```
reset_token = http_session_var.set(mockclient)
try:
    datapoints = await get_data_points("http://localhost", "")
finally:
    http_session_var.reset(reset_token)
```

EXERCISE 8-1: EXTENDING THE API

This chapter has introduced a lot of new concepts and involves some complex test setup. This code is complex, but we need to be confident in updating it when a new version is released.

Right now, we don't have any identifier for a sensor beyond its URL, and that can change over time as IP addresses are reallocated. We should create a way for a sensor endpoint to be identified, so we can more easily find data from a single sensor. Add a new v2.1 API to the apd.sensors package that provides a new endpoint. This endpoint should be

```
@version.route("/deployment_id")
def deployment_id() -> t.Tuple[t.Dict[str, t.Any], int, t.Dict[str, str]]:
    headers = {"Content-Security-Policy": "default-src 'none'"}
    data = {"deployment_id":
    flask.current_app.config["APD_SENSORS_DEPLOYMENT_ID"]}
    return data, 200, headers
```

You will need to modify many parts of the test setup to accommodate this change, including the fixture code for previous APIs. Remember, the intention isn't for the test code of old APIs to never change, just the user-facing API itself.

Once you've done this, update the apd.aggregation package to store deployment_id as an attribute of DataPoint, and use the v2.1 API to retrieve the deployment ID from the endpoint.

This is a significant change, equivalent to a major version bump for the apd.sensors package, and perhaps the most difficult exercise in this book. It is, however, the kind of change that you will have to make in real code sooner or later, so it's good to practice.

The completed versions of both of these changes are in the code that accompanies this chapter.

Summary

We've covered a lot of the practicalities of running asynchronous code in this chapter, especially some of the difficulties you may encounter when working with databases in an asynchronous context. The most important thing to remember, whether dealing with SQLAlchemy, the Django ORM, or connections to another database type that uses synchronous code, is that the run_in_executor pattern is necessary to avoid blocking behavior drastically reducing performance. There is a balance that needs to be drawn between the performance benefits and the code readability benefits, though. This is perhaps the most crucial balance that you should keep in mind when writing asynchronous code.

We also covered many techniques that are generally useful when writing Python code, asynchronous or otherwise. Custom data classes and context managers using `contextlib` are extremely useful pieces of functionality, which you will have use for in lots of different contexts. Context variables and efficient ORM queries are both very useful, but to a lesser degree.

The `apd.aggregation` package has grown a lot over the course of this chapter, to the point that it's of sufficient quality to be usable in production. In the next chapter, we'll look at analyzing the data and building useful user interfaces to display reports.

Additional resources

I recommend the following resources for more information on the topics covered in this chapter:

> For information on implementing custom SQL behavior in Django's ORM, see `https://docs.djangoproject.com/en/3.0/ref/models/expressions/`.

> The full SQLAlchemy documentation on hybrid attributes, including information on some less commonly used features, is at `https://docs.sqlalchemy.org/en/14/orm/extensions/hybrid.html`.

Django's documentation on mixing synchronous and asynchronous code is at `https://docs.djangoproject.com/en/3.0/topics/async/` which includes information on database operations and helper functions for bridging the gap between synchronous and asynchronous code in Django apps.

The web app at `https://explain.depesz.com/` is a useful tool to help understand the result of PostgreSQL EXPLAIN ANALYZE statements, by reformatting them as a table and color-coding timing information.

`https://github.com/getsentry/responses` is a useful library for creating mock HTTP responses when using the requests HTTP library.

CHAPTER 9

Viewing the data

We started investigating the types of queries we might be interested in at the end of the previous chapter, but we've not yet written any routines to help us make sense of the data we're collecting. In this chapter, we return to Jupyter notebooks, this time as a data analysis tool rather than a prototyping aid.

IPython and Jupyter seamlessly support both synchronous and asynchronous function calls. We have a (mostly) free choice between the two types of API. As the rest of the `apd.aggregation` package is asynchronous, I recommend that we create some utility coroutines to extract and analyze data.

Query functions

A Jupyter notebook would be able to import and use SQLAlchemy functions freely, but that would require users to understand a lot about the internals of the aggregation system's data structures. It would effectively mean that the tables and models that we've created become part of the public API, and any changes to them may mean incrementing the major version number and documenting changes for end-users.

Instead, let's create some functions that return `DataPoint` records for users to interact with. This way, only the `DataPoint` objects and the function signatures are part of the API that we must maintain for people. We can always add more functions later, as we discover additional requirements.

To begin with, the most important feature that we need is the ability to find data records, ordered by the time they were collected. This lets users write some analysis code to analyze the values of the sensors over time. We may also want to filter this by the sensor type, the deployment identifier, and a date range.

We have to decide what form we want the function to have. Should it return a list or tuple of objects or an iterator? A tuple would allow us to easily count the number of items we retrieved and to iterate over the list multiple times. On the other hand, an iterator

397

© Matthew Wilkes 2020
M. Wilkes, *Advanced Python Development*, https://doi.org/10.1007/978-1-4842-5793-7_9

would allow us to minimize RAM use, which may help us support much larger data sets, but restricts us to only being able to iterate over the data once. We'll create iterator functions, as they allow for more efficient code. The iterators can be converted to tuples by the calling code, so our users are able to choose to iterate over a tuple if they prefer.

Before we can write this function, we need a way for users to set up a database connection. As one of our aims is to hide the details of the database from our end-users, we don't want to require using a SQLAlchemy function for this. The custom function we create (Listing 9-1) for connecting to the database can also set up context variables to represent our connection and avoid the need for an explicit session argument to all of our search functions.

Listing 9-1. query.py with a context manager to connect to the database

```
import contextlib
from contextvars import ContextVar
import functools
import typing as t

from sqlalchemy import create_engine
from sqlalchemy.orm import sessionmaker
from sqlalchemy.orm.session import Session

db_session_var: ContextVar[Session] = ContextVar("db_session")

@contextlib.contextmanager
def with_database(uri: t.Optional[str] = None) -> t.Iterator[Session]:
    """Given a URI, set up a DB connection, and return a Session as a
    context manager """
    if uri is None:
        uri = "postgresql+psycopg2://localhost/apd"
    engine = create_engine(uri)
    sm = sessionmaker(engine)
    Session = sm()
    token = db_session_var.set(Session)
    try:
        yield Session
        Session.commit()
```

```
    finally:
        db_session_var.reset(token)
        Session.close()
```

This function acts as a (synchronous) context manager, setting up a database connection and an associated session and both returning that session and setting it as the value of the db_session_var context variable before entering the body of the associated with block. It also unsets this session, commits any changes, and closes the session when the context manager exits. This ensures that there are no lingering locks in the database, that data is persisted, and that if functions that use the db_session_var variable can only be used inside the body of this context manager.

If we ensure that the environment that we've installed the aggregation package into is registered as a kernel with Jupyter, we can start to experiment with writing utility functions in a notebook. I'd also recommend installing some helper packages so we can more easily visualize the results.

```
> pipenv install ipython matplotlib
> pipenv run ipython kernel install --user --name="apd.aggregation"
```

We can now start a new Jupyter notebook (Listing 9-2), select the apd.aggregation kernel and connect to the database, using the new with_database(...) decorator. To test the connection, we can manually query the database using the resulting session and our datapoint_table object.

Listing 9-2. Jupyter cell to find number of sensor records

```
from apd.aggregation.query import with_database
from apd.aggregation.database import datapoint_table

with with_database("postgresql+psycopg2://apd@localhost/apd") as session:
    print(session.query(datapoint_table).count())
```

We also need to write the function that returns DataPoint objects for the user to analyze. Eventually, we'll have to deal with performance issues due to processing large amounts of data, but the first code you write to solve a problem should not be optimized, a naïve implementation is both easier to understand and more likely not to suffer from being too *clever*. We'll look at some techniques for optimization in the next chapter.

PREMATURE OPTIMIZATION

Debugging is twice as hard as writing the code in the first place. Therefore, if you write the code as cleverly as possible, you are, by definition, not smart enough to debug it.

—Brian Kernighan

Python is not the fastest programming language; it can be tempting to write your code to minimize the inherent slowness, but I would strongly recommend fighting this urge. I've seen "highly optimized" code that takes an hour to execute, which, when replaced with a naïve implementation of the same logic, takes two minutes to complete.

It isn't common, but when you make your code more elaborate, you're making your job harder when it comes to improving it.

If you write the simplest version of a method, you can compare it to subsequent versions to determine if you're making code faster or just more complex.

The first version of get_data() that we'll implement is one that returns all the DataPoint objects in the database, without having to worry about dealing with any SQLAlchemy objects. We already decided that we would create a generator coroutine, rather than a function (or coroutine) that returns a list of DataPoint objects, so our initial implementation is the one in Listing 9-3.

Listing 9-3. Simplest implementation of get_data()

```
async def get_data() -> t.AsyncIterator[DataPoint]:
    db_session = db_session_var.get()
    loop = asyncio.get_running_loop()
    query = db_session.query(datapoint_table)
    rows = await loop.run_in_executor(None, query.all)
    for row in rows:
        yield DataPoint.from_sql_result(row)
```

This function gets the session from the context variable set up by `with_database(...)`, builds a query object, and then runs that object's all method using an executor, giving way to other tasks while the all method runs. Iterating over the query object rather than calling `query.all()` would cause database operations to be triggered as the loop runs, so we must be careful to only set up the query in asynchronous code and delegate the `all()` function call to the executor. The result of this is a list of SQLAlchemy's lightweight result named tuples in the rows variable, which we can then iterate over yielding the matching `DataPoint` object.

As `rows` variable contains a list of all the result objects, we know that all the data has been processed by the database and parsed SQLAlchemy in the executor before execution passes back to our `get_data()` function. This means that we're using all the RAM needed to store the full results set before the first `DataPoint` object is available to the end-user. Storing all this data when we don't know that we need all of it is a little memory and time inefficient, but elaborate methods to paginate the data in the iterator would be an example of premature optimization. Don't change this from the naïve approach until it becomes a problem.

We always have to deal with the memory and time overheads of retrieving the SQLAlchemy row objects, but the numbers in Table 9-1 give us an idea of how much overhead we are adding to the system by converting them to `DataPoint` classes. A million rows would involve an extra 152 megabytes of RAM and an additional 1.5 seconds of processing time. Both of these are well within the capacity of modern computers and appropriate for infrequent tasks, so they are not of immediate concern.

Table 9-1. *Comparison of RAM usage and instantiation time for the SQLAlchemy row and our DataPoint class*

Object	Size[1]	Time to instantiate[2]
SQLAlchemy result row	80 bytes	0.4 microseconds
DataPoint	152 bytes	1.5 microseconds

Results may vary between Python implementations and processing power available

However, because we're creating an iterator, there is no guarantee that our DataPoint objects will all be resident in memory at once. If the consuming code does not keep a reference to them, then they can be garbage collected immediately after they're used. For example, in Listing 9-4 we use our two new helper functions to count the rows without any data point objects being resident in memory.

Listing 9-4. Jupyter cell to count data points using our helper context manager

```
from apd.aggregation.query import with_database, get_data

with with_database("postgresql+psycopg2://apd@localhost/apd") as session:
    count = 0
    async for datapoint in get_data():
        count += 1
    print(count)
```

---

[1]Size is calculated using `sys.getsizeof(...)`. This does not include the size of attributes on an object, which can be found with `sys.getsizeof(obj.__dict__)` for simple objects.
[2]Estimated using `timeit.timeit(...)`, as follows:

```
setup = """
import datetime
import uuid
from sqlalchemy.util._collections import lightweight_named_tuple
result = lightweight_named_tuple("result", ["id", "collected_at", "sensor_name",
"deployment_id", "data",])
data = (1, datetime.datetime.now(), "Example", uuid.uuid4(), None)
"""

timeit.timeit("result(data)", setup)
```

Merely counting the data points isn't an interesting way of analyzing the data. We can start trying to make sense of the data by plotting values on a scatter plots. Let's start with a simple sanity check, plotting the value of the `RelativeHumidity` sensor against date (Listing 9-5). This is a good one to start with, as the stored data is a floating-point number rather than a dictionary-based structure, so we don't need to parse the values.

The matplotlib library is perhaps the most popular plotting library in Python. Its `plot_date(...)` function is a great fit for plotting a series of values against time. It takes a list of values for the x axis and a corresponding list of values for the y axis, as well as the style to be used when plotting a point[3] and a flag to set which axis contains the date values. Our `get_data(...)` function doesn't return what we need for the x and y parameters directly, it returns an async iterator of data point objects.

We can convert an async iterable of data point objects to a list of tuples containing date and value pairs from a single sensor using a list comprehension. At that point, we have a list of date and value pairs and can use the built-in `zip(...)`[4] function to invert the grouping to a pair of lists, one for date and the other for value.

Listing 9-5. Relative humidity plotting jupyter cell, with the output chart it generates

```
from apd.aggregation.query import with_database, get_data

from matplotlib import pyplot as plt

async def plot():
    points = [
        (dp.collected_at, dp.data)
        async for dp in get_data()
```

---

[3]The "o" style specifies a circular marker and no line. The string can contain a marker type, a line style, and a color. *r would plot red stars, - is a line in the default color with no markers, s--m is magenta squares connected by a dashed line, etc. The additional resource list in this chapter contains a link to the full specification.

[4]`zip(*iterables)` flips the way that an iterable of iterables is split up. I find it easiest to imagine this as equivalent to rotating a spreadsheet. If your input iterables are `["Matt", "Leeds"]`, `["Jesse", "Seattle"]`, and `["Nejc", "Ljubljana"]`, you can imagine that as being equivalent to a spreadsheet where the names are in column A and the cities in column B. In that case, Matt is row 1, Jesse is row 2, and Nejc is row 3. `tuple(zip(*names_and_cities))` reads out the *columns* in order, so it would be `(('Matt', 'Jesse', 'Nejc'), ('Leeds', 'Seattle', 'Ljubljana'))`.

```
        if dp.sensor_name=="RelativeHumidity"
    ]
    x, y = zip(*points)
    plt.plot_date(x, y, "o", xdate=True)
with with_database("postgresql+psycopg2://apd@localhost/apd") as session:
    await plot()
plt.show()
```

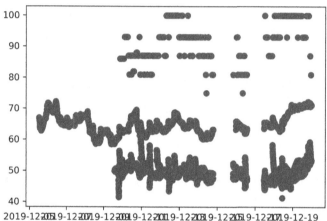

Filtering data

It would be nice to filter the data in the query stage, rather than just discarding all sensor data that doesn't meet our criteria when we are iterating through them. Right now, every piece of data is selected, a result object is created, then a DataPoint object, and only then are irrelevant entries skipped. To this end, we can add an additional parameter to the get_data(...) method that determines if a filter on sensor_data will be applied to the generated query.

```
async def get_data(sensor_name: t.Optional[str] = None) ->
t.AsyncIterator[DataPoint]:
    db_session = db_session_var.get()
    loop = asyncio.get_running_loop()
    query = db_session.query(datapoint_table)
    if sensor_name:
        query = query.filter(datapoint_table.c.sensor_name == sensor_name)
    query = query.order_by(datapoint_table.c.collected_at)
```

This approach saves a lot of overhead, as it means that only the relevant sensor data points are passed to the end-user, but also it's a more natural interface. Users expect to be able to specify what data they want, not to get absolutely all data and manually filter it. The version of the function in Listing 9-6 takes less than one second to execute with my sample data set (compared to over 3 seconds for the previous version) but shows the same chart.

Listing 9-6. Delegating filtering to the get_data function

```
from apd.aggregation.query import with_database, get_data

from matplotlib import pyplot as plt

async def plot():
    points = [(dp.collected_at, dp.data) async for dp in
    get_data(sensor_name="RelativeHumidity")]
    x, y = zip(*points)
    plt.plot_date(x, y, "o", xdate=True)

with with_database("postgresql+psycopg2://apd@localhost/apd") as session:
    await plot()
plt.show()
```

This plotting function is short and not overly complex; it represents quite a natural interface for loading data from the database. The downside is that having multiple deployments mixed in together results in unclear charts, where there are multiple data points for a given time. Matplotlib supports calling plot_date(...) multiple times with different logical result sets, which are then displayed using different colors. Our users can achieve this by creating multiple point lists as they iterate over the results of the get_data(...) call, as shown in Listing 9-7.

Listing 9-7. Plotting all sensor deployments independently

```
import collections

from apd.aggregation.query import with_database, get_data

from matplotlib import pyplot as plt

async def plot():
```

```
    legends = collections.defaultdict(list)
    async for dp in get_data(sensor_name="RelativeHumidity"):
        legends[dp.deployment_id].append((dp.collected_at, dp.data))

    for deployment_id, points in legends.items():
        x, y = zip(*points)
        plt.plot_date(x, y, "o", xdate=True)
with with_database("postgresql+psycopg2://apd@localhost/apd") as session:
    await plot()
plt.show()
```

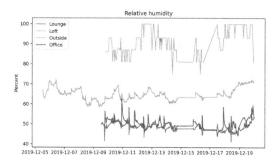 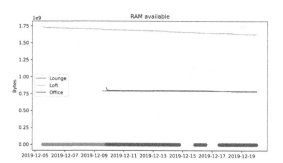

This one again makes the interface unnatural; it would be more logical for end-users to iterate over deployments and then iterate over sensor data values, rather than iterate over all data points and organize them into lists manually. An alternative would be to create a new function that lists all the deployment ids, then allow get_data(...) to filter by deployment_id. This would allow us to loop over the individual deployments and make a new get_data(...) call to get only that deployment's data. This is demonstrated in Listing 9-8.

Listing 9-8. Extended data collection functions for deployment_id filtering

```
async def get_deployment_ids():
    db_session = db_session_var.get()
    loop = asyncio.get_running_loop()
```

```
    query = db_session.query(datapoint_table.c.deployment_id).distinct()
    return [row.deployment_id for row in await loop.run_in_executor(None,
    query.all)]

async def get_data(
    sensor_name: t.Optional[str] = None,
    deployment_id: t.Optional[UUID] = None,
) -> t.AsyncIterator[DataPoint]:
    db_session = db_session_var.get()
    loop = asyncio.get_running_loop()
    query = db_session.query(datapoint_table)
    if sensor_name:
        query = query.filter(datapoint_table.c.sensor_name == sensor_name)
    if deployment_id:
        query = query.filter(datapoint_table.c.deployment_id == deployment_id)
    query = query.order_by(
        datapoint_table.c.collected_at,
    )
```

This new function can be used to loop over multiple calls to get_data(...), rather than the plot function looping and sorting the resulting data points into independent lists. Listing 9-9 demonstrates a very natural interface to looping over all the deployments for a single sensor, which behaves identically to the previous version.

Listing 9-9. Plotting all deploymens using the new helper functions

```
import collections

from apd.aggregation.query import with_database, get_data, get_deployment_ids

from matplotlib import pyplot as plt

async def plot(deployment_id):
    points = []
    async for dp in get_data(sensor_name="RelativeHumidity",
    deployment_id=deployment_id):
        points.append((dp.collected_at, dp.data))
```

```
    x, y = zip(*points)
    plt.plot_date(x, y, "o", xdate=True)

with with_database("postgresql+psycopg2://apd@localhost/apd") as session:
    deployment_ids = await get_deployment_ids()
    for deployment in deployment_ids:
        await plot(deployment)
plt.show()
```

This approach allows the end-user to interrogate each deployment individually, so only the relevant data for a combination of sensor and deployment is loaded into RAM at once. It's a perfectly appropriate API to offer the end-user.

Multilevel iterators

We previously reworked the interface for filtering by sensor name to do the filtering in the database to avoid iterating over unnecessary data. Our new deployment id filter isn't used to exclude data we don't need, it's used to make it easier to loop over each logical group independently. We don't need to use a filter here, we're using one to make the interface more natural.

If you've worked with the itertools module in the standard library much, you may have used the groupby(...) function. This takes an iterator and a key function and returns an iterator of iterators, the first being the value of the key function and the second being a run of values that match the given result of the key function. This is the same problem we've been trying to solve by listing our deployments and then filtering the database query.

The key function given to groupby(...) is often a simple lambda expression, but it can be any function, such as one of the functions from the operator module. For example, operator.attrgetter("deployment_id") is equivalent to lambda obj: obj.deployment_id, and operator.itemgetter(2) is equivalent to lambda obj: obj[2].

For this example, we'll define a key function that returns the value of an integer modulo 3 and a data() generator function that yields a fixed series of numbers, printing its status as it goes. This allows us to see clearly when the underlying iterator is advanced.

```
import itertools
import typing as t

def mod3(n: int) -> int:
    return n % 3

def data() -> t.Iterable[int]:
    for number in [0, 1, 4, 7, 2, 6, 9]:
        print(f"Yielding {number}")
        yield number
```

We can loop over the contents of the data() generator and print the value of the mod3 function, which lets us see that the first group has one item, then there's a group of three items, then a group of one, then a group of two.

```
>>> print([mod3(number) for number in data()])
data() is starting
Yielding 0
Yielding 1
Yielding 4
Yielding 7
Yielding 2
Yielding 6
Yielding 9
data() is complete
[0, 1, 1, 1, 2, 0, 0]
```

Setting up a groupby does not consume the underlying iterable; each item it generates is processed as the groupby is iterated over. To work correctly, the groupby only needs to decide if the current item is in the same group as the previous one or if a new group has started, it doesn't analyze the iterable as a whole. Items with the same value for the key function are only grouped together if they are a contiguous block in the input iterator, so it's common to ensure that the underlying iterator is sorted to avoid splitting groups up.

By creating a groupby over our data with the mod3(...) key function, we can create a two-level loop, first iterating over the values of the key function, then iterating over the values from data() that produce that key value.

```
>>> for val, group in itertools.groupby(data(), mod3):
...         print(f"Starting new group where mod3(x)=={val}")
...         for number in group:
...             print(f"x=={number} mod3(x)=={mod3(val)}")
...         print(f"Group with mod3(x)=={val} is complete")
...
data() is starting
Yielding 0
Starting new group where mod3(x)==0
x==0 mod3(x)==0
Yielding 1
Group with mod3(x)==0 is complete
Starting new group where mod3(x)==1
x==1 mod3(x)==1
Yielding 4
x==4 mod3(x)==1
Yielding 7
x==7 mod3(x)==1
Yielding 2
Group with mod3(x)==1 is complete
Starting new group where mod3(x)==2
x==2 mod3(x)==2
Yielding 6
Group with mod3(x)==2 is complete
Starting new group where mod3(x)==0
x==6 mod3(x)==0
Yielding 9
x==9 mod3(x)==0
data() is complete
Group with mod3(x)==0 is complete
```

From the output of the print statements, we can see that the groupby only ever pulls one item at a time, but manages the iterators it provides in such a way that looping over the values is natural. Whenever the inner loop requests a new item, the groupby function requests a new item from the underlying iterator and then decides its behavior based

410

on that value. If the key function reports the same value as the previous item, it yields the new value to the inner loop; otherwise, it signals that the inner loop is complete and holds the value until the next inner loop starts.

The iterators behave just as we'd expect if we had concrete lists of items; there is no requirement to iterate over the inner loop if we don't need to. If we don't iterate over the inner loop completely before advancing the outer loop, the groupby object will transparently advance the source iterable as though we had. In the following example, we skip the group of three where mod3(...)==1, and we can see that the underlying iterator is advanced three times by the groupby object:

```
>>> for val, group in itertools.groupby(data(), mod3):
...     print(f"Starting new group where mod3(x)=={val}")
...     if val == 1:
...         # Skip the ones
...         print("Skipping group")
...         continue
...     for number in group:
...         print(f"x=={number} mod3(x)=={mod3(val)}")
...     print(f"Group with mod3(x)=={val} is complete")
...
data() is starting
Yielding 0
Starting new group where mod3(x)==0
x==0 mod3(x)==0
Yielding 1
Group with mod3(x)==0 is complete
Starting new group where mod3(x)==1
Skipping group
Yielding 4
Yielding 7
Yielding 2
Starting new group where mod3(x)==2
x==2 mod3(x)==2
Yielding 6
Group with mod3(x)==2 is complete
Starting new group where mod3(x)==0
```

```
x==6 mod3(x)==0
Yielding 9
x==9 mod3(x)==0
data() is complete
Group with mod3(x)==0 is complete
```

The behavior is intuitive when we're using it, but it can be hard to follow how it's implemented. Figure 9-1 shows a pair of flow charts, one for the outer loop and one for each individual inner loop.

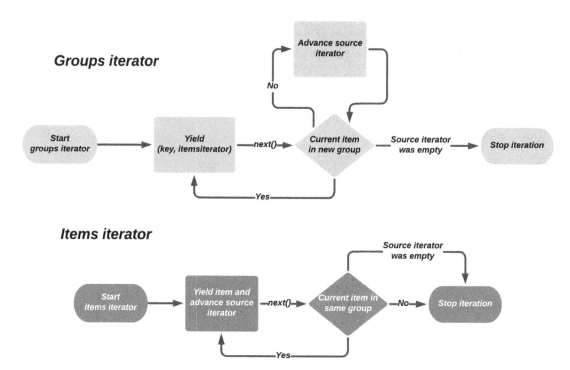

Figure 9-1. *Flow chart demonstrating how groupby works*

If we had a standard iterator (as opposed to an asynchronous iterator), we could sort the data by deployment_id and use itertools.groupby(...) to simplify our code to handle multiple deployments without needing to query for the individual deployments. Rather than making a new get_data(...) call for each, we could iterate over the groups and handle the internal iterator in the same way we already do, using list comprehensions and zip(...).

Unfortunately, there is no fully asynchronous equivalent of groupby at the time of writing. While we can write a function that returns an async iterator whose values are UUID and async iterator of DataPoint pairs, there is no way of grouping these automatically.

At the risk of writing clever code, we can write an implementation of groupby that works with asynchronous code ourselves using closures. It would expose multiple iterators to the end-user that work on the same underlying iterator, in just the same way as `itertools.groupby(...)`. It would be better to use a library function for this if one were available.

Each time we find a new value of the key function, we need to return a new generator function that maintains a reference to the underlying source iterator. This way, when someone advances an item iterator, it can choose to either yield the data point it receives or to indicate that it's the end of the item iterator, as the groupby function does. Equally, if we advance the outer iterator before an item iterator has been consumed, it needs to "fast-forward" through the underlying iterator until the start of a new group is found.

The code in Listing 9-10 is a single function that delegates to our get data function and wraps it in the appropriate groupby logic, as opposed to a generic function that can adapt any iterator.

Listing 9-10. An implementation of get_data_by_deployment that acts like an asynchronous groupby

```
async def get_data_by_deployment(
    *args, **kwargs
) -> t.AsyncIterator[t.Tuple[UUID, t.AsyncIterator[DataPoint]]]:
    """Return an Async Iterator that contains two-item pairs.
    These pairs are a string (deployment_id), and an async iterator that
    contains
    the datapoints with that deployment_id.

    Usage example:

        async for deployment_id, datapoints in get_data_by_deployment():
            print(deployment_id)
            async for datapoint in datapoints:
                print(datapoint)
            print()
```

```
    """

    # Get the data, using the arguments to this function as filters
    data = get_data(*args, **kwargs)

    # The two levels of iterator share the item variable, initialise it
    # with the first item from the iterator. Also set last_deployment_id
    # to None, so the outer iterator knows to start a new group.
    last_deployment_id: t.Optional[UUID] = None
    try:
        item = await data.__anext__()
    except StopAsyncIteration:
        # There were no items in the underlying query, return immediately
        return

    async def subiterator(group_id: UUID) -> t.AsyncIterator[DataPoint]:
        """Using a closure, create an iterator that yields the current
        item, then yields all items from data while the deployment_id matches
        group_id, leaving the first that doesn't match as item in the enclosing
        scope."""
        # item is from the enclosing scope
        nonlocal item
        while item.deployment_id == group_id:
            # yield items from data while they match the group_id this
            # iterator represents
            yield item
            try:
                # Advance the underlying iterator
                item = await data.__anext__()
            except StopAsyncIteration:
                # The underlying iterator came to an end, so end the
                # subiterator too
                return
```

```
while True:
    while item.deployment_id == last_deployment_id:
        # We are trying to advance the outer iterator while the
        # underlying iterator is still part-way through a group.
        # Speed through the underlying until we hit an item where
        # the deployment_id is different to the last one (or,
        # is not None, in the case of the start of the iterator)
        try:
            item = await data.__anext__()
        except StopAsyncIteration:
            # We hit the end of the underlying iterator: end this
            # iterator too
            return
    last_deployment_id = item.deployment_id
    # Instantiate a subiterator for this group
    yield last_deployment_id, subiterator(last_deployment_id)
```

This uses await data.__anext__() to advance the underlying data iterator, rather than an async for loop, to make the fact that the iterator is consumed in multiple places more obvious.

An implementation of this generator coroutine is in the code for this chapter. I'd encourage you to try adding print statements and breakpoints to it, to help understand the control flow. This code is more complex than most Python code you'll need to write (and I'd caution you against introducing this level of complexity into production code; having it as a self-contained dependency is better), but if you can understand how it works, you'll have a thorough grasp on the details of generator functions, asynchronous iterators, and closures. As asynchronous code is used more in production code, libraries to offer this kind of complex manipulation of iterators are sure to become available.

Additional filters

We've added get_data(...) filters for sensor_name and deployment_id, but it's also useful to choose the range of time that's being displayed. We can implement this with two datetime filters which are used to filter on the collected_at field.

The implementation of get_data(...) that supports this is shown in Listing 9-11, but because get_data_by_deployment(...) passes all arguments through to get_data(...) unchanged, we don't need to modify that function to allow date windows in our analysis.

Listing 9-11. get_data method with sensor, deployment, and date filters

```
async def get_data(
    sensor_name: t.Optional[str] = None,
    deployment_id: t.Optional[UUID] = None,
    collected_before: t.Optional[datetime.datetime] = None,
    collected_after: t.Optional[datetime.datetime] = None,
) -> t.AsyncIterator[DataPoint]:
    db_session = db_session_var.get()
    loop = asyncio.get_running_loop()
    query = db_session.query(datapoint_table)
    if sensor_name:
        query = query.filter(datapoint_table.c.sensor_name == sensor_name)
    if deployment_id:
        query = query.filter(datapoint_table.c.deployment_id == deployment_id)
    if collected_before:
        query = query.filter(datapoint_table.c.collected_at <
        collected_before)
    if collected_after:
        query = query.filter(datapoint_table.c.collected_at > collected_after)
    query = query.order_by(
        datapoint_table.c.deployment_id,
        datapoint_table.c.sensor_name,
        datapoint_table.c.collected_at,
    )

    rows = await loop.run_in_executor(None, query.all)
    for row in rows:
        yield DataPoint.from_sql_result(row)
```

Testing our query functions

The query functions need to be tested, just like any others. Unlike most of the functions we've written so far, the query functions take lots of optional arguments that significantly change the output of the returned data. Although we don't need to test a wide range of values for each filter (we can trust that our database's query support works correctly), we need to test that each option works as intended.

We need some setup fixtures to enable us to test functions that depend on a database being present. While we could mock the database connection out, I wouldn't recommend this, as databases are very complex pieces of software and not well suited to being mocked out.

The most common approach to testing database applications is to create a new, empty database and allow the tests to control the creation of tables and data. Some database software, like SQLite, allows for new databases to be created on the fly, but most require the database to be set up in advance.

Given that we're assuming there's an empty database available to us, we need a fixture to connect to it, a fixture to set up the tables, and a fixture to set up the data. The connect fixture is very similar to the `with_database` context manager,[5] and the function to populate the database will include sample data that we can insert using `db_session.execute(datapoint_table.insert().values(...))`.

The fixture to set up the database tables is the most difficult one. The easiest approach is to use `metadata.create_all(...)`, as we did before we had introduced alembic for database migrations. This works fine for most applications, so it's the best choice in general. Our application includes a database view that's not managed by SQLAlchemy, but by a custom migration in Alembic. Therefore, we need to use Alembic's upgrade functionality to set up our database tables. The relevant fixtures we need are given as Listing 9-12.

Listing 9-12. Database setup fixtures

```
import datetime
from uuid import UUID

from apd.aggregation.database import datapoint_table
```

---

[5]I'd recommend not adding a commit() call, as this will allow changes to the database to be rolled back between tests.

```
from alembic.config import Config
from alembic.script import ScriptDirectory
from alembic.runtime.environment import EnvironmentContext
import pytest

@pytest.fixture
def db_uri():
    return "postgresql+psycopg2://apd@localhost/apd-test"

@pytest.fixture
def db_session(db_uri):
    from sqlalchemy import create_engine
    from sqlalchemy.orm import sessionmaker

    engine = create_engine(db_uri, echo=True)
    sm = sessionmaker(engine)
    Session = sm()
    yield Session
    Session.close()

@pytest.fixture
def migrated_db(db_uri, db_session):
    config = Config()
    config.set_main_option("script_location", "apd.aggregation:alembic")
    config.set_main_option("sqlalchemy.url", db_uri)
    script = ScriptDirectory.from_config(config)

    def upgrade(rev, context):
        return script._upgrade_revs(script.get_current_head(), rev)

    def downgrade(rev, context):
        return script._downgrade_revs(None, rev)

    with EnvironmentContext(config, script, fn=upgrade):
        script.run_env()

    try:
        yield
```

```
    finally:
        # Clear any pending work from the db_session connection
        db_session.rollback()

        with EnvironmentContext(config, script, fn=downgrade):
            script.run_env()

@pytest.fixture
def populated_db(migrated_db, db_session):
    datas = [
        {
            "id": 1,
            "sensor_name": "Test",
            "data": "1",
            "collected_at": datetime.datetime(2020, 4, 1, 12, 0, 1),
            "deployment_id": UUID("b4c68905-b1e4-4875-940e-69e5d27730fd"),
        },
        # Additional sample data omitted from listing for brevity's sake
    ]
    for data in datas:
        insert = datapoint_table.insert().values(**data)
        db_session.execute(insert)
```

This gives us an environment where we can write tests that query a database that contains only known values, so we can write meaningful assertions.

Parameterized tests

Pytest has a special piece of functionality for generating multiple tests that do something very similar: the parameterize mark. If a test function is marked as parameterized, it can have additional arguments that do not correspond to fixtures, as well as a series of values for these parameters. The test function will be run multiple times, once for each different argument value function. We can use this feature to write functions that test various filtering methods of our functions without lots of duplication, as shown in Listing 9-13.

Listing 9-13. A parameterized get_data test to verify different filters

```
class TestGetData:
    @pytest.fixture
    def mut(self):
        return get_data

    @pytest.mark.asyncio
    @pytest.mark.parametrize(
        "filter,num_items_expected",
        [
        ({}, 9),
        ({"sensor_name": "Test"}, 7),
        ({"deployment_id": UUID("b4c68905-b1e4-4875-940e-69e5d27730fd")}, 5),
        ({"collected_after": datetime.datetime(2020, 4, 1, 12, 2, 1),}, 3),
        ({"collected_before": datetime.datetime(2020, 4, 1, 12, 2, 1),}, 4),
        (
            {
                "collected_after": datetime.datetime(2020, 4, 1, 12, 2, 1),
                "collected_before": datetime.datetime(2020, 4, 1, 12, 3, 5),
            },
            2,
        ),
        ],
    )
    async def test_iterate_over_items(
        self, mut, db_session, populated_db, filter, num_items_expected
    ):
        db_session_var.set(db_session)
        points = [dp async for dp in mut(**filter)]
        assert len(points) == num_items_expected
```

The first time this test is run, it has `filter={}`, `num_items_expected=9` as parameters. The second run has `filter={"sensor_name": "Test"}`, `num_items_expected=7`, and so on. Each of these test functions will run independently and will be counted as a new passing or failing test, as appropriate.

This will result in six tests being generated, with names like `TestGetData.test_iterate_over_items[filter5-2]`. This name is based on the parameters, with complex parameter values (like `filter`) being represented by their name and the zero-based index into the list, and simpler parameters (like `num_items_expected`) included directly. Most of the time, you won't need to care about the name, but it can be very helpful to identify which variant of a test is failing.

Displaying multiple sensors

We've now got three functions that help us connect to the database and iterate over `DataPoint` objects in a sensible order and with optional filtering. So far we've been using the `matplotlib.pyplot.plot_dates(...)` function to convert pairs of sensor values and dates to a single chart. This is a helper function that makes it easier to generate a plot by making various drawing functions available in a global namespace. It is not the recommended approach when making multiple charts.

We want to be able to loop over each of our sensor types and generate a chart for each. If we were to use the pyplot API, we would be constrained to using a single plot, with the highest values skewing the axes to make the lowest impossible to read. Instead, we want to generate an independent plot for each and show them side by side. For this, we can use the `matplotlib.pyplot.figure(...)` and `figure.add_subplot(...)` functions. A subplot is an object which behaves broadly like `matplotlib.pyplot` but representing a single plot inside a larger grid of plots. For example, `figure.add_subplot(3,2,4)` would be the fourth plot in a three-row, two-column grid of plots.

Right now, our `plot(...)` function assumes that the data it is working with is a number, which can be passed directly to matplotlib for display on our chart. Many of our sensors have different data formats though, such as the temperature sensor which has a dictionary of temperature and the unit being used as its value attribute. These different values need to be converted to numbers before they can be plotted.

We can refactor our plotting function out to a utility function in `apd.aggregation` to vastly simplify our Jupyter notebooks, but we need to ensure that it can be used with other formats of sensor data. Each plot needs to provide some configuration for the sensor to be graphed, a subplot object to draw the plot in, and a mapping from deployment ids to a user-facing name for populating the plot's legend. It should also accept the same filtering arguments as get_data(...), to allow users to constrain their charts by date or deployment id.

We'll pass this config data as an instance of a data class, which also contains a reference to a "clean" function. This clean function is what's responsible for converting a DataPoint instance to a pair of values that can be plotted by matplotlib. The clean function must transform an iterable of DataPoint objects to an iterable of (x, y) pairs that matplotlib can understand. For RelativeHumidity and RAMAvailable sensors, this is a simple matter of yielding the date/float tuple, like our code has done so far.

```
async def clean_passthrough(
    datapoints: t.AsyncIterator[DataPoint],
) -> t.AsyncIterator[t.Tuple[datetime.datetime, float]]:
    async for datapoint in datapoints:
        if datapoint.data is None:
            continue
        else:
            yield datapoint.collected_at, datapoint.data
```

The config data class also needs some string parameters, such as the title of the chart, the axis labels, and the sensor_name that needs to be passed to get_data(...) in order to find the data needed for this chart. Once we have the Config class defined, we can create two config objects that represent the two sensors which use raw floating-point numbers as their value type and a function to return all registered configs.

Combining the figure functions from matplotlib with our new config system allows us to write a new plot_sensor(...) function (Listing 9-14) that can generate any number of charts using only a few simple lines of code in the Jupyter notebook.

Listing 9-14. New config objects and plot function that uses it

```
@dataclasses.dataclass(frozen=True)
class Config:
    title: str
    sensor_name: str
    clean: t.Callable[[t.AsyncIterator[DataPoint]], t.AsyncIterator[
    t.Tuple[datetime.datetime, float]]]
    ylabel: str
```

```
configs = (
    Config(
        sensor_name="RAMAvailable",
        clean=clean_passthrough,
        title="RAM available",
        ylabel="Bytes",
    ),
    Config(
        sensor_name="RelativeHumidity",
        clean=clean_passthrough,
        title="Relative humidity",
        ylabel="Percent",
    ),
)

def get_known_configs() -> t.Dict[str, Config]:
    return {config.title: config for config in configs}

async def plot_sensor(config: Config, plot: t.Any, location_names:
t.Dict[UUID,str], **kwargs) -> t.Any:
    locations = []
    async for deployment, query_results in get_data_by_deployment(
    sensor_name=config.sensor_name, **kwargs):
        points = [dp async for dp in config['clean'](query_results)]
        if not points:
            continue
        locations.append(deployment)
        x, y = zip(*points)
        plot.set_title(config['title'])
        plot.set_ylabel(config['ylabel'])
        plot.plot_date(x, y, "-", xdate=True)
    plot.legend([location_names.get(l, l) for l in locations])
    return plot
```

With these new functions in place, we can modify the Jupyter notebook cell to call the plot_sensor(...) function instead of writing our own plotting function in Jupyter. The code that an end-user of apd.aggregation needs to write to connect to the database and render two charts (shown as Listing 9-15) is significantly shorter, thanks to these helper functions.

Listing 9-15. Jupyter cell to plot both Humidity and RAM Available, and their output

```
import asyncio

from matplotlib import pyplot as plt

from apd.aggregation.query import with_database
from apd.aggregation.analysis import get_known_configs, plot_sensor

with with_database("postgresql+psycopg2://apd@localhost/apd") as session:
    coros = []
    figure = plt.figure(figsize = (20, 5), dpi=300)
    configs = get_known_configs()
    to_display = configs["Relative humidity"], configs["RAM available"]
    for i, config in enumerate(to_display, start=1):
        plot = figure.add_subplot(1, 2, i)
        coros.append(plot_sensor(config, plot, {}))
    await asyncio.gather(*coros)

display(figure)
```

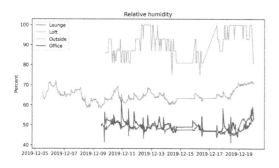 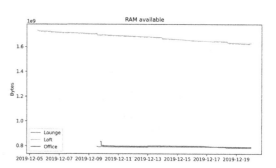

As the Temperature and SolarCumulativeOutput sensors return serialized objects from the pint package in the format {'unit': 'degC', 'magnitude': 8.4}, we can't use these with our existing clean_passthrough() function; we need to create a new one. The simplest is to assume that the units are always the same and extract the magnitude line only. This would chart any temperatures in a different scale incorrectly, as the units are not being corrected. For now, all of our sensors return values in degrees centigrade, so this isn't a serious concern.

```
async def clean_magnitude(datapoints):
    async for datapoint in datapoints:
        if datapoint.data is None:
            continue
        yield datapoint.collected_at, datapoint.data["magnitude"]
```

If we use this new cleaner function to add a new config object for temperature, we see the chart in Figure 9-2. It's clear from this data we can see that the temperature sensor is not entirely reliable: the temperature in my office rarely exceeds the melting point of steel.

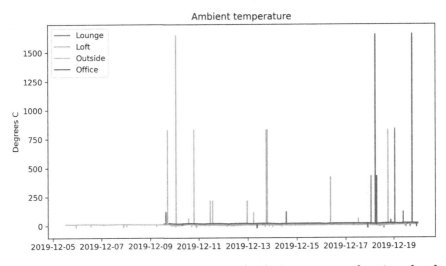

Figure 9-2.   *Temperature sensor output with obvious errors skewing the data*

Processing data

An advantage of the approach that we've taken is that we can perform relatively arbitrary transforms on the data that we're given, allowing us to discard data points that we consider to be incorrect. It's often better to discard data when analyzing than during collection, as bugs in the function to check a data point's validity won't cause data loss if it's only checked during analysis. We can always delete incorrect data after the fact, but we can never recollect data that we chose to ignore.

One way of fixing this problem with the temperature sensor would be to make the clean iterator look at a moving window on the underlying data rather than just one DataPoint at a time. This way, it can use the neighbors of a sensor value to discard values that are too different.

The collections.deque type is useful for this, as it offers a structure with an optional maximum size, so we can add each temperature we find to the deque, but when reading it, we only see the last n entries that were added. A deque can have items added or removed from either the left or right edges, so it's essential to be consistent about adding and popping from the same end when using it as a limited window.

We can begin by filtering out any values that are out of the supported range of the DHT22 sensors,[6] to remove the most egregious incorrect data. This removes many, but not all, of the incorrect readings. A simple way of filtering out single item peaks is to have a three-item window and yield the middle item unless it is too different to the average of the temperatures on either side, as shown in Listing 9-16. We don't want to remove all legitimate fluctuations, so our definition of "not too different" must take into account that a run of readings such as 21c, 22c, 21c are legitimate while excluding runs such as 20c, 60c, 23c.

Listing 9-16. An example implementation of a cleaner function for temperature

```python
async def clean_temperature_fluctuations(
    datapoints: t.AsyncIterator[DataPoint],
) -> t.AsyncIterator[t.Tuple[datetime.datetime, float]]:
    allowed_jitter = 2.5
    allowed_range = (-40, 80)
    window_datapoints: t.Deque[DataPoint] = collections.deque(maxlen=3)

    def datapoint_ok(datapoint: DataPoint) -> bool:
        """Return False if this data point does not contain a valid
        temperature"""
        if datapoint.data is None:
            return False
        elif datapoint.data["unit"] != "degC":
```

[6]The temperature sensor is intended as a measure of ambient temperature. If we write a new sensor type to collect a different type of temperature data, we may need to reconsider this filter.

426

```
        # This point is in a different temperature system. While it
        # could be converted
        # this cleaner is not yet doing that.
        return False
    elif not allowed_range[0] < datapoint.data["magnitude"] <
    allowed_range[1]:
        return False
    return True

async for datapoint in datapoints:
    if not datapoint_ok(datapoint):
        # If the datapoint is invalid then skip directly to the next item
        continue

    window_datapoints.append(datapoint)
    if len(three_temperatures) == 3:
        # Find the temperatures of the datapoints in the window, then
        # average
        # the first and last and compare that to the middle point.
        window_temperatures = [dp.data["magnitude"] for dp in
        window_datapoints]
        avg_first_last = (window_temperatures[0] +
        window_temperatures[2]) / 2
        diff_middle_avg = abs(window_temperatures[1] - avg_first_last)
        if diff_middle_avg > allowed_jitter:
            pass
        else:
            yield window_datapoints[1].collected_at, window_temperatures[1]
    else:
        # The first two items in the iterator can't be compared to both
        # neighbors
        # so they should be yielded
        yield datapoint.collected_at, datapoint.data["magnitude"]
# When the iterator ends the final item is not yet in the middle
# of the window, so the last item must be explicitly yielded
if datapoint_ok(datapoint):
    yield datapoint.collected_at, datapoint.data["magnitude"]
```

This cleaner function produces a much smoother temperature trend, as demonstrated in Figure 9-3. The cleaner filters out any data points where the temperature could not be found as well as any severe errors. It is retaining fine detail of temperature trends; as the window contains the last three data points recorded (even those which were not excluded from the data set), a sudden change in temperature will start to be reflected in the output data so long as it persists for at least two consecutive readings.

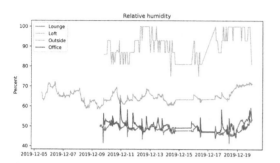 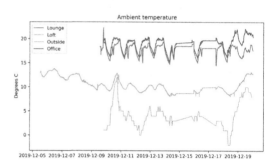

Figure 9-3. *Result of the same data with an appropriate cleaner*

EXERCISE 9-1: ADD A CLEANER FOR SOLARCUMULATIVEOUTPUT

The SolarCumulativeOutput sensor returns a number of watt-hours, serialized in the same way as the temperature sensor. If we chart this, we see an upward trending line that moves in irregular steps. It would be much more useful to see the power generated at a moment in time rather than the total up until that time.

To achieve this, we need to convert watt-hours to watts, which means dividing the number of watt-hours by the amount of time between data points.

Write a clean_watthours_to_watts(...) iterator coroutine that keeps track of the last time and watt-hour readings, finds the difference, and then returns watts divided by time elapsed.

For example, the following two date and value pairs should result in a single output entry at 1pm with a value of 5.0.

```
[
    (datetime.datetime(2020, 4, 1, 12, 0, 0), {"magnitude": 1.0, "unit":
    "watt_hour"}),
    (datetime.datetime(2020, 4, 1, 13, 0, 0), {"magnitude": 6.0, "unit":
    "watt_hour"})
]
```

The code accompanying this chapter contains a work environment for this exercise, consisting of a test setup with a series of unit tests for this function but no implementation. There is also an implementation of the cleaner as part of the final code for this chapter.

With these cleaners and config entries in place for solar power and temperature, we can draw a 2x2 grid of charts. As the charts are now showing the desired data, it's a good time to improve readability by adding in values for deployment names, which are passed as the final argument to plot_sensor(...) in Listing 9-17.

Listing 9-17. Final Jupyter cell to display 2x2 grid of charts

```python
import asyncio
from uuid import UUID

from matplotlib import pyplot as plt

from apd.aggregation.query import with_database
from apd.aggregation.analysis import get_known_configs, plot_sensor

location_names = {
  UUID('53998a51-60de-48ae-b71a-5c37cd1455f2'): "Loft",
  UUID('1bc63cda-e223-48bc-93c2-c1f651779d69'): "Living Room",
  UUID('ea0683de-6772-4678-bfe7-6014f54ffc8e'): "Office",
  UUID('5aaa901a-7564-41fb-8eba-50cdd6fe9f80'): "Outside",
}

with with_database("postgresql+psycopg2://apd@localhost/apd") as session:
    coros = []
    figure = plt.figure(figsize = (20, 10), dpi=300)
    configs = get_known_configs().values()
    for i, config in enumerate(configs, start=1):
        plot = figure.add_subplot(2, 2, i)
        coros.append(plot_sensor(config, plot, location_names))
    await asyncio.gather(*coros)

display(figure)
```

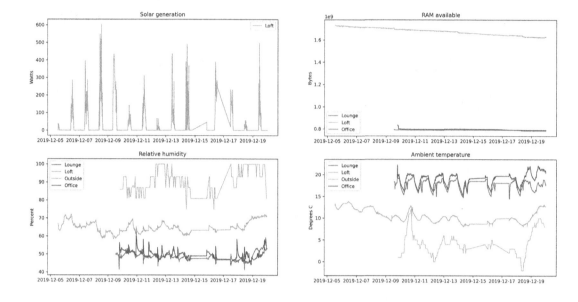

Interactivity with Jupyter widgets

So far, our code to generate the charts has no interactivity available to the end-user. We are currently displaying all data points ever recorded, but it would be handy to be able to filter to only show a time period without needing to modify the code to generate the chart.

To do this, we add an optional dependency on `ipywidgets`, using the `extras_require` functionality of `setup.cfg`, and reinstall the `apd.aggregation` package in our environment using `pipenv install -e .[jupyter]`.

You may also need to run the following, to ensure that the system-wide Jupyter installation has the support functionality for widgets enabled:

```
> pip install --user widgetsnbextension
> jupyter nbextension enable --py widgetsnbextension
```

With this installed, we can request that Jupyter create interactive widgets for each argument and call the function with the user-selected values. Interactivity allows the person viewing the notebook to choose arbitrary input values without needing to modify the code for the cell or even understand the code.

Figure 9-4 shows an example of a function which adds two integers and which has been connected to Jupyter's interactivity support. In this case, the two integer arguments are given a default value of 100 and are rendered as sliders. Users can manipulate these sliders, and the result of the function is recomputed automatically.

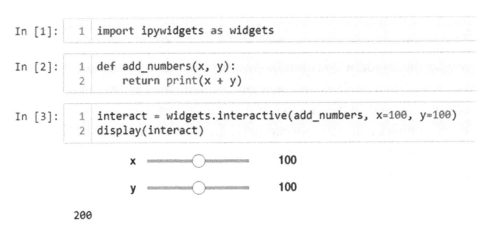

Figure 9-4. *Interactive view of an addition function*

Multiply nested synchronous and asynchronous code

We can't pass coroutines to the `interactive(...)` function as it's defined to expect a standard, synchronous function. It's a synchronous function itself, so it's not even possible for it to `await` the result of a coroutine call. Although IPython and Jupyter allow `await` constructs in places where they aren't usually permitted, this is done by wrapping the cell in a coroutine[7] and scheduling it as a task; it is not deep magic that truly marries synchronous and asynchronous code, it's a hack for convenience.

Our plotting code involves awaiting the `plot_sensor(...)` coroutine, so Jupyter must wrap the cell into a coroutine. Coroutines can only be called by coroutines or directly on an event loop's `run(...)` function, so asynchronous code generally grows to the point that the entire application is asynchronous. It's a lot easier to have a group of functions that are all synchronous or all asynchronous than it is to mix the two approaches.

---

[7]Specifically, IPython tries to compile the cell to bytecode and checks for a SyntaxError. If there is a SyntaxError, it will wrap the code in a coroutine and try again.

We can't do that here because we need to provide a function to `interactive(...)`, over which we have no control of the implementation. The way we get around this problem is that we must convert the coroutine into a new synchronous method. We don't want to rewrite all the code to a synchronous style just to accommodate the `interactive(...)` function, so a wrapper function to bridge the gap is a better fit.

The coroutine requires access to an event loop that it can use to schedule tasks and which is responsible for scheduling it. The existing event loop we have won't do, as it is busy executing the coroutine that's waiting for `interactive(...)` to return. If you recall, it's the `await` keyword that implements cooperative multitasking in asyncio, so our code will only ever switch between different tasks when it hits an `await` expression.

If we are running a coroutine, we can `await` another coroutine or task, which allows the event loop to execute other code. Execution won't return to our code until the function that was being awaited has completed execution, but other coroutines can run in the meantime. We *can* call synchronous code like `interactive(...)` from an asynchronous context, but that code can introduce blocking. As this blocking is not blocking on an `await` statement, execution cannot be passed to another coroutine during this period. Calling any synchronous function from an asynchronous function is equivalent to guaranteeing that a block of code does not contain an `await` statement, which guarantees that no other coroutine's code will be run.

Until now, we have used the `asyncio.run(...)` function to start a coroutine from synchronous code and block waiting for its result, but we're already inside a call to `asyncio.run(main())` so we cannot do this again.[8] As the `interactive(...)` call is blocking without an `await` expression, our wrapper will be running in a context where it's guaranteed that no coroutine code can run. Although the wrapper function that we use to convert our asynchronous coroutine to a synchronous function must arrange for that coroutine to be executed, it cannot rely on the existing event loop to do this.

To make this explicit, imagine a function that takes two functions as arguments, as shown in Listing 9-18. These functions both return an integer. This function invokes both of the functions that were passed as arguments, adds the results, and then returns the sum of those integers. If all the functions involved are synchronous, there are no problems.

---

[8]`asyncio.run(...)` is not *re-entrant*: calls cannot be nested.

Listing 9-18. Example of calling only synchronous functions from a synchronous context

```python
import typing as t

def add_number_from_callback(a: t.Callable[[], int], b: t.Callable[[],
int]) -> int:
    return a() + b()

def constant() -> int:
    return 5

print(add_number_from_callback(constant, constant))
```

We can even call this add_number_from_callback(...) function from an asynchronous context and get the right result, with the caveat that add_number_from_callback(...) blocks the entire process, potentially negating the benefits of asynchronous code.

```python
async def main() -> None:
    print(add_number_from_callback(constant, constant))

asyncio.run(main())
```

Our particular invocation is low risk because we know that there are no IO requests which could potentially block for a long time. However, we might want to add a new function that returns a number from a HTTP request. If we already had a coroutine to get the result of a HTTP request, we might want to use this rather than reimplementing this as a synchronous function. An example of a coroutine to get the number (in this case from the random.org random number generator service) is as follows:

```python
import aiohttp

async def async_get_number_from_HTTP_request() -> int:
    uri = "https://www.random.org/integers/?num=1&min=1&max=100&col=1"
    "&base=10&format=plain"
    async with aiohttp.ClientSession() as http:
        response = await http.get(uri)
        return int(await response.text())
```

As this is a coroutine, we can't pass it directly to the add_number_from_callback(...) function. If we were to try, we'd see Python error TypeError: unsupported operand type(s) for +: 'int' and 'coroutine'.[9]

You might write a wrapper function for async_get_number_from_HTTP_request to create a new task that we can wait for, but that would submit the coroutine to the existing event loop, which we've already decided isn't a possible solution. We would have no way of awaiting this task, as it's not valid to use await in a synchronous function, and it's not valid to call asyncio.run(...) in a nested fashion. The only way of waiting for this would be to loop doing nothing until the task is complete, but this loop prevents the event loop from scheduling the task, resulting in a contradiction.

```
def get_number_from_HTTP_request() -> int:
    task = asyncio.create_task(async_get_number_from_HTTP_request())
    while not task.done():
        pass
    return task.result()
```

The main() task constantly loops over the task.done() check, never hitting an await statement and so never giving way to the async_get_number_from_HTTP_request() task. This function results in a deadlock.

Tip   It's also possible to create blocking asynchronous code with any long-running loop that doesn't contain an explicit await statement or an implicit one such as async for and async with.

You shouldn't need to write a loop that checks for another coroutine's data, as we've done here. You should await that coroutine rather than looping. If you do ever need a loop with no awaits inside, you can explicitly give the event loop a chance to switch into other tasks by awaiting a function that does nothing, such as await asyncio.sleep(0), so long as you're looping in a coroutine rather than a synchronous function that a coroutine called.

---

[9] Mypy would word the error as

```
error: Argument 2 to "add_number_from_callback" has incompatible type "Callable[[],
Coroutine[Any, Any, int]]"; expected "Callable[[], int]"
```

We can't convert the entire call stack to the asynchronous idiom, so the only remaining way around this problem is to start a second event loop, allowing the two tasks to run in parallel. We've blocked our current event loop, but we *can* start a second one to execute the asynchronous HTTP code.

This approach makes it possible to call async code from synchronous contexts, but all tasks scheduled in the main event loop are still blocked waiting for the HTTP response. This only solves the problem of deadlocks when mixing synchronous and asynchronous code; the performance penalty is still in place. You should avoid mixing synchronous and asynchronous code wherever possible. The resulting code is difficult to understand, can introduce deadlocks, and negates the performance benefits of asyncio.

A helper function that takes a coroutine and executes it in a new thread, without involving the currently running event loop, is given as Listing 9-19. This also includes a coroutine that makes use of this wrapper to pass the HTTP coroutine as though it were a synchronous function.

Listing 9-19. Wrapper function to start a second event loop and delegate new async tasks there

```
def wrap_coroutine(f):
    @functools.wraps(f)
    def run_in_thread(*args, **kwargs):
        loop = asyncio.new_event_loop()
        wrapped = f(*args, **kwargs)
        with ThreadPoolExecutor(max_workers=1) as pool:
            task = pool.submit(loop.run_until_complete, wrapped)
        return task.result()
    return run_in_thread

async def main() -> None:
    print(
        add_number_from_callback(
            constant, wrap_coroutine(async_get_number_from_HTTP_request)
        )
    )
```

We can use this same approach to allow our plot_sensor(...) coroutine to be used in an interactive(...) function call, as shown in Listing 9-20.

Listing 9-20. Interactive chart filtering example, with output shown

```
import asyncio
from uuid import UUID

import ipywidgets as widgets
from matplotlib import pyplot as plt

from apd.aggregation.query import with_database
from apd.aggregation.analysis import (get_known_configs, plot_sensor,
wrap_coroutine)

@wrap_coroutine
async def plot(*args, **kwargs):
    location_names = {
      UUID('53998a51-60de-48ae-b71a-5c37cd1455f2'): "Loft",
      UUID('1bc63cda-e223-48bc-93c2-c1f651779d69'): "Living Room",
      UUID('ea0683de-6772-4678-bfe7-6014f54ffc8e'): "Office",
      UUID('5aaa901a-7564-41fb-8eba-50cdd6fe9f80'): "Outside",
    }

    with with_database("postgresql+psycopg2://apd@localhost/apd") as session:
        coros = []
        figure = plt.figure(figsize = (20, 10), dpi=300)
        configs = get_known_configs().values()
        for i, config in enumerate(configs, start=1):
            plot = figure.add_subplot(2, 2, i)
            coros.append(plot_sensor(config, plot, location_names, *args,
                **kwargs))
        await asyncio.gather(*coros)
    return figure

start = widgets.DatePicker(
    description='Start date',
)
end = widgets.DatePicker(
    description='End date',
)
```

```
out = widgets.interactive(plot, collected_after=start, collected_before=end)
display(out)
```

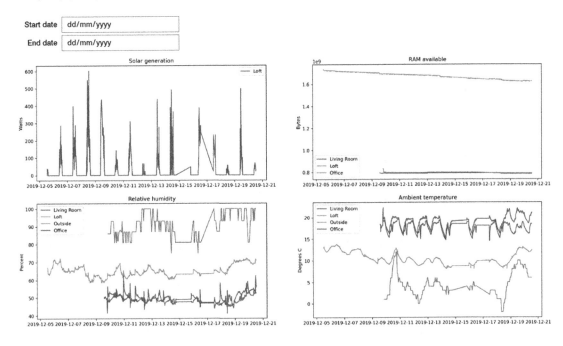

Tidying up

We now have lots of complex logic in the Jupyter cell. We should move this to some more general utility functions so that end-users don't need to deal with the details of how to plot charts. We don't want users to have to deal with the details of converting coroutines to wrapped functions to pass to the interactive system, so we can provide a helper function for them to use, as in Listing 9-21.

Listing 9-21. Genericized versions of the plot functions

```
async def plot_multiple_charts(*args: t.Any, **kwargs: t.Any) -> Figure:
    # These parameters are pulled from kwargs to avoid confusing function
    # introspection code in IPython widgets
    location_names = kwargs.pop("location_names", None)
    configs = kwargs.pop("configs", None)
    dimensions = kwargs.pop("dimensions", None)
    db_uri = kwargs.pop("db_uri", "postgresql+psycopg2://apd@localhost/apd")
```

```
    with with_database(db_uri):
        coros = []
        if configs is None:
            # If no configs are supplied, use all known configs
            configs = get_known_configs().values()
        if dimensions is None:
            # If no dimensions are supplied, get the square root of the
            # number
            # of configs and round it to find a number of columns. This will
            # keep the arrangement approximately square. Find rows by
            # multiplying out rows.
            total_configs = len(configs)
            columns = round(math.sqrt(total_configs))
            rows = math.ceil(total_configs / columns)
        figure = plt.figure(figsize=(10 * columns, 5 * rows), dpi=300)
        for i, config in enumerate(configs, start=1):
            plot = figure.add_subplot(columns, rows, i)
            coros.append(plot_sensor(config, plot, location_names, *args,
            **kwargs))
        await asyncio.gather(*coros)
    return figure

def interactable_plot_multiple_charts(
    *args: t.Any, **kwargs: t.Any
) -> t.Callable[..., Figure]:
    with_config = functools.partial(plot_multiple_charts, *args, **kwargs)
    return wrap_coroutine(with_config)
```

This leaves us with Jupyter code that instantiates the widgets and the location names, then calls interactable_plot_multiple_charts(...) to generate the function to pass to the interactive(...) function. The resulting Jupyter cell, which is equivalent to the previous implementation but significantly shorter, is as follows:

```
import ipywidgets as widgets
from apd.aggregation.analysis import interactable_plot_multiple_charts
```

```
plot = interactable_plot_multiple_charts(location_names=location_names)
out = widgets.interact(plot, collected_after=start, collected_before=end)
display(out)
```

Persistent endpoints

The next logical piece of cleanup we could do is to move the configuration of endpoints to a new database table. This would allow us to automatically generate the location_names variable, ensure the colors used on each chart are consistent across invocations, and also let us update all sensor endpoints without having to pass their URLs each time.

To do this, we'll create a new database table and data class to represent a deployment of apd.sensors. We also need command-line utilities to add and edit the deployment metadata, utility functions to get the data, and tests for all of this.

EXERCISE 9-2: IMPLEMENT STORED DEPLOYMENTS

The changes involved in storing deployments in the database require creating new tables, new console scripts, migrations, and some work on tests.

Implement any or all of the following features, according to what you would find useful:

- Deployment object and table that contains id, name, URI, and API key

- Command-line scripts to add, edit, and list deployments

- Tests for the command-line scripts

- Make servers and api_key arguments to collect_sensor_data optional, using the stored values if omitted

- Helper function to get a deployment record by its ID

- An additional field for the deployment table for the color that should be used to plot its data

- Modifications to plot functions to use a deployment's name and line color directly from its database record

All of these are included in the same implementation that accompanies this chapter.

Charting maps and geographic data

We've been focused on xy plots of value against time in this chapter, as it represents the test data we've been retrieving. Sometimes we need to plot data against other axes. The most common of these is latitude against longitude, so the plot resembles a map.

If we extract the latitude and longitude items from the data set (say, a dictionary mapping coordinates to a temperature record for places around Great Britain), we can pass these as the arguments to plot(...) to see them visualized, as shown in Listing 9-22.

Listing 9-22. Plotting lat/lons using matplotlib, and the resulting chart

```
import matplotlib.pyplot as plt
fig, ax = plt.subplots()
lats = [ll[0] for ll in datapoints.keys()]
lons = [ll[1] for ll in datapoints.keys()]
ax.plot(lons, lats, "o")
plt.show()
```

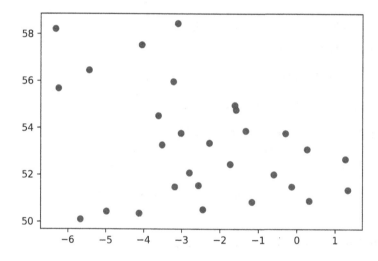

The shape of the data is only very approximately like an outline of Great Britain, which is shown in Figure 9-5. Most people who look at this plot would not recognize it as such.

Figure 9-5. *Outline of Great Britain, the island that comprises England, Wales, and Scotland*

The distortion is because we've plotted this according to the *equirectangular* map projection, where latitude and longitude are an equally spaced grid that does not take the shape of the earth into account. There is no one correct map projection; it very much depends on what the map's intended use is.

We need the map to look familiar to most people, who will be very familiar with the outline of whatever country they live in. We want people who look at it to look at the data, not the unusual projection. The most commonly used projection is the *Mercator* projection, which the OpenStreetMap (OSM) project provides implementations for in many programming languages, including Python.[10] The merc_x(...) and merc_y(...) functions to implement the projection won't be included in the listings, as they're rather complex mathematical functions.

Tip   When drawing maps that show areas of hundreds of square kilometers, it becomes more and more important to use a projection function, but for small-scale maps, it's possible to provide a more familiar view using the ax.set_aspect(...) function. Changing the aspect ratio moves the point where distortion is at a minimum from the equator to another latitude; it doesn't correct for the distortion. For example, ax.set_aspect(1.7) would move the point of least distortion to 54 degrees latitude, as 1.7 is equal to 1 / cos(54).

---

[10]https://wiki.openstreetmap.org/wiki/Mercator#Python_implementation

With the projection functions available, we can re-run the plotting function and see that the points match up much more closely with the outline that we expect, as shown in Figure 9-6. In this case, the labels on the axes no longer show coordinates; they show meaningless numbers. We should ignore these labels for now.

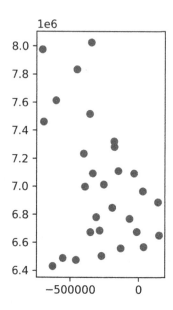

Figure 9-6. *Map using the merc_x and merc_y projections from OSM*

New plot types

This only shows us the position of each data point, not the value associated with it. The plotting functions we've used so far all plot two values, the x and y coordinates. While we could label the plot points with temperatures, or color code with a scale, the resulting chart isn't very easy to read. Instead, there are some other plot types in matplotlib that can help us: specifically `tricontourf(...)`. The tricontour family of plotting functions take three-dimensional input of `(x, y, value)` and interpolate between them to create a plot with areas of color representing a range of values.

While the tricontour functions plot the color areas, we should also plot the points where the measurements were taken, albeit less prominently (Listing 9-23). This works the same way as plotting multiple data sets on a chart; we can call the various plot functions as many times as needed to display all the data; they do not need to be the same type of plot, so long as the axes are compatible.

Listing 9-23. Color contours and scatter on the same plot

```
fig, ax = plt.subplots()

lats = [ll[0] for ll in datapoints.keys()]
lons = [ll[1] for ll in datapoints.keys()]
temperatures = tuple(datapoints.values())

x = tuple(map(merc_x, lons))
y = tuple(map(merc_y, lats))

ax.tricontourf(x, y, temperatures)
ax.plot(x, y, 'wo', ms=3)
ax.set_aspect(1.0)
plt.show()
```

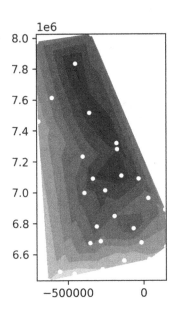

This is understandable once we know what we're looking at, but we can improve it further by plotting the coastline of the island of Great Britain on the map. Given the list of coordinates representing the coastline of Great Britain,[11] we can make a final call to the plot function, this time specifying that we want to draw a line rather than dots. The final version (Figure 9-7) of our plot is much easier to read, especially if we enable drawing a legend by calling `plt.colorbar(tcf)` where `tcf` is the result of the `ax.tricontourf(...)` function call.

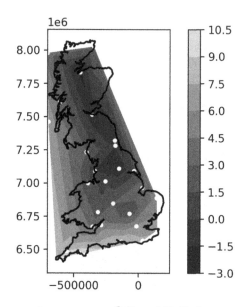

Figure 9-7. *Plot of temperatures around Great Britain on a typical winter's day*

---

[11]The code used to extract these is as follows. The data is from the `www.naturalearthdata.com` data set.

```
import fiona
path = "ne_10m_admin_0_countries.shp"
shape = fiona.open(path)
countries = tuple(shape)
UK = [country for country in countries if country['properties']['ADMIN'] == "United
Kingdom"][0]
coastlines = UK['geometry']['coordinates']
by_complexity = sorted(coastlines, key=lambda coords: len(coords[0]))
gb_boundary = by_complexity[-1][0]
```

This was omitted from the Jupyter notebook to reduce the dependencies needed to use it. In practice, this function would be used rather than literal tuples.

Tip   There are lots of GIS libraries for Python and Matplotlib that make more complex maps easier. If you're planning on drawing lots of maps, I'd encourage you to look at Fiona and Shapely for manipulating points and polygons easily. I strongly recommend these libraries to anyone working with geographic information in Python; they're very powerful indeed.

The basemap toolkit for matplotlib offers very flexible map drawing tools, but the maintainers have decided against distributing it like a standard Python package so I am unable to recommend it as a general solution to map drawing.

Supporting map type charts in apd.aggregation

We need to make some changes to our config object to support these maps, as they behave differently to all the other plots we've made so far. Previously, we've iterated over deployments and drawn a single plot for each deployment, representing a single sensor. To draw a map, we'd need to combine two values (coordinate and temperature) and draw a *single* plot representing all deployments. It's possible that our individual deployments would move around and would provide a coordinate sensor to record where they were at a given time. A custom cleaner function alone would not be sufficient to combine the values of multiple datapoints.

Backward compatibility in data classes

Our Config object contains a sensor_name parameter, which filters the output of the get_data_by_deployment(...) function call as part of the drawing process. We need to override this part of the system; we no longer want to pass a single parameter to the get_data_by_deployment(...) function; we want to be able to replace the entire call with custom filtering.

The sensor_name= parameter has been made optional and the type changed to an InitVar. We've also added a new get_data parameter, which is an optional callable with the same shape as get_data_by_deployment(...). InitVars are another useful feature of data classes, allowing parameters to be specified which are not stored but are available in a post-creation hook called __post_init__(...). In our case, shown in Listing 9-24, we can define such a hook to set up the new get_data= variable based on sensor_name=, maintaining backward compatibility with implementations that only pass a sensor_name=.

445

Listing 9-24. Data class with get_data parameter and backward compatibility hook

```
@dataclasses.dataclass
class Config:
    title: str
    clean: t.Callable[[t.AsyncIterator[DataPoint]], t.AsyncIterator[
    t.Tuple[datetime.datetime, float]]]
    get_data: t.Optional[
        t.Callable[..., t.AsyncIterator[t.Tuple[UUID,
        t.AsyncIterator[DataPoint]]]]
    ] = None
    ylabel: str
    sensor_name: dataclasses.InitVar[str] = None

    def __post_init__(self, sensor_name=None):
        if self.get_data is None:
            if sensor_name is None:
                raise ValueError("You must specify either get_data or
                sensor_name")
            self.get_data = get_one_sensor_by_deployment(sensor_name)

def get_one_sensor_by_deployment(sensor_name):
    return functools.partial(get_data_by_deployment,
    sensor_name=sensor_name)
```

The __post_init__(...) function is called automatically, passing any InitVar attributes to it. As we are setting get_data in the __post_init__ method, we need to ensure that the data class is not frozen, as this counts as a modification.

This change allows us to change which data is passed to the clean(...) function, but that function still expects to return a time and float tuple to be passed into the plot_date(...) function. We need to change the shape of the clean(...) function.

We will no longer only be using plot_date(...) to draw our points; some types of chart require contours and points, so we must also add another customization point to choose how data are plotted. The new draw attribute of the Config class provides this function.

To support these new function call signatures, we need to make `Config` a generic class, as shown in Listing 9-25. This makes it possible to specify the underlying data of the Config object (or have the type system infer it from context). The existing data types are of the type `Config[datetime.datetime, float]`, but our map `Config` will be `Config[t.Tuple[float, float], float]`. That is, some configs plot a float against a date, others plot a float against a pair of floats.

Listing 9-25. A generic Config type

```
plot_key = t.TypeVar("plot_key")
plot_value = t.TypeVar("plot_value")

@dataclasses.dataclass
class Config(t.Generic[plot_key, plot_value]):
    title: str
    clean: t.Callable[
        [t.AsyncIterator[DataPoint]], t.AsyncIterator[t.Tuple[plot_key,
        plot_value]]]
    ]
    draw: t.Optional[
        t.Callable[
            [t.Any, t.Iterable[plot_key], t.Iterable[plot_value],
            t.Optional[str]], None
        ]
    ] = None
    get_data: t.Optional[
        t.Callable[..., t.AsyncIterator[t.Tuple[UUID,
        t.AsyncIterator[DataPoint]]]]
    ] = None
    ylabel: t.Optional[str] = None
    sensor_name: dataclasses.InitVar[str] = None

    def __post_init__(self, sensor_name=None):
        if self.draw is None:
            self.draw = draw_date
```

```
if self.get_data is None:
    if sensor_name is None:
        raise ValueError("You must specify either get_data or
        sensor_name")
    self.get_data = get_one_sensor_by_deployment(sensor_name)
```

The Config class has lots of complex typing information in it now. This does have real benefits, though: the following code raises a typing error:

```
Config(
    sensor_name="Temperature",
    clean=clean_temperature_fluctuations,
    title="Ambient temperature",
    ylabel="Degrees C",
    draw=draw_map,
)
```

It also gives us confidence when we read the code; we know that the argument and return types of functions as specified match up. As this code involves lots of manipulating of data structures into iterators of iterators of tuples (*etc.*), it is easy to get confused about exactly what's required. This is a perfect use case for typing hints.

We expect users to be creating custom configuration objects with custom draw and clean methods. Having reliable typing information lets them find subtle errors much more quickly.

The config.get_data(...) and config.draw(...) functions we need to handle our existing two plot types are refactoring of code that we've already examined in depth in this chapter, but they are available to view in the code that accompanies this chapter for those who are interested in the details.

Drawing a custom map using the new configs

The changes to Config allow us to define map-based configurations, but our current data doesn't include any data that can be drawn as a map because none of our deployments includes a location sensor. We can use the new config.get_data(...) option to generate some static data rather than real, aggregated data to demonstrate the functionality. We can also add the custom coastline line by extending the draw_map(...) function (Listing 9-26).

Listing 9-26. Jupyter function to draw a custom map chart along with the registered charts

```python
def get_literal_data():
    # Get manually entered temperature data, as our particular deployment
    # does not contain data of this shape
    raw_data = {...}
    now = datetime.datetime.now()
    async def points():
        for (coord, temp) in raw_data.items():
            deployment_id = uuid.uuid4()
            yield DataPoint(sensor_name="Location",
            deployment_id=deployment_id,
            collected_at=now, data=coord)
            yield DataPoint(sensor_name="Temperature",
            deployment_id=deployment_id,
            collected_at=now, data=temp)
    async def deployments(*args, **kwargs):
        yield None, points()
    return deployments

def draw_map_with_gb(plot, x, y, colour):
    # Draw the map and add an explicit coastline
    gb_boundary = [...]
    draw_map(plot, x, y, colour)
    plot.plot(
        [merc_x(coord[0]) for coord in gb_boundary],
        [merc_y(coord[1]) for coord in gb_boundary],
        "k-",
    )

country = Config(
    get_data=get_literal_data(),
    clean=get_map_cleaner_for("Temperature"),
    title="Country wide temperature",
```

```
    ylabel="",
    draw=draw_map_with_gb,
)

out = widgets.interactive(interactable_plot_multiple_charts(configs=configs
+ (country, )), collected_after=start, collected_before=end)
```

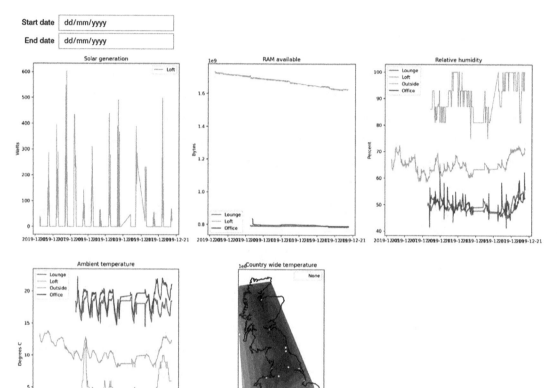

EXERCISE 9-3: ADD A BAR CHART FOR CUMULATIVE SOLAR POWER

We wrote a cleaner for the solar generation data to convert it to momentary power instead of cumulative power. This makes it much more evident when power is being generated over time, but it makes understanding the amount generated each day harder.

Write a new cleaner that returns cumulative power per day and a new draw function that displays this as a bar chart.

As always, the code accompanying this chapter includes a starting point and a sample completed version.

Summary

In this chapter, we've returned to Jupyter for the purpose that people are most familiar with, rather than purely as a prototyping tool. We've also used Matplotlib here, which many users of Jupyter will have come across already. Together, these two make a formidable tool for communicating data analysis outcomes.

We've written lots of helper functions to make it easy for people to build custom interfaces in Jupyter to view the data we are aggregating. This has allowed us to define a public-facing API while allowing us lots of flexibility to change the way things are implemented. A good API for end-users is vital for retaining users, so it's worth spending the time on.

The final version of the accompanying code for this chapter includes all the functions we've built up, many of which contain long blocks of sample data. Some of these were too long to include in print, so I recommend that you take a look at the code samples and try them out.

Finally, we've looked at some more advanced uses of some technologies we've used already, including using the __post_init__(...) hook of data classes to preserve backward compatibility when default arguments do not suffice, and more complex combinations of synchronous and asynchronous code.

Additional resources

The following links provide additional background information on the subjects covered in this chapter:

> Details on the formatting options available on matplotlib charts as well as links to other chart types are available at the matplotlib documentation, at `https://matplotlib.org/3.1.1/api/_as_gen/matplotlib.pyplot.plot.html#matplotlib.pyplot.plot`.

> A testing helper library to manage creating independent postgresql instances is testing.postgresql, available from `https://github.com/tk0miya/testing.postgresql`.

> OpenStreetMap's page on the Mercator projection, including details of different implementations, is `https://wiki.openstreetmap.org/wiki/Mercator`.

> The Fiona library, for parsing geographic information files in Python, is documented at `https://fiona.readthedocs.io/en/latest/README.html`.

> The Shapely library, for manipulating complex GIS objects in Python, is available at `https://shapely.readthedocs.io/en/latest/manual.html`. I particularly recommend this one; it's been useful to me on many occasions.

Speeding things up

There are two main approaches to improving the speed of code: optimizing the code we've written and optimizing the control flow of the program to run less code. People often focus on optimizing the code rather than the control flow because it's easier to make self-contained changes, but the most significant benefits are usually in changing the flow.

Optimizing a function

The first step to optimizing a function is having a good understanding of it's performance before making any changes. The Python standard library has a profile module to assist with this. Profile introspects code as it runs to build up an idea of the time spent on each function call. The profiler can detect multiple calls to the same function and monitor any functions called indirectly. You can then generate a report that shows the function call chart for an entire run.

We can profile a statement using the `profile.run(...)` function. This uses the reference profiler, which is always available, but most people use the optimized profiler at `cProfile.run(...)`[1]. The profiler will **exec** the string passed as the first argument, generate profiling information, and then automatically format the profile results into a report.

```
>>> from apd.aggregation.analysis import interactable_plot_multiple_charts
>>> import cProfile
>>> cProfile.run("interactable_plot_multiple_charts()()", sort="cumulative")
        164 function calls in 2.608 seconds

   Ordered by: cumulative time
```

---

[1] If you're using a Python implementation other than CPython (such as PyPy or Jython), this optimized profiler won't be available, and you'll need to use the reference implementation.

© Matthew Wilkes 2020

M. Wilkes, *Advanced Python Development*, https://doi.org/10.1007/978-1-4842-5793-7_10

ncalls	tottime	percall	cumtime	percall	filename:lineno(function)
1	0.001	0.001	2.608	2.608	{built-in method builtins.exec}
1	0.001	0.001	2.606	2.606	<string>:1(<module>)
1	0.004	0.004	2.597	2.597	analysis.py:327(run_in_thread)
9	2.558	0.284	2.558	0.284	{method 'acquire' of '_thread.lock' objects}
1	0.000	0.000	2.531	2.531	_base.py:635(__exit__)

...

The table displayed here shows the number of times a function was invoked (*ncalls*), the time spent executing that function (*tottime*), and that total time divided by the number of calls (*percall*). It also shows the cumulative time spent executing that function and all indirectly called functions, both as a total and divided by the number of calls (*cumtime* and the second *percall*). A function having a high cumtime and a low tottime implies that the function itself could not benefit from optimizing, but the control flow involving that function may.

Tip   Some IDEs and code editors have built-in support for running profilers and viewing their output. If you're using an IDE, then this may be a more natural interface for you. The behavior of the profilers is still the same, however.

When running code in a Jupyter notebook, you can also generate the same report using the "cell magic" functionality (Figure 10-1). A cell magic is an annotation on a cell to use a named plugin during execution, in this case a profiler. If you make the first line of your cell %%prun -s cumulative, then once the cell has completed executing, the notebook displays a pop-up window containing a profile report for the whole cell.

Caution   The "cell magic" approach is not currently compatible with top-level await support in IPython. If you use the %%prun cell magic, then that cell cannot await a coroutine.

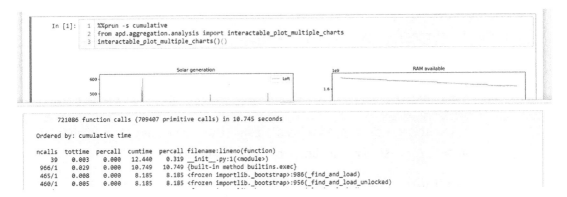

Figure 10-1. *Example of profiling a Jupyter notebook cell*

Profiling and threads

The preceding examples generate reports that list lots of threading
internal functions rather than our substantive functions. This is because our
`interactable_plot_multiple_charts(...)(...)` function[2] starts a new thread to handle
running the underlying coroutines. The profiler does not reach into the started thread to
start a profiler, so we only see the main thread waiting for the worker thread to finish.

We can fix this by changing the way our code wraps a coroutine into a thread, giving
us the opportunity to insert a profiler inside the child thread. For example, we could add
a debug= flag and then submit a different function to the thread pool if debug=True is
passed, as shown in Listing 10-1.

Listing 10-1. Example of wrap_coroutine to optionally include profiling

```
_Coroutine_Result = t.TypeVar("_Coroutine_Result")

def wrap_coroutine(
    f: t.Callable[..., t.Coroutine[t.Any, t.Any, _Coroutine_Result]],
    debug: bool=False,
) -> t.Callable[..., _Coroutine_Result]:
    """Given a coroutine, return a function that runs that coroutine
    in a new event loop in an isolated thread"""
```

---

[2]This function is called twice because it was written to be used as part of an interactive widget.
`interactable_plot_multiple_charts(...)` takes setup arguments and returns a function that
can be hooked up to widgets. We call it twice here because we want to set up the function and
call it once with no special arguments, rather than plumb it in to interactive widgets.

```python
    @functools.wraps(f)
    def run_in_thread(*args: t.Any, **kwargs: t.Any) -> _Coroutine_Result:
        loop = asyncio.new_event_loop()
        wrapped = f(*args, **kwargs)

        if debug:
            # Create a new function that runs the loop inside a cProfile
            # session, so it can be profiled transparently

            def fn():
                import cProfile

                return cProfile.runctx(
                    "loop.run_until_complete(wrapped)",
                    {},
                    {"loop": loop, "wrapped": wrapped},
                    sort="cumulative",
                )

            task_callable = fn
        else:
            # If not debugging just submit the loop run function with the
            # desired coroutine
            task_callable = functools.partial(loop.run_until_complete,
            wrapped)
        with ThreadPoolExecutor(max_workers=1) as pool:
            task = pool.submit(task_callable)
        # Mypy can get confused when nesting generic functions, like we do
        # here
        # The fact that Task is generic means we lose the association with
        # _CoroutineResult. Adding an explicit cast restores this.
        return t.cast(_Coroutine_Result, task.result())

    return run_in_thread

def interactable_plot_multiple_charts(
    *args: t.Any, debug: bool=False, **kwargs: t.Any
```

```
) -> t.Callable[..., Figure]:
    with_config = functools.partial(plot_multiple_charts, *args, **kwargs)
    return wrap_coroutine(with_config, debug=debug)
```

In Listing 10-1, we use the runctx(...) function from the profiler, rather than the run(...) function. runctx(...) allows passing global and local variables to the expression we're profiling.[3] The interpreter does not introspect the string representing the code to run to determine what variables are needed. You must pass them explicitly.

With this change in place, the same code we used to plot all the charts with interactive elements can also request that profiling information be collected, so users in Jupyter notebooks can easily debug new chart types theyre adding, as demonstrated in Figure 10-2.

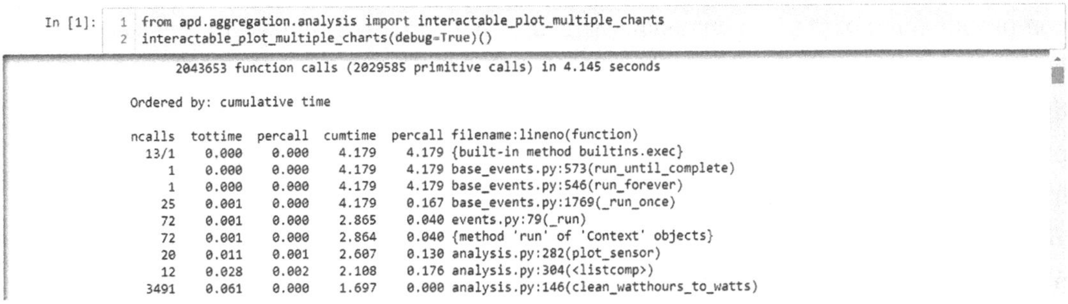

```
In [1]:   1  from apd.aggregation.analysis import interactable_plot_multiple_charts
          2  interactable_plot_multiple_charts(debug=True)()

              2043653 function calls (2029585 primitive calls) in 4.145 seconds

          Ordered by: cumulative time

          ncalls  tottime  percall  cumtime  percall filename:lineno(function)
            13/1    0.000    0.000    4.179    4.179 {built-in method builtins.exec}
               1    0.000    0.000    4.179    4.179 base_events.py:573(run_until_complete)
               1    0.000    0.000    4.179    4.179 base_events.py:546(run_forever)
              25    0.001    0.000    4.179    0.167 base_events.py:1769(_run_once)
              72    0.001    0.000    2.865    0.040 events.py:79(_run)
              72    0.001    0.000    2.864    0.040 {method 'run' of 'Context' objects}
              20    0.011    0.001    2.607    0.130 analysis.py:282(plot_sensor)
              12    0.028    0.002    2.108    0.176 analysis.py:304(<listcomp>)
            3491    0.061    0.000    1.697    0.000 analysis.py:146(clean_watthours_to_watts)
```

Figure 10-2. *Integrated profiling option being used from Jupyter*

The profiler running in the child thread still includes some overhead functions at the top, but we can now see the functions we wanted to profile rather than only thread management functions. If we only look at the functions relevant to our code, the output is as follows:

ncalls	tottime	percall	cumtime	percall	filename:lineno(function)
20	0.011	0.001	2.607	0.130	analysis.py:282(plot_sensor)
12	0.028	0.002	2.108	0.176	analysis.py:304(<listcomp>)
3491	0.061	0.000	1.697	0.000	analysis.py:146(clean_watthours_to_watts)
33607	0.078	0.000	0.351	0.000	query.py:114(subiterator)

---

[3]Providing the loop and wrapped variables as explicit local variables also ensures that Python knows how to create a closure over these variables and make them available to the profiled expression. If we passed locals=locals(), we wouldn't see these variables passed down unless we gave Python a hint that we needed them from the containing scope using nonlocal loop and nonlocal wrapped statements.

12	0.000	0.000	0.300	0.025 analysis.py:60(draw_date)
33603	0.033	0.000	0.255	0.000 query.py:39(get_data)
3	0.001	0.000	0.254	0.085 analysis.py:361(
				plot_multiple_charts)
16772	0.023	0.000	0.214	0.000 analysis.py:223(clean_passthrough)
33595	0.089	0.000	0.207	0.000 database.py:77(from_sql_result)
8459	0.039	0.000	0.170	0.000 analysis.py:175(
				clean_temperature_fluctuations)
24	0.000	0.000	0.140	0.006 query.py:74(get_deployment_by_id)
2	0.000	0.000	0.080	0.040 query.py:24(with_database)

It appears that the plot_sensor(...) function is called 20 times, the list comprehension points = [dp async for dp in config.clean(query_results)] is called 12 times, and the clean_watthours_to_watts(...) function is called 3491 times. The huge number of reported calls for the clean function is due to the way the profiler interacts with generator functions. Every time that a new item is requested from the generator, it is classed as a new invocation of the function. Equally, every time an item is yielded, it is classed as that invocation returning. This approach may seem more complex than measuring the time from the first invocation until the generator is exhausted, but it means that the tottime and cumtime totals do not include the time that the iterator was idle and waiting for other code to request the next item. However, it also means that the percall numbers represent the time taken to retrieve a single item, not the time taken for every time the function is called.

Caution   Profilers need a function to determine the current time. By default profile uses time.process_time() and cProfile uses time.perf_counter(). These measure very different things. The process_time() function measures time the CPU was busy, but perf_counter() measures real-world time. The real-world time is often called "wall time," meaning the time as measured by a clock on a wall.

Interpreting the profile report

The clean_watthours_to_watts(...) function should draw your eye immediately, as it's a relatively low-level function with a very high cumtime. This function is being used as a support function to draw one of four charts, but it's responsible for 65% of the total execution time of plot_sensor(...). This function is where we would start optimization, but if we compare the tottime and the cumtime, we can see that it only spends 2% of the total time in this function.

The discrepancy tells us that it's not the code we've directly written in this function thats introducing the slowdown, it's the fact that were calling other functions indirectly as part of our implementation of clean_watthours_to_watts(...). Right now, were looking at optimizing functions rather than optimizing execution flow. As optimizing this function requires optimizing the pattern of calling functions out of our control, well pass by it for now. The second half of this chapter covers strategies for improving performance by altering control flow, and well return to fix this function there.

Instead, lets concentrate on the items that have a high tottime rather than cumtime, representing that the time spent is in executing code that we wrote, rather than code that were using. These numbers are significantly lower than the times we looked at previously; theyre relatively simple functions and represent a smaller potential benefit, but that may not always be the case.

```
   12   0.103   0.009   2.448   0.204 analysis.py:304(<listcomp>)
33595   0.082   0.000   0.273   0.000 database.py:77(from_sql_result)
33607   0.067   0.000   0.404   0.000 query.py:114(subiterator)
```

We see that two functions related to the database interface are potential candidates. These are each run over 33,000 times and take less than a tenth of a second total time each, so they are not particularly tempting optimization targets. Still, they're the highest in terms of tottime of our code, so they represent the best *chance* we have to do the simple, self-contained type of optimization.

The first thing to do is to try changing something about the implementation and measuring any difference. The existing implementation is very short, containing only a single line of code. It's unlikely that we could optimize at all, but lets try.

```
@classmethod
def from_sql_result(cls, result) -> DataPoint:
    return cls(**result._asdict())
```

One thing thats not immediately clear in the preceding implementation that may cause slowdown is that a dictionary of values is generated and mapped dynamically to keyword arguments.[4] An idea to test would be to explicitly pass the arguments, as we know that they are consistent.

```
@classmethod
def from_sql_result(cls, result) -> DataPoint:
    if result.id is None:
        return cls(data=result.data, deployment_id=result.deployment_id,
                   sensor_name=result.sensor_name,
                   collected_at=result.collected_at)
    else:
        return cls(id=result.id, data=result.data,
            deployment_id=result.deployment_id, sensor_name=result.sensor_name,
            collected_at=result.collected_at)
```

The most important part of this process is to test our hypothesis. We need to re-run the code and compare the results. We also need to be aware of the fact that the code may vary in execution time because of external factors, such as load on the computer, so it's a good idea to try running the code a few times to see if the results are stable. Were looking

---

[4]The timeit profiler (explained in the next section) can be used to demonstrate this relationship:

```
>>> def func(a, b, c, d, e, f, g, h, i, j, k):
...     return a+b+c+d+e+f+g+h+i+j+k
...
>>> timeit.timeit("func(**vals)", "vals={'a':1, 'b':1, 'c':1, 'd':1, 'e':1, 'f':1,
    'g':1, 'h':1, 'i':1, 'j':1, 'k':1}", globals={'func':func})
0.7101785999999777
>>> timeit.timeit("func(a=1,b=1,c=1,d=1,e=1,f=1,g=1,h=1,i=1,j=1,k=1)",
    globals={'func':func})
0.6051479999999998
>>> timeit.timeit("a(1,1,1,1,1,1,1,1,1,1,1)", globals={'func':func})
0.479350299999993
```

The difference between these approaches is marginal for trivial functionals and irrelevant for more complex functions. You should continue to use the one that makes your code clearest; we're only trying this in our example as a last resort for performance improvements.

for a significant speedup here, as our change would introduce maintainability issues, so a trivially small speed boost isnt worth it.

```
33595    0.109    0.000    0.147    0.000 database.py:77(from_sql_result)
```

The result here shows that more time was spent in the `from_sql_result()` function than the previous implementation, but the cumulative time has decreased. This result tells us that the changes we made to `from_sql_result()` directly caused that function to take longer, but in doing so we changed the control flow to eliminate the call to `_asdict()` and pass values directly which more than made up for the slowdown we introduced.

In other words, this functions implementation has no definite improvement to performance other than by changing the control flow to avoid code in `_asdict()`. It also reduces maintainability of the code by requiring us to list the fields in use in multiple places. As a result, well stick with our original implementation rather than the "optimized" version.

Tip   There is another potential optimization to class creation, setting a `__slots__` attribute on the class, like `__slots__` = {`"sensor_name"`, `"data"`, `"deployment_id"`, `"id"`, `"collected_at"`}. This allows a developer to guarantee that only specifically named attributes will ever be set on an instance, which allows the interpreter to add many optimizations. At the time of writing, there are some incompatibilities between data classes and `__slots__` that make it less easy to use, but if you want to optimize instantiation of your objects, then I recommend taking a look.

The same is true of the other two: the `subiterator()` and list comprehension functions are very minimal; changes to them decrease readability and do not bring substantial performance improvements.

It's relatively rare for a small, easily understood function to be a candidate for significant performance improvement, as poor performance is often correlated with complexity. If the complexity in your system is due to the composition of simple functions, then performance improvements come from optimizing control flow. If you have very long functions that do complex things, then it's more likely that significant improvements can come from optimizing functions in isolation.

Other profilers

The profiler that comes with Python is enough to get useful information in most cases. Still, as code performance is such an important topic, there are other profilers available that have unique advantages and disadvantages.

timeit

The most important alternative profiler to mention is also from the Python standard library, called timeit. timeit is useful for profiling fast, independent functions. Rather than monitoring a program in normal operation, timeit runs given code repeatedly and returns the cumulative time taken.

```
>>> import timeit
>>> from apd.aggregation.utils import merc_y
>>> timeit.timeit("merc_y(52.2)", globals={"merc_y": merc_y})
1.8951617999996415
```

When called with the default arguments, as previously shown, the output is the number of seconds needed to execute the first argument one million times, measured using the most accurate clock available. Only the first argument (stmt=) is required, which is a string representation of the code to be executed each time. A second string argument (setup=) represents setup code that must be executed before the test starts, and a globals= dictionary allows passing arbitrary items into the namespace of the code being profiled. This is especially useful for passing in the function under test, rather than importing it in the setup= code. The optional number= argument allows us to specify how many times the code should be run, as one million executions is an inappropriate amount for functions that take more than about 50 microseconds to execute.[5]

Both the string representing the code to test and the setup= strings can be multiline strings containing a series of Python statements. Be aware, however, that any definitions or imports in the first string are run every time, so all setup code should be done in the second string or passed directly as a global.

---

[5]A function that takes 1 millisecond to execute translates to timeit taking over 15 minutes to execute with the default parameters.

line_profiler

A commonly recommended alternative profiler is line_profiler by Robert Kern.[6] It records information on a line-by-line basis rather than a function-by-function basis, making it very useful for pinpointing where exactly a functions performance issues are coming from.

Unfortunately, the trade-offs for line_profiler are quite significant. It requires modification to your Python program to annotate each function you wish to profile, and while those annotations are in place, the code cannot be run except through the line_profilers custom environment. Also, at the time of writing, it's not been possible to install line_profiler with pip for approximately two years. Although you will find many people recommending this profiler online, thats partially due to it being available before other alternatives. I would recommend avoiding this profiler unless absolutely necessary for debugging a complex function; you may find it costs you more time to set up than you save in convenience once installed.

yappi

Another alternative profiler is yappi,[7] which provides transparent profiling of Python code running across multiple threads and in asyncio event loops. Numbers such as the call count for iterators represent the number of times the iterator is called rather than the number of items retrieved, and no code modifications are needed to support profiling multiple threads.

The disadvantage to yappi is that it's a relatively small project under heavy development, so you may find it to be less polished than many other Python libraries. I would recommend yappi for cases where the built-in profiler is insufficient. At the time of writing, Id still recommend the built-in profiling tools as my first choice, but yappi is a close second.

The interface to yappi is somewhat different to the built-in profilers that we've used so far, as it doesnt offer an equivalent to the run(...) function call. The yappi profiler must be enabled and disabled around the code being profiled. There is an equivalent API for the default profiler, as shown in Table 10-1.

---

[6]https://github.com/rkern/line_profiler
[7]https://github.com/sumerc/yappi

Table 10-1. *Comparison of cProfile and yappi profiling*

cProfile using enable/disable API	Yappi-based profiling
import cProfile profiler = cProfile.Profile() profiler.enable() method_to_profile() profiler.disable() profiler.print_stats()	import yappi yappi.start() method_to_profile() yappi.stop() yappi.get_func_stats().print_all()

Using yappi in a Jupyter cell gives us the ability to call the functions in the underlying code without needing to work around threading and asyncio issues. We could have used yappi to profile our code without making the debug= parameter change earlier. In the preceding example, if method_to_profile() called interactable_plot_multiple_charts(...) and widgets.interactive(...), the resulting profile output would be as follows:

```
Clock type: CPU
Ordered by: totaltime, desc

name                                   ncall   tsub       ttot       tavg
..futures\thread.py:52 _WorkItem.run   17      0.000000   9.765625   0.574449
..rrent\futures\thread.py:66 _worker   5/1     0.000000   6.734375   1.346875
..38\Lib\threading.py:859 Thread.run   5/1     0.000000   6.734375   1.346875
..ndowsSelectorEventLoop.run_forever   1       0.000000   6.734375   6.734375
..b\asyncio\events.py:79 Handle._run   101     0.000000   6.734375   0.066677
..lectorEventLoop.run_until_complete   1       0.000000   6.734375   6.734375
..WindowsSelectorEventLoop._run_once   56      0.000000   6.734375   0.120257
..gation\analysis.py:282 plot_sensor   4       0.093750   6.500000   1.625000
..egation\analysis.py:304 <listcomp>   12      0.031250   5.515625   0.459635
...
```

The total times displayed by yappi are significantly higher than those from cProfile in this example. You should only ever compare the times produced by a profiler to results generated on the same hardware with the same tools, as performance can vary wildly[8] when profilers are enabled.

YAPPI HELPER FUNCTIONS

Yappi supports filtering stats by function and module out of the box. There is also an option to provide custom filter functions, to determine exactly which code should be displayed in performance reports. There are some other options available; you should check the documentation of yappi to find the recommended way to filter output to only show code you're interested in.

The code accompanying this chapter has some helper functions to make yappi profiling more comfortable from a Jupyter context. These are `profile_with_yappi`, a context manager to handle activating and deactivating the profiler; `jupyter_page_file`, a context manager to help display the profiling data in the same way as the %%prun cell magic, not merged in with cell output; and `yappi_package_matches`, a helper that uses the `filter_callback=` option to restrict the stats displayed to only show modules within a given Python package. An example of using these helper functions is shown as Listing 10-2.

Listing 10-2. Jupyter cell for yappi profiling, with part of the Jupyter output shown

```
from apd.aggregation.analysis import (interactable_plot_multiple_charts,
configs)
from apd.aggregation.utils import (jupyter_page_file, profile_with_yappi,
yappi_package_matches)
import yappi

with profile_with_yappi():
    plot = interactable_plot_multiple_charts()
    plot()
```

---

[8]I've seen real-world Python code that is an order of magnitude faster in a Linux VM on an OSX host than on the host itself, even running the same release of Python and all dependencies. Python build, OS version, and profiler can all make a big difference, so you should establish a baseline whenever you're doing benchmarking; don't rely on ones you've generated on previous days.

```
with jupyter_page_file() as output:
    yappi.get_func_stats(filter_callback=lambda stat:
        yappi_package_matches(stat, ["apd.aggregation"])
    ).print_all(output)
```

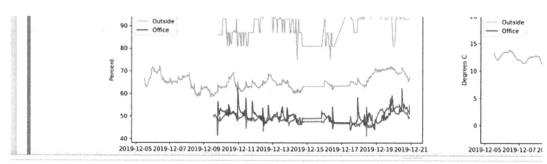

```
Clock type: CPU
Ordered by: totaltime, desc

name                                     ncall  tsub       ttot       tavg
..gation\analysis.py:282 plot_sensor     4      0.000000   6.312500   1.578125
..egation\analysis.py:304 <listcomp>     12     0.125000   5.437500   0.453125
..is.py:146 clean_watthours_to_watts     1      0.078125   4.296875   4.296875
..gregation\query.py:114 subiterator     12     0.218750   0.890625   0.074219
```

None of these three helpers are strictly needed, but they provide for a more user-friendly interface.

Tracemalloc

The profilers we've looked at so far all measure the CPU resources needed to run a piece of code. The other primary resource available to us is memory. A program that runs quickly but requires a large amount of RAM would run significantly more slowly on systems that have less RAM available.

Python has a built-in RAM allocation profiler, called tracemalloc. This module provides `tracemalloc.start()` and `tracemalloc.stop()` functions to enable and disable to profiler, respectively. A profile result can be requested at any time by using the `tracemalloc.take_snapshot()` function. An example of using this on our plotting code is given as Listing 10-3.

The result of this is a Snapshot object, which has a statistics(...) method to return a list of individual statistics. The first argument to this function is the key by which to group results. The most useful two keys to use are "lineno" (for line-by-line profiling) and "filename" (for whole file profiling). A cumulative= flag allows the user to choose between including the memory use of indirectly called functions or not. That is, should each statistic line represent what a line does directly or all the consequences of running that line?

Listing 10-3. Example script to debug memory usage after plotting the charts

```
import tracemalloc

from apd.aggregation.analysis import interactable_plot_multiple_charts

tracemalloc.start()
plot = interactable_plot_multiple_charts()()
snapshot = tracemalloc.take_snapshot()
tracemalloc.stop()
for line in snapshot.statistics("lineno", cumulative=True):
    print(line)
```

The documentation in the standard library provides some helper functions to provide for better formatting of the output data, especially the code sample for the display_top(...) function.[9]

Caution   The tracemalloc allocator only shows memory allocations that are still active at the time that the snapshot is generated. Profiling our program shows that the SQL parsing uses a lot of RAM but won't show our DataPoint objects, despite them taking up more RAM. Our objects are short-lived, unlike the SQL ones, so they have already been discarded by the time we generate the snapshot. When debugging peak memory usage, you must create a snapshot at the peak.

---

[9]https://docs.python.org/3/library/tracemalloc.html#pretty-top

New Relic

If youre running a web-based application, then the commercial service New Relic may provide useful profiling insights.[10] It provides a tightly integrated profiling system that allows you to monitor the control flow from web requests, the functions involved in servicing them, and interactions with databases and third-party services as part of the render process.

The trade-offs for New Relic and it's competitors are substantial. You gain access to an excellent set of profiling data, but it doesnt fit all application types and costs a significant amount of money. Besides, the fact that the actions of real users are used to perform the profiling means that you should consider user privacy before introducing New Relic to your system. That said, New Relics profiling has provided some of the most useful performance analyses Ive seen.

Optimizing control flow

More commonly, it's not a single function that is the cause of performance problems within a Python system. As we saw earlier, writing code in a naïve way generally results in a function that cannot be optimized beyond changing what it's doing.

In my experience, the most common source of low performance is a function that calculates more than it needs to. For example, in our first implementations of features to get collated data, we did not yet have database-side filtering, so we added a loop to filter the data we want from the data thats not relevant.

Filtering the input data later doesnt just move workaround; it can increase the total amount of work being done. In this situation, the work done is loading data from the database, setting up DataPoint records, and extracting the relevant data from those records. By moving the filtering from the loading step to the extracting step, we set up DataPoint records for objects that we know we dont care about.

---

[10]Other commercial profiling tools are available.

```
COMPLEXITY
```

The time taken by a function is not always directly proportional to the size of the input, but it's a good approximation for functions that loop over the data once. Sorting and other more complex operations behave differently.

The relationship between how long functions take (or how much memory they need) and their input size is called computational complexity. Most programmers never need to worry about the exact complexity class of functions, but it's worth being aware of the broad-strokes differences when optimizing your code.

You can estimate the relationship between input size and time using the timeit function with different inputs, but as a rule of thumb, it's best to avoid nesting loops within loops. Nested loops that always have a very small number of iterations are okay, but looping over user input within another loop over user input results in the time a function takes increasing rapidly[11] as the amount of user input increases.

The longer a function takes for a given input size, the more important it is to minimize the amount of extraneous data it processes.

In Figure 10-3, the horizontal axis maps to the time taken and the vertical axis to the amount of input a stage in the pipeline has to process. The width of a step, and therefore the time it takes to process, is proportional to the amount of data that it is processing.

These two flows illustrate the amount of work that needs to happen to process a single sensor, with the top flow having database-level filtering and the bottom having filtering in Python. In both cases, the total amount of output is the same, but the intermediate stages have different amounts of data to process and therefore take a different amount of time.

---

[11]Specifically, this is *polynomial* complexity, sometimes written as $O(n^c)$. The time taken is the time to execute the loop body, multiplied by each of the lengths of the loop.

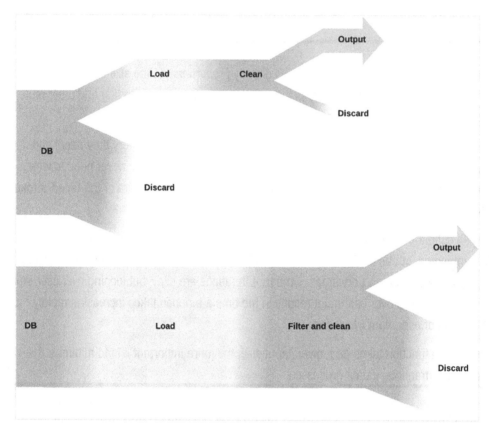

Figure 10-3. *Diagram of the size of data set for code that filters in the database vs. filtering during cleaning*

There are two places that we discard data: when we are finding only the data for the sensor in question and when discarding invalid data. By moving the sensor filter to the database, we reduce the amount of work done in the load step and therefore the amount of time needed. We are moving the bulk of the filtering, with the more complex filtering for removing invalid data still happening in the clean step. If we could move this filtering to the database, it would further decrease the time taken by the load step, albeit not as much.

We already assumed that wed need to filter in the database when we wrote the functions, partially to improve the usability of the API, but we can test the assumption that it improves performance by using the yappi profiler and the ability to provide explicit configurations to our drawing system. We can then directly compare the time taken to draw a chart with database-backed filtering with Python filtering. The implementation of the performance analysis for filtering in the database is shown in Listing 10-4.

Listing 10-4. Jupyter cell to profile a single chart, filtering in SQL

```
import yappi

from apd.aggregation.analysis import (interactable_plot_multiple_charts,
Config)
from apd.aggregation.analysis import (clean_temperature_fluctuations,
get_one_sensor_by_deployment)
from apd.aggregation.utils import profile_with_yappi

yappi.set_clock_type("wall")

filter_in_db = Config(
    clean=clean_temperature_fluctuations,
    title="Ambient temperature",
    ylabel="Degrees C",
    get_data=get_one_sensor_by_deployment("Temperature"),
)

with profile_with_yappi():
    plot = interactable_plot_multiple_charts(configs=[filter_in_db])
    plot()

yappi.get_func_stats().print_all()
```

The following statistics are a partial output from the cells output, showing some of the entries that are most interesting to us. We can see that 10828 data objects were loaded, that the get_data(...) function took 2.7 seconds, and that 6 database calls were made totaling 2.4 seconds. The list comprehension on line 304 of analysis.py (points = [dp async for dp in config.clean(query_results)]) is where the cleaner function is called. Cleaning the data took 0.287 seconds, but the time in the cleaning function itself was negligible.

name	ncall	tsub	ttot	tavg
..lectorEventLoop.run_until_complete	1	0.000240	3.001717	3.001717
..alysis.py:341 plot_multiple_charts	1	2.843012	2.999702	2.999702
..gation\analysis.py:282 plot_sensor	1	0.000000	2.720996	2.720996
..query.py:86 get_data_by_deployment	1	2.706142	2.706195	2.706195
..d\aggregation\query.py:39 get_data	1	2.569511	2.663460	2.663460

```
..lchemy\orm\query.py:3197 Query.all  6         0.008771  2.407840  0.401307
..lchemy\orm\loading.py:35 instances  10828  0.005485  1.588923  0.000147
..egation\analysis.py:304 <listcomp>  4         0.000044  0.286975  0.071744
..175 clean_temperature_fluctuations  4         0.000000  0.286888  0.071722
```

We can re-run the same test but with a new version of this same chart, where all the filtering happens in Python. Listing 10-5 demonstrates this, by adding a new cleaner function that does the filtering and using the existing get_data_by_deployment(...) function as the data source. This represents how we would need to filter data if we hadnt added a sensor_name= parameter to get_data(...).

Listing 10-5. Jupyter cell to profile drawing the same chart but without any database filtering

```
import yappi

from apd.aggregation.analysis import (interactable_plot_multiple_charts,
Config, clean_temperature_fluctuations, get_data_by_deployment)
from apd.aggregation.utils import (jupyter_page_file, profile_with_yappi,
YappiPackageFilter)

async def filter_and_clean_temperature_fluctuations(datapoints):
    filtered = (item async for item in datapoints if
    item.sensor_name=="Temperature")
    cleaned = clean_temperature_fluctuations(filtered)
    async for item in cleaned:
        yield item

filter_in_python = Config(
    clean=filter_and_clean_temperature_fluctuations,
    title="Ambient temperature",
    ylabel="Degrees C",
    get_data=get_data_by_deployment,
)

with profile_with_yappi():
    plot = interactable_plot_multiple_charts(configs=[filter_in_python])
    plot()

yappi.get_func_stats().print_all()
```

In this version, the filtering happens in
`filter_and_clean_temperature_fluctuations(...)`, so we expect this
to take a long time. The additional time taken is partially in the generator
expression in that function, but not entirely. The total time taken by
`plot_multiple_charts(...)` has increased from 3.0 seconds to 8.0 seconds,
of which 1.3 seconds are the filtering. This shows that by filtering in the database,
we've saved 3.7 seconds of overhead, which represents a 21% speedup.

name	ncall	tsub	ttot	tavg
..lectorEventLoop.run_until_complete	1	0.000269	7.967136	7.967136
..alysis.py:341 plot_multiple_charts	1	7.637066	7.964143	7.964143
..gation\analysis.py:282 plot_sensor	1	0.000000	6.977470	6.977470
..query.py:86 get_data_by_deployment	1	6.958155	6.958210	6.958210
..d\aggregation\query.py:39 get_data	1	6.285337	6.881415	6.881415
..lchemy\orm\query.py:3197 Query.all	6	0.137161	6.112309	1.018718
..lchemy\orm\loading.py:35 instances	67305	0.065920	3.424629	0.000051
..egation\analysis.py:304 <listcomp>	4	0.000488	1.335928	0.333982
..and_clean_temperature_fluctuations	4	0.000042	1.335361	0.333840
..175 clean_temperature_fluctuations	4	0.000000	1.335306	0.333826
..-input-4-927271627100>:7 <genexpr>	4	0.000029	1.335199	0.333800

Visualizing profiling data

Complex iterator functions are hard to profile, as seen with
`clean_temperature_fluctuations(...)` listing it's `tsub` time as exactly zero.
It is a complex function that calls other methods, but for it to spend exactly zero time
must be a rounding error. **Profiling running code can point you in the right direction,
but you'll only ever get indicative numbers from this approach**. It's also hard to see
how the 0.287 seconds total time breaks down by constituent functions from this view.

Both the built-in profile module and yappi support exporting their data in pstats
format, a Python-specific profile format that can be passed to visualization tools. Yappi
also supports the callgrind format from the Valgrind profiling tool.

We can save a callgrind profile from yappi using `yappi.get_func_stats().save(` `"callgrind.filter_in_db"`, `"callgrind"`) and then load it into a callgrind visualizer like KCachegrind.[12] Figure 10-4 shows an example of displaying the database-filtered version of this code in QCachegrind, where the area of the blocks corresponds to the time spent in the corresponding function.

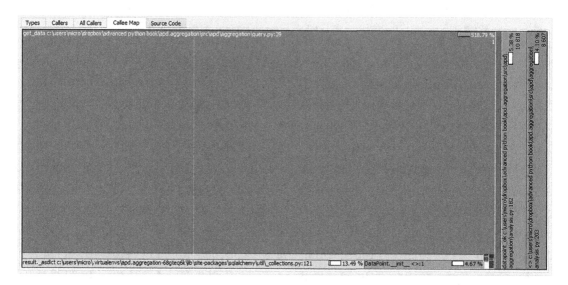

Figure 10-4. *Call chart for clean_temperature_fluctuations when filtering data in the database*

You may be surprised to learn that `get_data(...)` is not only present in this chart but is by far the largest single block. The `clean_temperature_fluctuations(...)` function doesnt appear to call the `get_data(...)` function, so it's not immediately obvious why this function should account for most of the time taken.

Iterators make reasoning about call flow difficult, as when you pull an item from an iterable in a loop, it doesnt look like a function call. Under the hood, Python is calling `youriterable.__next__()` (or `youriterable.__anext__()`), which passes execution back to the underlying function, completing the previous yield. A for loop can, therefore, cause any number of functions to be called, even if it's body is empty. The `async for` construction makes this a bit clearer, as it is explicitly saying that the underlying code may await. It wouldnt be possible for the underlying code to await unless control was

---

[12]The screenshot is from the Windows port, QCachegrind. As Valgrind is a Linux tool you'll find a wider range of utilities if you use Linux.

passing to other code rather than just interacting with a static data structure. When profiling code that consumes iterables, you will find the underlying data generation functions called by the functions that use the iterable are present in the output.

CONSUMING ITERABLES AND SINGLE DISPATCH FUNCTIONS

We can write a function that consumes an iterator as soon as possible, which simplifies the call stack somewhat. Consuming the iterator can reduce performance by preventing tasks running in parallel and requires that there is enough memory to contain the whole iterable, but it does greatly simplify the output of profiling tools. Simple functions for consuming an iterable and an async iterable while retaining the same interface are shown as Listing 10-6.

Listing 10-6. Pair of functions for consuming iterators in place

```
def consume(input_iterator):
    items = [item for item in input_iterator]
    def inner_iterator():
        for item in items:
            yield item
    return inner_iterator()

async def consume_async(input_iterator):
    items = [item async for item in input_iterator]
    async def inner_iterator():
        for item in items:
            yield item
    return inner_iterator()
```

This pair of functions takes an iterator (or async iterator) and consumes it as soon as it's called (or awaited), returning a new iterator that yields only from that preconsumed source. These functions are used as follows:

```
# Synchronous
nums = (a for a in range(10))
consumed = consume(nums)

# Async
async def async_range(num):
    for a in range(num):
        yield a
```

```
nums = async_range(10)
consumed = await consume_async(nums)
```

We can simplify this using the functools module in the standard library, specifically the @singledispatch decorator. Back in the second chapter, we looked at Python's dynamic dispatch functionality, which allows a function to be looked up by the class to which it's attached. We're doing something similar here; we have a pair of functions that are associated with an underlying data type, but these data types aren't classes we've written. We have no control over what functions are attached to them, as the two types are features of the core language rather than classes we've created and can edit.

The @singledispatch decorator marks functions as having multiple implementations differentiated on by the type of the first argument. Rewriting our functions to use this approach (Listing 10-7) only involves adding decorators to them to join the alternative implementations to the base one and a type hint to differentiate the variants.

Listing 10-7. Pair of functions for consuming iterators in place with single dipatch

```python
import functools

@functools.singledispatch
def consume(input_iterator):
    items = [item for item in input_iterator]
    def inner_iterator():
        for item in items:
            yield item
    return inner_iterator()

@consume.register
async def consume_async(input_iterator: collections.abc.AsyncIterator):
    items = [item async for item in input_iterator]
    async def inner_iterator():
        for item in items:
            yield item
    return inner_iterator()
```

These two functions behave in exactly the same way as the previous implementations, except that the consume(...) function can be used for either type of iterator. It transparently switches between synchronous and asynchronous implementations based on the type of its input. If the first argument is an AsyncIterator, then the `consume_async(...)` variant is used; otherwise the `consume(...)` variant is used.

```
nums = (a for a in range(10))
consumed = consume(nums)
nums = async_range(10)
consumed = await consume (nums)
```

The functions passed to register must have a type definition or a type passed to the register function itself. We've used `collections.abc.AsyncIterator` rather than `typing.AsyncIterator` as the type here, as the type must be *runtime checkable*. This means that `@singledispatch` is limited to dispatching on concrete classes or abstract base classes.

The `typing.AsyncIterator` type is a generic type: we can use `typing.AsyncIterator[int]` to mean an iterator of ints. This is used by mypy for static analysis, but isn't used at runtime. There's no way that a running Python program can know if an arbitrary async iterator is a `typing.AsyncIterator[int]` iterator without consuming the whole iterator and checking its contents.

`collections.abc.AsyncIterator` makes no guarantees about the contents of the iterator, so it is similar to `typing.AsyncIterator[typing.Any]`, but as it is an abstract base class, it can be checked with `isinstance(...)` at runtime.

Caching

Another way that we can improve performance is to cache the results of function calls. A cached function call keeps a record of past calls and their results, to avoid computing the same value multiple times. So far, we've been plotting temperatures using the centigrade temperature system, but a few countries have retained the archaic Fahrenheit system of measurement. It would be nice if we could specify which temperature system we want to use to display our charts, so users can choose the system with which they are most familiar.

The work of converting the temperature scale is orthogonal to the task done by the existing `clean_temperature_fluctuations(...)` method; we may want to convert temperatures without cleaning out fluctuations, for example. To achieve this, well create a new function that takes a cleaner and a temperature system and returns a new cleaner that calls the underlying one, then does a temperature conversion.

```
def convert_temperature(magnitude: float, origin_unit: str, target_unit:
str) -> float:
    temp = ureg.Quantity(magnitude, origin_unit)
    return temp.to(target_unit).magnitude

def convert_temperature_system(cleaner, temperature_unit):
    async def converter(datapoints):
        results = cleaner(datapoints)
        async for date, temp_c in results:
            yield date, convert_temperature(temp_c, "degC",
            temperature_unit)

    return converter
```

The preceding function does not have any type hints, as they are very verbose. Both the cleaner argument and the return value from convert_temperature_system(...) are of the type t.Callable[[t.AsyncIterator[DataPoint]], t.AsyncIterator[t.Tuple[datetime.datetime, float]]], which is a ridiculously complex construction to include twice in a single line of code. These types are used repeatedly in our analysis functions and, while hard to recognize at a glance, map to easily understood concepts. These are good candidates for factoring out into variables, the result of which is given as Listing 10-8.

Listing 10-8. Typed conversion functions

```
CLEANED_DT_FLOAT = t.AsyncIterator[t.Tuple[datetime.datetime, float]]
CLEANED_COORD_FLOAT = t.AsyncIterator[t.Tuple[t.Tuple[float, float], float]]

DT_FLOAT_CLEANER = t.Callable[[t.AsyncIterator[DataPoint]], CLEANED_DT_FLOAT]
COORD_FLOAT_CLEANER = t.Callable[[t.AsyncIterator[DataPoint]],
CLEANED_COORD_FLOAT]

def convert_temperature(magnitude: float, origin_unit: str, target_unit:
str) -> float:
    temp = ureg.Quantity(magnitude, origin_unit)
    return temp.to(target_unit).magnitude
```

```
def convert_temperature_system(
    cleaner: DT_FLOAT_CLEANER, temperature_unit: str,
) -> DT_FLOAT_CLEANER:
    async def converter(datapoints: t.AsyncIterator[DataPoint],) ->
    CLEANED_DT_FLOAT:
        results = cleaner(datapoints)
        reveal_type(temperature_unit)
        reveal_type(convert_temperature)
        async for date, temp_c in results:
            yield date, convert_temperature(temp_c, "degC",
            temperature_unit)

    return converter
```

TYPING PROTOCOLS, TYPEVARS AND VARIANCE

We have used t.TypeVar(...) before, to represent a placeholder in a generic type, such as when we defined the draw(...) function in our config class. We had to use T_key and T_value type variables there because some functions in the class used a tuple of key and value and others used a pair of key and value iterables.

That is, when a clean= function is of the type

```
t.Callable[t.AsyncIterator[DataPoint]],
t.AsyncIterator[t.Tuple[datetime.datetime, float]]
```

the corresponding draw= function is of the type

```
t.Callable[[t.Any, t.Iterable[datetime.datetime], t.Iterable[float],
t.Optional[str]], None]
```

We need to have access to both the datetime and float component types independently to build both type declarations. Type variables allow us to tell mypy that a type is a placeholder that will be supplied later; here we need both a T_key and a T_value type variable. We can also use them to define a pattern for a generic type called Cleaned and two instances of that type with specific values.

```
Cleaned = t.AsyncIterator[t.Tuple[T_key, T_value]]
CLEANED_DT_FLOAT = Cleaned[datetime.datetime, float]
CLEANED_COORD_FLOAT = Cleaned[t.Tuple[float, float], float]
```

If you're expecting there to be lots of different types of cleaned/cleaner types, then this approach is a bit clearer than explicitly assigning the full types to every function.

The cleaner functions that return this data are a bit more complicated, as mypy's ability to infer the use of generic types in callables has limits. To create complex aliases for callable and class types (as opposed to data variables), we must use the *protocol* feature. A protocol is a class that defines attributes that an underlying object must possess to be considered a match, very much like a custom abstract base class's subclasshook, but in a declarative style and for static typing rather than runtime type checking.

We want to define a callable that takes an `AsyncIterator` of datapoints and some other type. The other type here is being represented by the `T_cleaned_co` type variable, as follows:

```
T_cleaned_co = t.TypeVar("T_cleaned_co", covariant=True, bound=Cleaned)

class CleanerFunc(Protocol[T_cleaned_co]):
    def __call__(self, datapoints: t.AsyncIterator[DataPoint]) -> T_cleaned_co:
        ...
```

This `CleanerFunc` type can then be used to generate the `*_CLEANER` variables that match the `*_CLEANED` variables from earlier. The type used in square brackets for `CleanerFunc` is the variant of `Cleaned` that this particular function provides.

```
DT_FLOAT_CLEANER = CleanerFunc[CLEANED_DT_FLOAT]
COORD_FLOAT_CLEANER = CleanerFunc[CLEANED_COORD_FLOAT]
```

The `covariant=` argument in the `TypeVar` is a new addition, as is the `_co` suffix we used for the variable name. Previously, our type variables have been used to define both function parameters and function return values. These are *invariant* types: the type definitions must match exactly. If we declare a function that expects a `Sensor[float]` as an argument, we cannot pass a `Sensor[int]`. Normally, if we were to define a function that expects a `float` as an argument, it would be fine to pass an `int`.

This is because we haven't given mypy permission to use it's compatibility checking logic on the constituent types of the `Sensor` class. This permission is given with the optional `covariant=` and `contravariant=` parameters to type variables. A *covariant* type is one where the normal subtype logic applies, so if the Sensor's `T_value` were covariant, then functions that expect `Sensor[float]` can accept `Sensor[int]`, in the same way that functions that expect `float` can accept `int`. This makes sense for generic classes that have functions that **provide** data to the function they're passed to.

A *contravariant* type (usually named with the _contra suffix) is one where the inverse logic holds. If Sensor's T_value were contravariant, then functions that expect Sensor[float] cannot accept Sensor[int], but they must accept things more specific than float, such as Sensor[complex]. This is useful for generic classes that have functions that **consume** data from the function they're passed to.

We're defining a protocol that provides data,[13] so a covariant type is the natural fit. Sensors are simultaneously a provider (sensor.value()) and a consumer (sensor.format(...)) of data and so must be **invariant**.

Mypy detects the appropriate type of variance when checking a protocol and raises an error if it doesn't match. As we are defining a function that provides data, we must set covariant=True to prevent this error from showing.

The bound= parameter specifies a minimum specification that this variable can be inferred to be. As this is specified to be Cleaned, T_cleaned_co is only valid if it can be inferred to be a match to Cleaned[Any, Any]. CleanerFunc[int] is not valid, as int is not a subtype of Cleaned[Any, Any]. The bound= parameter can also be used to create a reference to the type of an existing variable, in which case it allows the definition of types that follow the signature of some externally provided function.

Protocols and type variables are powerful features that can allow for much simpler typing, but they can also make code look confusing if they're overused. Storing types as variables in a module is a good middle ground, but you should ensure that all typing boilerplate is well commented and perhaps even placed in a utility file to avoid overwhelming new contributors to your code.

With our new conversion code in place, we can create a plot configuration that draws the temperature chart in degrees Fahrenheit. Listing 10-9 shows how end-users of the apd.aggregation package can create a new Config object that behaves in the same way as the existing one but renders it's values in their preferred temperature scale.

---

[13]Although it consumes DataPoint objects, that's a fixed type. It's only the way the TypeVar object is used that matters.

Listing 10-9. Jupyter cell to generate a single chart showing temperature in degrees F

```
import yappi
from apd.aggregation.analysis import (interactable_plot_multiple_charts,
Config)
from apd.aggregation.analysis import (convert_temperature_system,
clean_temperature_fluctuations)
from apd.aggregation.analysis import get_one_sensor_by_deployment

filter_in_db = Config(
    clean=convert_temperature_system(clean_temperature_fluctuations,
    "degF"),
    title="Ambient temperature",
    ylabel="Degrees F",
    get_data=get_one_sensor_by_deployment("Temperature"),
)
display(interactable_plot_multiple_charts(configs=[filter_in_db])())
```

We've changed the control flow by adding this function, so we should do another profiling run to find what changes it made. We wouldnt want temperature conversion to take a significant amount of time.

```
..ation\analysis.py:191 datapoint_ok   10818  0.031250  0.031250  0.000003
..on\utils.py:41 convert_temperature   8455   0.078125  6.578125  0.000778
```

The `convert_temperature(...)` function itself is invoked 8455 times, although `datapoint_ok(...)` is invoked 10818 times. This tells us that by filtering through `datapoint_ok(...)` and the cleaning function before converting the temperature, we've avoided 2363 calls to `convert_temperature(...)` for data we dont need to know about to draw the current chart. However, the calls we did make still took 6.58 seconds, tripling the total time taken to draw this chart. This is excessive.

We can optimize this function by reimplementing it to remove the dependency on pint and therefore reducing the overhead involved. If `convert_temperature(...)` were a simple arithmetic function, the time taken would be reduced to 0.02 seconds, at the expense of a lot of flexibility. This is fine for a simple conversion where both units are needed; pint excels in situations where the exact conversion isnt known ahead of time.

Alternatively, we can cache the results of the convert_temperature(...) function. A simple cache can be achieved by creating a dictionary that maps between values keyed in degrees C and values in the chosen temperature system. The implementation in Listing 10-10 builds up a dictionary for every invocation of the iterator, preventing the same items being calculated multiple times.

Listing 10-10. A simple manual cache

```
def convert_temperature_system(
    cleaner: DT_FLOAT_CLEANER, temperature_unit: str,
) -> DT_FLOAT_CLEANER:
    async def converter(datapoints: t.AsyncIterator[DataPoint],) ->
    CLEANED_DT_FLOAT:
        temperatures = {}
        results = cleaner(datapoints)
        async for date, temp_c in results:
            if temp_c in temperatures:
                temp_f = temperatures[temp_c]
            else:
                temp_f = temperatures[temp_c] = convert_temperature(temp_c,
                "degC", temperature_unit)
            yield date, temp_f

    return converter
```

A caches efficiency[14] is usually measured by hit rate. If our data set were to be [21.0, 21.0, 21.0, 21.0], then our hit rate would be 75% (miss, hit, hit, hit). If it were [1, 2, 3, 4], then the hit rate would drop to zero. The preceding cache implementation assumes a reasonable hit rate, as it makes no effort to evict unused values from it's cache. A cache is always a trade-off between the extra memory used and time saving it allows. The exact tipping point where it becomes worth it depends on the size of the data being stored and your individual requirements for memory and time.

A common strategy for evicting data from a cache is that of an LRU (least recently used) cache. This strategy defines a maximum cache size. If the cache is full, when a new item is to be added, it replaces the one that has gone the longest without being accessed.

---

[14]That is, the use of a cache, not a type of cache. We can only talk about the efficiency of a cache if we know the information about the requests being made of it.

The functools module provides an implementation of an LRU cache as a decorator, which makes it convenient for wrapping our functions. We can also use it to create cached versions of existing functions by manually wrapping a function in an LRU cache decorator.

Caution   An LRU cache can be used if a function takes only hashable types as arguments. If a mutable type (such as a dictionary, list, set, or data class without frozen=True) is passed to a function wrapped in an LRU cache, a TypeError will be raised.

If we take our original, pint-based convert_temperature(...) function and add the LRU cache decorator, we can now benchmark the time it takes with a cache in place. The result of this is that the number of calls made to the function is drastically reduced but the time taken *per invocation* remains consistent. The 8455 invocations without the cache have become 67 invocations, corresponding to a hit rate of 99.2% and reducing the time overhead in offering this feature from 217% to 1%.

```
..on\utils.py:40 convert_temperature  67      0.000000  0.031250  0.000466
```

Its possible to retrieve additional information about the efficiency of an LRU cache without running a profiler, using the cache_info() method on the decorated function. This can be useful when debugging a complex system, as you can check which caches are performing well and which arent.

```
>>> from apd.aggregation.utils import convert_temperature
>>> convert_temperature.cache_info()
CacheInfo(hits=8455, misses=219, maxsize=128, currsize=128)
```

Figure 10-5 shows the time taken by all three approaches, on a logarithmic scale (the horizontal lines represent tenfold increases, not a linear increase). This helps demonstrate how close the caching and optimized approaches are; for our particular problem, caching a very expensive function results in performance in the same order of magnitude as an alternative, less flexible implementation.

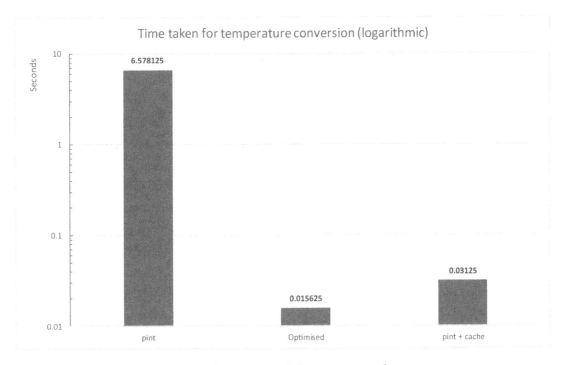

Figure 10-5. *Summary of performance of three approaches*

Rewriting the function to avoid using pint would still result in performance improvement, but caching the results provides an improvement of approximately the same magnitude for a much smaller change, both in terms of lines of code and conceptually.

As always, there is a balancing act at play here. It's likely that people would want temperature only in degrees Celsius or degrees Fahrenheit, so a conversion function that only provides those two is probably good enough. The conversion itself is straightforward and well understood, so the risk of introducing bugs is minimal. More complex functions may not be so easy to optimize, which makes caching a more appealing approach. Alternatively, they may process data that implies a lower hit rate, making refactoring more appealing.

The benefit of the `@lru_cache` decorator isnt in the inherent efficiency of the cache (its a rather bare-bones cache implementation), but in that it's easy to implement for Python functions. The implementation of a function decorated with a cache can be understood by everyone who needs to work with it as they can ignore the cache and focus on the function body. If youre writing a custom caching layer, for example, using systems like Redis as the storage rather than a dictionary, you should build your integration such that it doesnt pollute the decorated code with cache-specific instructions.

Cached properties

Another caching decorator available in the functools module is
@functools.cached_property. This type of cache is more limited than an LRU cache,
but it fits a use case thats common enough that it warrants inclusion in the Python
standard library. A function decorated with @cached_property acts in the same way as
one decorated with @property, but the underlying function is called only once.

The first time that the program reads the property, it is transparently replaced with
it's result of the underlying function call.[15] So long as the underlying function behaves
predictably and without side effects,[16] a @cached_property is indistinguishable from a
regular @property. Like @property, this can only be used as an attribute on a class and
must take the form of a function that takes no arguments except for self.

One place this can be of use is in the implementation of the DHT sensors back in the
apd.sensors package. The value() methods of these two sensors delegate heavily to the
DHT22 class from the Adafruit interface package. In the following method, only a small
fraction of the code is relevant to extracting the value; the rest is setup code:

```python
def value(self) -> t.Optional[t.Any]:
    try:
        import adafruit_dht
        import board

        # Force using legacy interface
        adafruit_dht._USE_PULSEIO = False

        sensor_type = getattr(adafruit_dht, self.board)
        pin = getattr(board, self.pin)
    except (ImportError, NotImplementedError, AttributeError):
        # No DHT library results in an ImportError.
        # Running on an unknown platform results in a
```

---

[15]This replacement is thread-safe, so even if multiple threads try to read the property, the function
won't be called multiple times for a given object.

[16]Side effects in a functional programming context are things a function does other than returning
an output variable. If a function manipulates mutable data, such as changing a global variable,
then returning a cached return value also prevents these changes from happening on future
invocations.

```
        # NotImplementedError when getting the pin
        return None
    try:
        return ureg.Quantity(sensor_type(pin).temperature,
        ureg.celsius)
    except (RuntimeError, AttributeError):
        return None
```

We can change this to factor out the common code for creating the sensor interface into a base class, which contains a sensor property. The temperature and humidity sensors can then drop all their interface code and instead rely on the existence of self.sensor.

```
class DHTSensor:

    def __init__(self) -> None:
        self.board = os.environ.get("APD_SENSORS_TEMPERATURE_BOARD",
        "DHT22")
        self.pin = os.environ.get("APD_SENSORS_TEMPERATURE_PIN", "D20")

    @property
    def sensor(self) -> t.Any:
        try:
            import adafruit_dht
            import board

            # Force using legacy interface
            adafruit_dht._USE_PULSEIO = False

            sensor_type = getattr(adafruit_dht, self.board)
            pin = getattr(board, self.pin)
            return sensor_type(pin)
        except (ImportError, NotImplementedError, AttributeError):
            # No DHT library results in an ImportError.
            # Running on an unknown platform results in a
            # NotImplementedError when getting the pin
            return None
```

```
class Temperature(Sensor[t.Optional[t.Any]], DHTSensor):
    name = "Temperature"
    title = "Ambient Temperature"

    def value(self) -> t.Optional[t.Any]:
        try:
            return ureg.Quantity(self.sensor.temperature, ureg.celsius)
        except RuntimeError:
            return None

    ...
```

The @property line in the DHTSensor class can be replaced with @cached_property to cache the sensor object between invocations. Adding a cache here doesnt impact the performance of our existing code, as we do not hold long-lived references to sensors and repeatedly query their value, but any third-party users of the sensor code may find it to be an advantage.

EXERCISE 10-1: OPTIMIZING CLEAN_WATTHOURS_TO_WATTS

At the start of this chapter, we identified the clean_watthours_to_watts(...) functions as the most in need of optimization. On my test data set, it was adding multiple seconds to the execution run.

In the accompanying code to this chapter, there are some extended tests to measure the behavior of this function and it's performance. Tests to validate performance are tricky, as they are usually the slowest tests, so I don't recommend adding them as a matter of course. If you do add them, make sure to mark them as such so that you can skip them in your normal test runs.

Modify the clean_watthours_to_watts(...) function so that the test passes. You will need to achieve a speedup of approximately 16x for the test to pass. The strategies discussed in this chapter are sufficient to achieve a speedup of about 100x.

Summary

The most important lesson to learn from this chapter is that no matter how well you understand your problem space, you should always measure your performance improvements, not just assume that they are improvements. There is often a range of options available to you to improve performance, some of which are more performant than others. It can be disappointing to think of a clever way of making something faster only to learn that it doesnt actually help, but it's still better to know.

The fastest option may require more RAM than can reasonably be assumed to be available, or it may require the removal of certain features. You must consider these carefully, as fast code that doesnt do what the user needs is not useful.

The two caching functions in functools are to be aware of for everyday programming. Use `@functools.lru_cache` for functions that take arguments and `@functools.cached_property` for calculated properties of objects that are needed in multiple places.

If your typing hints start to look cumbersome, then you should tidy them up. You can assign types to variables and represent them with classes like `TypedDict` and `Protocol`, especially when you need to define more complex structured types. Remember that these are not for runtime type checking and consider moving them to a typing utility module for clearer code. This reorganization has been applied in the sample code for this chapter.

Additional resources

The following links go into more depth on the topics covered in this section:

If youre interested in the logic of the different variances used in typing, Id recommend reading up on the Liskov Substitution Principle. The Wikipedia page at `https://en.wikipedia.org/wiki/Liskov_substitution_principle` is a good starting place, especially for links to computer science course materials on the subject.

More details on how mypy handles protocols and some advanced uses, such as allowing limited runtime checking of protocol types, are found at `https://mypy.readthedocs.io/en/stable/protocols.html`.

Beaker (`https://beaker.readthedocs.io/en/latest/`) is a caching library for Python that supports various back-end storages. It's especially aimed at web applications, but can be used in any type of program. It's useful for situations where you need multiple types of cache for different data.

The two third-party profiles we've used in this chapter are `https://github.com/rkern/line_profiler` and `https://github.com/sumerc/yappi`.

Documentation on how to customize the timer used with the built-in profiling tools is available in the standard librarys docs at `https://docs.python.org/3/library/profile.html#using-a-custom-timer`.

Fault tolerance

It's natural for developers to write code from an optimistic standpoint. We write code that doesn't work, and then we adjust it repeatedly until it gives us the result we want. Hopefully, we also write tests that allow us to verify that the code still works in the future and tests to check that we are handling any edge cases that we've become aware of correctly. We can never write tests to cover problems we haven't thought of yet, so being disciplined with how code is divided and handles the small problems it encounters is the best strategy we have for writing software that behaves as we expect.

Error handling

We've caught exceptions in the accompanying code to this book since the very beginning. Some have been exceptions that we know can be raised by code that we're using (e.g., the DHT interface code raising `RuntimeError` if it couldn't connect to the sensor). Others are exceptions implied by incorrect use of objects (such as `KeyError` in the solar generation sensor if we try to get a piece of data from the inverter that isn't present in the output).

We've also raised `NotImplementedError` as part of our `Sensor` base class to express that a method **must** be overridden by sensor developers and various `RuntimeError`s and `ValueError`s as part of the error handling for the command-line interface.

Programming languages usually follow either the "look before you leap" or "it's easier to ask forgiveness than permission" philosophies of error handling. A look before you leap philosophy means that you should use conditionals to determine if something is possible and leave exceptions to represent *unexpected* cases. The asking forgiveness philosophy means you should write code that expects the most common case and supplement this with exception handlers for the edge cases that you're aware of.

Python is very much in the latter camp; it's considered proper style when writing Python code to rely on exception handlers for control flow in many circumstances.

491

© Matthew Wilkes 2020
M. Wilkes, *Advanced Python Development*, https://doi.org/10.1007/978-1-4842-5793-7_11

Getting items from a container

One of the most common expressions we write in Python is getting an entry from a container type, such as a value from a dictionary or an item from a list. These both use variable[other] constructions. If other does not happen to point to a valid item in variable, then an exception is raised. Otherwise, the associated value is returned.

Although these actions use the same square bracket construction, both the underlying data types and the meaning of the variables are very different. When we write a function that uses this feature, we need to be aware of how different the possible outcomes are.

You will sometimes see dictionaries referred to as a *mapping*, but the terms are not interchangeable. A dictionary is an example of a mapping, which is the name for any object that maps keys to values and provides certain methods. If variable is a mapping (such as a dictionary), then other should be a *hashable* type: one where hash(other) is defined.

On the other hand, if variable is a list or tuple, then item access for *sequences* is the one that's used. In this case, other should be an integer that represents the index in the container that we're looking for. The reason we can't use the square bracket syntax for getting an item from a generator but we can use it for a list is because a generator isn't a sequence. All sequences (and, indeed, all mappings) are iterables, but not all iterables are sequences.

Abstract base classes

The definitions of mapping, sequence, and hashable are the corresponding Mapping, Sequence, and Hashable classes in the collections.abc module. Both Mapping and Sequence are subclasses of Collection. An object is a Collection if it implements the __len__(), __iter__(), and __contains__(...) magic methods. That is, if an object has a defined length, can be iterated over, and can be queried to see if a value is in the result of iterating over the object, then it is a collection.

Although the collections.abc.Sized, collections.abc.Iterable, collections.abc.Container,[1] and collections.abc.Collection objects are all abstract base classes that provide a subclass hook (meaning that any objects that implement the required methods are considered subclasses of the abstract base classes), Mapping and Sequence implementations are not detected automatically. Implementations of mapping or sequence must register against the appropriate base class.

---

[1]These are the three classes that correspond to the three methods that must be present for an object to be a collection.

Both mappings and sequences implement a __getitem__(...) method but with very different meanings. A Sequence is an object where variable[0] returns the first item in the underlying collection, whereas a Mapping is an object where variable[0] returns the value attached, the key 0.

The two different semantics of the __getitem__(...) method raise different exceptions when something goes wrong. The sequence version raises an IndexError when code tries to retrieve an item beyond the end of a sequence (such as variable[0] on an empty sequence). Conversely, KeyError is raised when code uses item access on a mapping that doesn't contain a value associated with that key.

Code that calls either type of __getitem__(...) causes a TypeError to be raised when the corresponding key is not of an appropriate type. For example, variable[1.2] on a sequence or variable[{}] on a mapping both raise TypeError. The Python interpreter also raises a TypeError when the variable being indexed has no __getitem__(...) method – for example, None[0].

You should expect the line variable[other] potentially to raise any of these three different exceptions. By knowing more about the underlying data type of the variables, we can exclude a TypeError and either IndexError or KeyError, but only by knowing more about the actual data can we be sure that no exception is raised.

For many simple tasks (such as the function in Table 11-1 that wraps __getitem__(...) to return a default value in the case where the requested item isn't available[2]), the "forgiveness" style is significantly more straightforward. It's not inherently simpler; it's entirely possible to write code that has confusing control flow by nesting many try/except blocks, but it usually simplifies code. Perhaps more importantly, it's the style that people expect from a Python program.

[2]Mappings provide some of this with their variable.get(key, default) method, but this can still raise a TypeError, and there is no built-in equivalent for Sequences.

Table 11-1. *Verbose implementations of a get with default function in both styles*

Look before you leap	Ask forgiveness

```python
from collections.abc import Sequence,
Mapping
from collections.abc import Hashable

def get_item(variable, key,
default=None):
    if isinstance(variable, Sequence):
        if isinstance(key, int):
            if (0 <= key <
            len(variable)):
                return variable[key]
            else:
                # key is too big
                return default
        else:
            # Key isn't an int
            return default

    elif isinstance(variable, Mapping):
        if isinstance(key, Hashable):
            if key in variable:
                return variable[key]
            else:
                # key is not known
                return default
        else:
            # Key isn't hashable
            return default
    else:
        # variable isn't a known type
        return default
```

```python
def get_item(variable, key,
default=None):
    try:
        return variable[key]
    except TypeError:
        # variable has no get item
        # method
        # or key isn't a valid type
        return default
    except KeyError:
        # Variable is a mapping but
        # doesn't contain key
        return default
    except IndexError:
        # Variable is a sequence
        # shorter than key
        return default
```

The problem comes in deciding where to catch exceptions and where to let them bubble up to calling code. The key difference in the two implementations mentioned earlier is that the left-hand side has two code paths for success and four for failure, whereas the one on the right has one for success and three for failure. If we want to customize the behavior for a specific condition, that's easier on the left than on the right, but only because the control flow on the left is more complex than the code on the right.

This complexity is also evident in the performance of this function, as shown in Figure 11-1; while some operations are about the same performance with either implementation, the exception handler route is sometimes much faster. In my experience, it's usually easier to avoid overly clever code when using the ask forgiveness method.

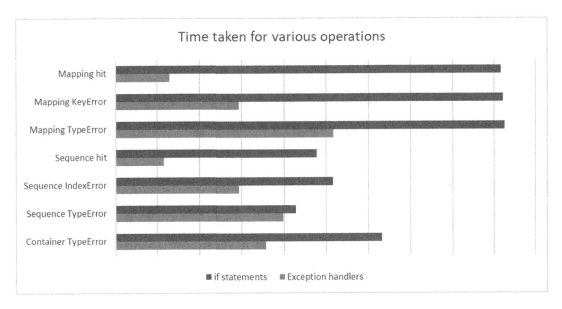

Figure 11-1. *Performance chart of the two implementations in each different case*

Imagine we want our `get_item(...)` function to raise a `TypeError` if the value of the `variable=` parameter is an object that doesn't support item access, but we still want the unknown key code paths to result in a default being returned. This corresponds to customizing the bottom condition on the left, but only one of the two sources of `TypeError` on the right. We can add a conditional to the `TypeError` exception handler to determine which code path caused the problem. To compensate for this increase in complexity, we can also coalesce the `KeyError` and `IndexError` exception handlers into one block, as they represent the same behavior, as shown in Listing 11-1.

Listing 11-1. A get with default function that raises on noncontainer arguments

```
def get_item(variable, key, default=None):
    try:
        return variable[key]
    except (KeyError, IndexError):
        # Key is invalid for variable, the error raised depends on the type
        # of variable
        return default
    except TypeError:
        if hasattr(variable, "__getitem__"):
            return default
        else:
            raise
```

Tip   Inside an exception handler, you can use `raise` without an explicit exception to reraise the same error currently being handled.

Exception types

Exceptions are classes with their own class hierarchy. All exceptions inherit from `BaseException`, but only those that also inherit from `Exception` are intended for developers to use.[3] When we catch exceptions, we need to specify which type of exception we want to catch. An `except` block that doesn't specify an exception type to catch is called a *bare except* and catches all exceptions, even the internal ones. As `KeyboardInterrupt` is one of these internal exceptions, a bare `try`/`except` has the effect of suppressing the user's ability to use `<CTRL+C>` to stop a program.

Tip   It's always better to catch multiple exception types rather than an overly broad superclass. You can specify many exception types in one block or use multiple `except` blocks to achieve this.

---

[3]The built-in exceptions that do not fit into this category are `GeneratorExit`, `KeyboardInterrupt`, and `SystemExit`.

The class hierarchy for exceptions is relatively shallow, but some superclasses are worth bearing in mind. The most useful is LookupError, which is a superclass of both KeyError and IndexError. LookupError specifically refers to cases where a requested key isn't present, so it's not overly broad. This allows us to simplify our get_item(...) function slightly, by replacing except (KeyError, IndexError) with except LookupError.

TypeError and ValueError

We often have to raise our own exceptions, rather than just reraising existing ones from lower down the call stack. In this case, we need to ensure that we pick an appropriate exception type and a useful message. TypeError and ValueError are good exception types to default to if it's unclear which exception class is the best fit.

A TypeError is appropriate at any time where the value passed to a function is of the wrong type, and a ValueError is appropriate when the value passed is of the correct type but is inappropriate in some way other than the cases covered by LookupErrors.

The four exceptions TypeError, ValueError, KeyError, and IndexError together represent most of the logical types of exception that you'll come across. If you need to raise an exception in your own code, the chances are that one of these is a good fit.

RuntimeError and SystemExit

There are also exception classes for nonspecific problematic behavior where the accompanying message is a description of the problem. RuntimeError is a last resort exception class, to cover errors that don't match any other category, but that might need to be caught by calling functions. SystemExit is raised internally by the sys.exit(...) function call to signal that the program should end.[4] In both cases, the argument given is critical, as it's the only information on what the problem is.

Generally speaking, except SystemExit: blocks are only appropriate as a way of customizing how to display a final error message to the end-user. It may make sense for code to catch RuntimeErrors and proceed with normal operation, but this depends heavily on the way the underlying code is structured and the meaning of the RuntimeError. It's usually better to create a new exception class than to rely on RuntimeError.

---

[4] SystemExit is also used for ending a program early, even if there have been no actual problems. It's usual to do this with sys.exit(0) rather than raising a SystemExit exception, though.

AssertionError

AssertionErrors are raised automatically by the interpreter when an assert statement fails. You often experience these when writing tests as it's in tests that most assert statements are written. It's entirely possible to add assert statements to arbitrary Python code, but it's vanishingly rare for developers to do this.

Python does not guarantee that it raises an AssertionError for any failed assert statement, so you can't rely on an assert statement for normal error handling. One possible use for assert statements in nontest code is to add assertions to cover your assumptions about things that must always be true. For example, you might use assert lines to verify some relationship between the arguments to a function that can't be expressed as a static typing declaration, or that an argument list is sorted correctly. Again, this is not a replacement for proper error handling in your functions, but having asserts can help to track down obscure errors.

The benefit to using assert statements is in the fact that they don't always raise an error. If you run your program with python -O or the PYTHONOPTIMIZE=1 environment variable, then the assert statements are ignored, allowing for potentially expensive sanity checks to be disabled except during debugging sessions.

It's incorrect to add assert statements to your code to implement checks that are *necessary* for the correct functioning of the program, precisely because there's no guarantee that they'll be run. This kind of check should be implemented with an if statement guarding a raise. You should only ever use assert for checks that you believe should always be true, but where you'd like to know if you were wrong.

Custom exceptions

Whenever you are working with a new third-party library, there are usually a variety of custom exceptions exposed to you. Pint offers UndefinedUnitError for cases where a unit isn't listed in pint's database and DimensionalityError for conversions that are not possible, for example. UndefinedUnitError is a type of AttributeError to match the ureg.watt method of accessing a unit. DimensionalityError is a subclass of TypeError, implying that the developers of the library want developers to think of quantities of different units as though they were different types.

Click has a series of exceptions for handling the parsing of command-line options which are not relevant to our code; requests provide specific exceptions in the requests.exception module (such as ConnectTimeout, ReadTimeout, InvalidSchema,

InvalidURL, etc.) that developers can catch to handle specific error cases, or through parent classes such as requests.exception.Timeout for all timeout errors, or even IOError as it is the base class of all requests-specific exceptions.

It's not always clear what type of exception third-party code raises; the intentions of the developer and how they see their code are a substantial influence. The only way to know which exceptions you're supposed to catch from third-party code is to read the documentation[5] and trust that it is accurate.

Creating new exception types

When you're writing library code that defines new exception types, you should put yourself in the shoes of your future users. Make sure that there is sufficient variety to communicate precisely which error has occurred but arrange them in such a way that they form a cohesive whole, both with the default exception types and each other. Like all API design, the most important success criterion is that your end-users find it intuitive.

Our apd.sensors package uses None as a signaling value for when a sensor's value cannot be determined. Sensors can fail to return a value for a range of reasons: there could be a temporary error in retrieving the value (such as a connection error in the solar output sensor) or a permanent error (such as the AC status sensor on a machine that doesn't have a battery charging circuit).

A sensor failing to return a data point isn't a LookupError of either type: the code *did* find the sensor, it's just not working correctly. It's not a TypeError or a ValueError, as no argument is either the wrong type or an unacceptable value. The closest match of the built-in exception types is RuntimeError, our exception type of last resort. To avoid raising RuntimeError directly, we can define some exception subclasses and rework our code to raise these exceptions rather than returning None as a sentinel object.

Listing 11-2 demonstrates new exceptions we can add to the apd.sensors package, including a base class for all apd.sensors exceptions, a more specific one for problems with data collection, and two subclasses for types of data collection problem. These classes allow users of the code to identify specific problems in their sensor code or to look for broad classes of sensor-related failures.

---

[5]And often, unfortunately, the code is the documentation.

Listing 11-2. New exceptions for apd.sensors, stored as exceptions.py

```
class APDSensorsError(Exception):
    """An exception base class for all exceptions raised by the
    sensor data collection system."""

class DataCollectionError(APDSensorsError, RuntimeError):
    """An error that represents the inability of a Sensor instance
    to retrieve a value"""

class IntermittentSensorFailureError(DataCollectionError):
    """A DataCollectionError that is expected to resolve itself
    in short order"""

class PersistentSensorFailureError(DataCollectionError):
    """A DataCollectionError that is unlikely to resolve itself
    if retried."""
```

These four exceptions allow end-users to catch errors intuitively. Wrapping sensor.value() with a try/except that catches any of RuntimeError, APDSensorsError, or DataCollectionError would all catch the failures. The fact that there is an IntermittentSensorFailureError also allows downstream code to identify that particular case and to retry the read, such as the example function in Listing 11-3.

Listing 11-3. Example function to retry a sensor read if there's an intermittent problem

```
from apd.sensors.base import Sensor, T_value
from apd.sensors.exceptions import IntermittentSensorFailureError

def get_value_with_retries(sensor: Sensor[T_value], retries: int=3) -> T_value:
    for i in range(retries):
        try:
            return sensor.value()
        except IntermittentSensorFailureError as err:
            if i == (retries - 1):
                # This is the last retry, reraise the underlying error
                raise
            else:
                continue
```

```
# It shouldn't be possible to get here, but it's better to
# fall through with an appropriate exception rather than a
# None
raise IntermittentSensorFailureError(f"Could not find a value "
f"after {retries} retries")
```

We can then use these errors in place of return None in the various sensors. This allows us to remove the t.Optional[...] constructions in the type of various sensors. Changing this type *does* mean that previously JSON-encoded sensor values are no longer valid, as None is no longer a valid sensor value for this sensor. Any code that calls sensor.from_json_compatible(...) or sensor.format(...) may raise an exception. When writing code that stores sensor values and then restores them later, it's important to ensure that any errors are caught, and the data point is discarded. If we wanted to ensure compatibility for future changes, we could write migration functions and store version numbers with the sensor data.

Additional metadata

We are already raising RuntimeError in the CLI interface to communicate an error message. This code path is another good use for a custom exception; we can create an exception in Listing 11-4 that is not of a commonly suppressed type[6] and stores additional metadata, such as the required exit status code.

Listing 11-4. A new exception type with additional metadata

```
@dataclasses.dataclass(frozen=True)
class UserFacingCLIError(APDSensorsError, SystemExit):
    """A fatal error for the CLI"""
    message: str
    return_code: int

    def __str__(self):
        return f"[{self.return_code}] {self.message}"
```

---

[6]Just inheriting directly from Exception would work well here, too. We keep APDSensorsError primarily for aesthetic reasons, as it's unlikely that this code would be called by a consumer that would want to silence any and all APD Sensor errors, but it does make it possible. The meaning of SystemExit matches closely, so that has also been included, but I want to store additional metadata that SystemExit doesn't provide.

It's usual to instantiate an exception with a single argument: a human-readable explanation of the exception. This approach isn't the only format for exceptions; for example, the OSError exception type has arguments for numeric error identifiers as well as the human-readable string.

Note   While most built-in exceptions accept an arbitrary number of arguments, I'd recommend against using this to store metadata about an exception. A custom exception type with well-defined parameters is always clearer than a convention for how a tuple's arguments are interpreted.

Exception types are Python classes so we can use any of our standard techniques to store additional information as part of an exception. I would recommend a data class, as we do with any Python class that primarily stores data. We can then extract this metadata during the handling of the exception, allowing us to consolidate the return code and the human-readable message for a failure into one object. Here, we're explicitly adding two items of metadata. The custom UserFacingCLIError.__str__() method is needed because casting an Exception to a string must return only the user-facing representation of the error, whereas the default implementation for dataclasses displays a tuple of all the arguments.

We can then use this exception to show a message to the user and to return the correct exit code to the operating system.

```
if develop:
    try:
        sensors = [get_sensor_by_path(develop)]
    except UserFacingCLIError as error:
        click.secho(error.message, fg="red", bold=True)
        sys.exit(error.return_code)
```

Tracebacks involving multiple exceptions

When we raise an exception from Python code which we don't subsequently catch, the interpreter prints a traceback. Tracebacks provide the end-user with information about what exception was raised and exactly what part of the code triggered it. The following is an example traceback obtained by deliberately introducing a bug into the IP address sensor:

```
Traceback (most recent call last):
  File "...\Scripts\sensors-script.py", line 11, in <module>
    load_entry_point('apd.sensors', 'console_scripts', 'sensors')()
  File "...\site-packages\click\core.py", line 764, in __call__
    return self.main(*args, **kwargs)
  File "...\site-packages\click\core.py", line 717, in main
    rv = self.invoke(ctx)
  File "...\site-packages\click\core.py", line 956, in invoke
    return ctx.invoke(self.callback, **ctx.params)
  File "...\site-packages\click\core.py", line 555, in invoke
    return callback(*args, **kwargs)
  File "...\src\apd\sensors\cli.py", line 72, in show_sensors
    click.echo(str(sensor))
  File "...\src\apd\sensors\base.py", line 31, in __str__
    return self.format(self.value())
  File "...\src\apd\sensors\sensors.py", line 41, in value
    addresses = socket.getaddrinfo("hostname", None)
  File "...\Lib\socket.py", line 748, in getaddrinfo
    for res in _socket.getaddrinfo(host, port, family, type, proto, flags):
socket.gaierror: [Errno 11001] getaddrinfo failed
```

Each pair of File and code lines in the traceback represents a function in the call stack. The bottom one is the line that raised the exception, with each pair above providing context as to in which part of the software the error occurred. In this case, the exception was raised in the standard library's socket.py, although it's not immediately obvious why. If we go back up one level, we see a call from code that we control into the standard library. If you assume that the libraries you're using are free from bugs (which is generally a fair assumption), then it's likely that the lowest stack entry that points to code we control is the culprit. It's not always this line, sometimes higher parts of the stack are responsible (e.g., due to setting a variable incorrectly), but this is usually the best place to begin debugging.

In this case, we can see from the stack trace that we have passed a string literal containing "hostname," but the first argument to getaddrinfo(...) should be an actual hostname. In this case, the error was caused by accidentally wrapping the variable name in quotation marks rather than passing the variable, something a linter may have caught.

An exception is usually one of the first things Python developers see (both in their careers and when solving a particular problem), so tracebacks are quite familiar to most developers; however, there are some minor variations on tracebacks that are much less commonly seen but very useful.

Exception in except or finally block

The first alternative form represents raising an exception while handling another exception. Usually, the only raise statement in an exception handler is a bare `raise` to reraise the caught exception, usually after introspecting the state of the system to determine if the exception should be suppressed. However, the introspection code itself could contain an error that causes an unhandled exception. It's also possible that code in a `finally:` block could cause an exception to be raised.

The error that was caused when we passed "hostname" rather than hostname exposed an error case that we aren't currently handling. If we pass a hostname that cannot be resolved through the DNS system, then an exception is raised. If we wanted to handle this case differently to other potential OSErrors raised here, we'd need to introspect the exception in the handler.

OSErrors provide an errno= attribute to get a numeric code to identify the particular problem, rather than subclasses for each possible error. When catching the exception, if we erroneously check for an err_no= attribute rather than errno=, then an AttributeError is raised. Both the original OSError exception and the AttributeError are useful information to pass to the end-user, so both tracebacks are provided.

The incorrect conditional code is given as follows:

```
41.         try:
42.             addresses = socket.getaddrinfo("hostname", None)
43.         except OSError as err:
44.             if err.err_no == 11001:
45.                 raise
```

The result is that two exceptions are shown, stacked, as follows:

```
Traceback (most recent call last):
  File "...\src\apd\sensors\sensors.py", line 42, in value
    addresses = socket.getaddrinfo("hostname", None)
  File "...\Lib\socket.py", line 748, in getaddrinfo
```

```
  for res in _socket.getaddrinfo(host, port, family, type, proto, flags):
socket.gaierror: [Errno 11001] getaddrinfo failed
```

During handling of the preceding exception, another exception occurred:

```
Traceback (most recent call last):
  File "...\Scripts\sensors-script.py", line 11, in <module>
    load_entry_point('apd.sensors', 'console_scripts', 'sensors')()
  File "...\site-packages\click\core.py", line 764, in __call__
    return self.main(*args, **kwargs)
  File "...\site-packages\click\core.py", line 717, in main
    rv = self.invoke(ctx)
  File "...\site-packages\click\core.py", line 956, in invoke
    return ctx.invoke(self.callback, **ctx.params)
  File "...\site-packages\click\core.py", line 555, in invoke
    return callback(*args, **kwargs)
  File "...\src\apd\sensors\cli.py", line 72, in show_sensors
    click.echo(str(sensor))
  File "...\src\apd\sensors\base.py", line 31, in __str__
    return self.format(self.value())
  File "...\src\apd\sensors\sensors.py", line 44, in value
    if err.err_no == 11001:
AttributeError: 'gaierror' object has no attribute 'err_no'
```

The first exception to be displayed is the first one that occurred: the lower-level exception that we were handling when we triggered the second exception. The traceback is much shorter because all lines of traceback that are common with the second exception are omitted. The topmost of the context lines in the first traceback (sensors.py, line 42) points to the try block of a try/except construction. There must be a single line in the second traceback that points to a line in an except block corresponding with the try. In this case, it's sensors.py, line 44. All lines above that one also apply as context to the first traceback.

The first and second tracebacks are separated with a line saying "During handling of the above exception, another exception occurred:". This makes it clear that the second exception happened inside a try block that contained the code which triggered the first exception. The interpreter prints the full traceback for the second exception in the same format as any normal exception traceback.

Any number of tracebacks can be shown as part of this format, although it's rare for there to be more than 2. This is only because it's considered good style to minimize the amount of code in an except or finally block, so it's not unheard of to see more.

raise from

Sometimes we want to replace an exception that we've caught with another one, such as replacing an ImportError for adafruit_dht in our temperature sensor with a PersistentSensorFailureError, indicating that the sensor can't provide a value and that it's not expected to change in short order. This is especially useful when we have defined new exception types for a library, as it lets us simplify the possible exceptions a function can raise.

If we write a try/except construction that directly raises the new PersistentSensorFailureError, then any traceback would separate the two saying that our exception was raised while handling the import error, as we saw earlier. This isn't an accurate description of the situation, as we're not really *handling* the exception from a user perspective. Python provides for a raise ... from ... construction here to mark an exception as being a replacement for another.

We should update the sensor property from the DHT sensor base class to use this approach, as shown in Listing 11-5.

Listing 11-5. New version of DHT base class

```
import os
import typing as t

from .exceptions import PersistentSensorFailureError

class DHTSensor:
    def __init__(self) -> None:
        self.board = os.environ.get("APD_SENSORS_TEMPERATURE_BOARD",
        "DHT22")
        self.pin = os.environ.get("APD_SENSORS_TEMPERATURE_PIN", "D20")

    @property
    def sensor(self) -> t.Any:
```

```
try:
    import adafruit_dht
    import board
    sensor_type = getattr(adafruit_dht, self.board)
    pin = getattr(board, self.pin)
    return sensor_type(pin)
except (ImportError, NotImplementedError, AttributeError) as err:
    # No DHT library results in an ImportError.
    # Running on an unknown platform results in a
    # NotImplementedError when getting the pin.
    # An unknown sensor type causes an AttributeError
    raise PersistentSensorFailureError(
    "Unable to initialise sensor interface") from err
```

This results in precisely the same formatting of output as without the `from err` clause, but with a different separator line. Rather than saying the second exception occurred while handling the first, the two tracebacks are separated by "`The above exception was the direct cause of the following exception:`".

As a special case to the preceding example, using `raise PersistentSensorFail ureError("Unable to initialise sensor interface") from None` would result in the original `ImportError` being completely suppressed. In this case, only our exception would be shown to the end-user, and it would contain the full context in the traceback lines.

Testing for exception handling

We have some tests that involve exceptions in the CLI tests. Specifically, we try calling the `get_sensor_by_path(...)` function with various invalid sensor paths and assert that `RuntimeError` is raised. Pytest's `raises(...)` context manager is used for asserting that we expect a block of code to raise a certain exception. It takes two arguments: the type of the exception and an optional `match=` parameter to define a regex filter on the string representation of the error.

```
with pytest.raises(RuntimeError, match="Could not import module"):
    subject("apd.nonsense.sensor:FakeSensor")
```

The context manager catches `RuntimeError` and checks if the string representation matches the `match=` parameter.[7] If any other exception is raised, including different `RuntimeErrors` which do not match the string, then the context manager reraises them as normal. If no matching exception has been raised by the time the `with pytest.raises(...):` block ends, then the context manager raises an `AssertionError`, meaning that the test fails.

This approach lets us test that code raises the exceptions we expect, so we can be confident that our functions raise exceptions in situations where we know the data to be bad. This is only half the battle; the other side to exceptions in testing is to inject exceptions in places where they might be raised and test that the calling code behaves correctly. For example, we might want to test that a sensor that raises `IntermittentSensorFailureError(...)` does not cause the whole data collection run to fail.

New behaviors

We've decided that Sensor's `value()` function should return either an object of the type specified in the generic `Sensor[type]` declaration or should raise `DataCollectionError`. We haven't defined what the CLI or API should do if a sensor fails. There's little point testing the exception behavior before we know what behavior we want.

We'll start with the CLI. When there's an error, I want to show the error string in the command-line interface and continue with the rest of the sensor lookups. It would also be very useful to have an optional flag to show the whole exception traceback, to help developers debug precisely why a sensor isn't working. The code to implement this is in Listing 11-6.

Listing 11-6. Updated command-line entrypoint with exception handling

```
@click.command(help="Displays the values of the sensors")
@click.option(
    "--develop", required=False, metavar="path",
    help="Load a sensor by Python path"
)
```

---

[7]The match parameter can be either a regex string or a compiled regex pattern. To match a string literal that means something different as a regex, use `re.escape(string_literal)`.

```
@click.option(
    "--verbose", is_flag=True, help="Show additional info"
)
def show_sensors(develop: str, verbose: bool) -> int:
    sensors: t.Iterable[Sensor[t.Any]]
    if develop:
        try:
            sensors = [get_sensor_by_path(develop)]
        except UserFacingCLIError as error:
            if verbose:
                tb = traceback.format_exception(type(error), error,
                error.__traceback__)
                click.echo("".join(tb))
            click.secho(error.message, fg="red", bold=True)
            return error.return_code
    else:
        sensors = get_sensors()
    for sensor in sensors:
        click.secho(sensor.title, bold=True)
        try:
            click.echo(str(sensor))
        except DataCollectionError as error:
            if verbose:
                tb = traceback.format_exception(type(error), error,
                error.__traceback__)
                click.echo("".join(tb))
                continue
            click.echo(error)
        click.echo("")
    return 0
```

Note The code we've written to format the entire exception is rather clunky. The `traceback.format_exception(...)` function has maintained its signature since the Python 1 era,[8] albeit with a few additions. Three arguments are required, but they can all be extracted from the exception object itself. The traceback object can be replaced by None to indicate that only the exception information should be formatted, not the whole traceback.

We should also modify the behavior of the API. To maintain backward compatibility, we should make the API substitute a None for any `DataCollectionError` in existing API versions. It's possible (although perhaps unlikely) that some user would have written code that monitors how often errors occur by looking for None values in the API response. Going forward, we'd want to create a new version of the API that handles errors intelligently, so API users get useful information about failures.

To test this new behavior, we need to create a testing `Sensor` subclass (Listing 11-7) that raises specific exceptions so that we can verify that the surrounding code behaves appropriately. This lets us reliably trigger sensor errors in our tests.

Listing 11-7. Definition of FailingSensor test sensor

```
from apd.sensors.base import JSONSensor
from apd.sensors.exceptions import IntermittentSensorFailureError

class FailingSensor(JSONSensor[bool]):

    title = "Sensor which fails"
    name = "FailingSensor"
```

---

[8]In Python 1.x exceptions were not objects that took a message as an argument. They were raised as `raise ValueError, "Value is out of range"` (for example). The traceback had to be extracted from the `sys.exc_traceback` global variable. To format an exception, you'd need its type, its string representation, and the traceback. The type and string representation were merged in Python 2, but it wasn't until Python 3 that exception objects started holding their own traceback information.

```
def __init__(self, n: int=3, exception_type:
Exception=IntermittentSensorFailureError):
    self.n = n
    self.exception_type = exception_type

def value(self) -> bool:
    self.n -= 1
    if self.n:
        raise self.exception_type(f"Failing {self.n} more times")
    else:
        return True

@classmethod
def format(cls, value: bool) -> str:
    raise "Yes" if value else "No"
```

In Listing 11-8, we will test the v1.0 API server but with the get_sensors(...) method mocked out to return the FailingSensor and PythonVersion sensors.

Listing 11-8. Test to verify the 1.0 API remains compatible

```
@pytest.mark.functional
def test_erroring_sensor_shows_None(self, api_server, api_key):
    from .test_utils import FailingSensor

    with mock.patch("apd.sensors.cli.get_sensors") as get_sensors:
        # Ensure the failing sensor is first, to test that subsequent
        # sensors are still processed
        get_sensors.return_value = [FailingSensor(10), PythonVersion()]
        value = api_server.get("/sensors/",
        headers={"X-API-Key": api_key}).json
    assert value['Sensor which fails'] == None
    assert "Python Version" in value.keys()
```

Advanced mocking with unittest.Mock

As we saw in Chapter 8, an alternative approach for creating mock objects is to use the mock support in the standard library's unittest package. Previously, we created raw Mock objects, but they can also be created with an optional spec= parameter. This causes them only to emulate the attributes of the object passed, rather than returning a new mock for any arbitrary attribute access. This approach is helpful, as any code that attempts to detect the presence of attributes on an object would behave the same when passed a mock as if a real object had been passed.

This makes the mock objects much closer to the real things being tested and fixes a whole class of testing bugs. If you're using isinstance(...) conditions, especially when combined with the use of abstract base classes that implement subclass hooks, then Mock objects that don't use a spec= parameter can cause the wrong code path to be taken, as in the example console session in the following:

```
>>> import collections.abc
>>> import unittest.mock
>>> from apd.sensors.base import Sensor

>>> unspecced = unittest.mock.MagicMock()
>>> isinstance(unspecced, Sensor)
False
>>> isinstance(unspecced, collections.abc.Container)
True

>>> specced = unittest.mock.MagicMock(spec=Sensor)
>>> isinstance(specced, Sensor)
True
>>> isinstance(specced, collections.abc.Container)
False
```

We can use this mock object to create mock sensors that trigger exceptions or return specific values. A slight problem with this approach is that none of the real Sensor base class code is involved, so we can't rely on our mock objects having helper methods provided by the base class. We need to customize the behavior of the whole user-facing API (such as the __str__() method) rather than only implementing the functions we need to customize, as we did with our first FailingSensor implementation, as in Listing 11-9.

Listing 11-9. An alternative way to create a FailingSensor object

```
from apd.sensors.base import Sensor
from apd.sensors.exceptions import IntermittentSensorFailureError

FailingSensor = mock.MagicMock(spec=Sensor)
FailingSensor.title = "Sensor which fails"
FailingSensor.name = "FailingSensor"
FailingSensor.value.side_effect = IntermittentSensorFailureError(
"Failing sensor")
FailingSensor.__str__.side_effect = IntermittentSensorFailureError(
"Failing sensor")
```

The title and name attributes need to be set as there are no title and name attributes on the Sensor base class, only type declarations that imply that they are available on subclasses. If we didn't set them here, then any attempt to access them would result in an AttributeError.

We've previously used the return_value attribute on a Mock object to define what value should be returned if an object is called: FailingSensor.__str__.return_value = "Yes" would configure the mock such that str(FailingSensor) == "Yes". We can't use this approach to raise an exception, though.

The side_effect attribute can contain an exception to be raised, an iterable of items to be returned from multiple invocations or a function that is called to determine the result. Setting the side effect to be an iterable is a convenient way to specify changing behavior. For example, with the following side-effect configuration, the first time str(FailingSensor) is used, it raises an IntermittentSensorFailureError telling the user that two more failures are expected. If str(FailingSensor) is repeatedly called, it works through the list raising the next two IntermittentSensorFailureErrors, then returning "Yes" on the fourth try.

```
FailingSensor.__str__.side_effect = [
    IntermittentSensorFailureError("Failing 2 more times"),
    IntermittentSensorFailureError("Failing 1 more times"),
    IntermittentSensorFailureError("Failing 0 more times"),
    "Yes"
]
```

Unfortunately, any further invocations result in a StopIteration error, as the side_effect method of specifying return values has a one-to-one mapping of list items to results of invocations. It's possible to use functions from the itertools module[9] to create an infinitely long iterable, allowing arbitrarily many calls to str(FailingSensor).

```
FailingSensor.__str__.side_effect = itertools.chain(
    [
        IntermittentSensorFailureError("Failing 2 more times"),
        IntermittentSensorFailureError("Failing 1 more times"),
        IntermittentSensorFailureError("Failing 0 more times"),
    ],
    itertools.cycle(["Yes"])
)
```

This example uses the itertools.cycle(...) function to create an infinitely long iterable that repeats the items from the iterable it was given as an argument, as well as the , which appends arbitrary iterables together. The result of which is an iterable that can be used as a side effect to raise exceptions three times, then consistently return "Yes".

Warnings

Warnings are implemented in a similar way to exceptions but behave very differently. Although developers sometimes talk about raising warnings, warnings aren't used with the raise keyword[10] but are triggered with the warnings.warn(...) function. The most common warning that developers come across is DeprecationWarning. You may well have seen some while running the example code for this book. This is inevitable, as the underlying libraries may deprecate features at any time or may themselves be using a deprecated feature to maintain support for older versions of code.

---

[9]We looked at itertools.groupby(...) previously, but the whole itertools module is worth learning about. It's one of my favorite modules in the standard library, as it provides helper functions for many of the common tasks involving generators.

[10]However, as they are part of the BaseException type hierarchy, it is technically possible to raise a warning with the raise keyword, but this is only there to support some internal implementation details of the warning framework. Warnings should *never* be raised directly; it's not meaningful and is very confusing.

For example, for a short time during the writing of this book, the aiohttp module triggered a deprecation warning when run in Python 3.8, warning that it uses an older signature for `asyncio.shield(...)`[11].

```
...\lib\site-packages\aiohttp\connector.py:944: DeprecationWarning: The
loop argument is deprecated since Python 3.8, and scheduled for removal
in Python 3.10.
 hosts = await asyncio.shield(self._resolve_host(
```

A `DeprecationWarning` is intended to tell developers that a pattern they are using is no longer considered best practice. It should be clear about what's wrong (in this case, the `loop=` argument shouldn't be passed), and it should give a clear timeframe for when the problem must be fixed (before upgrading to Python 3.10).

In this case, it's the Python standard library raising the deprecation warning, and the intended audience is the developer of aiohttp. As users of aiohttp, we're not the intended audience, and we shouldn't be concerned about seeing deprecation warnings, so long as the timeframe they specify isn't about to end. In this particular case, the aiohttp developers fixed this deprecation warning within 2 weeks of Python 3.8 being released.

The specific code from aiohttp's `connector.py` that triggered the problem is on line 944, as specified in the warning message. If we look at that code, we can see the code that triggered the exception.

```
944.              hosts = await asyncio.shield(self._resolve_host(
945.                  host,
946.                  port,
947.                  traces=traces), loop=self._loop)
```

The code in the Python standard library that implements the warning is as follows:

```
if loop is not None:
    warnings.warn("The loop argument is deprecated since Python 3.8, "
                  "and scheduled for removal in Python 3.10.",
                  DeprecationWarning, stacklevel=2)
```

---

[11]A function to prevent an asyncio task from being canceled if the calling task is canceled. In this case, it's used to allow DNS lookups to be shared between requests, as the lookup would need to be done even if the request that triggered it first was canceled.

The warn(...) function can either take a string and a type of warning as the first two arguments or a warning instance as the first argument. If only a string is passed with no warning type, it is assumed to be a UserWarning. The stacklevel= argument corresponds to how many rows from the bottom of a traceback the relevant code is. It's really important to get this right, as a warning should always implicate the user's code, not the code that's detecting the problem and raising the warning.

The default is stacklevel=1, which shows the source of the deprecation warning as the warnings.warn(...) call. Here, stacklevel=2 causes the context displayed to be the line of code that called the function that warnings.warn(...) is in. Similarly, stacklevel=3 would be one function further removed.

We made a change to our Config object in the apd.aggregation package when we added support for map-based images. We effectively deprecated the sensor_name= parameter in favor of a differently specified get_data= parameter, but we didn't expose this to the user. This is a good candidate for a DeprecationWarning, as shown in Listing 11-10.

Listing 11-10. Updated Config data class that issues a deprecation warning for sensor_name

```
@dataclasses.dataclass
class Config(t.Generic[T_key, T_value]):
    title: str
    clean: CleanerFunc[Cleaned[T_key, T_value]]
    draw: t.Optional[
        t.Callable[
            [t.Any, t.Iterable[T_key], t.Iterable[T_value],
            t.Optional[str]], None
        ]
    ] = None
    get_data: t.Optional[
        t.Callable[..., t.AsyncIterator[t.Tuple[UUID,
        t.AsyncIterator[DataPoint]]]]
    ] = None
    ylabel: t.Optional[str] = None
    sensor_name: dataclasses.InitVar[str] = None
```

```python
    def __post_init__(self, sensor_name: t.Optional[str] = None) -> None:
        if self.draw is None:
            self.draw = draw_date   # type: ignore
        if sensor_name is not None:
            warnings.warn(
                DeprecationWarning(
                    f"The sensor_name parameter is deprecated. Please pass "
                    f"get_data=get_one_sensor_by_deployment('{sensor_name}') "
                    f"to ensure the same behaviour. The sensor_name="
                    f"parameter "
                    f"will be removed in apd.aggregation 3.0."
                ),
                stacklevel=3,
            )
            if self.get_data is None:
                self.get_data = get_one_sensor_by_deployment(sensor_name)
        if self.get_data is None:
            raise ValueError("You must specify a get_data function")
```

Note   The `stacklevel=` parameter here is 3, not 2. We want this warning to be shown when a user instantiates a `Config` object. The `@dataclass` decorator generates an `__init__(...)` function which calls `__post_init__(...)`. A stacklevel of 2 would show the deprecation warning as being associated with the generated `__init__(...)` function rather than the calling code. If you're not sure, try raising an exception and looking at the stack trace.

The resulting warning shows where the incorrect code was (analysis.py, line 287), has exact instructions for what to fix, and includes a deadline for fixing it. It also shows the line in question, which in this case is the first line of a multiline `Config(...)` constructor call.

```
...\src\apd\aggregation\analysis.py:287: DeprecationWarning:
The sensor_name parameter is deprecated. Please pass
get_data=get_one_sensor_by_deployment('Temperature') to ensure
the same behaviour. The sensor_name= parameter will be removed
in apd.aggregation 3.0.
    Config(
```

Warning filters

It's possible to define new warning types to complement the built-in ones, but this is less useful than subclassing exceptions. The main reason to create new warning types is to allow end-users to make better use of warning filters. A warning filter changes the behavior of warnings away from the default, to make them more or less prominent.

Changing the filter can be used to control more accurately the set of warnings that are shown to end-users. If you're maintaining a tool that depends on a library which causes multiple deprecation warnings, then suppressing the warnings for end-users improves their confidence in the tool.[12]

```
warnings.simplefilter("ignore", DeprecationWarning)
```

Conversely, you could increase the severity of warnings to be exceptions to help you to debug what precisely their cause is. The action `"error"` for the warning filter causes any warnings to be treated as exceptions. That is, a full traceback is displayed, and execution stops once the code encounters its first warning.[13] Using the post-mortem debugger in combination with this option is an effective way of investigating the reason for warnings.

```
warnings.simplefilter("error", DeprecationWarning)
```

Tip   When running Python code directly as `python script.py`, you can set the default warning behavior with the `-W` command-line option, as `python -Werror script.py`. Setting the PYTHONWARNINGS environment variable has the same effect, but it works for Python-based executables that aren't invoked through the interpreter directly, such as our sensors command-line tool.

If a downstream component hasn't defined custom warnings (and most do not), you can also filter warnings by file, line number,[14] message, or any mixture of these. This flexibility allows you to suppress specific warnings that you're aware of without suppressing any others that you may not know about.

---

[12]Just don't forget to fix any problems before the deprecation warning expires, as if the tool stops working that will have a much more significant impact on users' confidence in it.

[13]This is the reason that warnings are a type of exception, so they can be raised by this filter action.

[14]Be aware that the filename and line number may change if a new version of the library is released.

```
import re, warnings

warnings.filterwarnings(
    "ignore",
    message=re.escape("The sensor_name parameter is deprecated"),
    category=DeprecationWarning,
    module=re.escape("apd.aggregation.analysis"),
    lineno=275
)
```

Finally, you can modify a warning filter temporarily and restore the old ones automatically. This can be useful if a single function raises lots of different warnings that you'd like to suppress, but without hiding them when triggered through different code paths.

```
import warnings

with warnings.catch_warnings():
    warnings.simplefilter("ignore")
    function_that_warns_a_lot()
```

The same context manager is useful in testing if you want to assert that a warning was raised in your code. This is useful if you want to be confident that warnings are shown in certain complex situations, but it's usually not necessary. The catch_warnings(...) function takes an optional record=True argument which allows access to a record of all warnings raised within the body of the context manager. You should make sure that the warning filter is not ignoring any warnings, as only warnings that are shown to the end-user are recorded. Listing 11-11 shows an example test that makes use of this functionality.

Listing 11-11. A test to ensure a warning is raised

```
def test_deprecation_warning_raised_by_config_with_no_getdata():
    with warnings.catch_warnings(record=True) as captured_warnings:
        warnings.simplefilter("always", DeprecationWarning)
        config = analysis.Config(
            sensor_name="Temperature",
            clean=analysis.clean_passthrough,
            title="Temperaure",
            ylabel="Deg C"
        )
```

```
    assert len(captured_warnings) == 1
    deprecation_warning = captured_warnings[0]
    assert deprecation_warning.filename == __file__
    assert deprecation_warning.category == DeprecationWarning
    assert str(deprecation_warning.message) == (
        "The sensor_name parameter is deprecated. Please pass "
        "get_data=get_one_sensor_by_deployment('Temperature') "
        "to ensure the same behaviour. The sensor_name= parameter "
        "will be removed in apd.aggregation 3.0."
    )
```

Logging

Applications of all types use logging extensively. It helps end-users debug problems and allows for more detailed bug reports, which in turn saves time trying to reproduce problems. Logging is used in much the same way as print(...) for debugging, but it has some significant advantages for large applications and libraries.

The most significant advantage of logging over print(...) debugging is that the logging framework associates every log entry with a severity. Users can choose a log level to control how much logging information is recorded, so they can choose to generate debug logs only when needed (for example).

Tip   If you're writing logging statements that help with debugging, provide an easy way for end-users to get the logs to you. Pipenv does this well with a --support flag, which prints all relevant data in markdown format for pasting into a GitHub issue. Consider adding a similar option, to set a low log level and output formatted version and configuration data along with the log file as part of your interface design. Just don't automatically collate logs from users' systems without their express permission, though, as that may be an invasion of their privacy.

The default levels of logging are debug, info, warning, error, and critical.[15] We can log a message using the matching functions in the logging module, such as logging.warning(...), to log a message at the warning level to the *root logger*.

```
>>> logging.warning("This is a warning")
WARNING:root:This is a warning
```

By default, Python discards debug and info log messages, only messages at the warning level and above are logged to the terminal with the format LEVEL:logger:message. The threshold at which the logger changes from discarding the messages to displaying them is that logger's level. The format used for display is set up the first time you use the root logger and can be adjusted by calling the logging.basicConfig(...) function with a new formatter.[16] This also allows you to change the filter threshold level for the root logger, such as setting it to debug in the following example:

```
logging.basicConfig(format="{asctime}: {levelname} - {message}", style="{",
level=logging.DEBUG)
```

Python has had many string formatting syntaxes over the years; to use the modern style, pass style="{" as another argument. You may see logging configuration in older programs use a different format, but the available keys are still the same. These keys are listed in the standard library's documentation under LogRecord attributes, but the most useful ones are

1. asctime – Formatted date/time

2. levelname – Name for the log level

3. pathname – Path to the file that raised the log message

4. funcName – Name of the function that raised the log message

5. message – The string that was logged

---

[15]New levels can be created with logging.addLevelName(level, levelName), where level is an integer that's compared to the logging.DEBUG, logging.INFO, and other integer constants for sorting. To log to this level, you must use logging.log(level, message) rather than logging.info(message) style convenience functions.

[16]It's best to do this before any log messages have been generated. If there is already a logging config in place, then the function will not do anything unless the force=True parameter has been passed. Before Python 3.8 the force= parameter was not available.

Nested loggers

It's common for a nested hierarchy of loggers to be used in a program. A logger can be retrieved with the `logging.getLogger(name)` function call, where name is the name of the logger to be retrieved.

When a logger is retrieved, the name is compared to existing loggers split by `.` characters. If there is an existing logger with a name that's a prefix of the new one, then it will become the parent. That is:

```
>>> import logging
>>> root_logger = logging.getLogger()
>>> apd_logger = logging.getLogger("apd")
>>> apd_aggregation_logger = logging.getLogger("apd.aggregation")

>>> print(apd_aggregation_logger)
<Logger apd.aggregation (WARNING)>

>>> print(apd_aggregation_logger.parent)
<Logger apd (WARNING)>

>>> print(apd_logger.parent)
<RootLogger root (WARNING)>
```

Caution   Had `apd_aggregation_logger` been created before `apd_logger`, then both would have the root logger as their parent. The easiest way to ensure this behaves correctly is to add `logger = logging.getLogger(__name__)` lines to all modules. This ensures that your logger structure will be the same as the structure of your code, making it easier to reason about. Make sure also to include it in any `__init__.py` if you want to be sure that all the parent loggers are set up correctly.

These loggers can each be used to log messages, with the logger that was used displayed as part of the log message (if the logger name is included in the formatter). Any messages a logger receives are also passed to its parent.[17] It's this behavior that allows us to configure the format of all loggers by configuring the root logger.

```
>>> apd_aggregation_logger.warning("a warning")
WARNING:apd.aggregation:a warning

>>> apd_logger.warning("a warning")
WARNING:apd:a warning

>>> root_logger.warning("a warning")
WARNING:root:a warning
```

Individual loggers can have a new level set, which propagates to all their children (unless they have their own level set). This allows configuring logging on a per-package basis by setting the level of named loggers.

```
>>> apd_logger.setLevel(logging.DEBUG)

>>> apd_aggregation_logger.debug("debugging")
DEBUG:apd.aggregation:debugging

>>> apd_logger.debug("debugging")
DEBUG:apd:debugging

>>> root_logger.debug("debugging")
(no output)
```

Custom actions

Up to now, we've been treating loggers as a glorified print statement, but they're much more flexible than that. When we log a string, the logging framework internally creates a LogRecord object, then that is passed to a handler that formats it and outputs onto the standard error stream.

---

[17]Unless the logger has the logger.propagate=False attribute set, in which case they are not. If you ever see duplicate log entries, there's a good chance you've configured a logger with custom output (as demonstrated later in this section), but have neglected to disable log propagation for that logger.

Loggers can also have custom handlers that record the information logged in some other way. The most commonly used handler is the StreamHandler, which formats log messages (potentially using custom formatters) and displays them in the terminal. We can use this to define that a custom log format is used for logging in the apd.aggregation package, but the default format is used for all other logging, for example.

Extra metadata

We can add application-specific aspects to the formatter using the extra dictionary of the log methods. The downside of this is that *all* log messages that follow that format must provide a value for the extra keys if they are part of the log format. If you set a custom format on the root logger that requires a specific extra piece of data, it would cause all logging calls not under your direct control to raise a KeyError. This is a good reason to only apply a custom formatter to your own loggers, and not the root logger.

In order to do this, we need to customize a single logger with a new formatter. We can't use the logging.basicConfig(...) function as that only manipulates the root logger; we need to provide a new function that sets up the handlers as we want them to be. Listing 11-12 has an example of this function.

Listing 11-12. Helper function to configure a logger with a specific formatter

```python
import logging

def set_logger_format(logger, format_str):
    """Set up a new stderr handler for the given logger
    and configure the formatter with the provided string
    """
    logger.propagate = False
    formatter = logging.Formatter(format_str, None, "{")

    std_err_handler = logging.StreamHandler(None)
    std_err_handler.setFormatter(formatter)

    logger.handlers.clear()
    logger.addHandler(std_err_handler)
    return logger
```

```
logger = set_logger_format(
    logging.getLogger(__name__),
    format_str="{asctime}: {levelname} - {message}",
)
```

Any additional fields that we add in the set_logger_format(...) call must also be provided in every logging call, as an extra= dictionary, as follows:

```
>>> logger = set_logger_format(
...         logging.getLogger(__name__),
...         format_str="[{sensorname}/{levelname}] - {message}",
... )
>>> logger.warn("hi", extra={"sensorname": "Temperature"})
[Temperature/WARNING] - hi
```

We can work around this limitation by manipulating log records before they are formatted. There are a few different ways we can inject variables into a log record: customizing the factory, adding an adapter, or adding a filter. Injecting the data automatically also allows for a more convenient interface when logging from our own code, as we no longer have to explicitly pass all the data our formatter might want as keyword arguments.

Logging adapter

A logging adapter is a piece of code that wraps a logger to allow for customization of any of its behaviors. It provides a process function that can be used to mutate both the message and arguments to the underlying log functionality and can be created as shown in Listing 11-13.

Listing 11-13. A log adapter that provides defaults for some additional keywords

```
import copy
import logging

class ExtraDefaultAdapter(logging.LoggerAdapter):
    def process(self, msg, kwargs):
        extra = copy.copy(self.extra)
        extra.update(kwargs.pop("extra", {}))
        kwargs["extra"] = extra
        return msg, kwargs
```

```
def set_logger_format(logger, format_str):
    """Set up a new stderr handler for the given logger
    and configure the formatter with the provided string
    """

    logger.propagate = False
    formatter = logging.Formatter(format_str, None, "{")

    std_err_handler = logging.StreamHandler(None)
    std_err_handler.setFormatter(formatter)

    logger.handlers.clear()
    logger.addHandler(std_err_handler)
    return logger
```

Using this adapter allows us to omit the extra dictionary unless we have data that we wish to add to this log message, allowing us to leave it out when it's not relevant. This also makes it much easier to add new items to the format string, as we don't need to change every logging function call to match.

```
>>> logger = set_logger_format(
...     logging.getLogger(__name__),
...     format_str=" [{sensorname}/{levelname}] - {message}",
... )
>>> logger = ExtraDefaultAdapter(logger, {"sensorname": "none"})
>>> logger.warn("hi")
[none/WARNING] - hi
>>> logger.warn("hi", extra={"sensorname": "Temperature"})
[Temperature/WARNING] - hi
```

The downside of this approach is that we need to wrap every logger with the adapter. It is a good fit for automatically populating additional data in a single module, but it doesn't help us to provide a default across multiple loggers because there is no guarantee that all code using the logger will also use the adapter (in fact, for the root logger, it's all but guaranteed that there will be code that uses logging that isn't aware of our custom adapter).

We can add whatever logic we want to the adapter itself. Instead of providing an explicit default for the sensorname, we could extract this from a context variable, for example. Adapters fit best for situations where only a single logger requires a custom piece of metadata. If you've defined a custom formatter for a logger that only you are logging to, then it's quite possible to ensure that all logging calls go through the adapter.

LogRecord factory

Another approach is to customize the creation of the internal log record objects themselves. Customizing the factory allows for arbitrary data to be stored on all LogRecords without the code that's logging being aware of any difference. This allows for custom metadata to be used in the format for loggers that third-party code uses, such as the root logger. Making this format common to all loggers means that there is no comingling of different log formats, which may be a significant advantage for users. The downside is that attributes set here cannot be passed in an extra dictionary.[18]

In the previous example, we had lots of flexibility with how we passed the additional data to the logging system. When overriding the LogRecord factory, we have little choice but to use a context variable to pass the additional data in. This limits the ways in which this method can be used, as we cannot simply pass the value we want as an argument.

Listing 11-14 shows example code for customizing the record factory to include the value from a sensorname_var context variable in all records.

Listing 11-14. Customizing a LogRecord factory to add contextual information and include in all logs

```
from contextvars import ContextVar
import functools
import logging

sensorname_var = ContextVar("sensorname", default="none")

def add_sensorname_record_factory(existing_factory, *args, **kwargs):
    record = existing_factory(*args, **kwargs)
    record.sensorname = sensorname_var.get()
    return record
```

---

[18]The code that merges the extra dictionary in explicitly checks for collisions and raises a KeyError if found.

```
def add_record_factory_wrapper(fn):
    old_factory = logging.getLogRecordFactory()
    wrapped = functools.partial(fn, old_factory)
    logging.setLogRecordFactory(wrapped)
```

```
add_record_factory_wrapper(add_sensorname_record_factory)
logging.basicConfig(
    format="[{sensorname}/{levelname}] - {message}", style="{",
    level=logging.INFO
)
```

This approach is quite different to the previous approaches in that it changes the logging configuration at a global level. The adapter example involved changes to each module to wrap the logger in the appropriate adapter, and each module can have its own adapted logger. Only one record factory can be active at a time. Although we can override it multiple times to provide additional data, all the overrides must be written in such a way so as not to conflict with each other. This approach can be used as follows:

```
>>> logger = logging.getLogger(__name__)
>>> logger.warning("hi")
[none/WARNING] - hi
>>> token = sensorname_var.set("Temperature")
>>> logging.warning("hi")
[Temperature/WARNING] - hi
>>> sensorname_var.reset(token)
```

Logging filters

In my opinion, logging filters provide a good middle ground between these two approaches. The name filter may make this approach a bit counterintuitive, as filters are intended to be used to discard log records dynamically, but it's also the most flexible way to mutate log records.

You can associate a logging filter with a logger, which causes it to be called for every log message that logger processes, but you can also register it against a handler. It's handlers that control the formatting, so associating a filter with a handler ensures that the custom format and the default value filter are closely associated. Whenever that handler is used, you know that the filter is also active.

This approach means that the default sensor name is only populated as part of the formatting process. The additional information can still be passed as part of the extra dictionary, as is normal, and it is available to all logging handlers when explicitly passed. Listing 11-15 shows an updated setup function that optionally associates a filter with the handler.

Listing 11-15. Using a handler filter to add a default sensorname

```
import logging

class AddSensorNameDefault(logging.Filter):
    def filter(self, record):
        if not hasattr(record, "sensorname"):
            record.sensorname = "none"
        return True

def set_logger_format(logger, format_str, filters=None):
    """Set up a new stderr handler for the given logger
    and configure the formatter with the provided string
    """
    logger.propagate = False
    formatter = logging.Formatter(format_str, None, "{")

    std_err_handler = logging.StreamHandler(None)
    std_err_handler.setFormatter(formatter)

    logger.handlers.clear()
    logger.addHandler(std_err_handler)
    if filters is not None:
        for filter in filters:
            std_err_handler.addFilter(filter)
    return logger
```

Setting up this logger is very similar to the adapter pattern, but with an important difference. The set_logger_format(...) call only needs to be made once. Any subsequent calls to logging.getLogger(...) return a correctly configured logger, without needing every user of the logger to configure the filter. The initial use is done as follows:

```
logger = set_logger_format(
    logging.getLogger(),
    "[{sensorname}/{levelname}] - {message}",
    filters=[AddSensorNameDefault(), ]
)
>>> logger.warning("hi")
[none/WARNING] - hi
>>> logger.warning("hi", extra={"sensorname": "Temperature"})
[Temperature/WARNING] - hi
```

Logging configuration

The downside to the preceding code is that, in order to change the formatter or add a filter, we've had to do quite a lot of setting up for the logging system. For all applications other than simple, self-contained tools, end-users likely want to configure their own handlers or log formatters. This is especially true of libraries used in larger applications.

As such, it's quite rare to configure logging with Python code in real-world applications. Normally, logging configuration is provided through a configuration system of some sort, such as the [logging] configuration section of the alembic.ini file that configures the migration system. The logging.config.fileConfig(...) helper function can be used to load logging configuration from a file, and a small amount of glue code (Listing 11-16) can be used to make any filters we've added available for end-users to take advantage of in ini-style log configuration (Listing 11-17).

Listing 11-16. Glue code to provide a handler that has a filter added by default

```
import logging

class AddSensorNameDefault(logging.Filter):
    def filter(self, record):
        if not hasattr(record, "sensorname"):
            record.sensorname = "none"
        return True
```

```
class SensorNameStreamHandler(logging.StreamHandler):
    def __init__(self, *args, **kwargs):
        super().__init__()
        self.addFilter(AddSensorNameDefault())
```

Listing 11-17. A sample logging configuration file that uses a filter to provide default values for the formatter

```
[loggers]
keys=root

[handlers]
keys=stderr_with_sensorname

[formatters]
keys=sensorname

[logger_root]
level=INFO
handlers=stderr_with_sensorname

[handler_stderr_with_sensorname]
class=apd.aggregation.utils.SensorNameStreamHandler
formatter = sensorname

[formatter_sensorname]
format = {asctime}: [{sensorname}/{levelname}] - {message}
style = {
```

Caution   The logging configuration file format allows for some logic to be embedded to make the setup of complex configurations easier. This makes it possible for arbitrary code to be run from the configuration file. It's rare for this to be a problem, but if you have tools that are run by system administrators, then only administrators should be able to edit the logging configuration.

Other handlers

There are other useful handlers apart from the `StreamHandler` that we've been using so far. The most common is `FileHandler` which outputs logging information to a named file. Setting this as a handler on the root logger is used to build persistent log files.

More complex handlers, such as `TimedRotatingFileHandler`, `SysLogHandler`, and `HTTPHandler`, are less commonly used but very powerful. These allow for the logs to be integrated into any manner of existing log management solutions. There are even commercial log management systems that integrate in the same way, such as Sentry with its custom `EventHandler` class.

Audit logs

Having custom loggers and handlers allows for writing audit logging systems that record user actions in a complex system. An audit log is a log which is intended to provide information about certain important actions that users have performed. It's not used for debugging, but for verifying that the system is not being abused.

To achieve this, you would usually get a new logger by name with `logging.getLogger("audit")` and configure this to be an audit logger. Unlike most loggers, most audit logs aren't named to match a Python module. Generally, audit loggers use special log handlers, such as handlers to append audit logging events to a system log or sending by email. I'd recommend also outputting audit log entries to the same output streams place as other log items. Having audit log entries comingled with debugging information adds high-level context that can be very useful when debugging problems.

Log handlers can be associated with multiple loggers, so custom log files can be configured to contain the output of multiple loggers by defining a handler for each file and associating it with each individual logger that should feed into that file. You can also use the nested structure of loggers to create log files for logical components of an application.

Log handlers are implemented with a Python class that provides an `emit(record)` function, so it's possible to write custom handlers to perform any application-specific audit logging actions that may be appropriate. In practice, there are handler implementations available for most common requirements.

Designing around problems

The preceding strategies allow us to communicate problems encountered within components of our program (using exceptions) and the end-users (using warnings and logging). They make it significantly easier for us to understand what problems our users are experiencing (when they're reported). However, most problems go unreported, and we can never think of every possible edge case ahead of time.

A crucial part of writing reliable software is to design processes that automatically compensate for problems encountered as part of its normal running. For us, any problem in communicating with a sensor results in a gap in the historical sensor data we are collecting.

There are two possible causes for such a failure. Either the sensor server is working correctly, and the aggregation process (or network) has failed, or the aggregation process (and network) is working correctly, and the sensor has failed.

Scheduling sensor lookups

The problem of the aggregator or network failing is the easiest to solve. Rather than the aggregation process pulling live data from sensors, we can modify the sensors to collect and store data periodically. It can then provide this collected data over an API. This allows the aggregation process to detect when data was collected but not downloaded and to correct the problem by downloading all the data since the last successful sync.

Achieving this involves significant changes to both the aggregation process and the sensors themselves. Not only do the servers involved need to trigger a sensor data collection at specific times, but it needs to be able to store the data and expose the set of stored data over the API.

We'll need to create a database integration in the same way that we did for the aggregation process. We also need a new command-line option to store data and add a set of dependencies for alembic and sqlalchemy to make sure we can store data to a database. These need to be optional dependencies: not all users of the apd.sensors package are necessarily using the aggregator, and it would be excessive to require users to install a full database system if they only need the command-line tool for checking current state. The optional dependency section of setup.cfg will look as shown in the following once this new feature has been added.

> **Note**   Some requirements are only relevant if we have both webapp and
> scheduled extras installed, as we'll use them to implement the database lookup
> later. We can create another extra for these, but that does make it harder for users
> to understand. You may prefer to add these dependencies to one or the other of
> the other extra definitions instead. As we're using a third extra, we'll have to bear
> in mind that not all dependencies may be available when writing code. Nothing is
> stopping a user from installing the extra for these additional dependencies without
> the two extras that it builds on.

```
[options.extras_require]
webapp = flask
scheduled =
  sqlalchemy
  alembic
storedapi =
  flask-sqlalchemy
  python-dateutil
```

We then need to ensure that our local development environment is marked as
needing this new set of optional dependencies using `pipenv install`. Just like the
aggregation process, we need to create a database table definition (Listing 11-18),
connect the metadata object to the alembic configuration, and generate an initial
alembic migration.

Listing 11-18. Database table for caching sensor values locally

```
from __future__ import annotations

import datetime
import typing as t

import sqlalchemy
from sqlalchemy.schema import Table
from sqlalchemy.orm.session import Session
```

```python
from apd.sensors.base import Sensor

metadata = sqlalchemy.MetaData()

sensor_values = Table(
    "recorded_values",
    metadata,
    sqlalchemy.Column("id", sqlalchemy.Integer, primary_key=True),
    sqlalchemy.Column("sensor_name", sqlalchemy.String, index=True),
    sqlalchemy.Column("collected_at", sqlalchemy.TIMESTAMP, index=True),
    sqlalchemy.Column("data", sqlalchemy.JSON),
)

def store_sensor_data(sensor: Sensor[t.Any], data: t.Any, db_session:
Session) -> None:
    now = datetime.datetime.now()
    record = sensor_values.insert().values(
        sensor_name=sensor.name, data=sensor.to_json_compatible(data),
        collected_at=now
    )
    db_session.execute(record)
```

The changes in Listing 11-19 add a command-line option for specifying which database should be connected to and a flag to mark that data should be saved to a local database rather than just output for the user's information. With this in place, our users can set up a scheduled task to call our script and save the data according to a schedule.

Listing 11-19. Updated command-line script to add saving of data

```python
@click.command(help="Displays the values of the sensors")
@click.option(
    "--develop", required=False, metavar="path",
    help="Load a sensor by Python path"
)
@click.option("--verbose", is_flag=True, help="Show additional info")
@click.option("--save", is_flag=True,
help="Store collected data to a database")
```

```python
@click.option(
    "--db",
    metavar="<CONNECTION_STRING>",
    default="sqlite:///sensor_data.sqlite",
    help="The connection string to a database",
    envvar="APD_SENSORS_DB_URI",
)
def show_sensors(develop: str, verbose: bool, save: bool, db: str) -> None:
    sensors: t.Iterable[Sensor[t.Any]]
    if develop:
        try:
            sensors = [get_sensor_by_path(develop)]
        except UserFacingCLIError as error:
            if verbose:
                tb = traceback.format_exception(type(error), error,
                error.__traceback__)
                click.echo("".join(tb))
            click.secho(error.message, fg="red", bold=True)
            sys.exit(error.return_code)
    else:
        sensors = get_sensors()

    db_session = None
    if save:
        from sqlalchemy import create_engine
        from sqlalchemy.orm import sessionmaker

        engine = create_engine(db)
        sm = sessionmaker(engine)
        db_session = sm()

    for sensor in sensors:
        click.secho(sensor.title, bold=True)
        try:
            value = sensor.value()
        except DataCollectionError as error:
            if verbose:
```

```
        tb = traceback.format_exception(type(error), error,
        error.__traceback__)
        click.echo("".join(tb))
        continue
    click.echo(error)
else:
    click.echo(sensor.format(value))
    if save and db_session is not None:
        store_sensor_data(sensor, value, db_session)
        db_session.commit()

click.echo("")
sys.exit(ReturnCodes.OK)
```

This is sufficient for ensuring that no data would be lost if there were to be a network or aggregation failure; however, it isn't enough to integrate the missing data once the error condition ends.

APIs and filtering

We need to update our API to make it possible to extract any data that was recorded in the past. At the same time, we can update the API to split out failed sensors into an independent list of errors, supplementing the exception handling we added earlier in this chapter.

Complex APIs often offer the ability for users to specify which data they need, allowing the API implementation to be more efficient by only calculating information that the end-user needs. More commonly, APIs offer some form of filtering option to reduce the amount of data that's passed on.

We need a new API endpoint that exposes the data that's been gathered so that the aggregation process can synchronize it to its database. The implementation of this endpoint is shown in Listing 11-20.

Listing 11-20. New historical values endpoint for the v3.0 API

```
@version.route("/historical")
@version.route("/historical/<start>")
@version.route("/historical/<start>/<end>")
@require_api_key
```

```
def historical_values(
    start: str = None, end: str = None
) -> t.Tuple[t.Dict[str, t.Any], int, t.Dict[str, str]]:
    try:
        import dateutil.parser
        from sqlalchemy import create_engine
        from sqlalchemy.orm import sessionmaker
        from apd.sensors.database import sensor_values
        from apd.sensors.wsgi import db
    except ImportError:
        return {"error": "Historical data support is not installed"}, 501, {}

    db_session = db.session
    headers = {"Content-Security-Policy": "default-src 'none'"}

    query = db_session.query(sensor_values)
    if start:
        query = query.filter(
            sensor_values.c.collected_at >= dateutil.parser.parse(start)
        )
    if end:
        query = query.filter(
            sensor_values.c.collected_at <= dateutil.parser.parse(end)
        )

    known_sensors = {sensor.name: sensor for sensor in cli.get_sensors()}
    sensors = []
    for data in query:
        if data.sensor_name not in known_sensors:
            continue
        sensor = known_sensors[data.sensor_name]
        sensor_data = {
            "id": sensor.name,
            "title": sensor.title,
            "value": data.data,
            "human_readable": sensor.format(
            sensor.from_json_compatible(data.data)),
```

```
        "collected_at": data.collected_at.isoformat(),
    }
    sensors.append(sensor_data)
data = {"sensors": sensors}
return data, 200, headers
```

The handlers to import this information into the aggregation process are very similar to the normal sensor collection, as the data is in the same format. The process could be implemented by adding a new command-line tool to synchronize any missing data in a timeframe or by detecting a long time since the last successful data collection and using the /historical endpoint instead of the normal one.

EXERCISE 11-1: SUPPORTING HISTORICAL DATA COLLECTION

This change doesn't directly help us with situations where the server running the sensor fails. It's not possible to recover from this for the sensor types that we have, but that is a property of our specific sensors rather than an immutable fact. Other sensors may be able to find a value at a point in time. For example, a sensor that reports on server status may be able to extract past state from existing system logs.

Consider what changes would need to be made to the codebase to support sensors that can report their value at points in the past. Consider how the existing classes could be modified to provide this extra functionality in a way that would be backward compatible with existing sensors.

As always, there is an example of how this could be achieved in the code accompanying this chapter. However, this won't be merged into the master branch of the code as it's too far away from the requirements for collating the kind of data that we're storing currently.

Summary

When writing libraries that you expect other developers to use, include custom exceptions and raise warnings when relevant; it's a more effective way to communicate with your audience than a README.txt file. In particular, plan any deprecations and ensure that warnings are shown when the old features are used.

Custom exception types allow downstream developers to write handlers for specific error conditions, just as the custom exceptions in the libraries you use allow you to catch errors in your dependencies.

Even if you're not writing a library for others to use, the logging framework allows for your users to configure what debugging information they'd like to store and how they'd like it to be handled. If you don't provide logging statements or you log them with `print(...)` alone, they are more likely to be discarded rather than passed back to you as a bug report.

While these features help with debugging and writing code to handle failures, the most important aspect of writing code that is robust against error cases is to design failover into the process itself.

Whatever combination of tactics you decide to use, make sure you test that your code is behaving correctly. Automated tests can and should verify that your code behaves in an acceptable way when things go wrong, not just when things work as expected.

Additional resources

The following links provide extra context on the subjects covered in this chapter:

As mentioned previously, the Python standard library's `itertools` module is one of the most underused. It's worth reading over the documentation at `https://docs.python.org/3.8/library/itertools.html` to learn the various tools it offers.

Also in the standard documentation, `https://docs.python.org/3.8/library/collections.abc.html` is a useful reference for what methods are required to implement the various types of Python data container.

The integration I'm using for flask and SQLAlchemy is documented at `https://flask-sqlalchemy.palletsprojects.com/en/2.x/`.

Details on the ini file format for logging configuration is at `https://docs.python.org/3.8/library/logging.config.html#logging-config-fileformat`.

CHAPTER 12

Callbacks and data analysis

Throughout the last 11 chapters, we've written a pair of utilities to collect data from various sources and aggregate it together. We've designed systems for displaying the aggregated data, recovering from error conditions, and enabling end-users to customize every step of the process for their own needs. However, the only way to interact with this data is to view it on a screen. There is no functionality available for actively analyzing the data as it comes in and reacting accordingly.

In this final chapter, we'll add a new concept to the aggregation process, allowing us to build both *triggers* that detect certain conditions in the input data and *actions* to run when those conditions are detected. Some potentially useful ones are threshold points for data (such as temperature above 18°C, solar panel output above 0.5 kW, or RAM available under 500MB). Alternatively, there are correlations between two sensors, such as the temperature on one sensor differing from the temperature of another by more than a threshold, or correlations across time, such as the solar power being significantly more or less than the previous day.

Generator data flow

All the analysis code we've written so far is passive; it is interposed between a data source and a consumer and modifies the data as the consumer pulls it through. These functions are all variations on a for loop; they iterate over the source data and may yield output. Generators are an excellent way of refactoring loops where both the input and output are iterables.

541

© Matthew Wilkes 2020
M. Wilkes, *Advanced Python Development*, https://doi.org/10.1007/978-1-4842-5793-7_12

The same code can be expressed in a few different ways, as a comprehension, a loop that modifies a shared variable, or as a generator function. For example, our clean_passthrough(...) function to get values from DataPoint objects is a generator function, as shown in Listing 12-1.

Listing 12-1. The passthrough cleaner generator function

```
async def clean_passthrough(
    datapoints: t.AsyncIterator[DataPoint],
) -> CLEANED_DT_FLOAT:
    async for datapoint in datapoints:
        if datapoint.data is None:
            continue
        else:
            yield datapoint.collected_at, datapoint.data
```

We can use this to convert an async iterator of data points to a list of date and value pairs by using values = [value async for value in clean_passthrough(datapoints)].

The same logic could be expressed directly as a list comprehension or as a loop that manipulates a list object. These are shown as the two implementations in Table 12-1.

Table 12-1. *Comprehension and loop implementations of the same logic*

```cleaned = [(datapoint.collected_at, datapoint.data) async for datapoint in datapoints if datapoint.data]```	```results = []async for datapoint in datapoints: if datapoint.data is None: continue else: results.append(datapoint.collected_at, datapoint.data)```

The critical difference is that by using a generator function, we can refer to the logic of the loop by the name of the function. With comprehensions and standard loops, we always define the logic in terms of the data we're working on. It's this property that made generator functions the best choice for us, as we need to pass a reference to the logic to the constructor of the Config object without having yet extracted any data.

In any case, the more complex cleaner functions we've written could not have been expressed as a comprehension. They need variables to keep track of state and to perform different operations conditionally. Any comprehension can be rewritten as a generator function,[1] but not all generator functions can be rewritten as comprehensions. If you have a comprehension that's becoming overly complex, you should consider refactoring it into a for loop or as a generator function.

Generators that consume their own output

The generator functions we've looked at so far have emulated a for loop. They have a source of data as an argument and can be iterated over. A generator function implements the logic of a loop, and a function calls it with the source data it wants to be processed. This looks like Listing 12-2, which shows a simple generator function for summing some numbers.

Listing 12-2. Generator to sum numbers

```
import typing as t

def sum_ints(source: t.Iterable[int]) -> t.Iterator[int]:
    """Yields a running total from the underlying iterator"""
    total = 0
    for num in source:
        total += num
        yield total

def numbers() -> t.Iterator[int]:
    yield 1
    yield 1
    yield 1
```

---

[1]However, you may need to convert the data type using a second comprehension of the right type, as we did to convert an async iterator to a list with a list comprehension.

```
def test():
    sums = sum_ints(numbers())
    assert [a for a in sums] == [1, 2, 3]
```

In this example, the numbers() function is used to provide an iterator of integers, and the sum_ints(...) function takes any iterable of integers and adds them up. Although the test() function is responsible for calling both functions and connecting them together, it iterates over the output of sum_ints(...) only. It's sum_ints(...) that iterates over the output of numbers(), not test(). In this way, the data flows from the numbers() function to the sum_ints(...) function to the test() function, as shown in Figure 12-1.

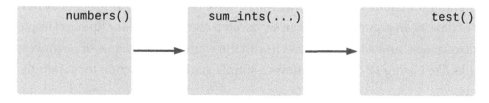

Figure 12-1. *The data flow behavior of a chain of iterators*

Although we can pass any arbitrary iterable to a function to iterate over, there are times where we want more explicit control over what the next piece of data to process should be. One of the hardest things to express with this pattern of consuming generator is priming a generator with an initial value, then feeding its own output back in as input (Figure 12-2).

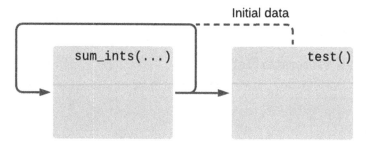

Figure 12-2. *An iterator that processes its own output, with an initial value*

Any time we want to have a generator that processes its own output, we'd have to code it to do so, rather than using an input iterator as the data source, as shown in Listing 12-3. This prevents it from being used in any way apart from on its own output.

Listing 12-3. A variant that has only a single start value, then processes its output

```python
import itertools
import typing as t

def sum_ints(start: int) -> t.Iterator[int]:
    """Yields a running total with a given start value"""
    total = start
    while True:
        yield total
        total += total

def test():
    sums = sum_ints(1)
    # Limit an infinite iterator to the first 3 items
    # itertools.islice(iterable, [start,] stop, [step])
    sums = itertools.islice(sums, 3)
    assert [a for a in sums] == [1, 2, 4]
```

There are real use cases for wanting to write functions that can work either on an input stream or on their own output. Any function that returns data in the same output format as its input can be written like this, but functions that iteratively *improve* their input are a good fit.

For example, if we have a function that reduces the size of an image by rescaling it to be 50% of its input size, we could write a generator function that, given an iterable of images, returns an iterator of resized images. Alternatively, if we could use that same generator on its own output, we could provide an input image and get a generator of progressively smaller versions of that same initial image.

The new function we've defined can no longer be used to add an arbitrary iterable of integers like we originally wanted. One way we can make the sum_ints(...) function work both on its own output and with arbitrary iterables is to define a new iterator that uses a closure to share state between the code that's consuming the generator and its function.

We can create a function that returns two iterators, one that delegates to the sum_ints(...) iterator and stashes a copy of the latest value and another iterator to be used as the input to sum_ints(...) that uses the shared value from the first function.[2] The data flow for this wrapper function is shown in Figure 12-3.

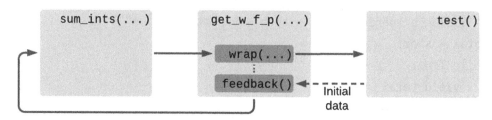

Figure 12-3. *Data flow using a wrapper function to generate an iterator that works on its own output*

Listing 12-4 demonstrates one way of writing this wrapper function. The get_wrap_feedback_pair(...) function provides the two generators, which are used in the test() method to create a version of sum_ints(...) with a known initial value that passes its own output back as input.

Listing 12-4. Helper function to feed a generator's output back as input

```
import itertools
import typing as t

def sum_ints(source: t.Iterable[int]) -> t.Iterator[int]:
    """Yields a running total from the underlying iterator"""
    total = 0
    for num in source:
        total += num
        yield total

def get_wrap_feedback_pair(initial=None):  # get_w_f_p(...) above
    """Return a pair of external and internal wrap functions"""
    shared_state = initial
```

---

[2]We did something similar with the get_data_by_deployment(...) iterator, which uses shared state to define a generator that impacts another. It's by far the most complex example of an iterator in this book.

546

```
    # Note, feedback() and wrap(...) functions assume that
    # they are always in sync
    def feedback():
        while True:
            """Yield the last value of the wrapped iterator"""
            yield shared_state
    def wrap(wrapped):
        """Iterate over an iterable and stash each value"""
        nonlocal shared_state
        for item in wrapped:
            shared_state = item
            yield item
    return feedback, wrap

def test():
    feedback, wrap = get_wrap_feedback_pair(1)
    # Sum the iterable (1, ...) where ... is the results
    # of that iterable, stored with the wrap method
    sums = wrap(sum_ints(feedback()))
    # Limit to 3 items
    sums = itertools.islice(sums, 3)
    assert [a for a in sums] == [1, 2, 4]
```

Now the sum_ints(...) function represents the logic being applied on each step of the loop, and get_wrap_feedback_pair(...) encodes the relationship between the output of the generator and the next value it should process. If we wanted to, for example, make a database query based on the results of the output and use that to supply the next value, we'd need to design a new variant of get_wrap_feedback_pair(...) that encodes the new relationship between input and output.

This approach gets us closer to being able to control the data flow in an iterator dynamically from the calling function, but it's still limited. It works perfectly well if we only ever want one relationship, but as the code is self-contained, the calling function (test(), in our case) can't influence the behavior. It relies on the wrapper function to implement the appropriate logic.

Enhanced generators

An alternative is to change the behavior of the generator to use the "enhanced generator" syntax.[3] This allows data to be sent into a running generator every time it yields an item. It's still rather limited, as you cannot send more data than is yielded, but it does allow for a more expressive way of customizing behavior.

So far we've been treating yield like an alternative to a return statement, but a yield expression resolves to a value that can be stored in a variable, as received = yield to_send. Under normal operation, the received value is always None, but it's possible to change this by advancing the generator using the send(...) method. This pattern allows for generator functions that loop over data explicitly provided by their caller each time they're advanced.

ENHANCED ASYNCHRONOUS GENERATORS

The same model of execution is available to iterators implemented in native coroutines, using the asend(...) coroutine on the asynchronous generator object. This behaves in the same way as the send(...) method, except that it must be awaited. This is needed as asynchronous iterators can block when yielding a new object, and both asend(...) and send(...) calls are special cases of requesting a new object.

The asend(...) result may not be awaited unless the underlying generator is at a yield statement. There is no synchronization involved in this call, so multiple calls cannot safely be scheduled in parallel. You must always await the result of one asend(...) call before making another to the same generator. As such, it's rare to schedule this as a task.

There is no asynchronous variant of the next(...) method for advancing a generator by one. Although you can manually use await gen.__anext__(), I'd recommend using await gen.asend(None) to advance an asynchronous iterator outside of a loop.

Listing 12-5 shows an example of the integer summing function that receives its data from yield statement return values rather than an input iterable.

---

[3]This name is taken from the Python Enhancement Proposal that added it, PEP342. Technically speaking, this software engineering pattern is a coroutine, which the title of PEP342 makes clear. This is an enhancement to Python from 2005, long before true coroutines using async def were introduced. I'll be calling these enhanced generators or referring to *sending* data to a generator, to avoid confusion between these and asynchronous functions.

Listing 12-5. Sending data to an in-progress generator

```python
import typing as t

def sum_ints() -> t.Generator[int, int, None]:
    """Yields a running total from the underlying iterator"""
    total = 0
    num = yield total
    while True:
        total += num
        num = yield total

def test():
    # Sum the iterable (1, ...) where ... is the results
    # of that iterable, stored with the wrap method
    sums = sum_ints()
    next(sums)  # We can only send to yield lines, so advance to the first
    last = 1
    result = []
    for n in range(3):
        last = sums.send(last)
        result.append(last)
    assert result == [1, 2, 4]

test()
```

Note   The type definition of the generator has changed from t.Iterable[int] to t.Generator[int, int, None]. The former is equivalent to t.Generator[int, None, None], meaning it yields ints, but it expects to be sent None and returns None as its final value.

The control flow, as shown in Figure 12-4, is much simpler in this case. Rather than data flowing only in one direction, or in loops through intermediate functions, the two functions pass data between themselves freely.

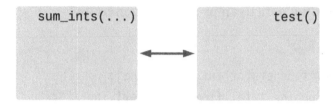

Figure 12-4. *Control flow using the enhanced generator method*

Enhanced generator functions encode the body of a loop, just like standard generators, but they are closer to the behavior of a while loop than a for loop. Rather than looping over some input data, it's looping with a condition and receiving intermediate values as it progresses.

This approach works well for situations where there is a stateful function that needs instructions from an outside source, such as image manipulation. An image editing enhanced generator could take an initial image as its input, then commands such as "resize", "rotate", "crop", and so on. The commands could be hard-coded; they could come from user input or from analyzing the last version it output.

Using classes

Enhanced generators can use the value they receive from the yield statement as the next piece of data to process or as an instruction to change what they're doing, or they can use a mixture of the two.

Code that's invoked multiple times with a variety of instructions and which shares state between invocations is commonly implemented as a class. In this case, the instance is responsible for storing the state, and the user of the class calls different methods to signal what code path is required.

Any code that uses this approach looks more natural than the enhanced generator syntax. For example, Listing 12-6 shows the same mean calculation behavior expressed as a class.

Listing 12-6. Class-based approach for long-running sets of asynchronous code

```python
class MeanFinder:
    def __init__(self):
        self.running_total = 0
        self.num_items = 0
```

```
    def add_item(self, num: float):
        self.running_total += num
        self.num_items += 1

    @property
    def mean(self):
        return self.running_total / self.num_items

def test():
    # Recursive mean from initial data
    mean = MeanFinder()
    to_add = 1
    for n in range(3):
        mean.add_item(to_add)
        to_add = mean.mean
    assert mean.mean == 1.0

    # Mean of a concrete data list
    mean = MeanFinder()
    for to_add in [1, 2, 3]:
        mean.add_item(to_add)
    assert mean.mean == 2.0
```

This approach is a particularly good fit for situations where you want to share code between multiple similar functions, as the class can be subclassed and individual methods overridden by each implementation. However, developers expect classes to be less stateful than enhanced generators. It's normal to call methods on an object knowing in advance how many arguments are needed and of what type. An enhanced generator allows developers to write programs where the receiving function decides what data to ask for from the calling function. This can be a good fit where the generator represents an algorithm for collating multiple pieces of data and keeping intermediate results.[4]

---

[4]For example, a program that arranges images into collages might be implemented as a class that has methods for supplying images and getting the arranged result out, or it might be implemented as an enhanced generator where whenever an image is added, a new result is returned.

Using an enhanced generator to wrap an iterable

As our enhanced generator changed the control flow to expect new items as the result of yield, we cannot use an enhanced generator in place of a standard generator. This method can be used to create functions that work collaboratively with their calling function to process data, but it's no longer usable as a simple wrapper around another iterable.

To get around this problem, we can write a wrapper function that converts the signature of an enhanced generator to that of a standard generator function. We can then use the enhanced generator in situations where we need to control the behavior interactively, and the wrapped one for when we have an input iterable, as demonstrated in Listing 12-7.

Listing 12-7. An enhanced generator that can be used as a standard generator

```
import typing as t

input_type = t.TypeVar("input_type")
output_type = t.TypeVar("output_type")

def wrap_enhanced_generator(
    input_generator: t.Callable[[], t.Generator[output_type, input_type,
    None]]
) -> t.Callable[[t.Iterable[input_type]], t.Iterator[output_type]]:
    underlying = input_generator()
    next(underlying)  # Advance the underlying generator to the first yield

    def inner(data: t.Iterable[input_type]) -> t.Iterator[output_type]:
        for item in data:
            yield underlying.send(item)

    return inner

def sum_ints() -> t.Generator[int, int, None]:
    """Yields a running total from the underlying iterator"""
    total = 0
    num = yield total
    while True:
        total += num
        num = yield total
```

```
def numbers() -> t.Iterator[int]:
    yield 1
    yield 1
    yield 1

def test() -> None:
    # Start with 1, feed output back in, limit to 3 items
    recursive_sum = sum_ints()
    next(recursive_sum)
    result = []
    last = 1
    for i in range(3):
        last = recursive_sum.send(last)
        result.append(last)
    assert result == [1, 2, 4]

    # Add 3 items from a standard iterable
    simple_sum = wrap_enhanced_generator(sum_ints)
    result_iter = simple_sum(numbers())
    assert [a for a in result_iter] == [1, 2, 3]
```

This approach lets us define an enhanced generator function to define the logic of a single step in a process and then use that logic either as a wrapper around an iterator or to process its own output. The data flow used when looping over an input iterable is shown in Figure 12-5.

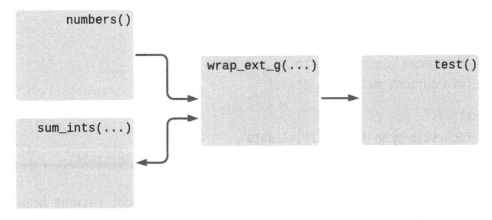

Figure 12-5. *Control flow of the wrapped enhanced generator*

Refactoring functions with excessive return values

Any enhanced generator can also be written as a series of functions, so long as all the required intermediate values are passed with each invocation. Functions that all require an argument are effectively sharing state, just in a more explicit way than usual.

Complex program structures do not fit this idiom well, so I wouldn't recommend rewriting an enhanced generator to use coroutines. If you see a set of functions in a loop, where the return values from one are immediately passed to another function call without being used, it might be a good candidate for refactoring.

Listing 12-8 demonstrates a pair of functions to calculate the mean of a series of numbers. The mean_ints_split_initial() function provides some initial values which the calling function passes to mean_ints_split(...) along with a new number to add. The mean_ints_split(...) function takes three arguments and returns two values, but the calling function only cares about one argument and one value.

Listing 12-8. Code to find the average of some numbers expressed as bare functions

```
import typing as t

def mean_ints_split_initial() -> t.Tuple[float, int]:
    return 0.0, 0

def mean_ints_split(
    to_add: float, current_mean: float, num_items: int
) -> t.Tuple[float, int]:
    running_total = current_mean * num_items
    running_total += to_add
    num_items += 1
    current_mean = running_total / num_items
    return current_mean, num_items

def test():
    # Recursive mean from initial data
    to_add, current_mean, num_items = mean_ints_split_initial()
    for n in range(3):
        current_mean, num_items = mean_ints_split(to_add, current_mean,
        num_items)
```

```
        to_add = current_mean
    assert current_mean == 1.0
    assert num_items == 3

    # Mean of concrete data list
    current_mean = num_items = 0
    for to_add in [1, 2, 3]:
        current_mean, num_items = mean_ints_split(to_add, current_mean,
        num_items)
    assert current_mean == 2.0
    assert num_items == 3
```

The num_items value being passed around here is only relevant to the implementation of mean_ints_split(...); it's not useful to the calling function. The API would be more straightforward if developers could instantiate a new mean calculation and then pass numbers in and access the revised mean, without needing to pass the additional context data each time. This is another good use of an enhanced generator, the code for which is shown as Listing 12-9.

Listing 12-9. Simplified mean calculation using an enhanced generator

```
import typing as t

def mean_ints() -> t.Generator[t.Optional[float], float, None]:
    running_total = 0.0
    num_items = 0
    to_add = yield None
    while True:
        running_total += to_add
        num_items += 1
        to_add = yield running_total / num_items

def test():
    # Recursive mean from initial data
    mean = mean_ints()
    next(mean)
    to_add = 1
```

```
    for n in range(3):
        current_mean = mean.send(to_add)
        to_add = current_mean
    assert current_mean == 1.0

    # Mean of a concrete data list
    # wrap_enhanced_generator would also work here
    mean = mean_ints()
    next(mean)
    for to_add in [1, 2, 3]:
        current_mean = mean.send(to_add)
    assert current_mean == 2.0
```

If you find yourself with a coroutine that is called multiple times and each time it is passed the results of the previous invocation, then it is a good match for an enhanced generator.

Queues

All of the approaches we've looked at so far assume that there is no need to push data to the iterator from multiple sources. As mentioned earlier, generators raise exceptions if another thread or task tries to send data before it's ready, which requires sophisticated use of locking to prevent. Equally, we cannot send data to a generator unless we also extract a piece of data. If multiple functions are trying to *send* data, then they must necessarily also be *extracting* data and would need to coordinate to ensure that the correct function gets any data intended for its use.

A better approach is to use a Queue object. We looked at these during the section on threading as a solution for passing work to a thread, but the asyncio module offers a Queue implementation that works in a similar way for asynchronous Python. Specifically, any methods that can block the thread in a standard queue are awaitable with asyncio queues. Listing 12-10 demonstrates an implementation of the sum_ints(...) function that uses a queue.

Listing 12-10. Sending work to a coroutine with a queue

```python
import asyncio
import itertools
import typing as t

async def sum_ints(data: asyncio.Queue) -> t.AsyncIterator[int]:
    """Yields a running total a queue, until a None is found"""
    total = 0
    while True:
        num = await data.get()
        if num is None:
            data.task_done()
            break
        total += num
        data.task_done()
        yield total

def numbers() -> t.Iterator[int]:
    yield 1
    yield 1
    yield 1

async def test():
    # Start with 1, feed output back in, limit to 3 items
    data = asyncio.Queue()
    sums = sum_ints(data)

    # Send the initial value
    await data.put(1)
    result = []
    async for last in sums:
        if len(result) == 3:
            # Stop the summer at 3 items
            await data.put(None)
        else:
            # Send the last value retrieved back
            await data.put(last)
```

```
            result.append(last)
    assert result == [1, 2, 4]

    # Add 3 items from a standard iterable
    data = asyncio.Queue()
    sums = sum_ints(data)

    for number in numbers():
        await data.put(number)
    await data.put(None)
    result = [value async for value in sums]
    assert result == [1, 2, 3]
```

This queue approach is very similar to the approach with a pair of wrapper functions, as can be seen if we compare Figures 12-3 and 12-6. The main difference is that the values being added to the queue are determined entirely by the containing test() function.

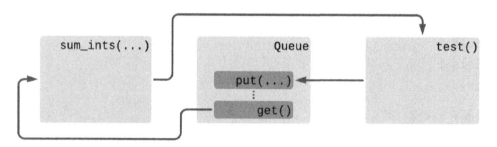

Figure 12-6. *Execution flow when using Queues*

A queue is purely a conduit for the data; it has no application-specific logic for where the data should come from. As with thread-based use of queues, I recommend using a sentinel value[5] to tell the coroutine when to end, as this makes it easier to clean up the iterators.

---

[5]We've been using None as our sentinel value, but if None is a valid value that the coroutine might expect from the queue, then we'd need to pick another. A common choice is to create a module-level instance of object, like END_OF_QUEUE_SENTINEL = object(). This can then be compared using

```
if value is END_OF_QUEUE_SENTINEL:
break
```

Choosing a control flow

I rarely use the enhanced generator approach, as there are usually ways of solving the problem with more commonly used Python control structures, like classes and queues. I find this clearer, but enhanced generators are very much worth knowing about, in case you have a problem that fits them particularly well.

The decision tree diagram in Figure 12-7 illustrates my process for deciding what structure to use. Unlike some of the other decision trees in this book, much of this choice comes down to aesthetics and readability. The chart will help you find the natural fit, but it's quite possible that you might make a different decision because you think it will improve maintainability.

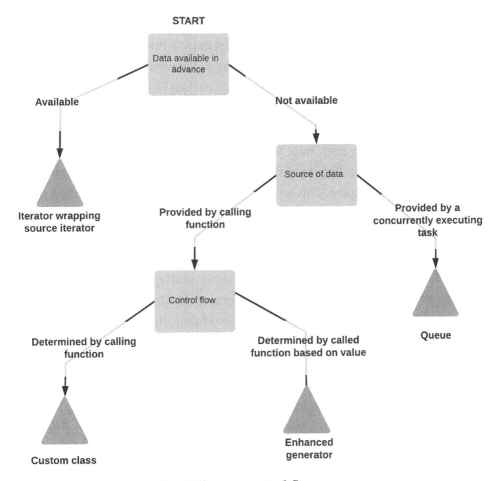

Figure 12-7. *Decision tree for different control flows*

Structure for our actions

We need to pick a method of passing data for our triggers and actions. Actions don't have data available in advance but have it passed by a single calling function. We will implement them as classes with a method to process a particular point.

Triggers are more difficult to design. They may well need to store state between datapoint checks. We expect to be loading data from a database, so we could create an async iterator that does a database query and yields the results, making more database queries whenever the end of the iterator is reached until more data is available. In this case, we would have the data available in advance, as we would have an iterator object that we trust to include all the necessary data. As such, we'd choose to implement triggers as an iterator wrapping another.

However, there is another potentially useful source of data: actions. For example, we might have a trigger object that compares "energy generated" and "energy used" DataPoints to produce an "energy purchased" value. We wouldn't want to add this value to the database, as it's just the difference of two other data points rather than a measured value, but we might want to create alerts if it's either too high or unusually high.

We could write PowerUsedTooHigh and PowerUsedHigherThanUsual triggers, but these would be very specific and share a lot of the same code. It would be better to be able to write a DifferenceBetweenSensors trigger as well as ValueTooHigh and ValueHigherThanUsual helpers. This would allow users to compose logic with any pair of sensors, but we'd need a way of sending the output of DifferenceBetweenSensors to both the ValueTooHigh and ValueHigherThanUsual stacks.

If data points can come from the database or the behavior of actions, then we cannot consider the source of data to be available in advance and must take the right-hand path at the first question of the decision tree. The source of data is the function that passes the collated data to the trigger, which means we should follow the left-hand path. As such, triggers will be implemented as classes.

Finally, we want to allow users to compose triggers and actions together into pipelines. Like the triggers, these objects don't have their data available in advance, but unlike triggers, they receive data from multiple places. It's this functionality that's responsible for receiving the data from the database as well as the data from the actions, so this will be Queue based.

In summary, our analysis code has Actions, Triggers, and DataProcessors. Actions and Triggers are both passed data from a single location, so they are both implemented as classes. DataProcessors can receive data from multiple sources and are responsible for passing it on to triggers and actions, so they use a Queue to receive data.

Analysis coroutines

To allow users to compose actions and triggers on the fly, we provide a DataProcessor class which represents a configured pipeline (Listing 12-11). This class is responsible for setting up the input queue for all data for this process and provides a simpler API for starting the various required tasks.

Listing 12-11. A class to represent a configured trigger and action pair

```
@dataclasses.dataclass
class DataProcessor:
    name: str
    action: Action
    trigger: Trigger[t.Any]

    def __post_init__(self):
        self._input: t.Optional[asyncio.Queue[DataPoint]] = None
        self._sub_tasks: t.Set = set()

    async def start(self) -> None:
        self._input = asyncio.Queue()
        self._task = asyncio.create_task(self.process(),
        name=f"{self.name}_process")
        await asyncio.gather(self.action.start(), self.trigger.start())

    @property
    def input(self) -> asyncio.Queue[DataPoint]:
        if self._input is None:
            raise RuntimeError(f"{self}.start() was not awaited")
        if self._task.done():
            raise RuntimeError("Processing has stopped") from (
            self._task.exception())
        return self._input
```

```python
async def idle(self) -> None:
    await self.input.join()

async def end(self) -> None:
    self._task.cancel()

async def push(self, obj: DataPoint) -> None:
    return await self.input.put(obj)

async def process(self) -> None:
    while True:
        data = await self.input.get()
        try:
            processed = await self.trigger.handle(data)
        except ValueError:
            continue
        else:
            action_taken = await self.action.handle(processed)
        finally:
            self.input.task_done()
```

The idle() method delegates to the join() method of the queue, which blocks until task_done() has been called the same number of times as get() was awaited. Therefore, await processor.idle() blocks until no items are waiting to be processed. This method is especially useful for writing test code, as it allows us to ensure that the processor has finished processing before we start to assert that the expected actions were taken.

Adding a queue between the raw data source and the triggers and actions allows us to guarantee that data is always processed in order and that failures do not stall the ability for other tasks to ingest data. We can only feed data into a group of triggers as quickly as the slowest one can process them unless we allow them to build up a backlog of data to process.

The problem with allowing a backlog to build up is that we could find ourselves using more and more memory to store the tasks for the slower tasks. The idle() method could be useful here, as it would allow us to block the ingesting coroutine periodically, so backlogs can only build up temporarily and must be cleared out before more data can be ingested. Alternatively, we could define a maximum length for the input queue, which would temporarily halt ingestion whenever a single sensor's backlog got too long.

With the data processor in place, we can also define the base classes for the trigger and action components to match its behavior, as shown in Listing 12-12.

Listing 12-12. Base classes for the Trigger and Action components

```python
import typing as t

from ..typing import T_value
from ..database import DataPoint
from ..exceptions import NoDataForTrigger

class Trigger(t.Generic[T_value]):
    name: str

    async def start(self) -> None:
        """ Coroutine to do any initial setup """
        return

    async def match(self, datapoint: DataPoint) -> bool:
        """ Return True if the datapoint is of interest to this
        trigger.
        This is an optional method, called by the default implementation
        of handle(...)."""
        raise NotImplementedError

    async def extract(self, datapoint: DataPoint) -> T_value:
        """ Return the value that this datapoint implies for this trigger,
        or raise NoDataForTrigger if no value is appropriate.
        Can also raise IncompatibleTriggerError if the value is not
        readable.

        This is an optional method, called by the default implementation
        of handle(...).
        """

        raise NotImplementedError

    async def handle(self, datapoint: DataPoint) -> t.Optional[DataPoint]:
        """Given a data point, optionally return a datapoint that
        represents the value of this trigger. Will delegate to the
        match(...) and extract(...) functions."""
```

563

```
        if not await self.match(datapoint):
            # This data point isn't relevant
            return None

        try:
            value = await self.extract (datapoint)
        except NoDataForTrigger:
            # There was no value for this point
            return None

        return DataPoint(
            sensor_name=self.name,
            data=value,
            deployment_id=datapoint.deployment_id,
            collected_at=datapoint.collected_at,
        )

class Action:
    async def start(self) -> None:
        return

    async def handle(self, datapoint: DataPoint):
        raise NotImplementedError
```

These two objects have a start() coroutine to allow for initial startup actions and a handle(...) method that takes a DataPoint object and processes it. In the case of a Trigger, the handle(...) method checks if the passed data point is relevant to the trigger, and if so, it returns a new data point, with the data specified by the extract(...) method. For an Action, the handle(...) coroutine returns a boolean representing if an action was taken. It also has side effects specific to the handler, such as database accesses.

A good first trigger to create is one that compares the value of a DataPoint to a threshold value, shown in Listing 12-13. This can be used to find temperatures that are too high, for example. As the ValueThresholdTrigger class is a rather complex class that takes many arguments, the data class functionality is useful to ensure that it has appropriate standard methods, such as __init__(...).

Listing 12-13. A trigger to check for a value having a certain relationship to a prespecified value

```
import dataclasses
import typing as t
import uuid

from ..database import DataPoint
from ..exceptions import IncompatibleTriggerError
from .base import Trigger

@dataclasses.dataclass(frozen=True)
class ValueThresholdTrigger(Trigger[bool]):
    name: str
    threshold: float
    comparator: t.Callable[[float, float], bool]
    sensor_name: str
    deployment_id: t.Optional[uuid.UUID] = dataclasses.field(default=None)

    async def match(self, datapoint: DataPoint) -> bool:
        if datapoint.sensor_name != self.sensor_name:
            return False
        elif (self.deployment_id and
        datapoint.deployment_id != self.deployment_id):
            return False
        return True

    async def extract(self, datapoint: DataPoint) -> bool:
        if datapoint.data is None:
            raise IncompatibleTriggerError("Datapoint does not contain data")
        elif isinstance(datapoint.data, float):
            value = datapoint.data
        elif (isinstance(datapoint.data, dict) and
        "magnitude" in datapoint.data):
            value = datapoint.data["magnitude"]
        else:
            raise IncompatibleTriggerError("Unrecognised data format")
        return self.comparator(value, self.threshold)  # type: ignore
```

565

The two arguments that control checking against the threshold are the `comparator=` and `threshold=` arguments. The `threshold` is a floating-point number, and `comparator=` is a function that takes two floating-point numbers and returns a boolean.

An example of a valid comparator would be `lambda x, y: x > y`, but there are some built-in versions of standard comparisons in the `operator` module.[6] Setting `comparator=operator.gt` is maybe a bit more explicit, and I prefer it. You should use whatever style feels more natural to you.

We also need at least one basic `Action` implementation, the simplest useful one being an action that calls a webhook to notify external services that the temperature is too high. An implementation for this is shown in Listing 12-14.

Listing 12-14. An action that calls a webhook, using the format expected by the IFTTT service

```
@dataclasses.dataclass
class WebhookAction(Action):
    """An action that runs a webhook"""
    uri: str

    async def start(self) -> None:
        return

    async def handle(self, datapoint: DataPoint) -> bool:
        async with aiohttp.ClientSession() as http:
            async with http.post(
                self.uri,
                json={
                    "value1": datapoint.sensor_name,
                    "value2": str(datapoint.data),
                    "value3": datapoint.deployment_id.hex,
                },
            ) as request:
```

---

[6]Lambda functions are unnamed functions that contain only a return expression. They're useful for writing trivial functions, especially trivial closures, but it can be tempting to overuse them. A concrete advantage of `operator.gt` is that tracebacks will display it as `<built-in function gt>` rather than `<function <lambda> at 0x00DD0858>`.

```
logger.info(
    f"Made webhook request for {datapoint} with status "
    f"{request.status}"
)
return request.status == 200
```

Another useful action is one that logs any data points that it is sent. While this isn't very helpful for production, it's invaluable as a way to debug our pipelines. This lets us see what the tool is doing in the terminal; the code to implement it is in Listing 12-15.

Listing 12-15. Action handler that logs to the standard error stream

```
class LoggingAction(Action):
    """An action that stores any generated data points back to the DB"""

    async def start(self) -> None:
        return

    async def handle(self, datapoint: DataPoint) -> bool:
        logger.warn(datapoint)
        return True
```

The code that accompanies this chapter includes some additional trigger and actions, and the released version of `apd.aggregation` may include yet more by the time you read this.

Ingesting data

We want to run many concurrent sets of triggers and actions, so we'll use a long-running coroutine to act as a controller for multiple subtasks. This coroutine manages setting up the triggers and actions and hands data off to each subtask.

The behavior of long-running coroutines is quite different to that of long-running threads, especially in how they terminate. When we looked at long-running threads, we needed to create a way to instruct the thread that there was no more data for it to process and that it should end. This was also true of enhanced iterators, and we used the same pattern with queue-based coroutines and functions, where sending a sentinel value was the only way of stopping the processing task.

Coroutines scheduled as tasks make this easier, as they have a cancel() method. The cancel() method allows developers to stop a task without adding a method to ask it to stop itself. This is especially useful for system designs where coroutines run for a long time, as it allows us to cleanly shut down parts of the program that are no longer needed. Any tasks that a coroutine has started are also canceled unless they were wrapped with asyncio.shield(...) when first created. It's also possible to write a coroutine that shuts down from a requested cancellation cleanly, using a try/finally block. Cancellation works by raising a CancelledError exception within the coroutine's code, which can be caught, and finalization code run before ending.

There are now handlers for an initial set of behaviors, but we need a way to push data into this process. We already have a function to load data from a database and asynchronously iterate over it; we can supplement this by placing it in an infinite loop that searches for any additional data once the first iteration has been consumed, as shown in Listing 12-16.

Listing 12-16. A version of get_data(...) that may block for new data while iterating

```
import asyncio

from apd.aggregation.query import db_session_var, get_data

async def get_data_ongoing(*args, **kwargs):
    last_id = 0
    db_session = db_session_var.get()
    while True:
        # Run a timer for 300 seconds concurrently with our work
        minimum_loop_timer = asyncio.create_task(asyncio.sleep(300))
        async for datapoint in get_data(*args, **kwargs):
            if datapoint.id > last_id:
                # This is the newest datapoint we have handled so far
                last_id = datapoint.id
            yield datapoint
            # Next time, find only data points later than the latest we've
            # seen
            kwargs["inserted_after_record_id"] = last_id
```

```
# Commit the DB to store any work that was done in this loop and
# ensure that any isolation level issues do not prevent loading more
# data
db_session.commit()
# Wait for that timer to complete. If our loop took over 5 minutes
# this will complete immediately, otherwise it will block
await minimum_loop_timer
```

Tip   This uses asyncio.sleep(…) to ensure a minimum time between loop iterations. If we were to await asyncio.sleep(300) directly at the end of the loop, there would always be at least 300 seconds between iterations, but it could be significantly more. Delegating this to a task at the start of the loop and then awaiting the completion of the task means that our 300-second wait is running in parallel to the productive work performed in the loop body. The same effect can be obtained through arithmetic on the current time to calculate the delay needed for each loop iteration, but this is much clearer.

The implementation here has a static delay between each database query. It isn't the most efficient method as it introduces a fixed period between data checks, so it can take up to 5 minutes for new data to become available. We can decrease the time between iterations, but this means correspondingly more load on the database server. This approach is called short polling, as it makes a short request on a regular basis to check for more data. Long polling is more efficient, as it involves making a request that doesn't complete until there is data available, but it requires that the back-end and interface library support it. Short polling is the most compatible approach, so it is a good default in the absence of evidence that it's too inefficient.

```
┌─────────────────────────────────────────────────────────────────┐
│                       POSTGRES PUBSUB                              │
└─────────────────────────────────────────────────────────────────┘
```

If we're using a database that offers pubsub,[7] we could avoid polling entirely and rewrite this to listen for a notification topic being sent by the data aggregation process.

The PostgreSQL pubsub functionality is enabled with the LISTEN and NOTIFY commands. SQLAlchemy does not tightly integrate this functionality, but the underlying connection libraries support it so we can take advantage if it's useful to us.

We'd first modify the CLI to send a notification after adding new data if the connected database is PostgreSQL:

```
if "postgresql" in db_uri:
    # On Postgres sent a pubsub notification, in case other processes are
    # waiting for this data
    Session.execute("NOTIFY apd_aggregation;")
```

Next, we'd create an alternative implementation of get_data_ongoing(...) that looks for notifications. This function must call Session.execute("LISTEN apd_aggregation;") to ensure that the connection is receiving notifications on the relevant topic.

As we're not using a fully asynchronous PostgreSQL library, we can't just await a notification, so we must create a shim function that is awaitable and handles reading notifications from the database connection.

```
async def wait_for_notify(loop, raw_connection):
    waiting = True
    while waiting:
        # The database connection isn't asynchronous, poll in a new thread
        # to make sure we've received any notifications
        await loop.run_in_executor(None, raw_connection.poll)
        while raw_connection.notifies:
            # End the loop after clearing out all pending
            # notifications
            waiting = False
            raw_connection.notifies.pop()
```

---

[7]Publish/subscribe. This feature allows a connection to request to be given messages on a given "topic" and other connections to send messages.

```
    if waiting:
        # If we had no notifications wait 15 seconds then
        # re-check
        await asyncio.sleep(15)
```

This still requires actively checking the database state, but the poll() function does not make a database query so it is a much more lightweight solution. The reduction in database load makes it more efficient to reduce the time between checks, down to seconds from minutes.

Running the analysis process

The final component to complete this feature is to write a new command-line utility to run the processing. This utility is responsible for setting up the database connection, loading the user's configuration, and connecting the handlers they've defined to the feed of information from the database, then starting the long-running coroutine.

Listing 12-17 shows a new click command that takes a path to a python-based configuration file and a database connection string and executes all the data processors in that file.

Listing 12-17. Command-line tool to run the management pipeline

```
import asyncio
import importlib.util
import logging
import typing as t

import click

from .actions.runner import DataProcessor
from .actions.source import get_data_ongoing
from .query import with_database

logger = logging.getLogger(__name__)

def load_handler_config(path: str) -> t.List[DataProcessor]:
    # Create a module called user_config backed by the file specified, and
    # load it
    # This uses Python's import internals to fake a module in a known
    # location
```

```
    # Based on an StackOverflow answer by Sebastian Rittau and sample code
    # from Brett Cannon
    module_spec = importlib.util.spec_from_file_location("user_config", path)
    module = importlib.util.module_from_spec(module_spec)
    module_spec.loader.exec_module(module)
    return module.handlers

@click.command()
@click.argument("config", nargs=1)
@click.option(
    "--db",
    metavar="<CONNECTION_STRING>",
    default="postgresql+psycopg2://localhost/apd",
    help="The connection string to a PostgreSQL database",
    envvar="APD_DB_URI",
)
@click.option("-v", "--verbose", is_flag=True, help="Enables verbose mode")
def run_actions(config: str, db: str, verbose: bool) -> t.Optional[int]:
    """This runs the long-running action processors defined in a config file.

    The configuration file specified should be a Python file that defines a
    list of DataProcessor objects called processors.n
    """

    logging.basicConfig(level=logging.DEBUG if verbose else logging.WARN)

    async def main_loop():
        with with_database(db):
            logger.info("Loading configuration")
            handlers = load_handler_config(config)

            logger.info(f"Configured {len(handlers)} handlers")
            starters = [handler.start() for handler in handlers]
            await asyncio.gather(*starters)

            logger.info(f"Ingesting data")
            data = get_data_ongoing()
            async for datapoint in data:
```

```
        for handler in handlers:
            await handler.push(datapoint)

    asyncio.run(main_loop())
    return True
```

The configuration file we're using here is a Python file, loaded explicitly by the load_handler_config(...) function. The configuration for this tool involves composing different Python classes, lambda functions, and other callables, so it's not suitable for nontechnical end-users to edit directly. We could have created a config file format that offers these options, but for now, at least, a Python-based configuration is sufficient. An example of this config file is shown in Listing 12-18.

Listing 12-18. A config file that uses a variety of actions and handlers from the accompanying code

```
import operator

from apd.aggregation.actions.action import (
    OnlyOnChangeActionWrapper,
    LoggingAction,
)
from apd.aggregation.actions.runner import DataProcessor
from apd.aggregation.actions.trigger import ValueThresholdTrigger

handlers = [
    DataProcessor(
        name="TemperatureBelow18",
        action=OnlyOnChangeActionWrapper(LoggingAction()),
        trigger=ValueThresholdTrigger(
            name="TemperatureBelow18",
            threshold=18,
            comparator=operator.lt,
            sensor_name="Temperature",
        ),
    )
]
```

Process status

A long-running process can be difficult to monitor. The most common way of showing users the status of such a process is by showing a progress bar, but this only works so long as we know the amount of data to be processed in advance. Our system is specifically designed to run indefinitely, waiting for new data. Even when no data is waiting to be processed, we are not 100% complete as we can reasonably expect more data to arrive soon.

A more appropriate approach would be to gather statistics about the work that's being done and display them to the user. We can keep track of the total number of data points read by each data processor and the total that were successfully handled by its action, as well as a rolling average of the time taken. These three items allow us to generate useful statistics (Listing 12-19) that gives the end-user a good idea of how efficient each handler is.

Listing 12-19. A data processor that generates statistics as it's used

```python
@dataclasses.dataclass
class DataProcessor:
    name: str
    action: Action
    trigger: Trigger[t.Any]

    def __post_init__(self):
        self._input: t.Optional[asyncio.Queue[DataPoint]] = None
        self._sub_tasks: t.Set = set()
        self.last_times = collections.deque(maxlen=10)
        self.total_in = 0
        self.total_out = 0

    async def process(self) -> None:
        while True:
            data = await self.input.get()
            start = time.time()
            self.total_in += 1
```

```
        try:
            processed = await self.trigger.handle(data)
        except ValueError:
            continue
        else:
            action_taken = await self.action.handle(processed)
            if action_taken:
                elapsed = time.time() - start
                self.total_out += 1
                self.last_times.append(elapsed)
        finally:
            self.input.task_done()

def stats(self) -> str:
    if self.last_times:
        avr_time = sum(self.last_times) / len(self.last_times)
    elif self.total_in:
        avr_time = 0
    else:
        return "Not yet started"
    return (
        f"{avr_time:0.3f} seconds per item. {self.total_in} in, "
        f"{self.total_out} out, {self.input.qsize()} waiting."
    )
```

The standard way of determining when to display statistics on UNIX-like systems is to register a signal handler that returns the information. Signals are how processes are informed about various operating system events, for example, when a user presses <CTRL+c>. Not all platforms support the same set of signals, so it's usual for different signals to be used on different operating systems.

For operating systems that provide a signal to request statistics (called SIGINFO), we should ensure that the program reacts appropriately. To achieve this, we update the CLI tool with a function to iterate over the data processors and output their statistics to the user, as shown in Listing 12-20.

Listing 12-20. Example of a statistics signal handler

```
import signal
def stats_signal_handler(sig, frame, data_processors=None):
    for data_processor in data_processors:
        click.echo(
            click.style(data_processor.name, bold=True, fg="red") + " " +
            data_processor.stats()
        )
    return

signal_handler = functools.partial(stats_signal_handler,
data_processors=handlers)
signal.signal(signal.SIGINFO, signal_handler)
```

A signal handler is registered against a signal using the `signal.signal(...)` function, which takes a signal number and a handler. The handler must be a function that takes two arguments: the signal that is being handled and the frame that was executing at the time the signal was received.

Note   The signal value is an integer, but if you run `print(signal.SIGINT)` (for example), you'll see `Signals.SIGINT`. This is because it's implemented with an Enum object. We used `IntEnum` to create the return code structure in Chapter 4, so this is quite familiar. There are a few variants of Enum available; the most interesting is `Flag`. This further extends Enum by allowing bitwise combinations of items, such as `Constants.ONE | Constants.TWO`.

The `SIGINFO` signal is only available on operating systems based on the BSD Unix operating system, such as FreeBSD and macOS.[8] It is raised by pressing <CTRL+t> when viewing the program output. This handler intercepts any use of <CTRL+t> on a compatible operating system and triggers displaying the statistics. On Linux systems, where SIGINFO is not available, it's common to use SIGUSR1, which can be sent using the `kill` command:

```
kill -SIGUSR1 pid
```

---

[8]Other BSD-inspired operating systems are available.

This signal is a lot less useful as it's not possible to generate with a key combination, but it is a standard so we should support it too. Windows offers no signals intended to request a status update, so we coopt the <CTRL+c> handler[9] instead. The new behavior of <CTRL+c> is to print the stats the first time it is pressed, and then the second press in quick succession causes the program to end. We'll achieve this by creating a signal handler that unsets itself and schedules a task to reattach the handler a short time later (Listing 12-21).

Listing 12-21. Signal handler functions to show statistics

```python
def stats_signal_handler(sig, frame, original_sigint_handler=None,
data_processors=None):
    for data_processor in data_processors:
        click.echo(
            click.style(data_processor.name, bold=True, fg="red") + " " +
            data_processor.stats()
        )
    if sig == signal.SIGINT:
        click.secho("Press Ctrl+C again to end the process", bold=True)
        handler = signal.getsignal(signal.SIGINT)
        signal.signal(signal.SIGINT, original_sigint_handler)
        asyncio.get_running_loop().call_later(5,
            install_ctrl_c_signal_handler, handler)
    return

def install_ctrl_c_signal_handler(signal_handler):
    click.secho("Press Ctrl+C to view statistics", bold=True)
    signal.signal(signal.SIGINT, signal_handler)

def install_signal_handlers(running_data_processors):
    original_sigint_handler = signal.getsignal(signal.SIGINT)
    signal_handler = functools.partial(
        stats_signal_handler,
```

---

[9]Jupyter also coopts the <CTRL+c> handler, to give information on the number of kernels running and prevent accidental termination, so this is not unprecedented.

```
        data_processors=running_data_processors,
        original_sigint_handler=original_sigint_handler,
    )

    for signal_name in "SIGINFO", "SIGUSR1", "SIGINT":
        try:
            signal.signal(signal.Signals[signal_name], signal_handler)
        except KeyError:
            pass
```

This uses the `loop.call_later(...)` method of the current event loop to restore the signal handler. This method schedules a new task that waits a given amount of time, then calls a function. The function being called is not a coroutine to be awaited but a standard function, so it must not be used for anything that could block.

The intention of this method, along with `loop.call_soon(...)`, is to allow for callbacks to be scheduled by asynchronous code without first having to wrap them in a coroutine and then scheduling it as a task.

Caution   Signal handlers registered with `signal.signal(...)`run immediately after the signal is received, interrupting any concurrent asyncio processes. It's important that any handlers minimize their interaction with the rest of the program, as it could cause undefined behavior. There's a `loop.add_signal_handler(...)` function that has the same signature as `signal.signal(...)` but guarantees that the signal handler is called once when it's safe to do so. Not all event loop implementations support this: this method does not work on Microsoft Windows, for example. If you need Windows compatibility, you must ensure that your signal handlers don't interfere with your async tasks.

Callbacks

This approach of defining functions and passing them to other functions is something we've used already as part of the chart configuration objects. For the analysis program, we're using `Handler` and `Action` objects, which maintain state and have multiple callable methods. On the other hand, we defined `clean(...)`, `get_data(...)`, and `draw(...)` functions, rather than custom classes for the three functions.

We could have created, for example, a Cleaner object that has a single clean(...) method rather than passing a function. There's no particular advantage to using a function instead of a class, so long as only one callable is needed.

A very common use case for passing functions is to implement callbacks. A callback is a function used to hook into an event in an intermediate function. The three functions we passed to our chart configuration are core to the functionality of the charting and are not callbacks.

A true callback function has no effect on the function that's running, only external side effects. For example, the plot_sensor(...) method checks for the case where a particular deployment has no points for a given sensor and skips adding that sensor to the legend if it's empty. We might imagine wanting to hook into this to tell the user when this case occurs, as it might be confusing to have a different number of deployments visible when filtering a view. The function that is called when that happens would be an example of a callback function.

We could implement this by adding a log_skipped callback function to the signature of this method, which is passed a message to be shown to the user. The message would be added as follows:

```
if log_skipped:
    log_skipped(f"No points for {name} in {config.title} chart")
```

The function could then have any number of different callables passed as log_skipped= to customize how the user is to be notified. For example, it could be printed to the screen, it could be made into a log message, or it could be appended to a list for display elsewhere.

```
plot_sensor(config, plot, location_names, *args, log_skipped=print, **kwargs)
plot_sensor(config, plot, location_names, *args, log_skipped=logger.info,
**kwargs)

messages = []
plot_sensor(config, plot, location_names, *args,
log_skipped=messages.append, **kwargs)
```

This isn't to say that callbacks implement unimportant functions, but they are never the core functionality *of the function that's triggering them*. Resetting our signal handlers after a delay is a core functionality of the application, but it's incidental to the work of the event loop, so it is also considered a callback.

Another example of a callback being part of the core functionality is our
`process(...)` method. We've not scheduled actions in parallel so that we can ensure
that they happen in order, but if we *had* scheduled actions as tasks, then we'd have
moved on to the next loop iteration before that task finished. This would have made it
impossible to record the time it took to complete each action.

Listing 12-22 shows a way of handling this by adding a callback to a task that is run
on completion. It doesn't matter when the task is awaited; the callback runs very soon
after the task completes.

Listing 12-22. Example of using a callback to record the time taken for a task

```
def action_complete(self, start, task):
    action_taken = task.result()
    if action_taken:
        elapsed = time.time() - start
        self.total_out += 1
        self.last_times.append(elapsed)
    self.input.task_done()

async def process(self) -> None:
    while True:
        data = await self.input.get()
        start = time.time()
        self.total_in += 1
        try:
            processed = await self.trigger.handle(data)
        except ValueError:
            self.input.task_done()
            continue
        else:
            result = asyncio.create_task(self.action.handle(processed))
            result.add_done_callback(functools.partial(
                self.action_complete, start))
```

It's also possible to implement this without add_done_callback(...), by wrapping
the handle(...) coroutine in another that gathers the relevant statistics, but this is very
much a matter of style. Most of the things that can be achieved with asyncio callbacks

can be rewritten more clearly by wrapping coroutines. It's rare for a task callback to be the best approach in anything other than low-level integrations of blocking code with the asyncio framework, but it can be useful on occasion.

We won't be applying either of these changes: we don't want to lose any guarantee that actions are processed in date order, as it could be confusing for end-users to get out of order notifications.

Extending the actions available

The actions and triggers we have available are a reasonable basis for demonstration, but they're not enough to meet real-world user needs. Although we could release the software as is, by going further and building some things that we expect real users to need, it's much easier for us to find pain points in the implementation.

EXERCISE 12-1: A TRIGGER THAT SUBTRACTS TWO SENSOR VALUES

Earlier in this chapter, we said that it would be useful to compare two deployments of the same sensor. For example, if the humidity of the upstairs of a house is significantly higher than the humidity downstairs, it suggests that the shower has recently been used. This isn't something that can be detected just by thresholding the upstairs sensor without false positives being very likely.

Write a new handler that compares two deployments of the same sensor and returns the difference between the two values. There is a branch point in the code for this chapter that provides a good starting point, with an updated get_data(...) method that does not sort data inappropriately for this task.

Once we have a trigger that calculates the difference between two sensors, we can create the functionality to allow Actions to pass the output of a trigger back to the set of all DataProcessors to be reanalyzed. In this way, we're merging the two approaches to data handling from the start of the chapter, and we are processing an iterable of data queried from the database, but also occasionally the output of the process itself. We can use another Queue object to represent ephemeral data points that we want to pass back to the handlers. The get_data_ongoing(...) function (Listing 12-23) would also pull data from this queue, not just the database.

Listing 12-23. Updated version of get_data that includes data points from a context variable

```
import asyncio
from contextvars import ContextVar

from apd.aggregation.query import db_session_var, get_data

refeed_queue_var = ContextVar("refeed_queue")

async def queue_as_iterator(queue):
    while not queue.empty():
        yield queue.get_nowait()

async def get_data_ongoing(*args, historical=False, **kwargs):
    last_id = 0
    if not historical:
        kwargs["inserted_after_record_id"] = last_id = (
        await get_newest_ record_id())
    db_session = db_session_var.get()
    refeed_queue = refeed_queue_var.get()

    while True:
        # Run a timer for 300 seconds concurrently with our work
        minimum_loop_timer = asyncio.create_task(asyncio.sleep(300))
        import datetime
        async for datapoint in get_data(*args,
        inserted_after_record_id=last_id, order=False, **kwargs):
            if datapoint.id > last_id:
                # This is the newest datapoint we have handled so far
                last_id = datapoint.id
            yield datapoint

        while not refeed_queue.empty():
            # Process any datapoints gathered through the refeed queue
            async for datapoint in queue_as_iterator(refeed_queue):
                yield datapoint
```

```
# Commit the DB to store any work that was done in this loop and
# ensure that any isolation level issues do not prevent loading more
# data
db_session.commit()
# Wait for that timer to complete. If our loop took over 5 minutes
# this will complete immediately, otherwise it will block
await minimum_loop_timer
```

The code in Listing 12-23 assumes that there is a queue in the context variable and pulls items from that queue so long as some are available. This processes all the DataPoints from a database query and then all the generated points before making the next query. Listing 12-24 shows the action needed to add items to this queue.

Listing 12-24. The relevant refeed action

```
from .source import refeed_queue_var

class RefeedAction(Action):
    """An action that puts data points into a special queue to be consumed
    by the analysis programme"""

    async def start(self) -> None:
        return

    async def handle(self, datapoint: DataPoint) -> bool:
        refeed_queue = refeed_queue_var.get()
        if refeed_queue is None:
            logger.error("Refeed queue has not been initialised")
            return False
        else:
            await refeed_queue.put(datapoint)
            return True
```

The refeed_queue_var variable is not set in either of these code paths. This is because the individual handlers and get_data_ongoing(...) functions are running in different contexts, so they cannot set the context variable globally. The iterator is running in the context of the main_loop() in the command-line tool, but each handler has its own individual context due to being started as a task running in parallel.

We need to set up the context variable *before* the handlers are branched off as new tasks so that they maintain a reference to the same task. We'll add it to the `main_loop()` function itself. While it would be possible to write this code using a global variable rather than a context variable, it would make testing and potential multithreading in the future more difficult.

Summary

In this chapter, we've applied many of the techniques we covered in past chapters to extend the functionality of the aggregation program greatly. A lot of the power of Python comes from being able to use a relatively small amount of features to achieve different results.

The most important feature for enabling this, in my opinion, is the ability to write code that takes an implementation of logic as an argument, either as a class, a function, or a generator function. This is perfect for the kind of work we've done in the analysis section of this book, as it allows us to create data pipelines and supply application-specific logic where needed.

Additional resources

There are a few more links I'd like to share, covering additional reading on this chapter's topics, listed as follows:

> More documentation on how Python handles signals can be found in the standard library's documentation, at `https://docs.python.org/3/library/signal.html`. This is especially useful information for writing cross-platform applications, as Microsoft Windows behaves quite differently.

> Details on how PostgreSQL's pub/sub handling works are at `www.postgresql.org/docs/12/sql-listen.html` and `www.postgresql.org/docs/12/sql-notify.html`.

> I'm using IFTTT's webhook support as a place to send notifications to. Details on this service are at `https://ifttt.com/` and `https://ifttt.com/maker_webhooks`.

In addition, there are a couple of links I'd like to share in general, not specific to this chapter:

The Python Software Foundation's list of upcoming events at `www.python.org/events/`.

The Advent of Code project (`https://adventofcode.com/`) releases 25 puzzles intended to be solved by coding every December. I find these to be very well written and a great way of trying out new techniques or languages. I'd encourage you to try some of the techniques this book covers with those puzzles, especially if you don't have a chance in your day-to-day programming work.

Epilogue

This long-running process is the final feature for the example code of this book. With it, we have a system that has a lightweight component that can be deployed to multiple servers, which optionally can record data over time and serve it over a HTTP interface, but alone is a useful debugging tool. We have a central aggregation process that maintains a list of known HTTP endpoints to query, a Jupyter notebook that draws charts of the aggregated data, and an analysis process that processes incoming data to add synthesized data to the shared database or trigger external actions.

At the start of this book, I listed some examples of real-world applications where this type of application can be useful. The obvious one is the smart home example that I've focused on, where our work allows us to chart energy usage and temperature over time. The trigger system can be used to detect when one room's temperature and humidity is closer to the outside temperature than the others, indicating a window has been left open, and we can use actions to push notifications to mobile devices using a webhook.

An urban sensor network, such as the one used in Amsterdam for monitoring airplane noise, can have sound levels plotted on a map at any given time, and a custom trigger could be written to detect moving sources of noise, for correlating with known flight data.

For server monitoring, we can draw charts of RAM and disk usage and send notifications to Slack when a server drops below a threshold on any of its monitored items. The notification action is especially useful for deployments like the arcade, where nontechnical staff can be alerted about an alarm condition on a specific machine and a report generated after the fact by maintenance staff.

The code for this project will continue to evolve over time. Both the website (`https://advancedpython.dev`) and this book's section on the Apress website offer the source code for this book on a chapter-by-chapter basis. Any contributions to the current version of the software are welcome.

As well as building a piece of legitimately useful software, we've explored a large portion of the Python standard library on the way while focusing on tools and techniques that are not commonly used in example software. We've used cookiecutter and Pipenv to create projects and set up build environment and Jupyter to prototype software and to build one-off dashboards and analysis scripts, and we've built a web service.

We wrote a synchronous piece of code for the satellite processes and an asynchronous tool for the aggregation software. Both used SQLAlchemy and Alembic for database connectivity and pytest for testing, covering using both from synchronous and asynchronous contexts.

The example code extensively uses relatively new language features, such as context variables, data classes, and typing, to make our code more expressive, and we've explored the appropriate places to use features like asyncio, iterators, and concurrency. Some of these techniques may be very familiar to you; others may have been entirely foreign. Python's ecosystem is broad with lots of smaller communities working to create exciting new tools. Only by engaging with all these communities would you be aware of what they're developing. It's much easier to stay up to date by joining your local Python community. There are Python conferences in countries all over the world and user groups in many cities. There are also chat rooms, forums, and question and answer boards where all parts of the community interact.

I once heard someone boast they could probably learn Python in 24 hours. I couldn't disagree more. I've been learning Python for 16 years now and feel that I still have much left to learn. Python is a well-designed language and therefore quite intuitive; a beginner can certainly write a simple program in 24 hours, and an experienced programmer can write correspondingly more complex programs in a short period. However, learning enough to be productive isn't the same as having learned everything.

Thousands of people work on Python's ecosystem to improve it over time, by contributing bug reports, documentation, libraries, and core code. Everyday Python programming is subtly different; although it's not likely to impact your day-to-day work, there's a chance that today was the day that somebody released a tool that makes your job easier. You won't know unless you look.

Learning from your peers is one of the most rewarding parts of open source software; I hope this book has helped you, and I hope to meet you and learn from you at a Python event sometime soon.

Index

A

Abstract base classes, 223
    @abc.abstractmethod decorator, 224
    __subclasshook__(...) method, 224
    vs. typing module types, 477
    virtual subclasses, 223

Actions, 560
    analysis process, 571, 572
    config file, 573, 575
    DataProcessor class, 561
    extending, 581
    IFTTT service, 566
    ingesting data, 567, 571
    logs, 567
    trigger, 563, 564

Adafruit, 42, 486

Adapter pattern, 229

__aenter__() method, 331, 365

__aexit__(...) method, 331, 365

Aggregation process, 533

aiohttp library, 336

__aiter__() method, 330

Alembic, 264
    ambiguous changes, 268
    creating a new revision, 265
    current version, 269
    downgrading, 268, 270
    irreversible, migrations, 270
    listing migrations, 269
    merging, migrations, 269
    migration metadata, 266
    running migrations, 268, 269
    setting up a new project, 264
    using constants in migrations, 267

__anext__() method, 330

apd.aggregation package, 397, 516, 524
    clean functions (*see* clean functions)
    database, 254
    get_data_by_deployment(...)
        function, 413, 416
    get_data(...) function, 415
    plot_sensor(...) function, 458
    plotting data, 429
    plotting functions, 421
    query functions, 417

apd.sensors package, 106
    APDSensorsError, 500
    DataCollectionError, 500
    directory structure, 108
    extending, 149
    IntermittentSensorFailureError, 500
    making releases, 141
    sensors script, 32, 36, 130, 147, 148,
        153, 155, 156, 535
    UserFacingCLIError, 502

apd.sunnyboy_solar package, 148,
        155, 173

API design, 190
    authentication, 190
    versioning, 240, 241, 243

B

F

Printed in the United States
By Bookmasters